"Clear, complete, compelling—this terrific resource will help both Christians and seekers understand the rational basis for Christianity. I wish it had been available when I was an atheist—it would have saved a lot of time in my spiritual journey toward God!"

—LEE STROBEL
author of *The Case for Christ* and *The Case for Faith*

"This extremely readable book brilliantly builds the case for Christianity from the question of truth all the way to the inspiration of the Bible. And the verdict is in: Christians stand on mounds of solid evidence while skeptics cling to nothing but their blind, dogmatic faith. If you're still a skeptic after reading *I Don't Have Enough Faith to Be an Atheist,* then I suspect you're living in denial!"

—JOSH MCDOWELL
speaker and author of *Evidence That Demands a Verdict*

"It is really true that atheism requires gobs of blind faith while the path of logic and reason leads straight to the gospel of Jesus Christ. Norman Geisler and Frank Turek convincingly show why."

—PHILLIP E. JOHNSON
author, *Darwin on Trial, Reason in the Balance,* and
The Wedge of Truth

"*I Don't Have Enough Faith to Be an Atheist* will equip, exhort, and encourage you 'to give the reason for the hope that you have . . . with gentleness and respect.'"

—HANK HANEGRAAFF
President, The Christian Research Institute, and
host of the *Bible Answer Man* broadcast

"No amount of evidence can convert an unbeliever to belief. That is solely the work of God. But what Norm Geisler and Frank Turek have done in this book should disturb anyone claiming to be an atheist . . . perhaps enough to persuade them to begin a search for the God who has been there all along."

—CAL THOMAS
Syndicated columnist and host of *After Hours*
on the Fox News Channel

Foreword by David Limbaugh

I Don't Have Enough
FAITH
to Be an
ATHEIST

Norman L. Geisler
Frank Turek

CROSSWAY BOOKS
WHEATON, ILLINOIS

Published by Crossway Books
        a publishing ministry of Good News Publishers
        1300 Crescent Street
        Wheaton, Illinois 60187

Cover design: Josh Dennis

Cover photo: Getty Images

First printing 2004

Printed in the United States of America

Library of Congress Cataloging-in-Publication Data
Geisler, Norman L.
   I don't have enough faith to be an atheist / Norman L. Geisler and
Frank Turek.
     p. cm.
   Includes bibliographical references and index.
   ISBN 13: 978-1-58134-561-2 (TPB: alk. paper)
   ISBN 10: 1-58134-561-5
   1. Apologetics. I. Turek, Frank. II. Title.
BT1103.G45   2004
239—dc22   2003023631

DP		16	15	14	13	12	11	10	09
21	20	19	18	17	16	15	14	13	

Contents

Foreword

As ONE WHO CAME TO Christ after years of skepticism, I have a particular affection for Christian apologetics. It is one of my passions. There is an abundance of evidence for the reliability of Scripture, for the authority of the Bible as the inspired Word of God, and that the Bible accurately portrays the historical events it covers, including the earthly life of Jesus Christ. Indeed, powerful and convincing proof exists that Christianity is the one true religion, that the triune God who reveals himself in its pages is the one and only God of the universe, and that Christ died for our sins so that we may live.

Proof, of course, is no substitute for faith, which is essential to our salvation and for our communion with God. Nor is the study of apologetics disrespectful to our faith. Rather, it augments it, informs it, bolsters it, and reinvigorates it. Were it otherwise, the Bible would not say, "Always be prepared to give an answer to everyone who asks you to give the reason for the hope that you have" (1 Pet. 3:15).

I Don't Have Enough Faith to Be an Atheist is the best single book I've seen to prepare believers to give the reasons for their faith, and for skeptics who are open to the truth. This book will serve as an indispensable evangelism tool, especially when dealing with nonbelievers with "intellectual" obstacles to the faith. As we know, the intellectual obstacles are usually just an excuse for nonbelievers, but when you remove the substance of their excuse they are left naked to confront their real obstacles, their real demons.

But I believe there's another important reason for the scriptural mandate to "be prepared to give an answer." It's not just to help us effectively communicate the gospel. Being prepared will also arm us with the tools to resist certain nagging doubts that we encounter in moments of weakness. It will—because it marshals the evidence for Christianity—fortify our faith.

Who can doubt that we need to be better equipped with the evidence, whether to help us better evangelize or to strengthen our own faith? As if the temptations of the flesh weren't enough for us to contend with, we are also confronted daily with negative external influences. In modern times these influences have grown increasingly sinister and insidious, as the Bible warned they would.

In times past nonbelievers had to decide whether Christianity was the one true religion, whether any of them were true, or whether God existed at all. But they generally were not saddled with the burden of determining whether there was such a thing as truth.

Our postmodern culture has done a number on the idea of truth. It teaches that truth and morality are relative, that there is no such thing as absolute truth. To the intellectual elite dominating our universities and the mainstream media, these ideas are considered enlightened and progressive, even though we all intuitively understand that absolute truth exists, and more importantly, we all conduct our lives with that recognition.

If you encounter one of these geniuses who is so certain that truth is a social construct defined by the powerful to remain in power, ask him if he would be willing to test his theory by leaping from the tallest building around. You might also want to quiz him on the Law of Noncontradiction. Ask him whether he believes that two contradictory things can be true at the same time. If he has the intellectual dishonesty to say "yes," ask him how certain he is that absolute truth does not exist. Is he absolutely certain?

Yes, truth is a casualty of our popular culture. And when truth goes, the authority of the gospel is undermined, because the gospel tells us all about the Truth. We can see evidence of this everywhere today. The modern notions of "tolerance" and "pluralism" are a direct result of the culture's assault on truth.

Liberal secularists insist that tolerance is the highest virtue. But they don't tell you what they mean by "tolerance." To them, tolerance doesn't simply involve treating those with different ideas respectfully and civilly. It means affirming their ideas as valid, which Christians can't do without renouncing their own beliefs. If, for example, you subscribe to the biblical prohibition on homosexual behavior as sinful, you cannot at the same time affirm that such behavior is not sinful.

The postmodern secularist doesn't have to confront these questions because he rejects the idea of absolute truth and the Law of Noncontradiction. He can just go on his merry way moralizing to everyone about tolerance and never having to explain the intrinsic contradictions in his views.

The tolerance peddlers are further exposed as frauds when you consider that they simply will not practice what they preach—at least toward those annoyingly stubborn Christians. They are absolutely unwilling to "tolerate" the Christian premise that Jesus Christ is the Way, the Truth, and the Life. For them to acknowledge this would necessarily refute their concept of tolerance, which holds that all ideas are of equal merit. In their infinite resourcefulness, they carve out an exception to their demand for universal tolerance when it comes to their treatment of Christians.

To them, Christianity's exclusive truth claims are simply beyond the pale—so bad as to disqualify Christians from receiving tolerance from others. One secularist university administrator, for instance, disciplined a conservative professor for exposing her class to literature from a Christian viewpoint, which included an article about how teachers should approach homosexuality. The administrator exclaimed, "We cannot tolerate the intolerable." You see, it's fairly easy for these types to extricate themselves from their indefensible positions. They simply move the goalposts. Talk about defining truth through power!

But the Christians' belief that theirs is the one true religion doesn't make them intolerant of others or disrespectful of their right to believe and worship how they choose. Our modern culture is woefully confused about these distinctions, and they use the Christians' confidence in their own belief system to paint Christians as intolerant of others with different belief systems. Nothing could be more inaccurate. Besides, for the record, Christianity isn't the only religion with exclusive truth claims. All major religions have such claims. Many of the central ideas of the major religions cannot be reconciled, which gives the lie to the trendy tenet of pluralism that all religions at their core are the same.

We often hear or read that all people wherever located worship the same God through different languages and cultures. This idea, with all due respect, is absurd on its face. For example, Islam teaches that Christ was a mere prophet, not deity. As C. S. Lewis observed, if Christ is not God, then he could not have been an exemplary prophet or a great moral teacher, because he claimed to be God. If he was not who he said he was, then he was either a liar or a lunatic, hardly a great moral teacher or prophet.

As another obvious example, the claims of certain Eastern religions that God is in everything and that there is no discrete distinction between the Creator and creation is utterly irreconcilable with Christianity. The examples are endless, but the point is that while various religions may share some overlapping values, many of their fundamental beliefs cannot be squared. It may make people feel better to pretend that all religions are essentially the same, but this concept is demonstrably false.

But political correctness in our culture generally carries the day. Even many of our churches have become corrupted with these misguided notions of tolerance and pluralism. They have allowed their theology to be diluted and have permitted the authority of Scripture to be denigrated in favor of society's "evolved" ideas about morality. Only a version of Christianity that preaches that all religions are the same is tolerant and loving. Traditional, Bible-based Christianity is intolerant, insensitive, exclusive, and unloving.

How loving, though, is it to become an accomplice to the destruction of truth itself—to the evisceration of the gospel? How sensitive is it to aid people away from the path of Life? As a Christian, how can you explain Christ's decision voluntarily to subject himself to the indignities and humiliation of human form, to experience wholesale separation from the Father, to physically accept all of the real wrath of the Father for all of mankind's past, present, and future sins, and to suffer the indescribable torment and death on the cross if all other paths to God are the same? What an immeasurable insult to the finished work of Christ on the cross! What an act of deliberate disobedience to Christ's direction that we spread the gospel to the corners of the earth! For if all religions are the same, then we've made a liar out of Christ and rendered his Great Commission a useless farce because we have removed all incentive to evangelize.

I'm not suggesting that Christians should approach evangelism stridently or disrespectfully. We should certainly honor the principle that all people are equal in God's sight and entitled to equal protection of the laws as well as fair, courteous, and respectful treatment. But there is no moral imperative that we adopt the notion that all belief systems are equally true. There is a moral imperative that we do not.

The above referenced scriptural passage instructing us to be prepared to give the reasons for our faith is immediately followed by the caution: "But do this with gentleness and respect, keeping a clear conscience, so that those who speak maliciously against your good behavior in Christ may be ashamed of their slander" (vv. 15b-16).

We must be mindful of the next sentence as well. "It is better, if it is God's will, to suffer for doing good than for doing evil. For Christ died for sins once for all, the righteous for the unrighteous, to bring you to God" (vv. 17-18). We must preach the truth, even if it makes us unpopular, even if it leads to the charge that we are intolerant or insensitive, even if it leads to our suffering or persecution. Yes, we must evangelize with gentleness and respect, but above all, we must evangelize. We must not be silenced by the tolerance police.

I frequently come into contact with people who either don't believe in Christianity or who do but have serious problems with parts of the Bible or elements of Christian doctrine. I'm certainly no expert in theology. So what do I tell these people? Beyond suggesting the daunting task of reading the Bible from start to finish, how do I help them to discover the truths that I belatedly discovered?

There are so many wonderful books available that will help, but there seem to be drawbacks with each one. They are too scholarly or too incomplete or too difficult to read. To get the complete package I usually have to recommend more than one book, which significantly decreases the chances that any of them will be read.

Not long ago a friend asked me for resources on apologetics that he could share with his nonbelieving sibling. I knew that we'd probably only have one shot at this in the immediate future; so I had to come up with just the perfect book. Frankly, I put off the decision because I couldn't decide among three or four of my favorite sources, none of which, by itself, would have been sufficient, in my opinion.

Just as I was preparing to cop out and make a recommendation of multiple books instead of just one, I received a note from Frank Turek, asking me to review *I Don't Have Enough Faith to Be an Atheist*. After reading the first few chapters of the book I was convinced my receipt of the book was providential.

Finally, I thought, there is one book that covers the gamut in a highly readable format. After reading it I told Frank that this is the one book I've been waiting for as an evangelical tool—to explain the ideas and unveil the truth in a way that is far above my pay grade. As of the printing of this book there will now be one source I can recommend to skeptics, doubters, or Christians who need some reinforcing evidence. I already know ten people to whom I will give this book. It's truly a godsend.

Frank Turek, whom I've now come to know as a tremendous gentleman and Christian scholar, coauthored this book with the giant among giants in the field of Christian apologetics—Dr. Norman Geisler. I have a number of Dr. Geisler's other works, including *Christian Apologetics, When Critics Ask,* and *When Skeptics Ask.* Interestingly, I was first exposed to Dr. Geisler through my friend and former neighbor Dr. Steve Johnson, a graduate of Dallas Theological Seminary and one of my spiritual mentors. Steve loaned me (I can't remember if I ever returned it!) a videotape in which Dr. Geisler was explaining the truths of Christianity in a most entertaining and captivating way. It was at that point that I decided to purchase and consume a number of his incredible books on apologetics.

I would recommend any and all of Dr. Geisler's books. But *I Don't Have Enough Faith to Be an Atheist* is just what the doctor ordered for a one-stop source for those who might not be willing to wade through a number of books. I have to admit, the title particularly intrigued me since I have long believed that it does take more faith to be an atheist. It certainly takes more faith to believe that human beings evolved from the random interaction of molecules (which somehow had to come into existence themselves) than to believe in a Creator.

This book also appealed to me because before tackling the issue of the truth of Christianity, it addresses the issue of truth itself, conclusively proving the existence of absolute truth. It demolishes the follies of moral relativism and postmodernism, then proceeds systematically to march toward the inescapable truths of the Christian religion. This is a book that had to be written and even more has to be published. So I'll stop the gushing now and let this book go to press. Many a hungry soul awaits the truths that are brilliantly set out in this work.

—David Limbaugh

Preface

How Much Faith Do You Need to Believe This Book?

RELIGIOUS SKEPTICS BELIEVE that books like this one can't be trusted for objective information because such books are written by religious people who have an agenda. In fact, that's the way skeptics view the Bible—it's a biased book written by biased people. Their assessment may be true for some books about religion, but it's not true for them all. If it were, you couldn't trust anything you read concerning religion—including books written by atheists or skeptics—because every writer has a viewpoint on religion.

So what does this mean to you, the reader? Should you disbelieve what an atheist writes about Christianity just because he's an atheist? Not necessarily, because he could be telling the truth. Should you disbelieve what a Christian writes about atheism just because he's a Christian? Again, not necessarily—he too could be telling the truth.

But what about an author's agenda? Does an agenda fatally taint his objectivity? If so, no book is objective, including those by atheists and skeptics. Why? Because *all* books are written for a reason, all authors have an agenda, and all (or at least most) authors believe what they write! However, that doesn't mean what they write is false or not objective. While authors are almost never neutral about their topics (personal interest is what drives them), they nevertheless can present their topics objectively.

For example, survivors of the Holocaust who wrote of their experiences certainly were not neutral bystanders. They believed passionately that the Nazis were wrong, and they were driven to record their experiences so the world would never forget the Holocaust and, hopefully, never repeat it. Did their passion or their agenda cause them to bend the facts? Not necessarily. In fact, their passion may have produced the opposite effect. While passion may induce some people to exaggerate, it may drive others to be all the more meticulous and accurate so as not to compromise the credibility of the message they wish to communicate.

As you'll see, we think the authors of the Bible took this meticulous and accurate road. It's also the road we're trying to take in this book. (And when you're done reading, we hope you'll let us know if you think we've actually taken that road.)

In the meantime, if you're a skeptic, please keep in mind that you should believe or disbelieve what we say because of the evidence we present, not because we have a certain set of religious beliefs. We are both Christians, but we were not always Christians. We came to believe through evidence. So, the fact *that* we are Christians is not the issue: *why* we are Christians is the important point. And that's the focus of this book.

—Norm Geisler and Frank Turek
January 2004

Acknowledgments

THERE ARE A NUMBER OF fine people who had enough faith to see this book through. Our wives, Barbara Geisler and Stephanie Turek, are at the top of the list. Without their love and support this book would not exist.

Several scholars and friends reviewed portions of the manuscript and offered many helpful suggestions. Wayne Frair graciously took several hours to critique the two chapters dealing with evolution. Fred Heeren did the same on the chapter dealing with the Big Bang. J. Budziszewski provided valuable insights on the Moral Law chapter (nobody understands that topic better than he). Barry Leventhal offered his personal recollections and expertise on the chapter about his conversion experience and messianic prophecies. Other important suggestions came from Bill Dembski, Mark Pustaver, Stephanie Turek, and Randy and Luci Hough. Of course, the full and final responsibility for the contents of this book rests with us.

Thanks to Wes Yoder of the Ambassador Speaker Bureau for his encouragement and for introducing us to Marvin Padgett of Crossway Books. Marvin had enough faith to take on this project and to stick with the unusual title. Bill Deckard of Crossway also deserves thanks for his skillful editing job. And thanks to Josh Dennis, who created the stunning cover.

Finally, we are grateful to David Limbaugh, who not only wrote the foreword but did so with great zeal and insight. His enthusiasm for Christ and his desire to defend the faith inspire us. We hope this book will in some small way help produce more Christians who share those same passions.

Introduction

Finding the Box Top to the Puzzle of Life

"One who claims to be a skeptic of one set of beliefs is actually a true believer in another set of beliefs."
—PHILLIP E. JOHNSON

THE UNIVERSITY RELIGION professor gave his wide-eyed undergraduate class a clear warning the very first day of the semester. "Please leave your religious beliefs at home!" he demanded. "As we look at the Old Testament, I may make some observations that will run contrary to what you've been taught in Sunday school. It's not my purpose to offend anyone, but it *is* my purpose to be as objective as possible in analyzing the text."

That sounded great to me. After all, I (Frank) enrolled in that class because I was in the midst of a spiritual search. I didn't want any religious party line. I just wanted to know if there was a God or not. What better place, I thought, to get some objectivity about God and the Bible than a secular school like the University of Rochester?

From the beginning, the professor took a very skeptical view of the Old Testament. He immediately affirmed the theory that Moses did not write the first five books of the Bible, and that many of the Bible's supposed prophetic passages were written after the fact. He also suggested that the Jews originally believed in many gods (polytheism), but that one God ultimately won the day because the final editors of the Old Testament were "religious-fanatic monotheists."

Most of the students had no trouble with his analysis, except one young man a couple of rows ahead of me. As the semester wore on, that student became visibly more agitated with the professor's skeptical theories. One day, when the professor began to criticize sections of Isaiah, the student could no longer moderate his displeasure.

"That's not right!" he blurted out. "This is the Word of God!"

"That guy's too religious," I quietly whispered to the person sitting next to me.

"Look," the professor reminded everyone, "I told you all at the beginning that you must leave your religious beliefs at home. We will not be able to be objective if you can't do that."

"But you're not being objective," charged the student as he stood up. "You're being overly skeptical."

Some in the class began to heckle the student.

"Let the professor teach!"

"Sit down!"

"This isn't Sunday school!"

The professor tried to defuse the situation, but the flustered student stormed out and never returned.

While I had some sympathy for the student and could see that the professor had his own anti-religious bias, I also wanted to hear more of what he had to say about the Old Testament, and particularly about God. When the semester ended, I was somewhat convinced that the professor was right—the Old Testament was not to be taken at face value. However, I still didn't have an answer to my most basic question: Does God exist? I felt completely unfulfilled when the last class ended. I had no closure, no answer. So I approached the professor, who was surrounded by students asking final questions.

"Professor," I said, after waiting until just about everyone else had left, "thanks for the class. I think I've learned a new perspective. But I still have one huge question."

"Sure, go ahead," he said.

"I enrolled in this class to find out if there really is a God or not. Well . . . is there?"

Without a moment's hesitation he snapped, "I don't know."

"You don't know?"

"No, I have no idea."

I was stunned. I felt like scolding him by saying, "Wait a minute, you're teaching that the Old Testament is false, and you don't know whether there's a God or not? The Old Testament could be true if God actually exists!" But since final grades were not in, I thought better of it. Instead, I simply walked out, frustrated with the entire semester. I could have respected a qualified "yes" or "no" with some reasons given, but not "I don't know"—I could get that from an uninformed man on the street. I expected a lot more from a university religion professor.

I later learned that my expectations were too high for the modern university. The term "university" is actually a composite of the words "unity" and "diversity." When one attends a university, he is supposed to be guided in the quest to find unity in diversity—namely, how all the diverse fields of knowledge (the arts, philosophy, the physical sciences, mathematics, etc.) fit together to provide a unified picture of life. A tall task indeed, but one that the modern university has not only abandoned but reversed. Instead of *uni*versities, we now have *plura*versities, institutions that deem every viewpoint, no matter how ridiculous, just as valid as any other—that is, except the viewpoint that just one religion or worldview could be true. That's the one viewpoint considered intolerant and bigoted on most college campuses.

Despite the denials streaming from our universities, we believe that there *is* a way to discover unity in diversity. And if one were to discover such unity, it would be like seeing the box top of a jigsaw puzzle. Just as the pieces of a jigsaw puzzle are difficult to put together without the picture on the box top, the many diverse pieces of life make no sense without some kind of unifying big picture. The question is, does anyone have the box top to this puzzle we call life? Many world religions claim that they do. Are any of them correct?

Fig. I.1

Religion and the Box Top

World religions are often attempts to provide a box top that allows you to see how the many pieces of life's puzzle make a complete, cohesive picture. This picture usually—and for good reason—begins with some sort of claim about God. What someone believes about God affects everything else that he or she believes. When Mortimer Adler was asked why the "God" section was the largest in the Great Books of the Western World series (which he edited), he insightfully observed that it's because more implications flow from the subject of God than from any other subject. Indeed, the five most consequential questions in life are these:

1. Origin: Where did we come from?
2. Identity: Who are we?
3. Meaning: Why are we here?
4. Morality: How should we live?
5. Destiny: Where are we going?

The answers to each of these questions depend on the existence of God. If God exists, then there's ultimate meaning and purpose to your life. If there's a real purpose to your life, then there's a real right and wrong way to live it. Choices you make now not only affect you here but will affect you in eternity. On the other hand, if there is no God, then your life ultimately means nothing. Since there is no enduring purpose to life, there's no right or wrong way to live it. And it doesn't matter how you live or what you believe—your destiny is dust.

So which world religion, if any, answers the God question correctly? Does any religion provide the true box top for life? The common wisdom says no, for a number of reasons.

First, many say it is unreasonable to believe that one religion could be exclusively true. If one religion were really true, it would mean that billions of religious people from every other religious faith are wrong today and have been wrong throughout the centuries. (And that's a big problem if Christianity is true because Christianity seems to teach that non-Christians are going to hell!) There's also the not unfounded fear that those who think they have the truth will be intolerant of those who won't accept it.

Easygoing Americans are more apt to believe that no religion is *the* truth. This sentiment is often illustrated by the favorite parable of many university professors: the parable of the six blind men and the elephant. This is where each blind man feels a different part of the elephant and therefore reaches a different conclusion about the object in front of him. One grabs the tusk and says, "This is a spear!" Another feels the trunk and says, "This is a snake!" The one hugging the leg claims, "This is a tree!" The blind man holding the tail thinks, "I have a rope!" The one feeling the ear believes, "This is a fan!" And the one leaning on the elephant's side is certain, "This is a wall!" These blind men are said to represent world religions because they each come to a different conclusion about what they are sensing. Like each blind man, we are told, no one religion has *the* truth. No one religion has the complete box top. Religions are simply different paths up the same mountain. This, of course, greatly appeals to the broadly tolerant American mind.

In America, truth in religion is considered an oxymoron. There is no truth in religion, we are told. It's all a matter of taste or opinion. You like chocolate, I like vanilla. You like Christianity, I like Islam. If Buddhism works for you, then it's true for you. Besides, you ought not judge me for my beliefs!

The second major problem with truth in religion is that some pieces of life seem to defy explanation—they don't appear to fit any religious box top. These include the existence of evil and the silence of God in the face of that evil. These are especially powerful objections to anyone claiming that an all-powerful (theistic) God exists. Many skeptics and atheists argue that if one true, powerful God actually exists, then he would intervene to clear up all the confusion. After all, if God is really out there, then why does he seem to hide himself? Why doesn't he just show up to debunk the false religions and end all the controversy? Why doesn't he intervene to stop all the evil in the world, including all the religious wars that are such a black mark on his name? And why does he allow bad things to happen to good people? These are difficult questions for anyone claiming that their theistic religion is true.

Finally, many modern intellectuals imply that any box top based on religion wouldn't be legitimate anyway. Why? Because, they say, only science yields truth. Not only has evolution removed the need for God, they say, but only what is testable in a laboratory can be considered true. That is, only science deals in matters of fact, while religion stays merely in the realm of faith. So there's no sense trying to muster evidence or facts to support religion, because that would be like mustering facts to prove that chocolate ice cream tastes better than vanilla ice cream. You can't prove preferences. Therefore, since they insist that religion is never a matter of objective fact but merely subjective taste, any box top derived from religion couldn't provide the objective picture of life we're looking for.

So where does all this leave us? Is the search for God and for life's box top hopeless? Should we assume that there's no objective meaning to life, and each invent our own subjective box top? Should we be content with the professor's "I don't know" answer?

We don't think so. We believe that there is a real answer. And despite the powerful objections we have identified (which we will address in later chapters), we believe that the answer is very reasonable. In fact, we believe this answer is more reasonable and requires less faith than any other possible answer, including that of an atheist. Let's begin to show you what we mean.

WHAT KIND OF GOD?

Before we go any further, let's be sure we're clear on terminology. Most of the world's major religions fall into one of these three religious world-views: theism, pantheism, and atheism.

A *theist* is someone who believes in a personal God who created the universe but is not part of the universe. This would be roughly equivalent to a painter and a painting. God is like the painter, and his creation is like the painting. God made the painting, and his attributes are expressed in it, but God is not the painting. Major theistic religions are Christianity, Judaism, and Islam.

By contrast, a *pantheist* is someone who believes in an impersonal God that literally *is* the universe. So, rather than *making* the painting, pantheists believe God *is* the painting. In fact, pantheists believe that God is everything that exists: God is the grass; God is the sky; God is the tree; God is this book; God is you; God is me; etc. Major pantheistic religions are of the Eastern variety such as Hinduism, some forms of Buddhism, and many forms of the "New Age."

An *atheist,* of course, is someone who does not believe in any type of God. To follow our analogy, atheists believe that what looks like a painting has always existed and no one painted it. Religious humanists would fall into this category.

Here's an easy way to remember these three religious worldviews: theism—God *made* all; pantheism—God *is* all; atheism—*no* God at all. In fig. I.2 theism is depicted as the hand *holding up* the world, pantheism as the hand *in* the world, and atheism as *nothing but* the world.

The Three Major Religious Worldviews

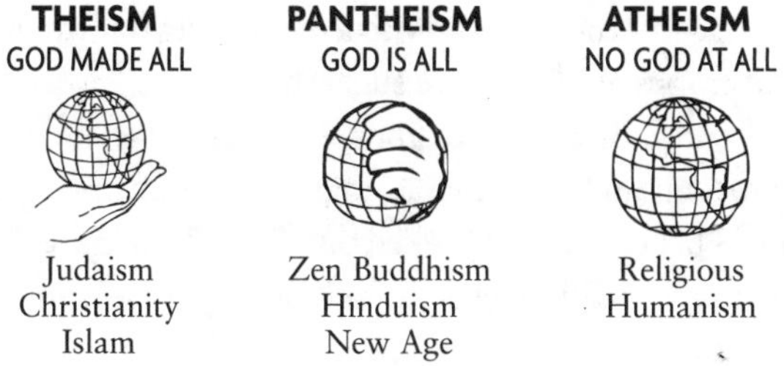

THEISM	PANTHEISM	ATHEISM
GOD MADE ALL	GOD IS ALL	NO GOD AT ALL

Judaism	Zen Buddhism	Religious
Christianity	Hinduism	Humanism
Islam	New Age	

Fig. I.2

One other term that we will use frequently is *agnostic*. That's someone who is unsure about the question of God.

So now that we've defined our terms, let's get back to this issue of faith and religion.

FAITH AND RELIGION

Despite its apparent persuasiveness, the claim that religion is simply a matter of faith is nothing more than a modern myth—it's just not true. While religion certainly requires faith, religion is not *only* about faith. *Facts* are also central to all religions because all religious worldviews—including atheism—make truth claims, and many of those truth claims can be evaluated through scientific and historical investigation.

For example, theists (e.g., Christians, Muslims, Jews) say that the universe had a beginning, while many atheists and pantheists (e.g., New Agers, Hindus) say that it did not (the universe is eternal). These are mutually exclusive claims. They can't both be right. Either the universe had a beginning or it did not. By investigating the nature and history of the universe, we can reasonably conclude that one view is right and the other wrong.

The alleged resurrection of Christ presents another example.

Christians claim that Jesus rose from the dead, while Muslims say that Jesus never even died. Again, one of these views is right and the other wrong. How can we know which one is right? By evaluating each of these conflicting truth claims against the historical evidence.

Notice that not only do different religions attempt to answer these questions, but scientists also have something to say about these matters. That is, science and religion often address the same questions: Where did the universe come from? Where did life come from? Are miracles possible? and so on. In other words, science and religion are not mutually exclusive categories as some have suggested.

Certainly not all religious claims are open to scientific or historic investigation. Some are unverifiable dogma. Nevertheless, the validity of many religious beliefs can be checked out. Some beliefs are reasonable— they can be proven with a high degree of certainty—while others are clearly unreasonable.

The Problems with Christianity

Is Christianity reasonable? We believe it is. However, unless one makes a thorough investigation of the evidence with an open mind, belief in Christianity may appear to be problematic. First, there are many perceived *intellectual* objections, like those mentioned above (the problem of evil, and the objections of many scientists).

Second, there are *emotional* obstacles that sometimes obstruct the acceptance of Christianity. Christian exclusivism, the doctrine of hell, and the hypocrisy of Christians are emotional roadblocks to just about everyone. (In fact, hypocrisy in the church probably repels people more than any other factor. Someone once said the biggest problem with Christianity is Christians!)

Finally, there are *volitional* reasons to reject Christianity, namely, Christian morality, which seems to restrict our choices in life. Since most of us don't want to answer to anyone, yielding our freedom to an unseen God is not something we naturally want to do.

Yet despite these intellectual, emotional, and volitional obstacles, we submit that it's not faith in Christianity that's difficult but faith in atheism or any other religion. *That is, once one looks at the evidence, we think it takes more faith to be a non-Christian than it does to be a Christian.* This may seem like a counterintuitive claim, but it's simply rooted in the fact that every religious worldview requires faith—even the worldview that says there is no God.

Why? Because as limited human beings, we do not possess the type of knowledge that will provide us with absolute proof of God's existence or nonexistence. Outside of the knowledge of our own existence (I know I exist because I have to exist in order to ponder the question), we deal in the realm of probability. Whatever we've concluded about the existence of God, it's always possible that the opposite conclusion is true. In fact, it is possible that our conclusions in this book are wrong. We don't think they are because we have good evidence to support them. Indeed, we think our conclusions are true beyond a reasonable doubt. (This type of certainty, say, 95-plus percent certain, is the best that fallible and finite human beings can attain for most questions, and it is more than sufficient for even the biggest decisions in life.) Nevertheless, some faith is required to overcome the possibility that we are wrong.

THE FAITH OF AN ATHEIST

While some faith is required for our conclusions, it's often forgotten that faith is also required to believe any worldview, including atheism and pantheism. We were reminded of this recently when we met an atheist named Barry at one of our seminars. Barry was incredulous that a mutual friend, Steve, had become a Christian.

He said, "I can't figure Steve out. He claims to be intellectual, but he can't answer all the objections I pose to him about Christianity. He says he doesn't have all the answers because he's new and still learning."

I (Frank) said, "Barry, it's virtually impossible to know *everything* about a particular topic, and it's certainly impossible when that topic is an infinite God. So there has to come a point where you realize you have enough information to come to a conclusion, even if unanswered questions remain."

Barry agreed but still didn't realize that he was doing exactly what he was chiding Steve for doing. Barry had decided his view—atheism—was correct even though he did not have exhaustive information to support it. Did he know for sure there is no God? Had he investigated every argument and evidence for the existence of God? Did he possess exhaustive information on the question of God? Could he answer every objection to atheism? Of course not. Indeed, it would be impossible to do so.

Since Barry, like Steve, is dealing in the realm of probability rather than absolute certainty, he has to have a certain amount of faith to believe that God does *not* exist.

Although he claimed to be an agnostic, Carl Sagan made the ultimate statement of *faith in atheistic materialism* when he claimed that "the Cosmos is all that is or ever was or ever will be."[1] How did he *know* that for sure? He didn't. How could he? He was a limited human being with limited knowledge. Sagan was operating in the realm of probability just like Christians are when they say God exists. The question is, who has more evidence for their conclusion? Which conclusion is more reasonable? As we'll see when we look at the evidence, the atheist has to muster a lot more faith than the Christian.

You may be thinking, "The atheist has to muster a lot more faith than the Christian! What possibly could Geisler and Turek mean by that?" We mean that the less evidence you have for your position, the more faith you need to believe it (and vice versa). Faith covers a gap in knowledge. And it turns out that atheists have bigger gaps in knowledge because they have far less evidence for their beliefs than Christians have for theirs. In other words, the empirical, forensic, and philosophical evidence strongly supports conclusions consistent with Christianity and inconsistent with atheism. Here are a few examples of that evidence that we'll unpack in the ensuing chapters:

1. The scientific evidence overwhelmingly confirms that the universe exploded into being out of nothing. Either someone created something out of nothing (the Christian view), or no one created something out of nothing (the atheistic view). Which view is more reasonable? The Christian view. Which view requires more faith? The atheistic view.

2. The simplest life form contains the information-equivalent of 1,000 encyclopedias. Christians believe only an intelligent being can create a life form containing the equivalent of 1,000 encyclopedias. Atheists believe nonintelligent natural forces can do it. Christians have evidence to support their conclusion. Since atheists don't have any such evidence, their belief requires a lot more faith.

3. Hundreds of years beforehand, ancient writings foretold the coming of a man who would actually be God. This man-God, it was foretold, would be born in a particular city from a par-

ticular bloodline, suffer in a particular way, die at a particular time, and rise from the dead to atone for the sins of the world. Immediately after the predicted time, multiple eyewitnesses proclaimed and later recorded that those predicted events had actually occurred. Those eyewitnesses endured persecution and death when they could have saved themselves by denying the events. Thousands of people in Jerusalem were then converted after seeing or hearing of these events, and this belief swept quickly across the ancient world. Ancient historians and writers allude to or confirm these events, and archaeology corroborates them. Having seen evidence from creation that God exists (point 1 above), Christians believe these multiple lines of evidence show beyond a reasonable doubt that God had a hand in these events. Atheists must have a lot more faith to explain away the predictions, the eyewitness testimony, the willingness of the eyewitnesses to suffer and die, the origin of the Christian church, and the corroborating testimony of the other writers, archeological finds, and other evidence that we'll investigate later.

Now perhaps these three points have raised in your mind some questions and objections. They should, because we're leaving out a lot of the detail that we'll unpack throughout the book. The main point for now is that you see what we mean when we say that every worldview—including atheism—requires some degree of faith.

Even skeptics have faith. They have faith that skepticism is true. Likewise, agnostics have faith that agnosticism is true. There are no neutral positions when it comes to beliefs. As Phillip Johnson so aptly put it, "One who claims to be a skeptic of one set of beliefs is actually a true believer in another set of beliefs."[2] In other words, atheists, who are naturally skeptical of Christianity, turn out to be true believers in atheism. As we shall see, if they are honest with the evidence, they need a lot more faith to maintain their atheistic beliefs than Christians need to maintain theirs.

DISCOVERING THE BOX TOP

We claim that there is strong evidence supporting Christianity. How will we proceed through this evidence? Since about 1996, we have traveled together around the country conducting a seminar called, "The Twelve Points That Show Christianity Is True." In it, we proceed logically from the question of truth all the way to the conclusion that the Bible is the Word of God. This book generally will follow this same logical, twelve-point progression:

1. Truth about reality is knowable.
2. The opposite of true is false.
3. It is true that the theistic God exists. This is evidenced by the:
   a. Beginning of the universe (Cosmological Argument)
   b. Design of the universe (Teleological Argument/ Anthropic Principle)
   c. Design of life (Teleological Argument)
   d. Moral Law (Moral Argument)
4. If God exists, then miracles are possible.
5. Miracles can be used to confirm a message from God (i.e., as acts of God to confirm a word from God).
6. The New Testament is historically reliable. This is evidenced by:
   a. Early testimony
   b. Eyewitness testimony
   c. Uninvented (authentic) testimony
   d. Eyewitnesses who were not deceived
7. The New Testament says Jesus claimed to be God.
8. Jesus' claim to be God was miraculously confirmed by:
   a. His fulfillment of many prophecies about himself;
   b. His sinless life and miraculous deeds;
   c. His prediction and accomplishment of his resurrection.
9. Therefore, Jesus is God.
10. Whatever Jesus (who is God) teaches is true.
11. Jesus taught that the Bible is the Word of God.
12. Therefore, it is true that the Bible is the Word of God (and anything opposed to it is false).

Before we begin presenting this line of reasoning, please note five points:

First, we are not suggesting that the above points are true by definition. Most of these points are premises that need to be justified by evidence. For example, point 3 claims, "It is true that the theistic God exists." That claim isn't true just because we say so. It needs to be backed up by good evidence, by good reasons. We'll give those good reasons when we get to that point in the book.

Second, notice that we are starting at the point of complete skepticism. That is, we are starting with a person who says he doesn't even believe in truth. We need to start there because if the prevailing view of the culture is right—that there is no truth—then it can't be *true* that a theistic God exists or that there is a *true* word from that God. However, if there is truth, and that truth can be known, then we can go on to investigate the truth of God's existence and the other points that follow (e.g., miracles are possible; the New Testament is historically reliable; and so forth).

Third, *if* this line of reasoning is sound (and that's a big "if" that this book will attempt to show), it necessarily disproves other religions where they differ from the Bible. (This sounds incredibly arrogant and presumptuous, but we'll address that later.) This would *not* mean that all other religions are completely false or that they have no truth. Nearly all religions have some truth. We are simply saying that *if the Bible is true,* then any specific claim that contradicts the Bible must be false. For example, if the Bible is true, and it says that there is a God beyond the universe who created and sustains the universe (theism), then any claim that denies theism (e.g., atheism) must be false. Likewise, if the Bible is true, and it claims that Jesus rose from the dead, then the Qur'anic denial of that fact must be false. (By the way, the reverse would also be true. If the evidence showed that the Qur'an was true, then the Bible would be false wherever it contradicted the Qur'an.)

Fourth, we give evidence for Christianity because we ought to live our lives based on truth. Socrates once said that the unexamined life is not worth living.[3] We believe that the unexamined faith is not worth believing. Furthermore, contrary to popular opinion, Christians are not supposed to "just have faith." Christians are *commanded* to know what they believe and why they believe it. They are commanded to give answers to those who ask (1 Pet. 3:15), and to demolish arguments against the Christian faith (2 Cor. 10:4-5). Since God is reasonable (Isa. 1:18) and wants us to use our reason, Christians don't get brownie points for being stupid. In fact, using reason is part of the greatest commandment which, according to Jesus, is to "Love the Lord your God with all your heart and with all your soul and with all your *mind*" (Matt. 22:37).[4]

Finally, we are often asked, "If Christianity has so much evidence behind it, then why don't more people believe it?" Our answer: Although we believe the evidence we're about to present shows that the Bible is true beyond reasonable doubt, no amount of evidence can compel anyone to believe it. Belief requires assent not only of the mind but also of the will. While many non-Christians have honest intellectual questions, we have found that many more seem to have a volitional resistance to Christianity. In other words, it's not that they don't have evidence to believe, it's that they don't *want* to believe. The great atheist Friedrich Nietzsche exemplified this type of person. He wrote, "If one were to prove this God of the Christians to us, we should be even less able to believe in him"[5]; and "It is our preference that decides against Christianity, not arguments."[6] Obviously, Nietzsche's disbelief was based on his will, not just his intellect.

At this point a skeptic might reverse the argument by claiming that it's the Christian who simply *wants* to believe. True, many Christians believe only because they want to, and cannot justify their belief with evidence. They simply have faith that the Bible is true. And merely wanting something to be true doesn't make it so. However, what we are saying is that many non-Christians do the same thing: they take a "blind leap of faith" that their non-Christian beliefs are true simply because they *want* them to be true. In the ensuing chapters, we'll take a hard look at the evidence to see who has to take the bigger leap.

The skeptic might then ask, "But why would anyone *want* Christianity to be false? Why would anyone not want the free gift of forgiveness?" Good question, but we think the answer lies in the volitional factors we touched on earlier. Namely, many believe that accepting the truth of Christianity would require them to change their thinking, friends, priorities, lifestyle, or morals, and they are not quite willing to give up control over their lives in order to make those changes. They believe that life would be easier and more fun without such changes. Perhaps they realize that while Christianity is all about forgiveness, it's also about denying yourself and carrying your cross. Indeed, Christianity is free, but it can cost you your life.

There's a difference between *proving* a proposition and *accepting* a proposition. We might be able to prove Christianity is true beyond reasonable doubt, but only *you* can choose to accept it. Please consider this question to see if you are open to acceptance: If someone could provide reasonable answers to the most significant questions and objections you have about Christianity—reasonable to the point that Christianity seems true beyond a reasonable doubt—would you then become a Christian? Think about that for a moment. If your *honest* answer is no, then your resistance to Christianity is emotional or volitional, not merely intellectual. No amount of evidence will convince you because evidence is not what's in your way—*you* are. In the end, only you know if you are truly open to the evidence for Christianity.

One beauty of God's creation is this: if you're not willing to accept Christianity, then you're free to reject it. This freedom to make choices—even the freedom to reject truth—is what makes us moral creatures and enables each of us to choose our ultimate destiny. This really hits at the heart of why we exist at all, and why God might not be as overt in revealing himself to us as some would like. For if the Bible is true, then God has provided each of us with the opportunity to make an eternal choice to either accept him or reject him. And in order to ensure that our choice is truly free, he puts us in an environment that is filled with evidence of his existence, but without his *direct* presence—a presence so powerful that it could overwhelm our freedom and thus negate our ability to reject him. In other words, *God has provided enough evidence in this life to convince anyone willing to believe, yet he has also left some ambiguity so as not to compel the unwilling.* In this way, God gives us the opportunity either to love him or to reject him without violating our freedom. In fact, the purpose of this life is to make that choice freely and without coercion. For love, by definition, must be freely given. It cannot be coerced. That's why C. S. Lewis wrote, "the Irresistible and the Indisputable are the two weapons which the very nature of [God's] scheme forbids Him to use. Merely to over-ride a human will (as His felt presence in any but the faintest and most mitigated degree would certainly do) would be for Him useless. He cannot ravish. He can only woo."[7]

We hope the evidence we present in this book will, in some small way, woo you to God. Keep in mind that it's not our evidence, it's *his*. We are simply compiling it in a logical order. By using real-world stories and illustrations as often as possible, we intend to make this book readable and its reasoning easily accessible.

Summary and Conclusion

As we have seen, many religious truth claims can be investigated and their plausibility determined. Since all conclusions about such claims are based on probability rather than absolute certainty, they all—including atheistic claims—require some amount of faith. As we look at the evidence in the ensuing chapters, we'll see that conclusions such as "God exists" and "the Bible is true" are certain beyond reasonable doubt. *Therefore, it takes a lot more faith to be a non-Christian than it does to be a Christian.*

However, we have also acknowledged that evidence alone cannot convince someone to become a Christian. Some atheists and non-Christians may reject Christianity not because the evidence is inadequate but because they don't *want* to accept it. Some people choose to suppress the truth rather than live by it. *In fact, we humans have a fatal tendency to try to adjust the truth to fit our desires rather than adjusting our desires to fit the truth.*

But wait. Isn't there a third alternative? What about remaining agnostic like the Old Testament professor at the beginning of this chapter? He said he didn't know if God exists. Some may think that such a person is open-minded. Perhaps. But there's a big difference between being *open-minded* and being *empty-minded.* In light of the evidence, we think agnosticism is a decision to be empty-minded. After all, isn't the reason we should be open-minded so that we can recognize truth when we see it? Yes. So what are we to do when there's enough evidence to point us to the truth? For example, what should we do when we see evidence beyond a reasonable doubt that George Washington was the first president of the United States? Should we remain "open-minded" as to who the first president was? No, that would be *empty*-minded. Some questions are closed. As we'll see, there's enough evidence regarding Christianity to draw a reasonably certain conclusion.

As Mortimer Adler observed, our conclusion about God impacts every area of our lives. It is the key to finding unity and diversity and ultimate meaning in life. It is literally the most important question for every human being to address. Fortunately, if our reasoning is correct, we will discover the box top to life's puzzle at the end of our journey. So let's take the first step on that journey. It begins with the question of truth.

Chapters 1–2 will cover:

➤ 1. Truth about reality is knowable.
2. The opposite of true is false.
3. It is true that the theistic God exists. This is evidenced by the:
   a. Beginning of the universe (Cosmological Argument)
   b. Design of the universe (Teleological Argument/ Anthropic Principle)
   c. Design of life (Teleological Argument)
   d. Moral Law (Moral Argument)
4. If God exists, then miracles are possible.
5. Miracles can be used to confirm a message from God (i.e., as acts of God to confirm a word from God).
6. The New Testament is historically reliable. This is evidenced by:
   a. Early testimony
   b. Eyewitness testimony
   c. Uninvented (authentic) testimony
   d. Eyewitnesses who were not deceived
7. The New Testament says Jesus claimed to be God.
8. Jesus' claim to be God was miraculously confirmed by:
   a. His fulfillment of many prophecies about himself;
   b. His sinless life and miraculous deeds;
   c. His prediction and accomplishment of his resurrection.
9. Therefore, Jesus is God.
10. Whatever Jesus (who is God) teaches is true.
11. Jesus taught that the Bible is the Word of God.
12. Therefore, it is true that the Bible is the Word of God (and anything opposed to it is false).

1

Can We Handle the Truth?

"Men stumble over the truth from time to time, but most pick themselves up and hurry off as if nothing happened."
—WINSTON CHURCHILL

IN THE MOVIE *A Few Good Men*, Tom Cruise plays a Navy lawyer who questions a Marine colonel, played by Jack Nicholson, about the murder of one of Nicholson's men. The dramatic courtroom scene turns into a shouting match as Cruise accuses Nicholson of being complicit in the murder:

> Cruise: "Colonel, did you order the Code Red!"
> Judge: "You don't have to answer that question!"
> Nicholson: "I'll answer the question . . . you want answers?"
> Cruise: "I think I'm entitled to them."
> Nicholson: "You want answers!"
> Cruise: "I want the truth!"
> Nicholson: "You can't handle the truth!"

Nicholson might as well have been yelling at all of America rather than Cruise because it seems that many in our country can't handle the truth. On one hand, we demand truth in virtually every area of our lives. For example; we demand the truth from:

- loved ones (no one wants lies from a spouse or a child)
- doctors (we want the right medicine prescribed and the right operations performed)
- stock brokers (we demand that they tell us the truth about companies they recommend)
- courts (we want them to convict only the truly guilty)
- employers (we want them to tell us the truth and pay us fairly)
- airlines (we demand truly safe planes and truly sober pilots)

We also expect to be told the truth when we pick up a reference book, read an article, or watch a news story; we want the truth from advertisers, teachers, and politicians; we assume road signs, medicine bottles, and food labels reveal the truth. In fact, we demand the truth for almost every facet of life that affects our money, relationships, safety, or health.

On the other hand, despite our unwavering demands for truth in those areas, many of us say we aren't interested in truth when it comes to morality or religion. In fact, many downright reject the idea that any religion can be true.

As we're sure you've noticed, there's a huge contradiction here. Why do we demand truth in everything but morality and religion? Why do we say, "That's true for you but not for me," when we're talking about morality or religion, but we never even think of such nonsense when we're talking to a stock broker about our money or a doctor about our health?

Although few would admit it, our rejection of religious and moral truth is often on volitional rather than intellectual grounds—we just don't *want* to be held accountable to any moral standards or religious doctrine. So we blindly accept the self-defeating truth claims of politically correct intellectuals who tell us that truth does not exist; everything is relative; there are no absolutes; it's all a matter of opinion; you ought not judge; religion is about faith, not facts! Perhaps Augustine was right when he said that we love the truth when it enlightens us, but we hate it when it convicts us. Maybe we can't handle the truth.

In order to resolve our cultural schizophrenia, we need to address four questions concerning truth:

1. What is truth?
2. Can truth be known?
3. Can truths about God be known?
4. So what? Who cares about truth?

We'll cover these questions in this chapter and the next.

What Is Truth? The Truth About Truth

What is truth? Very simply, truth is "telling it like it is." When the Roman governor Pilate asked Jesus "What is truth?" nearly 2,000 years ago, he didn't wait for Jesus to respond. Instead, Pilate immediately acted as if he knew at least some truth. Concerning Jesus, he declared, "I find no fault in this man" (see John 18:38). By exonerating Jesus, Pilate was "telling it like it is."

Truth can also be defined as "that which corresponds to its object" or "that which describes an actual state of affairs." Pilate's judgment was true because it matched its object; it described an accurate state of affairs. Jesus really was innocent.

Contrary to what is being taught in many public schools, truth is not relative but absolute. If something is true, it's true for all people, at all times, in all places. All truth claims are absolute, narrow, and exclusive. Just think about the claim "everything is true." That's an absolute, narrow, and exclusive claim. It excludes its opposite (i.e., it claims that the statement "everything is *not* true" is wrong). In fact, all truths exclude their opposites. Even religious truths.

This became comically clear when a number of years ago I (Norm) debated religious humanist Michael Constantine Kolenda. Of the many atheists I debated, he was one of the few who actually read my book *Christian Apologetics* prior to the debate.

When it was his turn to speak, Kolenda held up my book and declared, "These Christians are very narrow-minded people. I read Dr. Geisler's book. Do you know what he believes? He believes that Christianity is true and everything opposed to it is false! These Christians are very narrow-minded people!"

Well, Kolenda had also written a book which I had read beforehand. It was titled *Religion Without God* (which is sort of like romance without a spouse!). When it was my turn to speak, I held up Kolenda's book and declared, "These humanists are very narrow-minded people. I read Dr. Kolenda's book. Do you know what he believes? He believes that humanism is true and everything opposed to it is false! These humanists are very narrow-minded people!"

The audience chuckled because they could see the point. Humanist truth claims are just as narrow as Christian truth claims. For if H (humanism) is true, then anything opposed to H is false. Likewise, if C (Christianity) is true, then anything opposed to C is false.

There are many other truths about truth. Here are some of them:

• Truth is discovered, not invented. It exists independent of anyone's knowledge of it. (Gravity existed prior to Newton.)

- Truth is transcultural; if something is true, it is true for all people, in all places, at all times (2+2=4 for everyone, everywhere, at every time).
- Truth is unchanging even though our *beliefs* about truth change. (When we began to believe the earth was round instead of flat, the *truth* about the earth didn't change, only our *belief* about the earth changed.)
- Beliefs cannot change a fact, no matter how sincerely they are held. (Someone can sincerely believe the world is flat, but that only makes that person sincerely mistaken.)
- Truth is not affected by the attitude of the one professing it. (An arrogant person does not make the truth he professes false. A humble person does not make the error he professes true.)
- All truths are absolute truths. Even truths that appear to be relative are really absolute. (For example, "I, Frank Turek, feel warm on November 20, 2003" may appear to be a relative truth, but it is actually absolutely true for everyone, everywhere that Frank Turek had the sensation of warmth on that day.)

In short, contrary *beliefs* are possible, but contrary *truths* are not possible. We can *believe* everything is true, but we cannot *make* everything true.

This seems obvious enough. But how do we deal with the modern assertion that there is no truth? A couple of cartoon characters can help us.

The Road Runner Tactic

If someone said to you, "I have one insight for you that absolutely will revolutionize your ability to quickly and clearly identify the false statements and false philosophies that permeate our culture," would you be interested? That's what we're about to do here. In fact, if we had to pick just one thinking ability as the most valuable we've learned in our many years of seminary and postgraduate education, it would be this: how to identify and refute self-defeating statements. An incident from a recent talk-radio program will demonstrate what we mean by self-defeating statements.

The program's liberal host, Jerry, was taking calls on the subject of morality. After hearing numerous callers boldly claim that a certain moral position was true, one caller blurted out, "Jerry! Jerry! There's no such thing as truth!"

I (Frank) scrambled for the phone and began to dial furiously. Busy. Busy. Busy. I wanted to get on and say, "Jerry! To the guy who said, 'there is no such thing as truth'—is *that* true?"

I never did get through. And Jerry, of course, agreed with the caller, never realizing that his claim could not possibly be true—because it was self-defeating.

A self-defeating statement is one that fails to meet its own standard. As we're sure you realize, the caller's statement "there is no truth" claims to be true and thus defeats itself. It's like saying, "I can't speak a word in English." If someone ever said that, you obviously would respond, "Wait a minute! Your statement must be false because you just uttered it in English!"

Self-defeating statements are made routinely in our postmodern culture, and once you sharpen your ability to detect them, you'll become an absolutely fearless defender of truth. No doubt you've heard people say things like, "All truth is relative!" and "There are no absolutes!" Now you'll be armed to refute such silly statements by simply revealing that they don't meet their own criteria. In other words, by turning a self-defeating statement on itself, you can expose it for the nonsense it is.

We call this process of turning a self-defeating statement on itself the "Road Runner" tactic because it reminds us of the cartoon characters Road Runner and Wile E. Coyote. As you may remember from Saturday morning cartoons, the Coyote's one and only quest is to chase down the speedy Road Runner and make him his evening meal. But the Road Runner is simply too fast and too smart. Just when the Coyote is gaining ground, the Road Runner stops short at the cliff's edge leaving the passing Coyote momentarily suspended in midair, supported by nothing. As soon as the Coyote realizes he has no ground to stand on, he plummets to the valley floor and crashes in a heap.

Well, that's exactly what the Road Runner tactic can do to the relativists and postmodernists of our day. It helps them realize that their arguments cannot sustain their own weight. Consequently they crash to the ground in a heap. This makes you look like a super genius! Let's take the Road Runner tactic to college to show you what we mean.

The Road Runner Goes to College

The Road Runner tactic is especially needed by today's college students. Why? Because if you listen to many of our university professors, they'll tell you that there is no truth. What amazes us is that parents all over the world are literally paying thousands of dollars in college tuition so that their sons and daughters can be taught the *"truth" that there is no truth*, not to mention other self-defeating postmodern assertions such as: "All truth is relative" (Is *that* a relative truth?); " There are no absolutes" (Are you *absolutely* sure?); and, "It's true for you but not for me!" (Is that statement true just for you, or is it true for everyone?) "True for you but not for me" may be the mantra of our day, but it's not how the world really works. Try saying that to your bank teller, the police, or the IRS and see how far you get!

Of course these modern mantras are false because they are self-defeating. But for those who still blindly believe them, we have a few questions: If there really is no truth, then why try to learn anything? Why should any student listen to any professor? After all, the professor doesn't have the truth. What's the point of going to school, much less paying for it? And what's the point of obeying the professor's moral prohibitions against cheating on tests or plagiarizing term papers?

Ideas have consequences. Good ideas have good consequences, and bad ideas have bad consequences. Indeed, many students realize the implications of these bad postmodern ideas and behave accordingly. If we teach students that there is no right and wrong, why are we surprised when a couple of students gun down their classmates or a teenage mother leaves her baby in a trash can? Why should they act "right" when we teach them that there is no such thing as "right"?

C. S. Lewis revealed the absurdity of expecting virtue from people who are taught that no virtue exists: "In a sort of ghastly simplicity we remove the organ and demand the function. We make men without chests and expect of them virtue and enterprise. We laugh at honor and are shocked to find traitors in our midst. We castrate and bid the geldings be fruitful."[1]

The truth of the matter is this: false ideas about truth lead to false ideas about life. In many cases, these false ideas give apparent justification for what is really immoral behavior. For if you can kill the concept of truth, then you can kill the concept of any true religion or any true morality. Many in our culture have been attempting to do this, and the past forty years of religious and moral decline trumpet their success. Unfortunately, the devastating consequences of their efforts are not just true for them—they are also true for all of us.

So truth exists. It cannot be denied. Those who deny truth make the self-defeating truth claim that there is no truth. In this regard, they are a lot like Winnie the Pooh—they answer a knock at the door by saying, "No one is home!"

Now, let's see how the Road Runner tactic can help us answer the skeptical truth claim that "truth cannot be known!"

CAN TRUTH BE KNOWN? KNOCK, KNOCK . . .

Evangelical Christians believe that they ought to obey Jesus' command to "make disciples of all nations" (Matt. 28:19). In order to help Christians carry out this "Great Commission," D. James Kennedy created a door-to-door evangelism technique called "Evangelism Explosion" (EE). If you're a Christian, the EE technique allows you to quickly ascertain where a person is spiritually. After introducing yourself, you are to ask questions like these to the person answering the door:

1. Can I ask you a spiritual question?

And

2. If you were to die tonight and stand before God, and God were to ask you, "Why should I let you into my heaven?" what would you say?

Most people are curious enough to say yes to question 1. (If they say, "What do you mean by 'a spiritual question'?" you go ahead and ask them the second question.) As for the second question, the EE manual predicts that the non-Christian will usually give the "good works" answer. You know, something like, "God will accept me because I'm basically a good person. I haven't killed anybody; I go to church; I give to the poor . . ." In that case, the EE manual tells you to respond with the gospel (literally the "good news"): that all (including you) have fallen short of God's perfect standard, and no good work can erase the fact that you've already sinned; but the good news is that you can be saved from punishment by trusting in Christ, who was punished in your place.

While this technique has been very successful, some non-Christians do not respond to the two questions as expected. For example, one evening I (Norm) decided to take EE to the streets along with a fellow member of my church. Here's how it went:

Knock, Knock.

"Who's there?" (A man came to the door.)

I stuck out my hand and said, "Hi! My name is Norm Geisler, this is my partner, Ron, and we're from the church at the end of the street."

"I'm Don," the man replied, his eyes quickly sizing us up.

Immediately I jumped into action with question 1: "Don, do you mind if we ask you a spiritual question?"

"No, go ahead," Don said boldly, apparently eager to have a Bible thumper for dessert.

I laid question 2 on him: "Don, if you were to die tonight and stand before God, and God were to ask you, 'Why should I let you into my heaven?' what would you say?"

Don snapped back, "I'd say to God, 'Why *shouldn't* you let me into your heaven?'"

Gulp . . . he wasn't supposed to say that! I mean, that answer wasn't in the book!

After a split second of panic, I offered up a quick prayer and replied, "Don, if we knocked on your door seeking to come into your house, and you said to us, 'Why should I let you into my house?' and we responded, 'Why *shouldn't* you let us in?' what would you say?"

Don pointed his finger at my chest and sternly replied, "I would tell you where to go!"

I immediately shot back, "That's exactly what God is going to say to you!"

Don looked stunned for a second but then narrowed his eyes and said, "To tell you the truth: I don't believe in God. I'm an atheist."

"You're an atheist?"

"That's right!"

"Well, are you absolutely sure there is no God?" I asked him.

He paused, and said, "Well, no, I'm not *absolutely* sure. I guess it's possible there might be a God."

"So you're not really an atheist, then—you're an agnostic," I informed him, "because an atheist says, 'I know there is no God,' and an agnostic says 'I don't know whether there is a God.'"

"Yeah . . . alright; so I guess I'm an agnostic then," he admitted.

Now this was real progress. With just one question we moved from atheism to agnosticism! But I still had to figure out what kind of agnostic Don was.

So I asked him, "Don, what kind of agnostic are you?"

He laughed as he asked, "What do you mean?" (He was probably thinking, "A minute ago, I was an atheist—I have no idea what kind of agnostic I am now!")

"Well, Don, there are two kinds of agnostics," I explained. "There's the *ordinary* agnostic who says he *doesn't* know anything for sure, and then there's the *ornery* agnostic who says he *can't* know anything for sure."

Don was sure about this. He said, "I'm the ornery kind. You can't know anything for sure."

Recognizing the self-defeating nature of his claim, I unleashed the Road Runner tactic by asking him, "Don, if you say that you can't know anything for sure, then how do you know *that* for sure?"

Looking puzzled, he said, "What do you mean?"

Explaining it another way, I said, "How do you *know* for sure that you can't *know* anything for sure?"

I could see the lightbulb coming on but decided to add one more point: "Besides, Don, you can't be a skeptic about everything because that would mean you'd have to doubt skepticism; but the more you doubt skepticism the more sure you become."

He relented. "Okay, I guess I really *can* know something for sure. I must be an *ordinary* agnostic."

Now we were really getting somewhere. With just a few questions, Don had moved from atheism through *ornery* agnosticism to *ordinary* agnosticism.

I continued, "Since you admit now that you *can* know, why *don't* you know that God exists?"

Shrugging his shoulders, he said, "Because nobody has shown me any evidence, I guess."

Now I launched the million-dollar question: "Would you be willing to look at some evidence?"

"Sure," he replied.

This is the best type of person to talk to: someone who is willing to take an honest look at the evidence. Being willing is essential. Evidence cannot convince the unwilling.

Since Don was willing, we gave him a book by Frank Morison titled *Who Moved the Stone?*[2] Morison was a skeptic who set out to write a book refuting Christianity but instead became convinced by the evidence that Christianity was indeed true. (In fact, the first chapter of *Who Moved the Stone?* is called "The Book That Refused to Be Written.")

We visited Don a short time later. He described the evidence presented by Morison as "very convincing." Several weeks later, in the middle of a study of the Gospel of John, Don accepted Jesus Christ as his personal Lord and Savior.

Today Don is a deacon in a Baptist church near St. Louis, Missouri. Every Sunday morning, for years, he's driven the church bus through the local neighborhood to pick up those kids whose parents wouldn't come to church. His ministry has special meaning to me (Norm) because two men like Don (Mr. Costie and Mr. Sweetland) picked me up with a church bus more than 400 times—every Sunday from when I was nine until I was seventeen. I was in a position to accept Christ at seventeen largely because of that bus ministry. I guess it's true what they say, "What goes around comes around," even if it's just the Sunday school bus.

CAN ALL RELIGIONS BE TRUE?

The moral of the EE story is that complete agnosticism or skepticism is self-defeating. Agnostics and skeptics make the truth claim that truth claims cannot be made. They say that truth can't be known but then claim that their view is true. You can't have it both ways.

So we've established that truth can be known. In fact, it's undeniable. But so what? Can't all religions be true? Unfortunately, it's not just the secular world that's confused about this question; even some church pastors have trouble with it.

Seminary professor Ronald Nash heard of a good example of this. He told us of a student of his who went home to Bowling Green, Kentucky, for Christmas break a couple of years ago. While on break, this Bible-believing student decided to be adventurous one Sunday and attend a church that he had never attended before. But as soon as the pastor uttered the first sentence of his sermon, the student realized he had made a mistake—the pastor was contradicting the Bible.

"The theme of my sermon this morning," the pastor began, "is that all religious beliefs are true!" The student squirmed in his seat as the pastor went on to assure each member of the congregation that every religious belief they had was "true!"

When the sermon was over, the student wanted to slip out unnoticed, but the heavy-set, robed pastor was waiting at the door bear-hugging each passing congregant.

"Son," the pastor boomed upon greeting the student, "where are you from?"

"Actually, I'm from Bowling Green, sir. I'm home on break from seminary."

"Seminary! Good. So what religious beliefs do you have, Son?"

"I'd rather not say, sir."

"Why not, Son?"

"Because I don't want to offend you, sir."

"Oh, Son, you can't offend me. Besides, it doesn't matter what your beliefs are—they're true. So what do you believe?"

"Okay," the student relented. He leaned toward the pastor, cupped his hand around his mouth, and whispered, "Sir, I believe that you are going to hell!"

The pastor's face turned bright red as he struggled to respond. "I, ah, guess I, ah, made a mistake! All religious beliefs can*not* be true because yours certainly aren't true!"

Indeed, as the pastor realized, religious beliefs cannot all be true, because many religious beliefs are contradictory—they teach opposites. For example, conservative Christians believe that those who haven't accepted Christ as their Savior have chosen hell as their ultimate destination. It's often overlooked, but many Muslims believe the same about non-Muslims—they're headed for hell as well. And Hindus generally believe that everyone, regardless of beliefs, is caught in an indefinite cycle of reincarnation based on works. These contradictory beliefs can't all be true.

In fact, world religions have more contradictory beliefs than complementary ones. The notion that all religions teach basically the same thing—that we ought to love one another—demonstrates a serious misunderstanding of world religions. While most religions have some kind of similar moral code because God has implanted right and wrong on our consciences (we'll discuss that in chapter 7), they disagree on virtually every major issue, including the nature of God, the nature of man, sin, salvation, heaven, hell, and creation!

Think about it: *the nature of God, the nature of man, sin, salvation, heaven, hell,* and *creation.* Those are the biggies! Here are a few of those big differences:

- Jews, Christians, and Muslims believe in different versions of a theistic God, while most Hindus and New Agers believe that everything that exists is part of an impersonal, pantheistic force they call God.
- Many Hindus believe that evil is a complete illusion, while Christians, Muslims, and Jews believe that evil is real.
- Christians believe that people are saved by grace while all other religions, if they believe in salvation at all, teach some kind of salvation by good works (the definition of "good" and what one is saved from varies greatly).

These are just a few of the many essential differences. So much for the idea that all religions teach basically the same things!

Truth vs. Tolerance

While most *religions* have some beliefs that are true, not all religious *beliefs* can be true because they are mutually exclusive—they teach opposites. In other words, some religious beliefs must be wrong. But you're not supposed to say that in America today. You're supposed to be "tolerant" of all religious beliefs. And in our culture today, tolerance no longer means to put up with something you believe to be false (after all, you don't tolerate things you agree with). *Tolerance now means that you're supposed to accept every belief as true!* In a religious context, this is known as religious pluralism—the belief that all religions are true. There are a number of problems with this new definition of tolerance.

First, let us say that we are thankful that we have religious freedom in this country, and we don't believe in imposing a religion legislatively (see our book *Legislating Morality*).[3] We are well aware of the dangers of religious intolerance and believe that we should accept and respect people who have different religious beliefs. But that doesn't mean that personally we ought to embrace the impossible notion that all religious beliefs are true. Since mutually exclusive religious beliefs cannot be true, it makes no sense to pretend that they are. In fact, on an individual level it can be dangerous to do so. If Christianity is true, then it's dangerous to your eternal destiny not to be a Christian. Likewise, if Islam is true, then it's dangerous to your eternal destiny not to be a Muslim.

Second, the claim that "you ought not question someone's religious beliefs" is itself a religious belief for pluralists. But this belief is just as exclusive and "intolerant" as any religious belief of a Christian or Muslim. In other words, pluralists think all non-pluralist beliefs are wrong. So pluralists are just as dogmatic and closed-minded as anyone else making truth claims in the public square. And they want everyone who disagrees with them to see things *their* way.

Third, the prohibition against questioning religious beliefs is also an absolute moral position. Why shouldn't we question religious beliefs? Would it be immoral to do so? And if so, by whose standard? Do pluralists have any good reasons supporting *their belief* that we ought not question religious beliefs, or is it just their own personal opinion that they want to impose on the rest of us? Unless they can give us good reasons for such a moral standard, why should we allow them to impose it on us? And why are pluralists trying to impose that moral position on us anyway? That's not very "tolerant" of them.

Fourth, the Bible commands Christians to question religious beliefs (e.g., Deut. 13:1-5; 1 John 4:1; Gal. 1:8; 2 Cor. 11:13; etc.). Since Christians have a religious belief that they ought to question religious beliefs, then pluralists—according to their own standard—should accept this Christian belief as well. But of course they do not. Ironically, pluralists—advocates of the new tolerance—are not really tolerant at all. They only "tolerate" those who already agree with them, which by anyone's definition is not tolerance.

Fifth, the pluralist's claim that we ought not question religious beliefs is a derivative of the false cultural prohibition against making judgments. The prohibition against judging is false because it fails to meet its own standard: "you ought not judge" is itself a judgment! (Pluralists misinterpret Jesus' comments on judging [Matt. 7:1-5]. Jesus did not prohibit judging as such, only judging hypocritically.) Indeed, everyone—the pluralist, the Christian, the atheist, the agnostic—makes judgments. So the issue isn't whether or not we make judgments, but whether or not we make the *right* judgments.

Finally, are pluralists ready to accept as true the religious beliefs of Muslim terrorists—especially when those beliefs say that all non-Muslims (including pluralists) should be killed? Are they ready to accept as true the religious beliefs of those who believe in child sacrifice or other heinous acts? We hope not.

While we should respect the rights of others to believe what they want, we are foolish, and maybe even unloving, to tacitly accept every religious belief as true. Why is this unloving? Because *if* Christianity is true, then it would be unloving to suggest to anyone that their opposing religious beliefs are true as well. Affirming such error might keep them on the road to damnation. Instead, if Christianity is true, we ought to kindly tell them the truth because only the truth can set them free.

Once I Was Blind but Now I See

What does the vast plurality of religious beliefs tell us about truth in religion? At first glance, it might appear that the existence of so many contradictory beliefs just reinforces the elephant parable we mentioned in the introduction—namely, that truth in religion cannot be known. But exactly the opposite is the case.

To refresh your memory, in this parable an elephant is being examined by six blind men. Each man feels a different part of the elephant and thus reaches a different conclusion about the object in front of him. One grabs the tusk and says, "This is a spear!" Another holds the trunk and says, "This is a snake!" The one hugging the leg claims, "This is a tree!" The blind man holding the tail thinks, "I have a rope!" The one feeling the ear believes, "This is a fan!" And the one leaning on the elephant's side is certain, "This is a wall!" These blind men are said to represent world religions, because they each come to a different conclusion about what they are sensing. Like each blind man, we are told, no one religion has *the* truth. Religious truth is relative to the individual. It is subjective, not objective.

This may seem persuasive until you ask yourself one question: "What's the perspective of the one telling the parable?" Hmmmm, let's see, the one telling the parable. . . . He appears to have an *objective* perspective of the entire proceeding because he can see that the blind men are mistaken. Exactly! In fact, he wouldn't know that the blind men were wrong unless he had an objective perspective of what was right!

So if the person telling the parable can have an objective perspective, why can't the blind men? They could—if the blind men suddenly could see, they too would realize that they were originally mistaken. That's really an elephant in front of them and not a wall, fan, or rope.

We too can see the truth in religion. Unfortunately, many of us who deny there's truth in religion are not *actually* blind but only *willfully* blind. We may not want to admit that there's truth in religion because that truth will convict us. But if we open our eyes and stop hiding behind the self-defeating nonsense that truth cannot be known, then we'll be able to see the truth as well. And not just truth in the areas where we demand it—money, relationships, health, law, etc.—but truth in religion as well. As the blind man healed by Jesus said, "Once I was blind, but now I see."

The skeptic may say, "Wait a minute! The elephant parable may be a bad parable, but that still doesn't prove that truth in religion can be known. You've proven that truth can be known, but not necessarily truth in religion. In fact, didn't David Hume and Immanuel Kant disprove the idea of truth in religion?"

Not at all, and we'll discuss why in the next chapter.

SUMMARY

1. Despite the relativism that emanates from our culture, truth is absolute, exclusive, and knowable. To deny absolute truth and its knowability is self-defeating.
2. The "Road Runner" tactic turns a statement on itself and helps expose the self-defeating (and thus false) statements that are so common today. These include statements such as, "There is no truth!" (Is *that* true?); "All truth is relative!" (Is *that* a relative truth?); and "You can't know truth!" (Then how do you know *that?*). Basically, any statement that is unaffirmable (because it contradicts itself) must be false. Relativists are defeated by their own logic.
3. Truth is not dependent on our feelings or preferences. Something is true whether we like it or not.

4. Contrary to popular opinion, major world religions do not "all teach the same things." They have essential differences and only superficial agreements. All religions cannot be true, because they teach opposites.

5. Since, logically, all religions cannot be true, we cannot subscribe to the new definition of tolerance that demands that we accept the impossible idea that all religious beliefs are true. We are to respect the beliefs of others, but lovingly tell them the truth. After all, if you truly love and respect people, you will tactfully tell them the truth about information that may have eternal consequences.

2

Why Should Anyone Believe Anything At All?

People almost invariably arrive at their beliefs not on the basis of proof but on the basis of what they find attractive.

—BLAISE PASCAL

AUTHOR AND SPEAKER James Sire conducts an eye-opening interactive seminar for students at colleges and universities across the country. The seminar is called *Why Should Anyone Believe Anything At All?*

With such an intriguing title, the event usually attracts a large audience. Sire begins by asking those in attendance this question: "Why do people believe what they believe?" Despite the wide variety of answers, Sire shows that each answer he gets fits into one of these four categories: sociological, psychological, religious, and philosophical.[1]

Sociological Reasons	Psychological Reasons	Religious Reasons	Philosophical Reasons
Parents	Comfort	Scripture	Consistency
Friends	Peace of Mind	Pastor/Priest	Coherence
Society	Meaning	Guru	Completeness (best
Culture	Purpose	Rabbi	explanation of all
	Hope	Imam	the evidence)
	Identity	Church	

Table 2.1

Beginning on the left, Sire goes through the reasons in each category by asking students, "Is that a good reason to believe something?" If he gets sharp students (like he would at Southern Evangelical Seminary!), the dialog might go something like this:

> Sire: I see that many of you cited sociological factors. For example, many people have beliefs because their parents have those same beliefs. Do you think that alone is a good enough reason to believe something?

> Students: No, parents can sometimes be wrong!

> Sire: Okay, what about cultural influences? Do you think people ought to believe something just because it's accepted culturally?

> Students: No, not necessarily. The Nazis had a culture that accepted the murder of all Jews. That sure didn't make it right!

> Sire: Good. Now, some of you mentioned psychological factors such as comfort. Is that a good enough reason to believe something?

> Students: No, we're not 'comfortable' with that! Seriously, comfort is not a test for truth. We might be comforted by the belief that there's a God out there who cares for us, but that doesn't necessarily mean he really exists. Likewise, a junkie might be temporarily comforted by a certain type of drug, but that drug might actually kill him.

> Sire: So you're saying that truth is important because there can be consequences when you're wrong?

> Students: Yes, if someone is wrong about a drug, they might take too much and die. Likewise, if someone is wrong about the thickness of the ice, they might fall in and freeze to death.

> Sire: So for pragmatic reasons it makes sense that we should only believe things that are true.

> Students: Of course. Over the long run, truth protects and error harms.

> Sire: Okay, so sociological and psychological reasons alone are not adequate grounds to believe something. What about religious reasons? Some mentioned the Bible; others mentioned the Qur'an; still others got their beliefs from priests or gurus. Should you believe something just because some religious source or holy book says so?

Students: No, because the question arises, "Whose scripture or whose source should we believe?" After all, they teach contradictory things.

Sire: Can you give me an example?

Students: Well, the Bible and the Qur'an, for example, can't both be true because they contradict one another. The Bible says that Jesus died on the cross and rose three days later (1 Cor. 15:1-8), while the Qur'an says he existed but didn't die on the cross (Sura 4:157). If one's right, the other one is wrong. Then again, if Jesus never existed, both of them are wrong.

Sire: So how could we adjudicate between, say, the Bible and the Qur'an?

Students: We need some proofs outside those so-called scriptures to help us discover which, if either, is true.

Sire: From which category could we derive such proofs?

Students: All we have left is the philosophical category.

Sire: But how can someone's philosophy be a proof? Isn't that just someone's opinion?

Students: No, we don't mean philosophy in *that* sense of the word, but in the classic sense of the word where philosophy means finding truth through logic, evidence, and science.

Sire: Excellent! So with that definition in mind, let's ask the same question of the philosophical category. Is something worth believing if it's rational, if it's supported by evidence, and if it best explains all the data?

Students: That certainly seems right to us!

By exposing inadequate justifications for beliefs, the way is cleared for the seeker of truth to find adequate justifications. This is what an apologist does. An apologist is someone who shows how good reason and evidence support or contradict a particular belief. That's what we're attempting to do in this book, and it's what Sire sets up in his seminar.

Sire's Socratic approach helps students realize at least three things. First, any teaching—religious or otherwise—is worth trusting only if it points to the truth. Apathy about truth can be dangerous. In fact, believing error can have deadly consequences, both temporally and—if any one of a number of religious teachings are true—eternally as well.

Second, many beliefs that people hold today are not supported by evidence, but only by the subjective preferences of those holding them. As Pascal said, people almost invariably arrive at their beliefs not on the basis of proof but on the basis of what they find attractive. But truth is not a subjective matter of taste—it's an objective matter of fact.

Finally, in order to find truth, one must be ready to give up those subjective preferences in favor of objective facts. And facts are best discovered through logic, evidence, and science.

While using logic, evidence, and science seems the best way to get at truth, there are some who still have an objection. That objection concerns logic—namely, whose logic should we use, Eastern or Western? Ravi Zacharias tells a humorous anecdote that will reveal the answer.

WESTERN LOGIC VS. EASTERN LOGIC?

As a Christian apologist, author, and native of India, Ravi Zacharias travels the world giving evidence for the Christian faith. He has an incisive intellect and an engaging personality, which makes him a favorite on college and university campuses.

Following a recent presentation on an American campus regarding the uniqueness of Christ, Ravi was assailed by one of the university's professors for not understanding Eastern logic. During the Q&A period the professor charged, "Dr. Zacharias, your presentation about Christ claiming and proving to be the only way to salvation is wrong for people in India because you're using 'either-or' logic. In the East we don't use 'either-or' logic—that's Western. In the East we use 'both-and' logic. So salvation is not *either* through Christ *or* nothing else, but *both* Christ *and* other ways."

Ravi found this very ironic because, after all, he grew up in India. Yet here was a Western-born, American professor telling Ravi that he didn't understand how things really worked in India! This was so intriguing that Ravi accepted the professor's invitation to lunch in order to discuss it further.

One of the professor's colleagues joined them for lunch, and as he and Ravi ate, the professor used every napkin and place mat on the table to make his point about the two types of logic—one Western and one Eastern.

"There are two types of logic," the professor kept insisting.

"No, you don't mean that," Ravi kept replying.

"I absolutely do!" maintained the professor.

This went on for better than thirty minutes: the professor lecturing, writing, and diagramming. He became so engrossed in making his points that he forgot to eat his meal, which was slowly congealing on his plate.

Upon finishing his own meal, Ravi decided to unleash the Road Runner tactic to rebut the confused but insistent professor. He interrupted, "Professor, I think we can resolve this debate very quickly with just one question."

Looking up from his furious drawing, the professor paused and said, "Okay, go ahead."

Ravi leaned forward, looked directly at the professor, and asked, "Are you saying that when I'm in India, I must use *either* the 'both-and logic' *or* nothing else?"

The professor looked blankly at Ravi, who then repeated his question with emphasis: "Are you saying that when I'm in India, I must use *either*," Ravi paused for effect, "the 'both-and logic' *or*," another pause, "nothing else?"

Ravi later commented to us that the next words out of the professor's mouth were worth the time listening to his incoherent ramblings. After glancing sheepishly at his colleague, the professor looked down at his congealed meal and mumbled, "The *either-or* does seem to emerge, doesn't it." Ravi added, "Yes, even in India we look both ways before we cross the street because it is *either* me *or* the bus, not both of us!"

Indeed, the *either-or* does seem to emerge. The professor was using the either-or logic to try and prove the both-and logic, which is the same problem everyone experiences who tries to argue against the first principles of logic. They wind up sawing off the very limb upon which they sit.

Imagine if the professor had said, "Ravi, your math calculations are wrong in India because you're using Western math rather than Eastern math." Or suppose he had declared, "Ravi, your physics calculations don't apply to India because you're using Western gravity rather than Eastern gravity." We would immediately see the folly of the professor's reasoning.

In fact, despite what the relativists believe, things work in the East just like they work everywhere else. In India, just like in the United

States, buses hurt when they hit you, 2+2=4, and the same gravity keeps everyone on the ground. Likewise, murder is wrong there just as it is here. Truth is truth no matter what country you come from. And truth is truth no matter what you believe about it. Just as the same gravity keeps all people on the ground whether they believe in it or not, the same logic applies to all people whether they believe it or not.

So what's the point? The point is that there's only one type of logic that helps us discover truth. It's the one built into the nature of reality that we can't avoid using. Despite this, people will try to tell you that logic doesn't apply to reality, or logic doesn't apply to God, or there are different types of logic,[2] and so on. But as they say such things, they use the very logic they are denying. This is like using the laws of arithmetic to prove that arithmetic cannot be trusted.

It's important to note that we are not simply engaging in word games here. The Road Runner tactic uses the undeniable laws of logic to expose that much of what our common culture believes about truth, religion, and morality is undeniably false. That which is self-defeating cannot be true, but many Americans believe it anyway. We contradict ourselves at our own peril.

To Be Burned or Not to Be Burned, That Is the Question

The Road Runner tactic is so effective because it utilizes the Law of Noncontradiction. The Law of Noncontradiction is a self-evident first principle of thought that says contradictory claims cannot both be true at the same time in the same sense. In short, it says that the opposite of true is false. We all know this law intuitively, and use it every day.

Suppose you see a married couple on the street one day—friends of yours—and you ask the wife if it's true that she's expecting a baby. If she says "yes" and her husband says "no," you don't say, "Thanks a lot, that really helps me!" You think, "Maybe she hasn't told him, or maybe they misunderstood the question (or maybe something worse!)." There's one thing you know for sure: they can't both be right! The Law of Noncontradiction makes that self-evident to you.

When investigating any question of fact, including the question of God, the same Law of Noncontradiction applies. Either the theists are right—God exists—or the atheists are right—God doesn't exist. Both can't be correct. Likewise, either Jesus died and rose from the dead as the Bible claims, or he did not as the Qur'an claims. One is right, and the other is wrong.

In fact, a medieval Muslim philosopher by the name of Avicenna suggested a surefire way to correct someone who denies the Law of Noncontradiction. He said that anyone who denies the Law of Noncontradiction should be beaten and burned until he admits that to be beaten is not the same as not to be beaten, and to be burned is not the same as not to be burned! (A bit extreme, but you get the point!)

While reasonable people have no problem with the Law of Noncontradiction, some very influential philosophers have denied it implicitly in their teachings. Perhaps the two most influential of these are David Hume and Immanuel Kant. Many people have never heard of Hume and Kant, but their teachings have affected the modern mind greatly. That's why it's important that we take a brief look at each one of them. We'll start with Hume.

HUME'S SKEPTICISM: SHOULD WE BE SKEPTICAL ABOUT IT?

Perhaps more than any other person, David Hume is responsible for the skepticism prevalent today. As an empiricist, Hume believed that all meaningful ideas were either true by definition or must be based on sense experience. Since, according to Hume, there are no sense experiences for concepts beyond the physical, any metaphysical claims (those about concepts beyond the physical, including God) should not be believed—because they are meaningless. In fact, Hume asserted that propositions can be meaningful only if they meet one of the following two conditions:

- the truth claim is abstract reasoning such as a mathematical equation or a definition (e.g., "2+2=4" or "all triangles have three sides"); or
- the truth claim can be verified empirically through one or more of the five senses.

While he claimed to be a skeptic, Hume certainly wasn't skeptical about these two conditions—he was absolutely convinced he had the truth. In fact, he concludes his *Inquiry Concerning Human Understanding* with this emphatic assertion: "If we take in our hand any volume—of divinity or school metaphysics, for instance—let us ask, 'Does it contain any abstract reasoning concerning quantity or number?' No. 'Does it contain any experimental reasoning concerning matter of fact and existence?' No. Commit it then to the flames, for it can contain nothing but sophistry and illusion."[3]

Do you see the implications of Hume's two conditions? If he's correct, then any book talking about God is meaningless. You might as well use all religious writings for kindling!

Nearly two hundred years later, Hume's two conditions were converted into the "principle of empirical verifiability" by twentieth-century philosopher A. J. Ayer. The principle of empirical verifiability claims that a proposition can be meaningful only if it's true by definition or if it's empirically verifiable.

By the mid-1960s this view had become the rage in university philosophy departments across the country, including the University of Detroit where I (Norm) was a student. In fact, I took an entire class on Logical Positivism, which was another name for the brand of philosophy espoused by Ayer. The professor of that class, a Logical Positivist, was a strange breed. Though he claimed to be a Catholic, he refused to believe it was meaningful to speak about the existence of reality beyond the physical (i.e., metaphysics, God). In other words, he was an admitted atheist who told us that he wanted to convert the entire class to his brand of semantical atheism. (I once asked him, "How can you be both a Catholic and an atheist?" Ignoring two millennia of official Catholic teaching, he replied, "You don't have to believe in God to be a Catholic—you just have to keep the rules!")

On the first day of that class, this professor gave the class the task of giving presentations based on chapters in Ayer's book *Logic, Truth, and Language*. I volunteered to do the chapter titled "The Principle of Empirical Verifiability." Now keep in mind, this principle was the very foundation of Logical Positivism and thus of the entire course.

At the beginning of the next class, the professor said, "Mr. Geisler, we'll hear from you first. Keep it to no more than twenty minutes so we can have ample time for discussion."

Well, since I was using the lightning-fast Road Runner tactic, I had absolutely no trouble with the time constraints. I stood up and simply said, "The principle of empirical verifiability states that there are only two kinds of meaningful propositions: 1) those that are true by defini-tion and 2) those that are empirically verifiable. Since the principle of empirical verifiability itself is neither true by definition nor empirically verifiable, it cannot be meaningful."

That was it, and I sat down.

There was a stunned silence in the room. Most of the students could see the Coyote dangling in midair. They recognized that the principle of empirical verifiability could not be meaningful based on its own stan-dard. It self-destructed in midair! In just the second class period, the foundation of that entire class had been destroyed! What was the pro-fessor going to talk about for the next fourteen weeks?

I'll tell you what he was going to talk about. Instead of admitting that his class and his entire philosophical outlook was self-defeating and thus false, the professor suppressed that truth, hemmed and hawed, and then went on to suspect that I was behind everything that went wrong for him the rest of the semester. His allegiance to the principle of empir-ical verifiability—despite its obvious fatal flaw—was clearly a matter of the will, not of the mind.

There's a lot more to Hume, particularly his anti-miracle arguments, which we'll address when we get to chapter 8. But for now the point is this: Hume's hard empiricism, and that of his devotee A. J. Ayer, is self-defeating. The claim that "something can only be meaningful if it's empirically verifiable or true by definition" excludes itself because that statement is neither empirically verifiable nor true by definition. In other words, Hume and Ayer try to prove too much because their method of discovering meaningful propositions excludes too much. Certainly claims that are empirically verifiable or true by definition are meaning-ful. However, such claims don't comprise *all* meaningful statements as Hume and Ayer contend. So instead of committing all books about God "to the flames" as Hume suggests, you may want to consider using Hume's books to get your fire going.

KANT'S AGNOSTICISM: SHOULD WE BE AGNOSTIC ABOUT IT?

Immanuel Kant's impact has been even more devastating to the Christian worldview than David Hume's. For if Kant's philosophy is right, then there is no way to know *anything* about the real world, even empirically verifiable things! Why? Because according to Kant the structure of your senses and your mind forms all sense data, so you never really know the thing *in itself*. You only know the thing *to you* after your mind and senses form it.

To get a handle on this, look for a second out the window at a tree. Kant is saying that the tree you think you are looking at appears the way it does because your mind is forming the sense data you're getting from the tree. You really don't know the tree in itself; you only know the phenomena your mind categorizes about the tree. In short, you "kant" know the real tree in itself, only the tree as it appears to you.

Whew! Why is it that the average person on the street doesn't doubt what he sees with his own two eyes, but supposedly brilliant philosophers do? The more we study philosophy, the more we are convinced of this: if you want to make the obvious seem obscure, just let a philosopher get ahold of it!

Nevertheless, we can't avoid studying philosophy because, as C. S. Lewis said, "good philosophy must exist, if for no other reason, because bad philosophy needs to be answered."[4] Kant's philosophy is bad philosophy, yet it has convinced many people that there is an unbridgeable gulf between them and the real world; that there's no way you can get any reliable knowledge about what the world is really like, much less what God is really like. According to Kant, we are locked in complete agnosticism about the real world.

Thankfully, there's a simple answer to all of this—the Road Runner tactic. Kant commits the same error as Hume—he violates the Law of Noncontradiction. He contradicts his own premise by saying that *no one can know* the real world while *he claims to know* something about it, namely that the real world is unknowable! In effect, Kant says the *truth* about the real world is that there are *no truths* about the real world.

Since these self-defeating statements can stump even the sharpest minds, let's look at Kant's error another way. Kant is also making a logical fallacy called the "nothing-but" fallacy. This is a fallacy because "nothing-but" statements imply "more than" knowledge. Kant says he knows the data that gets to his brain is *nothing but* phenomena. But in order to know this, he would have to be able to see *more than* just the phenomena. In other words, in order to differentiate one thing from another thing, you have to be able to perceive where one ends and the other begins. For example, if you put a white piece of paper on a black desk, the only way you can tell where the paper ends is by seeing some of the desk that borders it. The contrast between the paper and the desk allows you to see the boundaries of the paper. Likewise, in order for Kant to differentiate the thing in the real world from that which his mind perceives, he would have to be able to see both. But this is exactly what he says can't be done! He says only the *phenomena* of the mind can be known, not the *noumena* (his term for the real world).

If there's no way to distinguish between the phenomena and noumena, then you can't see how they might differ. And if you can't see how they might differ, then it makes much more sense to assume that they are the same—in other words, that the idea in your mind accurately represents the thing in the real world.

What we are saying is that you really *do* know the thing in itself. You really *do know* the tree you are seeing because it is being impressed on your mind through your senses. In other words, Kant was wrong: your mind doesn't mold the tree, *the tree molds your mind.* (Just think about a wax seal: it's not the wax that impresses the seal; it's the seal that impresses the wax.) There's no gulf between your mind and the real world. In fact, your senses are your windows to the world. And senses, like windows, are that *through which* we look at the outside world. They are not that *at which* we are looking.

In a philosophy class I (Norm) was teaching, I pointed out the flaws in Kant's philosophy this way. I said, "First, if Kant claims that he can't know anything about the real world (the thing in itself) then how does he know the real world is there? And second, his view is self-defeating because he claims that you *can't know* anything about the real world while asserting that he *knows* that the real world is unknowable!"[5]

One student blurted out, "No! It can't be that easy, Dr. Geisler. You can't destroy the central tenet of the last hundred-plus years of philosophical thought in just a couple of simple sentences!"

Quoting my favorite source—*The Reader's Digest*—I responded, "'That's what happens when a beautiful theory meets a brutal gang of facts.' Besides, whoever said that a refutation has to be complex? If someone makes a simple mistake, it only takes a simple correction to point it out." There's nothing complex about the Road Runner; he's simply fast and effective.

Hume and Kant Are Wrong. So What?

Since Hume and Kant violate the Law of Noncontradiction, their attempts to destroy all "religious" truths fail. However, just because Hume and Kant are wrong, that doesn't necessarily mean that we have positive evidence for, say, the existence of God. The Road Runner tactic can only reveal that a proposition is false. It does not provide positive evidence that any particular claim is true.

So is it true that a theistic God exists? Is there any knowable evidence that will give us reasonable certainty one way or the other? Is there such a thing as knowable evidence for an unseen God? To answer those questions, we need to investigate how truth itself can be known.

How Is Truth Known?

Let's sum up what we've seen so far: truth exists, and it is absolute and undeniable. To say "truth cannot be known" is self-defeating because that very statement claims to be a *known, absolute* truth. In fact, anytime we say anything, we are implying that we know at least some truth because *any* position on *any* subject implies some degree of knowledge. If you say that someone's position is wrong, you must *know* what is right in order to say that (you can't know what is wrong unless you know what is right). Even if you say, "I don't know," you are admitting that you know something; namely, you *know* you don't know something else about the topic in question, not that you don't know anything *at all.*

But just how does one know truth? In other words, by what process do we discover truths about the world? The process of discovering truth begins with the self-evident laws of logic called first principles. They are called first principles because there is nothing behind them. They are not proved by other principles; they are simply inherent in the nature of reality and are thus self-evident. So you don't learn these first principles; you just know them. Everyone intuitively knows these principles even if they haven't thought about them explicitly.

Two of these principles are the Law of Noncontradiction and the Law of the Excluded Middle. We've already seen the reality and value of the Law of Noncontradiction. The Law of the Excluded Middle tells us that something either *is* or is *not.* For example, either God exists or he does not. Either Jesus rose from the dead or he did not. There are no third alternatives.

These first principles are the tools we use to discover all other truths. In fact, without them you couldn't learn anything else. First principles are to learning what your eyes are to seeing. Just as your eyes must be built into your body for you to see anything, first principles must be built into your mind for you to learn anything. It is from these first principles that we can learn about reality and ultimately discover the box top to this puzzle we call life.

Although we use these first principles to help us discover truth, they alone cannot tell us whether or not a particular proposition is true. To see what we mean, consider the following logical argument:

1. All men are mortal.
2. Spencer is a man.
3. Therefore Spencer is mortal.

The self-evident laws of logic tell us that the conclusion, Spencer is mortal, is a valid conclusion. In other words, the conclusion follows necessarily from the premises. *If* all men are mortal and *if* Spencer is a man, then Spencer is mortal. However, the laws of logic do not tell us whether those premises, and thus the conclusion, is true. Maybe all men are *not* mortal; maybe Spencer is not a man. Logic by itself can't tell us one way or the other.

This point is more easily seen by looking at a valid argument that isn't true. Consider the following:

1. All men are four-legged reptiles.
2. Zachary is a man.
3. Therefore Zachary is a four-legged reptile.

Logically, this argument is valid, but we all know it isn't true. The argument is valid because the conclusion follows from the premises. But the conclusion is false because the first premise is false. In other words, an argument can be logically sound but still be false because the premises of the argument do not correspond to reality. So logic only gets us so far. Logic can tell us that an argument is false, but it cannot tell us by itself which premises are true. How do we know that Zachary is a man? How do we know that men are not four-legged reptiles? We need some more information to discover those truths.

We get that information from observing the world around us and then drawing general conclusions from those observations. When you observe something over and over again, you may conclude that some general principle is true. For example, when you repeatedly drop an object off a table, you naturally observe that the object always falls to the floor. If you do that enough, you finally realize that there must be some general principle in place known as gravity.

This method of drawing general conclusions from specific observations is called induction (which is commonly equated with the scientific method). In order to be clear, we need to distinguish induction from deduction. The process of lining up premises in an argument and arriving at a valid conclusion is called deduction. That's what we did in the arguments above. But the process of discovering whether the *premises* in an argument are true usually requires induction.

Much of what you know, you know by induction. In fact, you've already used induction intuitively to investigate the truth of the premises in the arguments above. Namely, you determined that since every man you've observed has been a two-legged mammal, the man Zachary cannot be a four-legged reptile. You did the same thing with the question of Spencer's mortality. Since all men you've heard about ultimately die, you made the general conclusion that all men are mortal including a specific individual man named Spencer. These conclusions—two-legged men, gravity, and human mortality—are all inductive conclusions.

Most conclusions based on induction cannot be considered absolutely certain but only highly probable. For example, are you absolutely, 100 percent certain that gravity makes all objects drop? No, because you haven't observed all objects being dropped. Likewise, are you absolutely certain that all men are mortal? No, because you haven't observed all men die. Perhaps there's someone somewhere who hasn't died or will not die in the future.

So if inductive conclusions are not certain, can they be trusted? Yes, but to varying degrees of certainty. As we have said before, since no human being possesses infinite knowledge, most of our inductive conclusions can be wrong. (There is one important exception. It's called the "perfect induction," where all the particulars are known. For example, "all the letters on this page are black." This perfect induction yields certainty about the conclusion because you can observe and verify that every letter is indeed black.)

But even when we don't have complete or perfect information, we often have enough information to make reasonably certain conclusions on most questions in life. For example, since virtually everyone has been observed to die, your conclusion that all men are mortal is considered true beyond a reasonable doubt; it's 99-plus percent sure, but it's not beyond any doubt. It takes some faith—albeit a very small amount—to believe it.[6] The same can be said for concluding that gravity affects all objects, not just some. The conclusion is practically certain but not absolutely certain. In other words, we can be sure beyond a *reasonable* doubt, but not sure beyond *all* doubt.

HOW ARE TRUTHS ABOUT GOD KNOWN?

So what does observation and induction have to do with discovering the existence of God? Everything. In fact, observation and induction help us investigate the ultimate religious question: "Does God exist?"

You say, "Wait a minute! How can we use observation to investigate an unobservable being called God? After all, if God is invisible and immaterial as most Christians, Jews, and Muslims claim, then how can our senses help us gather information about him?"

The answer: we use induction to investigate God the same way we use it to investigate other things we can't see—by observing their effects. For example, we can't observe gravity directly; we can only observe its effects. Likewise, we can't observe the human mind directly, but only its effects. From those effects we make a rational inference to the existence of a cause.

In fact, the book you are now reading is a case in point. Why do you assume that this book is an effect of a human mind? Because all your observational experience tells you that a book is an effect that results only from some preexisting intelligence (i.e., an author). You've never seen the wind, the rain, or other natural forces produce a book; you've only seen people do so. So despite the fact that you didn't see anyone writing this book, you've concluded that it must have at least one author.

By reasoning that this book has an author, you are naturally putting observation, induction, and deduction together. If we were to write out your thoughts in logical form, they would look like this deductive argument:

1. All books have at least one author (premise based on inductive investigation).

2. *I Don't Have Enough Faith to Be an Atheist* is a book (premise based on observation).

3. Therefore, *I Don't Have Enough Faith to Be an Atheist* has at least one author (conclusion).

You know the argument is valid because of deduction, and you know the argument is true because the premises are true (which you have verified through observation and induction).

Now here's the big question: Just as a book requires preexisting human intelligence, are there any observable effects that seem to require some kind of preexisting supernatural intelligence? In other words, are there effects that we can observe that point to God? The answer is yes, and the first effect is the universe itself. An investigation of its beginning is the next step on our journey to discover the box top.

But before we look at that evidence for the beginning of the universe, we need to address one more objection to truth. And that is, "So what? Who cares about truth?"

So What? Who Cares About Truth?

We sometimes ask our students, "What's the greatest problem in America today? Is it ignorance or is it apathy?" One time a student answered, "I don't know, and I don't care!"

That sums up the problem in America today. Many of us are ignorant and apathetic about truth—but not when it comes to money, medicine, or the other tangible items we mentioned earlier. We care passionately about those things. But many people are ignorant and apathetic about truth in morality and religion (we know you're not, because you're taking the time to read this book). Are the people who have adopted the "whatever" theme of the culture right, or does truth in morality and religion really matter?

It really matters. How do we know? First, even though people may *claim* that truth in morality doesn't matter, they don't really believe that when someone treats them immorally. For example, they might claim that lying isn't wrong, but just watch how morally outraged they get when you lie to them (especially if it's about their money!).

We often hear that "it's the economy, Stupid!" But just think about how much better the economy would be if everyone told the truth. There would be no Enrons or Tycos. There would be no scandals or scams.

There would be no burdensome government regulations. Of course the economy is important, but it's directly affected by morality! Morality undergirds virtually everything we do. It not only affects us financially, but, in certain circumstances, it also affects us socially, psychologically, spiritually, and even physically.

A second reason truth in morality matters is because success in life is often dependent on the moral choices a person makes. These include choices regarding sex, marriage, children, drugs, money, business dealings, and so on. Some choices bring prosperity, others result in ruin.

Third, as we pointed out in a previous book, *Legislating Morality,*[7] all laws legislate morality. The only question is, "Whose morality will be legislated?" Think about it. Every law declares one behavior right and its opposite wrong—that's morality. Whose morality should be legislated on issues such as abortion or euthanasia? These are issues that directly impact the lives and health of real people. If it's morally wrong to kill innocent people, shouldn't that truth be legislated? Likewise, whose morality should be legislated on other issues of public policy that may affect your life, health, or finances? The answers we legislate can dramatically affect every citizen's life, liberty, and pursuit of happiness.

There's no doubt that what we believe to be true about morality directly impacts lives. Did it matter that the United States Supreme Court (as reflected in the 1857 *Dred Scott* decision) believed that blacks were not citizens but the property of their slave owners? Did it matter that the Nazis believed the Jews were inferior to the Aryan race? Does it matter today what we think about the moral status of people in other racial or religious categories? Of course! Truth in morality matters.

What about truth in religion? That truth can impact us even more profoundly than truth in morality. A fellow naval officer helped me (Frank) realize this back in 1988 when I was a new Christian.

At that time, we were deployed with a U.S. Navy flight crew to a Persian Gulf country. It was near the end of the Iran-Iraq war, and tensions were still high. When you're in a foreign and dangerous place, you tend to ponder your life and your mortality more seriously and frequently.

One day we were doing just that—talking about God and the afterlife. During our conversation my friend made a comment that has stuck with me to this day. Referring to the Bible, he said, "I don't believe the Bible. But if it *is* true, then I'll be in big trouble."

Of course he was right. If the Bible is *true,* then my friend has *chosen* an unpleasant eternal destiny. In fact, if the Bible is true, then everyone's eternal destiny can be read from its pages. On the other hand, if the Bible is not true, then many Christians are unwittingly wasting a lot of time, money, and, in some cases, even their lives by preaching Christianity in hostile territories. Either way, truth in religion matters.

It also matters if some other religion is true. For example, if the Qur'an is true, then I'm in just as much eternal trouble as my non-Christian Navy friend. On the other hand, if the atheists are right, then we might as well lie, cheat, and steal to get what we want because this life is all there is, and there are no consequences in eternity.

But forget eternity for a minute. Consider the temporal implications of religious teachings around the world. In Saudi Arabia, some schoolchildren are being taught that Jews are pigs and that non-Muslims (infidels) should be killed (while, thankfully, a majority of Muslims do not believe that non-Muslims should be killed, militant Muslims teach that type of *Jihad* straight from the Qur'an[8]). Is it really true that there's a God up there by the name of Allah who wants Muslims to kill all non-Muslims (which probably includes you)? Does this religious "truth" matter? It does when those kids grow up to fly planes into buildings and blow themselves up in populated areas. Wouldn't it be better to teach them the religious truth that God wants them to love their neighbor?

The Saudis may be teaching that Jews are pigs, but in our country, by means of a one-sided biology curriculum, we teach kids that there's really no difference between *any* human being and a pig. After all, if we're merely the product of blind naturalistic forces—if no deity created us with any special significance—then we are nothing more than pigs with big brains. Does this religious (atheistic) "truth" matter? It does when kids carry out its implications. Instead of good citizens who see people made in the image of God, we are producing criminals who see no meaning or value in human life. Ideas have consequences.

On the positive side, Mother Teresa helped improve conditions in India by challenging the religious beliefs of many in the Hindu culture. The Hindu belief in karma and reincarnation leads many Hindus to ignore the cries of the suffering. Why? Because they believe that those who suffer deserve their plight for doing something wrong in a previous life. So, if you help suffering people, you are interfering with their karma.

Mother Teresa taught Hindus in India the Christian principles of caring for the poor and suffering. Does that religious idea matter? Ask the millions whose lives she touched. Does the religious teaching of karma matter? Ask the millions still suffering.

The bottom line is this: regardless of what the real truth is concerning religion and morality, our lives are greatly affected by it today and perhaps even in eternity. Those who cavalierly say, "So what? Who cares about truth in morality and religion?" are ignoring reality and are blindly skating on thin ice. We owe it to ourselves and others to find the real truth, and then act on it. So let's get started with the question, "Does God exist?"

SUMMARY

1. People often get their beliefs from their parents, friends, childhood religion, or culture. Sometimes they simply formulate their beliefs on the basis of their feelings alone. While such beliefs could be true, it's also possible they may not be. The only way to be reasonably certain is to test beliefs by the evidence. And that is done by utilizing sound philosophical principles including those found in logic and science.[9]

2. Logic tells us that opposites cannot be true at the same time in the same sense. Logic is part of reality itself, and is thus the same in America, India, and everywhere in the universe.

3. By use of the Road Runner tactic, we can see that Hume is not skeptical about skepticism, and Kant is not agnostic about agnosticism. Therefore, their views defeat themselves. It is possible to know truths about God.

4. Many truths about God can be known by his effects, which we can observe. Through many observations (induction) we can draw reasonable conclusions (deductions) about the existence and nature of God (which we will do in subsequent chapters).

5. Truth in morality and religion has temporal and maybe even eternal consequences. Apathy and ignorance can be fatal. What you don't know, or don't care to know, *can* hurt you.

6. So why should anyone believe anything at all? Because they have evidence to support those beliefs, and because beliefs have consequences.

Chapters 3–7
will cover:

1. Truth about reality is knowable.
2. The opposite of true is false.
➤ **3. It is true that the theistic God exists. This is evidenced by the:**
   a. Beginning of the universe (Cosmological Argument)
   b. Design of the universe (Teleological Argument/ Anthropic Principle)
   c. Design of life (Teleological Argument)
   d. Moral Law (Moral Argument)
4. If God exists, then miracles are possible.
5. Miracles can be used to confirm a message from God (i.e., as acts of God to confirm a word from God).
6. The New Testament is historically reliable. This is evidenced by:
   a. Early testimony
   b. Eyewitness testimony
   c. Uninvented (authentic) testimony
   d. Eyewitnesses who were not deceived
7. The New Testament says Jesus claimed to be God.
8. Jesus' claim to be God was miraculously confirmed by:
   a. His fulfillment of many prophecies about himself;
   b. His sinless life and miraculous deeds;
   c. His prediction and accomplishment of his resurrection.
9. Therefore, Jesus is God.
10. Whatever Jesus (who is God) teaches is true.
11. Jesus taught that the Bible is the Word of God.
12. Therefore, it is true that the Bible is the Word of God (and anything opposed to it is false).

3

In the Beginning There Was a Great SURGE

"Science without religion is lame; religion without science is blind."

—ALBERT EINSTEIN

"IRRITATING" FACTS

It was 1916 and Albert Einstein didn't like where his calculations were leading him. If his theory of General Relativity was true, it meant that the universe was not eternal but had a beginning. Einstein's calculations indeed were revealing a definite beginning to all time, all matter, and all space. This flew in the face of his belief that the universe was static and eternal.

Einstein later called his discovery "irritating." He wanted the universe to be self-existent—not reliant on any outside cause—but the universe appeared to be one giant effect. In fact, Einstein so disliked the implications of General Relativity—a theory that is now proven accurate to five decimal places—that he introduced a cosmological constant (which some have since called a "fudge factor") into his equations in order to show that the universe is static and to avoid an absolute beginning.

But Einstein's fudge factor didn't fudge for long. In 1919, British cosmologist Arthur Eddington conducted an experiment during a solar eclipse which confirmed that General Relativity was indeed true—the universe wasn't static but had a beginning. Like Einstein, Eddington wasn't happy with the implications. He later wrote, "Philosophically, the notion of a beginning of the present order of nature is repugnant to me. . . . I should like to find a genuine loophole."[1]

By 1922, Russian mathematician Alexander Friedmann had officially exposed Einstein's fudge factor as an algebraic error. (Incredibly, in his quest to avoid a beginning, the great Einstein had divided by zero—something even schoolchildren know is a no-no!) Meanwhile, Dutch astronomer Willem de Sitter had found that General Relativity required the universe to be expanding. And in 1927, the expanding of the universe was actually observed by astronomer Edwin Hubble (namesake of the space telescope).

Looking through the 100-inch telescope at California's Mount Wilson Observatory, Hubble discovered a "red shift" in the light from every observable galaxy, which meant that those galaxies were moving away from us. In other words, General Relativity was again confirmed—the universe appears to be expanding from a single point in the distant past.[2]

In 1929 Einstein made a pilgrimage to Mount Wilson to look through Hubble's telescope for himself. What he saw was irrefutable. The *observational* evidence showed that the universe was indeed expanding as General Relativity had predicted. With his cosmological constant now completely crushed by the weight of the evidence against it, Einstein could no longer support his wish for an eternal universe. He subsequently described the cosmological constant as "the greatest blunder of my life," and he redirected his efforts to find the box top to the puzzle of life. Einstein said that he wanted "to know how God created the world. I am not interested in this or that phenomenon, in the spectrum of this or that element. I want to know His thought, the rest are details."[3]

Although Einstein said that he believed in a pantheistic God (a god that *is* the universe), his comments admitting creation and divine thought better describe a theistic God. And as "irritating" as it may be, his theory of General Relativity stands today as one of the strongest lines of evidence for a theistic God. Indeed, General Relativity supports what is one of the oldest formal arguments for the existence of a theistic God—the Cosmological Argument.

THE COSMOLOGICAL ARGUMENT—THE BEGINNING OF THE END FOR ATHEISM

Don't be put off by the technical-sounding name: "cosmological" comes from the Greek word *cosmos,* which means "world" or "universe." That is, the Cosmological Argument is the argument from the beginning of the universe. If the universe had a beginning, then the universe had a cause. In logical form, the argument goes like this:

1. Everything that had a beginning had a cause.
2. The universe had a beginning.
3. Therefore the universe had a cause.

As we showed in the last chapter, for an argument to be true it has to be logically valid, and its premises must be true. This is a valid argument, but are the premises true? Let's take a look at the premises.

Premise 1—Everything that had a beginning had a cause—is the Law of Causality, which is *the* fundamental principle of science. Without the Law of Causality, science is impossible. In fact, Francis Bacon (the father of modern science) said, "True knowledge is knowledge by causes."[4] In other words, science is a search for causes. That's what scientists do—they try to discover what caused what.

If there's one thing we've observed about the universe, it's that things don't happen without a cause. When a man is driving down the street, a car never appears in front of his car out of nowhere, with no driver or no cause. We know many a police officer has heard this, but it's just not true. There's always a driver or some other cause behind that car appearing. Even the great skeptic David Hume could not deny the Law of Causality. He wrote, "I never asserted so absurd a proposition as that something could arise without a cause."[5]

In fact, to deny the Law of Causality is to deny rationality. The very process of rational thinking requires us to put together thoughts (the causes) that result in conclusions (the effects). So if anyone ever tells you he doesn't believe in the Law of Causality, simply ask that person, "What *caused* you to come to that conclusion?"

Since the Law of Causality is well established and undeniable, premise 1 is true. What about premise 2? Did the universe have a beginning? If not, then no cause was needed. If so, then the universe must have had a cause.

Until about the time of Einstein, atheists could comfort themselves with the belief that the universe is eternal, and thus did not need a cause. But since then, five lines of scientific evidence have been discovered that prove beyond a reasonable doubt that the universe did indeed have a beginning. And that beginning was what scientists now call "The Big

Bang." This Big Bang evidence can be easily remembered by the acronym SURGE.

IN THE BEGINNING THERE WAS A GREAT SURGE

Every several years or so, the major news magazines—*Time, Newsweek,* and the like—run a cover story about the origin and fate of the universe. "When did the universe begin?" and "When will it end?" are two of the questions investigated in such articles. The fact that the universe had a beginning and will ultimately die is not even up for debate in these reports. Why? Because modern scientists know that a beginning and an ending are demanded by one of the most validated laws in all of nature—the Second Law of Thermodynamics.

S—The Second Law of Thermodynamics

The Second Law of Thermodynamics is the S in our SURGE acronym. Thermodynamics is the study of matter and energy, and the Second Law states, among other things, that the universe is running out of usable energy. With each passing moment, the amount of usable energy in the universe grows smaller, leading scientists to the obvious conclusion that one day all the energy will be gone and the universe will die. Like a running car, the universe will ultimately run out of gas.

You say, "So what? How does that prove that the universe had a beginning?" Well, look at it this way: the *First* Law of Thermodynamics states that the total amount of energy in the universe is constant.[6] In other words, the universe has only a finite amount of energy (much as your car has only a finite amount of gas). Now, if your car has only a finite amount of gas (the First Law), and whenever it's running it continually consumes gas (the Second Law), would your car be running right now if you had started it up an infinitely long time ago? No, of course not. It would be out of gas by now. In the same way, the universe would be out of energy by now if it had been running from all eternity. But here we are—the lights are still on, so the universe must have begun sometime in the finite past. That is, the universe is not eternal—it had a beginning.

A flashlight is another way to think about the universe. If you leave a flashlight on overnight, what's the intensity of the light in the morning? It is dim, because the batteries have used up most of their energy.

Well, the universe is like a dying flashlight. It has only so much energy left to consume. But since the universe still has some battery life left (it's not quite dead yet), it can't be eternal—it must have had a beginning— for if it were eternal, the battery would have died by now.

The Second Law is also known as the Law of Entropy, which is a fancy way of saying that nature tends to bring things to disorder. That is, with time, things naturally fall apart. Your car falls apart; your house falls apart; your body falls apart. (In fact, the Second Law is the reason many of us get "dresser disease" when we get older—our chest falls into our drawers!) But if the universe is becoming less ordered, then where did the original order come from? Astronomer Robert Jastrow likens the universe to a wound-up clock.[7] If a wind-up clock is running down, then someone must have wound it up.

This aspect of the Second Law also tells us that the universe had a beginning. Since we still have some order left—just like we still have some usable energy left—the universe cannot be eternal, because if it were, we would have reached complete disorder (entropy) by now.

A number of years ago, a student from a Christian ministry on an Ivy League campus invited me (Norm) to speak there on a related topic. During the lecture, I basically told the students what we've written here but in a lot more detail. After the lecture, the student who had invited me there asked me to have lunch with him and his physics professor.

As we sat down to eat, the professor made it clear that he was skeptical of my argument that the Second Law requires a beginning for the universe. In fact, he said he was a materialist who believed that only material exists and that it has existed from all eternity.

"If matter is eternal, what do you do with the Second Law?" I asked him.

He replied, "Every law has an exception. This is my exception."

I could have countered by asking him if it's really good science to assume that every law has an exception. That doesn't seem very scientific and may even be self-defeating. It may be self-defeating when you ask, "Does the law that 'every law has an exception' have an exception?" If it does, maybe the Second Law is the exception to the law that every law must have an exception.

I didn't go down that road, because I thought he would take exception. Instead, I backed off the Second Law for a moment and decided to question him about materialism.

"If everything is material," I asked, "then what is a scientific theory? After all, the theory about everything being material isn't material; it's not made out of molecules."

Without a moment's hesitation he quipped, "A theory is magic."

"Magic?" I repeated, not really believing what I was hearing. "What's your basis for saying that?"

"Faith," he quickly replied.

"Faith in magic?" I thought to myself. "I can't believe what I'm hearing! If faith in magic is the best the materialists have to offer, then *I don't have enough faith to be a materialist!*"

In retrospect, it seemed to me that this professor had a brief moment of complete candor. He knew he couldn't answer the overwhelming evidence in support of the Second Law, so he admitted that his position had no basis in evidence or good reason. In doing so, he provided another example of the will refusing to believe what the mind knows to be true, and how the atheists' view is based on sheer faith.

The professor was right about one thing: having faith. In fact, he needed a *leap* of faith to willingly ignore the most established law in all of nature. That's how Arthur Eddington characterized the Second Law more than eighty years ago:

> The Law that entropy increases—the Second Law of Thermodynamics—holds, I think, the supreme position among the laws of Nature. If someone points out to you that your pet theory of the universe is in disagreement with Maxwell's equations—then so much for Maxwell's equations. If it is found to be contradicted by observation— well, these experiments do bungle things sometimes. But *if your theory is found to be against the Second Law of Thermodynamics I can give you no hope; there is nothing for it but to collapse in deepest humiliation.*[8]

Since I could see that the professor was not really interested in accepting the truth, I didn't ask him any more potentially humiliating questions. But since we couldn't ignore the power of the Second Law on our own bodies, we both ordered dessert. Neither of us was willing to deny that we needed to replace the energy we had just used up!

U—The Universe Is Expanding

Good scientific theories are those that are able to predict phenomena that have not yet been observed. As we have seen, General Relativity predicted an expanding universe. But it wasn't until legendary astronomer Edwin Hubble looked through his telescope more than a decade later that scientists finally confirmed that the universe is expanding and that it's expanding from a single point. (Astronomer Vesto Melvin Slipher was hot on the trail of this expanding universe as early as 1913, but it was Hubble who put all the pieces together, in the late 20s.) This expanding universe is the second line of scientific evidence that the universe had a beginning.

How does the expanding universe prove a beginning? Think about it this way: if we could watch a video recording of the history of the universe in reverse, we would see all matter in the universe collapse back to a point, not the size of a basketball, not the size of a golf ball, not even the size of a pinhead, but mathematically and logically to a point that is actually nothing (i.e., no space, no time, and no matter). In other words, once there was nothing, and then, BANG, there was something—the entire universe exploded into being! This, of course, is what is commonly called "the Big Bang."

It's important to understand that the universe is not expanding into empty space, but space itself is expanding—there was no space before the Big Bang. It's also important to understand that the universe did not emerge from existing material but from nothing—there was no matter before the Big Bang. In fact, chronologically, there was no "before" the Big Bang because there are no "befores" without time, and there was no time until the Big Bang.[9] Time, space, and matter came into existence at the Big Bang.

These facts give atheists a lot of trouble, as they did on a rainy night in Georgia in April of 1998. That night I (Frank) attended a debate in Atlanta on the question, "Does God exist?" William Lane Craig took the affirmative position, and Peter Atkins took the negative position. The debate was highly spirited and even humorous at times, partially due to the moderator, William F. Buckley, Jr. (Buckley did not hide his favoritism for Craig's pro-God position: after introducing Craig and his impressive credentials, Buckley began to introduce Atkins by cracking, "On the side of the Devil is Dr. Peter Atkins!")

One of Craig's five arguments for the existence of God was the Cosmological Argument as supported by the Big Bang evidence we've been discussing here. He pointed out that the universe—all time, all matter, and all space—exploded out of nothing, a fact that Atkins had conceded in his book and reaffirmed later in the debate that night.

Since Craig spoke first, he informed the audience how Atkins attempts to explain the universe from an atheistic perspective: "In his book *The Creation Revisited*, Dr. Atkins struggles mightily to explain how the universe could come into existence, uncaused out of nothing. But in the end he finds himself trapped in self-contradiction. He [writes], 'Now we go back in time beyond the moment of creation to when there was no time, and to where there was no space.' At this time before time, he imagines a swirling dust of mathematical points which recombine again and again and again and finally come by trial and error to form our space time universe."[10]

Craig went on to point out that Atkins's position is not a scientific theory but is actually self-contradictory pop-metaphysics. It is pop-metaphysics because it's a made-up explanation—there's absolutely no scientific evidence supporting it. And it's self-contradictory because it assumes time and space before there was time and space.

Since Craig did not get a chance to dialogue with Atkins directly on this point, Ravi Zacharias and I stood in the question line near the end of the debate to ask Atkins about his position. Unfortunately, time expired before either of us could ask a question, so we approached Atkins backstage afterwards.

"Dr. Atkins," Ravi started, "you admit that the universe exploded out of nothing, but your explanation for the beginning equivocates on what 'nothing' is. Swirling mathematical points are not nothing. Even they are something. How do you justify this?"

Instead of addressing the issue, Atkins verbally succumbed to the Second Law of Thermodynamics. He said, "Look, gentlemen, I am very tired. I can't answer any more questions now." In other words, his decrease of energy proved the Second Law was at work. Atkins literally had nothing to say!

Well, according to the modern cosmological evidence, the universe literally had nothing from which to emerge. Yet when it came to giving an atheistic explanation for this, Atkins didn't really begin with nothing but with mathematical points and time. Of course, one can't imagine how mere mathematical points and time could actually cause the universe anyway. Nevertheless, we wanted to press the fact that atheists like Atkins must be able to explain how the universe began from absolutely nothing.

What is nothing? Aristotle had a good definition: he said that *nothing is what rocks dream about!* The nothing from which the universe emerged is not "mathematical points" as Atkins suggested or "positive and negative energy" as Isaac Asimov, who is also an atheist, once wrote.[11] Nothing is literally *no thing*—what rocks dream about.

British author Anthony Kenny honestly described his own predicament as an atheist in light of evidence for the Big Bang. He wrote, "According to the Big Bang Theory, the whole matter of the universe began to exist at a particular time in the remote past. A proponent of such a theory, at least if he is an atheist, must believe that the matter of the universe came from nothing and by nothing."[12]

R—*Radiation from the Big Bang*

The third line of scientific evidence that the universe had a beginning was discovered by accident in 1965. That's when Arno Penzias and Robert Wilson detected strange radiation on their antenna at Bell Labs in Holmdel, New Jersey. No matter where they turned their antenna, this mysterious radiation remained. They initially thought it might be the result of bird droppings deposited on the antenna by nesting Jersey Shore pigeons, so they had the birds and the droppings removed. But when they got back inside, they found that the radiation was still there, and it was still coming from all directions.

What Penzias and Wilson had detected turned out to be one of the most incredible discoveries of the last century—one that would win them Nobel Prizes. These two Bell Lab scientists had discovered the afterglow from the Big Bang fireball explosion!

Technically known as the cosmic background radiation, this afterglow is actually light and heat from the initial explosion. This light is no longer visible because its wavelength has been stretched by the expanding universe to wavelengths slightly shorter than those produced by a microwave oven. But the heat can still be detected.

As early as 1948, three scientists predicted that this radiation would be out there if the Big Bang did really occur. But for some reason no one attempted to detect it before Penzias and Wilson stumbled upon it by accident nearly twenty years later. When the discovery was confirmed, it laid to rest any lingering suggestion that the universe is in an eternal steady state. Agnostic astronomer Robert Jastrow put it this way:

> No explanation other than the Big Bang has been found for the fireball radiation. The clincher, which has convinced almost the last Doubting Thomas, is that the radiation discovered by Penzias and Wilson has exactly the pattern of wavelengths expected for the light and heat produced in a great explosion. Supporters of the steady state theory have tried desperately to find an alternative explanation, but they have failed. At the present time, the Big Bang theory has no competitors.[13]

In effect, the discovery of the fireball radiation burned up any hope in the Steady State. But that wasn't the end of the discoveries. More Big Bang evidence would follow. In fact, if cosmology were a football game, believers in the Big Bang would be called for "piling on" with this next discovery.

G—Great Galaxy Seeds

After finding the predicted expanding universe and radiation afterglow, scientists turned their attention to another prediction that would confirm the Big Bang. If the Big Bang actually occurred, scientists believed that we should see slight variations (or ripples) in the temperature of the cosmic background radiation that Penzias and Wilson had discovered. These temperature ripples enabled matter to congregate by gravitational attraction into galaxies. If found, they would comprise the fourth line of scientific evidence that the universe had a beginning.

In 1989 the search for these ripples was intensified when NASA launched the $200 million satellite aptly called COBE for Cosmic Background Explorer. Carrying extremely sensitive instruments, COBE was able to see whether or not these ripples actually existed in the background radiation and how precise they were.

When the project leader, astronomer George Smoot, announced COBE's findings in 1992, his shocking characterization was quoted in newspapers all over the world. He said, "If you're religious, it's like looking at God." University of Chicago astrophysicist Michael Turner was no less enthusiastic, claiming, "The significance of this [discovery] cannot be overstated. They have found the Holy Grail of Cosmology." Cambridge astronomer Stephen Hawking also agreed, calling the findings "the most important discovery of the century, if not of all time."[14] What did COBE find to merit such momentous descriptions?

COBE not only found the ripples, but scientists were amazed at their precision. The ripples show that the explosion and expansion of the universe was precisely tweaked to cause just enough matter to congregate to allow galaxy formation, but not enough to cause the universe to collapse back on itself. Any slight variation one way or the other, and none of us would be here to tell about it. In fact, the ripples are so exact (down to one part in one hundred thousand) that Smoot called them the "machining marks from the creation of the universe" and the "fingerprints of the maker."[15]

But these temperature ripples are not just dots on a scientist's graph somewhere. COBE actually took infrared pictures of the ripples. Now keep in mind that space observations are actually observations of the past because of the long time it takes light from distant objects to reach us. So COBE's pictures are actually pictures of the past. That is, the infrared pictures taken by COBE point to the existence of matter from the very early universe that would ultimately form into galaxies and clusters of galaxies. Smoot called this matter "seeds" of the galaxies as they exist today (these pictures can be seen at COBE's website, http://Lambda.gsfc.nasa.gov). These "seeds" are the largest structures ever detected, with the biggest extending across one-third of the known universe. That's 10 billion light years or 60 billion trillion (60 followed by 21 zeros) miles.[16]

Now you can see why some scientists were so grandiose in their description of the discovery. Something predicted by the Big Bang was again found, and that something was so big and so precise that it made a big bang with scientists!

E—Einstein's Theory of General Relativity

The E in SURGE is for Einstein. His theory of General Relativity is the fifth line of scientific evidence that the universe had a beginning, and its discovery was the beginning of the end for the idea that the universe is eternal. The theory itself, which has been verified to five decimal places, demands an absolute beginning for time, space, and matter. It shows that time, space, and matter are co-relative. That is, they are interdependent—you can't have one without the others.

From General Relativity, scientists predicted and then found the expanding universe, the radiation afterglow, and the great galaxy seeds that were precisely tweaked to allow the universe to form into its present state. Add these discoveries to the Second Law of Thermodynamics, and we have five lines of powerful scientific evidence that the universe had a beginning—a beginning, we might say, that came in a great SURGE.

GOD AND THE ASTRONOMERS

So the universe had a beginning. What does that mean for the question of God's existence? The man who now sits in Edwin Hubble's chair at the Mount Wilson observatory has a few things to say about that. His name is Robert Jastrow, an astronomer we've already quoted in this chapter. In addition to serving as the director of Mount Wilson, Jastrow is the founder of NASA's Goddard Institute of Space Studies. Obviously his credentials as a scientist are impeccable. That's why his book *God and the Astronomers* made such an impression on those investigating the implications of the Big Bang, namely those asking the question, "Does the Big Bang point to God?"

Jastrow reveals in the opening line of chapter 1 that he has no religious axe to grind. He writes, "When an astronomer writes about God, his colleagues assume he is either over the hill or going bonkers. In my case it should be understood from the start that I am an agnostic in religious matters."[17]

In light of Jastrow's personal agnosticism, his theistic quotations are all the more provocative. After explaining some of the Big Bang evidence we've just reviewed, Jastrow writes, "Now we see how the astronomical evidence leads to a biblical view of the origin of the world. The details differ, but the essential elements in the astronomical and biblical accounts of Genesis are the same: the chain of events leading to man commenced suddenly and sharply at a definite moment in time, in a flash of light and energy."[18]

The overwhelming evidence for the Big Bang and its consistency with the biblical account in Genesis led Jastrow to observe in an interview, "Astronomers now find they have painted themselves into a corner because they have proven, by their own methods, that the world began abruptly in an act of creation to which you can trace the seeds of every star, every planet, every living thing in this cosmos and on the earth. And they have found that all this happened as a product of forces they cannot hope to discover. . . . *That there are what I or anyone would call supernatural forces at work is now, I think, a scientifically proven fact.*"[19]

By evoking the supernatural, Jastrow echoes the conclusion of Einstein contemporary Arthur Eddington. As we mentioned earlier, although he found it "repugnant," Eddington admitted, "The beginning seems to present insuperable difficulties unless we agree to look on it as frankly supernatural."[20]

Now why would Jastrow and Eddington admit that there are "supernatural" forces at work? Why couldn't natural forces have produced the universe? Because these scientists know as well as anyone that natural forces—indeed all of nature—were created at the Big Bang. In other words, the Big Bang was the beginning point for the entire physical universe. Time, space, and matter came into existence at that point. There was no natural world or natural law prior to the Big Bang. Since a cause cannot come after its effect, natural forces cannot account for the Big Bang. Therefore, there must be something *outside of nature* to do the job. That's exactly what the word *supernatural* means.

The discoverers of the afterglow, Robert Wilson and Arno Penzias, were not Bible-thumpers either. Both initially believed in the Steady State Theory. But due to the mounting evidence, they've since changed their views and acknowledged facts that are consistent with the Bible. Penzias admits, "The Steady State theory turned out to be so ugly that people dismissed it. The easiest way to fit the observations with the least number of parameters was one in which the universe was created out of nothing, in an instant, and continues to expand."[21]

Wilson, who once took a class from Fred Hoyle (the man who popularized the Steady State Theory in 1948), said, "I philosophically liked the Steady State. And clearly I've had to give that up."[22] When science writer Fred Heeren asked him if the Big Bang evidence is indicative of a Creator, Wilson responded, "Certainly there was something that set it all off. Certainly, if you are religious, I can't think of a better theory of the origin of the universe to match with Genesis."[23] George Smoot echoed Wilson's assessment. He said, "There is no doubt that a parallel exists between the big bang as an event and the Christian notion of creation from nothing."[24]

The Empire Strikes Back (but Fizzles Out)

What do atheists have to say about this? We've already seen the shortcomings in the explanations of Atkins and Isaac Asimov—they start with *something* rather than literally nothing. Are there any other atheistic explanations out there that may be plausible? Not that we've seen. Atheists have come up with other theories, but all of them have their fatal flaws.[25] Let's take a brief look at a few of them.

The Cosmic Rebound Theory—This is the theory that suggests the universe has been expanding and contracting forever. This helps its proponents avoid a definite beginning. But the problems with this theory are numerous, and for those reasons it has fallen out of favor.

First, and most obviously, there's no evidence for an infinite number of bangs (after all, it's not the Big Bang, Bang, Bang, Bang, Bang . . . Theory!). The universe appears to have exploded once from nothing, not repeatedly from existing material.

Second, there's not enough matter in the universe to pull everything back together. The universe seems poised to continue expanding indefinitely.[26] This was confirmed in 2003 by Charles Bennett of NASA's Goddard Space Flight Center. After looking at readings from NASA's latest space probe, he said, "The universe will expand forever. It will not turn back on itself and collapse in a great crunch."[27] In fact, astronomers are now finding that the universe's expansion speed is actually accelerating, making a collapse even more improbable.[28]

Third, even if there were enough matter to cause the universe to contract and "bang" again, the Cosmic Rebound Theory contradicts the Second Law of Thermodynamics because the theory falsely assumes that no energy would be lost in each contraction and explosion. A universe "banging" repeatedly would eventually fizzle out just as a dropped ball eventually fizzles out. So if the universe has been expanding and contracting *forever*, it would have fizzled out already.

Finally, there's no way that today would have gotten here if the universe had been expanding and contracting forever. An infinite number of big bangs is an actual impossibility (we'll elaborate on this in a couple of pages). And even if there were a *finite* number of bangs, the theory cannot explain what caused the first one. There was nothing to "bang" before the first bang!

Imaginary Time—Other atheistic attempts at explaining how the universe exploded into being out of nothing are just as flawed. For example, in an effort to avoid an absolute beginning of the universe, Stephen Hawking made up a theory that utilizes "imaginary time." We could just as well call it an "imaginary theory" because Hawking himself admits that his theory is "just a [metaphysical] proposal" that cannot explain what happened in real time. "In real time," he concedes, "the universe has a beginning. . . ."[29] In fact, according to Hawking, "Almost everyone now believes that the universe, and time itself, had a beginning at the Big Bang."[30] So by his own admission Hawking's imaginary theory fizzles when applied to the real world. Imaginary time is just that—purely imaginary.

Uncertainty—With the evidence for the beginning of the universe so strong, some atheists question the first premise of the Cosmological Argument—the Law of Causality. This is dangerous ground for atheists, who typically pride themselves on being champions of reason and science. As we have pointed out before, the Law of Causality is the foundation of all science. Science is a search for causes. If you destroy the Law of Causality, then you destroy science itself.

Atheists attempt to cast doubt on the Law of Causality by citing quantum physics, specifically Heisenberg's Uncertainty Principle. This principle describes our inability to simultaneously predict the location and speed of subatomic particles (i.e., electrons). The atheist's contention here is this: if causality at the subatomic realm isn't necessary, then maybe causality of the entire universe isn't necessary either.

Fortunately for science, this atheistic attempt to cast doubt on the Law of Causality fails. Why? Because it confuses *causality* and *predictability*. The Heisenberg Uncertainty Principle does *not* prove that the movement of electrons is uncaused; it only describes our inability to *predict* their location and speed at any given time. The mere fact that we can't predict something doesn't mean that something has no cause. In fact, quantum theorists acknowledge that we might not be able to predict the simultaneous speed and location of electrons because our very attempts at observing them are the cause of their unpredictable movements! Like a beekeeper putting his head in a beehive, we must stir them up in order to observe them. Hence, the disturbance may be a case of the scientist looking at his own eyelashes in the microscope.

In the end, no atheistic theory adequately refutes either premise of the Cosmological Argument. The universe had a beginning and therefore it needs a cause.

The Religion of Science

So why don't all scientists just accept this conclusion instead of attempting to avoid the facts and their implications with wild and implausible explanations? Jastrow's comments are again insightful (remember, Jastrow is an agnostic). Jastrow observes,

> Theologians generally are delighted with the *proof* that the Universe had a beginning, but astronomers are curiously upset. Their reactions provide an interesting demonstration of the response of the scientific mind—supposedly a very objective mind—when evidence uncovered by science itself leads to a conflict with *the articles of faith in our profession.* It turns out that the scientist behaves the way the rest of us do when our beliefs are in conflict with the evidence. We become irritated, we pretend the conflict does not exist, or we paper it over with meaningless phrases.[31]

The phrases we have seen used by Atkins and Asimov to explain the beginning of the universe—"mathematical points" and "positive and negative energy" respectively—certainly seem meaningless to us. Indeed, they explain nothing.

Regarding Einstein's "irritating" feelings about General Relativity and the expanding universe, Jastrow writes: "This is curiously emotional language for a discussion of some mathematical formulas. I suppose that the idea of a beginning in time annoyed Einstein because of its theological implications."[32]

Everyone knows that theists have theological beliefs. But what's often overlooked is that atheistic and pantheistic scientists also have theological beliefs. As noted above, Jastrow calls some of these beliefs "the articles of faith in our profession," and he asserts that some of these beliefs comprise the "religion in science." He writes:

> There is a kind of religion in science . . . every effect must have its cause; there is no First Cause. . . . This religious faith of the scientist is violated by the discovery that the world had a beginning under conditions in which the known laws of physics are not valid, and as a product of forces or circumstances we cannot discover. When that happens, the scientist has lost control. If he really examined the implications, he would be traumatized. As usual when faced with trauma, the mind reacts by ignoring the implications—in science this is known as "refusing to speculate"—or trivializing the origin of the world by calling it the Big Bang, as if the Universe were a firecracker.[33]

Traumatized or not, scientists must come to grips with the implications of the Big Bang evidence. They may not like the evidence or its implications, but that won't change the facts. Since the evidence shows that time, space, and matter were created at the Big Bang, the most probable scientific conclusion is that the universe was caused by something *outside* of time, space, and matter (i.e., an Eternal Cause). When scientists stop short of that conclusion by papering it over with "meaningless phrases" or by "refusing to speculate," it seems that they are simply refusing to accept the facts and the most reasonable conclusions that come from them. This is a matter of the will, not the mind. The evidence is objective; it's the disbelieving scientists who are not.

WHAT IF THE BIG BANG THEORY IS WRONG?

So far we've given solid scientific evidence (SURGE) for the fact that the universe had a beginning. But suppose scientists wake up one day and find out that all of their calculations have been wrong—there was no Big Bang. Given the wide scope of the evidence and the ability of the theory to correctly predict so much observable phenomena, a total abandonment of the Big Bang would be extremely unlikely.

This is admitted even by atheists. Victor Stenger, a physicist who taught at the University of Hawaii, once wrote that "the universe exploded out of nothingness."[34] Stenger recently acknowledged that the Big Bang is looking more probable all the time. "We have to leave open the possibility that [the Big Bang] could be wrong," he said, "but . . .

every year that goes by, and more astronomical data comes in, it's more and more consistent with at least the general Big Bang picture."[35]

Indeed, in 2003 more evidence came forth that the Big Bang is correct. NASA's WMAP satellite (Wilkinson Microwave Anisotropy Probe) confirmed the findings of its predecessor COBE and returned pictures thirty-five times sharper than COBE's of the background radiation ripples.[36] In fact, space observations are becoming so supportive of the theistic worldview that George Will muses, "Soon the American Civil Liberties Union, or People for the American Way, or some similar faction of litigious secularism will file suit against NASA, charging that the Hubble Space Telescope unconstitutionally gives comfort to the religiously inclined."[37]

Nevertheless, let's play skeptic's advocate for a second. Let's suppose that at some point in the future the Big Bang Theory is deemed wrong. Would that mean that the universe is eternal? No, for a number of reasons.

First, the Second Law of Thermodynamics (the S in SURGE) supports the Big Bang but is not dependent on it. The fact that the universe is running out of usable energy and heading toward disorder is not even up for debate. In Eddington's words, the Second Law "holds the supreme position among the laws of nature." It is true even if the Big Bang is not.

Second, the same can be said for Einstein's theory of General Relativity (the E in SURGE). This theory, well verified by observation, requires a beginning to space, matter, and time whether or not it all began with a bang.

Third, there's also scientific evidence from geology that the universe had a beginning. As many of us learned in high school chemistry, radioactive elements decay over time into other elements. For example, radioactive uranium eventually turns into lead. This means that if all uranium atoms were infinitely old, they would all be lead by now, but they're not. So the earth cannot be infinitely old.

Finally, there's a philosophical line of evidence for the beginning of the universe. This line of evidence is so rationally inescapable that some consider it the strongest argument of all. It's called the *Kalam* (from the Arabic word for "eternal") Cosmological Argument, and it goes like this:

1. An infinite number of days has no end.
2. But today is the end day of history (history being a collection of all days).

3. Therefore, there were not an infinite number of days before today (i.e., time had a beginning).

To grasp this argument, see the timeline below, marked in segments of days (fig. 3.1). The further left you go, the further back in history you go. Now, assume for a moment that this line extends to the left indefinitely, so that you can't see if or where it begins. But as you look to the right you can see the end of the line because the last segment of the line represents today. Tomorrow isn't here yet, but when it gets here we'll add one more segment (i.e., a day) to the right end of the line.

Fig. 3.1

Now, here's how this proves that time had a beginning: since the line certainly ends on the right, the timeline cannot be infinite because something that is infinite has no end. Moreover, you can't add anything to something that is infinite, but tomorrow we will add another day to our timeline. So our timeline is undeniably finite.

Let's consider this argument from a different angle. If there were an infinite number of days before today, then today would never have arrived. But here we are! So there must have been only a *finite* number of days before today. In other words, even though we may not be able to see, as we look to the left, where the line begins, we know it had to begin at some point because only a finite amount of time could be passed for today to arrive. You can't traverse an infinite number of days. Thus time must have had a beginning.

Some may say that infinite numbers can exist, so why can't infinite days? Because there's a difference between an abstract infinite series and a concrete one. The one is purely theoretical, the other is actual. Mathematically, we can conceive of an infinite number of days, but actually we could never count or live an infinite number of days. You can conceive of an infinite number of mathematical points between two bookends on a shelf, but you could not fit an infinite number of books between them. That's the difference between an abstract and a concrete.

Numbers are abstract. Days are concrete. (By the way, this amplifies our answer above as to why there could not have been an infinite number of bangs in the cosmological history of the universe. An infinite number of actual events is impossible.)

What we are saying here is that the universe, Big Bang or not, had a beginning. That is, the Cosmological Argument is true because both premises of the argument are true: everything that comes to be has a cause, and the universe came to be. Since the universe had a beginning, it must have had a Beginner.

Who Made God?

In light of all the evidence for a beginning of the space-time universe, the Beginner must be outside the space-time universe. When God is suggested as the Beginner, atheists are quick to ask the age-old question, "Then who made God? If everything needs a cause, then God needs a cause too!"

As we have seen, the Law of Causality is the very foundation of science. Science is a search for causes, and that search is based on our consistent observation that everything that has a beginning has a cause. In fact, the question "Who made God?" points out how seriously we take the Law of Causality. It's taken for granted that virtually everything needs a cause.

So why then doesn't God need a cause? Because the atheist's contention misunderstands the Law of Causality. The Law of Causality does not say that *everything* needs a cause. It says that everything *that comes to be* needs a cause. God did not come to be. No one made God. He is unmade. As an eternal being, God did not have a beginning, so he didn't need a cause.

"But wait," the atheist will protest, "if you can have an eternal God, then I can have an eternal universe! After all, if the universe is eternal, then it did not have a cause." Yes, it is logically possible that the universe is eternal and therefore didn't have a cause. In fact, it is one of only two possibilities: either the universe, or something outside the universe, is eternal. (Since something undeniably exists today, then something must have always existed; we have only two choices: the universe, or something that caused the universe.) The problem for the atheist is that while it is *logically* possible that the universe is eternal, it does not seem to be *actually* possible. For all the scientific and philosophical evidence (SURGE, radioactive decay, and the *Kalam* Cosmological Argument) tells us the universe cannot be eternal. So by ruling out one of the two options, we are left with the only other option—something outside the universe is eternal.

When you get right down to it, there are only two possibilities for anything that exists: either 1) it has always existed and is therefore uncaused, or 2) it had a beginning and was caused by something else (it can't be self-caused, because it would have had to exist already in order to cause anything). According to the overwhelming evidence, the universe had a beginning, so it must be caused by something else—by something outside itself. Notice that this conclusion is consistent with theistic religions, but it is not based on those religions—it is based on good reason and evidence.

So what is this First Cause like? One might think you need to rely on a Bible or some other so-called religious revelation to answer that question, but, again, we don't need anyone's scripture to figure that out. Einstein was right when he said, "Science without religion is lame; religion without science is blind."[38] Religion can be informed and confirmed by science, as it is by the Cosmological Argument. Namely, we can discover some characteristics of the First Cause just from the evidence we've discussed in this chapter. From that evidence alone, we know the First Cause must be:

- self-existent, timeless, nonspatial, and immaterial (since the First Cause created time, space, and matter, the First Cause must be outside of time, space, and matter). In other words, he is without limits, or infinite;
- unimaginably powerful, to create the entire universe out of nothing;
- supremely intelligent, to design the universe with such incredible precision (we'll see more of this in the next chapter);
- personal, in order to choose to convert a state of nothingness into the time-space-material universe (an impersonal force has no ability to make choices).

These characteristics of the First Cause are exactly the characteristics theists ascribe to God. Again, these characteristics are not based on someone's religion or subjective experience. They are drawn from the scientific evidence we have just reviewed, and they help us see a critically important section of the box top to this puzzle we call life.

Conclusion: If There Is No God, Why Is There Something Rather than Nothing?

Years ago, I (Norm) debated an atheist at the University of Miami on the question "Does God exist?" After I presented much of the evidence we have reviewed here, I had the opportunity to ask my opponent some questions. Here's what I asked him:

"Sir, I have some questions for you: First, 'If there is no God, why is there something rather than nothing at all?'" I then proceeded to ask a few more questions, thinking he would answer them in sequence.

Now, usually when you debate someone, you're trying to persuade the audience. You don't expect to get your opponent to admit he's wrong. He's got too much invested in his position, and most debaters have too much ego to admit an error. But this guy was different. He surprised me when he said, "Regarding the first question, that's a good question. That's a *really* good question." And without any other comment, he went on to answer my second question.

After hearing the evidence for the existence of God, this debater was left questioning his own beliefs. He even attended a follow-up meeting and expressed that he had doubts about atheism. His faith in atheism was waning. Indeed.

"If there is no God, why is there something rather than nothing?" is a question that we all have to answer. And in light of the evidence, we are left with only two options: either *no one* created something out of nothing, or else *someone* created something out of nothing. Which view is more reasonable? Nothing created something? No. Even Julie Andrews knew the answer when she sang, "Nothing comes from nothing. Nothing ever could!" And if you can't believe that nothing caused something, *then you don't have enough faith to be an atheist!*

The most reasonable view is God. Robert Jastrow suggested this when he ended his book *God and the Astronomers* with this classic line: "For the scientist who has lived by his faith in the power of reason, the story ends like a bad dream. He has scaled the mountains of ignorance; he is about to conquer the highest peak; as he pulls himself over the final rock, he is greeted by a band of theologians who have been sitting there for centuries."[39]

4

Divine Design

"Only a rookie who knows nothing about science would say science takes away from faith. If you really study science, it will bring you closer to God."
—JAMES TOUR, NANOSCIENTIST

THE ASTRONOMICAL EVIDENCE for God *must* be strong when atheistic physicists admit that "the universe exploded out of nothingness," and agnostic astronomers claim that "supernatural forces" were so at work in the beginning that scientists are led back to "a band of theologians who have been sitting there for centuries" (see chapter 3). But the scientific evidence for God does not end with the Cosmological Argument. For many, the *precision* with which the universe exploded into being provides even more persuasive evidence for the existence of God.

This evidence, technically known as the Teleological Argument, derives its name from the Greek word *telos*, which means "design." The Teleological Argument goes like this:

1. Every design had a designer.
2. The universe has highly complex design.
3. Therefore, the universe had a Designer.

Isaac Newton (1642–1727) implicitly confirmed the validity of the Teleological Argument when he marveled at the design of our solar system. He wrote, "This most beautiful system of the sun, planets and comets, could only proceed from the counsel and dominion of an intelligent and powerful Being."[1] Yet it was William Paley (1743–1805) who made the argument famous by his commonsense assertion that every watch requires a watchmaker. Imagine you're walking along in the woods and you find a diamond-studded Rolex on the ground. What do you conclude is the cause of that watch: The wind and the rain? Erosion?

Some combination of natural forces? Of course not! There's absolutely no question in your mind that some intelligent being made that watch, and that some unfortunate individual must have accidentally dropped it there.

Scientists are now finding that the universe in which we live is like that diamond-studded Rolex, except the universe is even more precisely designed than the watch. In fact, the universe is specifically tweaked to enable life on earth—a planet with scores of improbable and inter-dependent life-supporting conditions that make it a tiny oasis in a vast and hostile universe.

These highly precise and interdependent environmental conditions (which are called "anthropic constants") make up what is known as the "Anthropic Principle." "Anthropic" comes from a Greek word that means "human" or "man." The Anthropic Principle is just a fancy title for the mounting evidence that has many scientists believing that the universe is extremely fine-tuned (designed) to support human life here on earth.

In this vast and hostile universe, we earthlings are much like astronauts who can survive only in the small confines of their spaceship. Like a spaceship, our earth supports life as it hurls through lifeless space. But also like a spaceship, a slight change or malfunction in any one of a number of factors—in either the universe or the earth itself—could fatally alter the narrowly defined environmental conditions we need to survive.

Apollo 13, one of the most challenging and famed missions in the history of NASA, will help drive this point home. We're going spend the next few pages aboard *Apollo 13*. And as we do, we'll point out some of the anthropic constants that make our lives possible.

Houston, We Have a Problem!

It's April 13, 1970, more than two days since Mission Commander Jim Lovell and two other astronauts blasted out of the earth's atmosphere on *Apollo 13*. They are now flying through space at more than 2,000 miles an hour, eagerly anticipating a walk that only a few men had taken—a walk on the surface of the moon. Everything is going as planned on their magnificently designed spacecraft. In Lovell's own words, he and his crew are "fat, dumb, and happy." But all of that is about to change.

At 55 hours and 54 minutes into the mission, shortly after completing a TV broadcast back to earth, Lovell is putting wires away when he hears a loud bang. He initially thinks it's just Pilot Jack Swigert playing a joke by secretly actuating a noisy valve. But when he sees the concerned expression on Swigert's face—an expression that reveals "It's not my fault!"—Lovell quickly realizes that this is no joke.

The dialog between Astronauts Lovell, Swigert, Fred Haise, and Charlie Duke (Duke being on the ground in Houston) goes like this:

Swigert: Houston, we've had a problem here.

Duke: This is Houston. Say again, please.

Lovell: Houston, we've had a problem. We've had a main B bus undervolt.

Duke: Roger. Main B undervolt.

Haise: Okay. Right now, Houston, the voltage is . . . looking good. We had a pretty large bang associated with the caution and warning there. And as I recall, main B was the one that had an amp spike on it once before.

Duke: Roger, Fred.

Haise: That jolt must have rocked the sensor on oxygen quantity 2. It was oscillating down around 20 to 60 percent. Now it's full-scale high.

At this point, the astronauts are not entirely sure what is happening. Oxygen tank sensors appear to be erratic. They're showing the tanks have as little as 20 percent to the impossible quantity of over 100 percent. Meanwhile, despite Haise's initial observation that "the voltage is looking good," multiple Master Caution warnings on the ship's electrical systems are telling the opposite story.

Within a few minutes, the dire nature of the problem becomes apparent. *Apollo 13* doesn't have just a sensor problem. It has an actual problem. Their spacecraft—now nearly 200,000 nautical miles from earth and heading away from home—is quickly losing oxygen and power. Two of the three fuel cells are dead, and the third one is depleting rapidly. Haise notifies Houston about the power situation:

Haise: AC 2 is showing zip. . . . We got a main bus A undervolt now. . . . It's reading about 25 and a half. Main B is reading zip right now.

Lovell then reports the oxygen problem:

> Lovell: And our O_2 quantity number 2 tank is reading zero.
>   Did you get that?
> Houston: O_2 quantity number 2 is zero.

Then, as Lovell looks out a hatch, he sees what appears to be a gas venting into space from the side of their spacecraft.

> Lovell: And it looks to me, looking out the hatch, that we are
>   venting something.
> Houston: Roger.

> Lovell: We are . . . we are venting something out into the, into
>   space.
> Houston: Roger. We copy, you're venting.

> Lovell: It's a gas of some sort.

That gas is later confirmed to be oxygen. Although the crew doesn't know this yet, oxygen tank 2 has just exploded and damaged oxygen tank 1 in the process. Lovell can't see the damage, just the venting gas.

Anthropic Constant 1: Oxygen Level—On earth, oxygen comprises 21 percent of the atmosphere. That precise figure is an anthropic constant that makes life on earth possible. If oxygen were 25 percent, fires would erupt spontaneously; if it were 15 percent, human beings would suffocate. Lovell and his crew must now find a way to maintain the right level of oxygen in their ship.

But oxygen is not their only problem. Like the atmosphere on earth, a change in one constant on the spacecraft can affect several others that are also necessary for life. The explosion creates a shortage not only of oxygen but also of electricity and water. On *Apollo 13,* water and electricity are produced by combining oxygen with hydrogen in the fuel cells. Without oxygen, there will be no way to manufacture air, water, or power. And since they are in the vacuum of space, there's no source of oxygen from the outside.

The situation is so unimaginable that Jack Swigert would later say, "If somebody had thrown that at us in the simulator," meaning a quadruple failure of fuel cells 1 and 3 and oxygen tanks 1 and 2, "we'd have said, 'Come on, you're not being realistic.'"

Unfortunately, this isn't the simulator but a real emergency in a spacecraft two-thirds of the way to the moon. What can they do?

Fortunately, there's a lifeboat. The Lunar Module (LM, known as "the lem") has provisions that can be used in an emergency. The LM is the craft attached to the top of the Command Module (CM) that two of the astronauts are scheduled to ride down to the moon while the third astronaut orbits above. Of course, the moon landing is about to be called off: saving the lives of the astronauts is now the new mission of *Apollo 13*.

In an effort to save power for reentry, the astronauts quickly power down the Command Module and climb into the LM. But even with the LM, the astronauts are by no means out of the woods. They still have to sling around the moon in order to get back to earth. This will take time—time they don't have. The LM has provisions designed to sustain two men for about forty hours, but they need to sustain *three* men for *four days!*

As a result, every effort is made to conserve water, oxygen, and electricity. All nonessential systems are shut down—including heat—and the astronauts decrease their water consumption to one small cup per day. Haise, feeling ill, soon begins to run a fever, and all three of the astronauts slowly begin dehydrating. This makes concentration more difficult.

Unfortunately, with most automated systems shut down, concentration becomes more and more critical. Besides slinging around the moon, the crew needs to make several manual course corrections to ensure they hit the proper reentry angle and to speed up their trip home. To do so, they'll have to manually navigate by the stars. But since debris from the explosion continues to envelop the ship in the vacuum of space, the astronauts can't distinguish the stars from sunlight reflecting off the debris. Consequently, they are reduced to using the earth and the sun as navigational reference points by lining them up in a spacecraft window.

Using this rather crude method, they check their calculations again and again to ensure they are correct. They have little room for error. In fact, they must aim the ship for reentry at a point no less than 5.5 degrees and no more than 7.3 degrees below the earth's horizon (from the spacecraft's point of view). Any deviation from that range, and their ship will either skip off the earth's atmosphere or burn up in too steep a descent.

Anthropic Constant 2: Atmospheric Transparency—The small window the astronauts must hit reflects the exacting standards by which the universe has been designed. While the atmosphere presents a reentry problem for the astronauts, its present qualities are absolutely essential for life here on earth. The degree of transparency of the atmosphere is an anthropic constant. If the atmosphere were less transparent, not enough solar radiation would reach the earth's surface. If it were more transparent, we would be bombarded with far too much solar radiation down here. (In addition to atmospheric transparency, the atmospheric composition of precise levels of nitrogen, oxygen, carbon dioxide, and ozone are in themselves anthropic constants.)

Anthropic Constant 3: Moon-Earth Gravitational Interaction—As the astronauts begin to sling around the moon, they encounter another anthropic constant.[2] This one regards the gravitational interaction that the earth has with a moon. If the interaction were greater than it currently is, tidal effects on the oceans, atmosphere, and rotational period would be too severe. If it were less, orbital changes would cause climatic instabilities. In either event, life on earth would be impossible.

Following their close encounter with the moon, the astronauts are finally heading toward home. However, still another problem arises. The delicate living conditions inside the spacecraft are becoming contaminated. As oxygen is being consumed, the astronauts are producing a new problem simply by exhaling. That is, carbon dioxide is beginning to reach dangerous levels inside the ship. If they can't find a way to change the carbon dioxide filters in the LM, the three astronauts will be poisoned by their own breaths!

Mission Control tells the astronauts to unpack extra filters designed for the Command Module (the part of the ship that has been evacuated and powered down) to see if they can be used in the LM. But instead of getting some much needed good news, the astronauts soon realize that the CM filters are the wrong size and shape for the LM! Contractor A apparently had not coordinated with contractor B! Frustrated Flight Director Gene Krantz—who famously inspired Mission Control with "failure is not an option!"—barks, "Tell me this isn't a government project!"

Scrambling for a solution, NASA engineers on the ground begin what is known as a "workaround"—they brainstorm a way to rig the square CM filters to fit the round hole in the LM with just materials that can be scrounged up on the spacecraft. They design a fix that they think will work and then talk the crew through the rigging process. Their workaround involves the ingenious use of cardboard, space-suit hoses, stowage bags, and duct tape (yes, it also fixes anything in space too— don't leave home without it!).

Anthropic Constant 4: Carbon Dioxide Level—Of course such a rig is not necessary here on earth because just the right level of carbon dioxide is maintained naturally in the earth's atmosphere. This is another anthropic constant. If the CO_2 level were higher than it is now, a runaway greenhouse effect would develop (we'd all burn up). If the level were lower than it is now, plants would not be able to maintain efficient photosynthesis (we'd all suffocate—the same fate the astronauts are trying to avoid).

Thankfully, the rigged filters work and buy the crew valuable time (and breathable air). Soon the time arrives to jettison the crippled service module. As the service module falls away, the crew sees for the first time the extent of the damage: the oxygen tank explosion blew a twelve-by-six-foot panel off the side of the service module, tilted the fuel cells, and damaged an antenna. Had an explosion *less than half that magnitude* occurred near the heat shield of the Command Module, it would have resulted in a catastrophic failure of the spacecraft and loss of the crew.

As they approach reentry, the crew climbs back into the Command Module in an attempt to power it up. This is their only hope of getting home (the LM doesn't have a heat shield). But with all three fuel cells dead and only battery power available, the normal CM power-up procedure will not work. Not every system can be brought on line because there simply isn't enough juice in the batteries! As a result, they have to rely on a new power-up procedure that other NASA engineers and astronauts have just finished developing on the ground.

To complicate matters, condensed water is now dripping from the CM's control panels where the temperature is a frigid 38 degrees. Will the panels short? Will the necessary systems come on line? This is a dangerous environment in which to apply power, but they have no choice.

Despite the danger, the new power-up sequence succeeds, and the astronauts strap themselves in for reentry. Back on earth, the world fixates on the fate of the three men. News bulletins and press conferences give timely updates. Congress passes a resolution for the American people to pray, and the pope urges the world to pray as the three brave

Americans, in a damaged space capsule, accelerate toward the earth's atmosphere at a tremendous speed. In a short time they will be pulled by the earth's gravity to a maximum velocity of nearly 25,000 miles per hour. That's almost 7 miles *per second!*

Anthropic Constant 5: Gravity—The gravity that is pulling the astronauts back home is still another anthropic constant. Its strength may be terrifying, but it couldn't be any different for life to exist here on earth. If the gravitational force were altered by 0.00000000000000000000000000000000000001 percent, our sun would not exist, and, therefore, neither would we.[3] Talk about precision!

As the astronauts plummet to earth in their crippled spacecraft, no one is certain if they will survive the violent and intensely hot reentry. Too many questions remain unanswered: Is the heat shield fully intact? Is the ship really on the right entry angle? Will the entry batteries on the CM work? Will the parachutes deploy properly? To make matters worse, there's a typhoon warning in the recovery area.

In light of all the uncertainty, the astronauts pay their respects to the ground crew just prior to the three-minute radio blackout that accompanies reentry:

Swigert: Hey, I want to say you guys are doing real good work.
Houston: So are you guys, Jack.
Swigert: I know all of us here want to thank all of you guys down there for the very fine job you did.
Lovell: That's affirm, Joe.
Houston: I tell you, we all had a good time doing it.
Lovell: You have a good bedside manner.
Houston: That's the nicest thing anybody's ever said.
Houston: Okay. Loss of signal in a minute . . . welcome home.
Swigert: Thank you.

During reentry, a C-135 aircraft is circling in the recovery area to provide the necessary communication link back to Mission Control. But after three minutes, there is no contact with the astronauts. Tension rises:

Houston: *Apollo 13* should be out of blackout at this time. We are standing by for any reports of ARIA (Apollo Range Instrumentation Aircraft) acquisition.

Flight: Network, no ARIA contact yet?

Network: Not at this time, Flight. (long pause)

Four minutes since reentry—still no contact. No reentry has ever taken this long.

Houston: Standing by for any reports of acquisition. (pause)

Finally, the aircraft receives a signal from the capsule:

Houston: We got a report that ARIA 4 aircraft has acquisition of signal.

But there's no confirmation yet that anyone is alive.

Houston: Odyssey, Houston. Standing by. Over.

To the relief of everyone, Swigert finally speaks up.

Swigert: Okay, Joe.

Houston: Okay. We read you, Jack!

The astronauts are alive, but one last hurdle remains: two stages of parachutes, first the drogue and then the main, must work or all will be lost. Without successful parachute deployment, the astronauts will be obliterated as their capsule impacts the ocean at 300 miles per hour.

Houston: Less than two minutes now till time of drogue deployment.

Waiting . . .

Houston: Report of two good drogues. Coming up now on main chutes. (Pause) Standing by for confirmation of main chutes deploy.

The main parachutes deploy as designed, and Houston gains visual contact.

Houston: Odyssey, Houston. We show you on the mains. It really looks great!

Finally, after four days of nail-biting suspense, the astronauts, Mission Control, and the rest of the world breathe a sigh of relief:

> Houston: Extremely loud applause here in Mission Control! . . .
> Extremely loud applause as *Apollo 13* on main chutes
> comes through loud and clear on the television display
> here.

Splashdown occurs at 1:07 P.M. EST on April 17, 1970.

THE ANTHROPIC PRINCIPLE: THE DESIGN IS IN THE DETAILS

When some in Mission Control began to express doubts that the astronauts would return alive, Flight Director Gene Krantz countered their pessimism with, "Gentlemen, I think this is going to be our finest hour." Indeed it was. *Apollo 13* became known as a "successful failure." The astronauts failed to walk on the moon, but they successfully returned to earth despite nearly lethal conditions.

Just as the crew survived against all odds through those lethal conditions, we too survive against all odds on this tiny planet called earth. The Apollo spacecrafts, like our earth, were designed to maintain human life in the very hostile environment of space. Since human beings can only survive in a very narrow envelope of environmental conditions, these ships must be designed with incredible precision and thousands of components. If one small thing goes wrong, human life is in jeopardy.

On *Apollo 13* the one small thing that put the crew in jeopardy seems too minor to matter—oxygen tank number 2 had been accidentally dropped two inches at some point prior to its installation. That mere two-inch drop damaged the tank's thin wall and began a cascade of events that ultimately led to its explosion.[4] Due to the interdependent nature of the components, the failure of the oxygen system led to the failure of other systems and almost to the loss of the spacecraft and crew. Think of it— that one little two-inch drop led to all the problems the astronauts had to overcome in order to survive. It resulted in too little oxygen, water, and power, and too much carbon dioxide and navigation error.

Like a small change in the spaceship, a small change in the universe would result in big problems for us as well. As we have seen, scientists have discovered that the universe—like a spacecraft—is precisely designed to create the very narrow envelope of life-supporting conditions here on earth. Any slight deviation in any one of a number of environmental and physical factors (what we've been calling "constants") would preclude us from even existing. And like the components on *Apollo 13,* these constants are interdependent—a small change in one might affect others and could prevent or destroy the conditions necessary for life.

The extent of the universe's fine-tuning makes the Anthropic Principle perhaps the most powerful argument for the existence of God. It's not that there are just a few broadly defined constants that may have resulted by chance. No, there are more than 100 very narrowly defined constants that strongly point to an intelligent Designer.[5] We've already identified five of them. Here are ten more:

1. If the centrifugal force of planetary movements did not precisely balance the gravitational forces, nothing could be held in orbit around the sun.

2. If the universe had expanded at a rate one millionth more slowly than it did, expansion would have stopped, and the universe would have collapsed on itself before any stars had formed. If it had expanded faster, then no galaxies would have formed.

3. Any of the laws of physics can be described as a function of the velocity of light (now defined to be 299,792,458 meters per second). Even a slight variation in the speed of light would alter the other constants and preclude the possibility of life on earth.

4. If water vapor levels in the atmosphere were greater than they are now, a runaway greenhouse effect would cause temperatures to rise too high for human life; if they were less, an insufficient greenhouse effect would make the earth too cold to support human life.

5. If Jupiter were not in its current orbit, the earth would be bombarded with space material. Jupiter's gravitational field acts as a cosmic vacuum cleaner, attracting asteroids and comets that might otherwise strike earth.

6. If the thickness of the earth's crust were greater, too much oxygen would be transferred to the crust to support life. If it were thinner, volcanic and tectonic activity would make life impossible.

7. If the rotation of the earth took longer than twenty-four hours, temperature differences would be too great between night and day. If the rotation period were shorter, atmospheric wind velocities would be too great.

8. The 23-degree axil tilt of the earth is just right. If the tilt were altered slightly, surface temperatures would be too extreme on earth.

9. If the atmospheric discharge (lightning) rate were greater, there would be too much fire destruction; if it were less, there would be too little nitrogen fixing in the soil.

10. If there were more seismic activity, much more life would be lost; if there was less, nutrients on the ocean floors and in river runoff would not be cycled back to the continents through tectonic uplift. (Yes, even earthquakes are necessary to sustain life as we know it!)

Astrophysicist Hugh Ross has calculated the probability that these and other constants—122 in all—would exist today *for any planet in the universe* by chance (i.e., without divine design). Assuming there are 10^{22} planets in the universe (a very large number: 1 with 22 zeros following it), his answer is shocking: one chance in 10^{138}—that's one chance in one with 138 zeros after it![6] There are only 10^{70} *atoms* in the entire universe. In effect, there is *zero* chance that any planet in the universe would have the life-supporting conditions we have, *unless* there is an intelligent Designer behind it all.

Nobel Laureate Arno Penzias, codiscoverer of the radiation afterglow, put it this way: "Astronomy leads us to a unique event, a universe which was created out of nothing and delicately balanced to provide exactly the conditions required to support life. In the absence of an absurdly-improbable accident, the observations of modern science seem to suggest an underlying, one might say, supernatural plan."[7]

Cosmologist Ed Harrison uses the word "proof" when he considers the implications of the Anthropic Principle on the question of God. He writes, "Here is the cosmological proof of the existence of God—the design argument of Paley—updated and refurbished. The fine-tuning of the universe provides *prima facie* evidence of deistic design."[8]

PROOF FOR GOD! HOW DO ATHEISTS RESPOND?

How do atheists respond to this "proof for God"? Some atheists admit there's some kind of Designer out there. Astronomer Fred Hoyle had his atheism shaken by the Anthropic Principle and the complexity he saw in life (which we'll cover in the next two chapters). Hoyle concluded, "A commonsense interpretation of the facts suggests that a super intellect has monkeyed with physics, as well as chemistry and biology, and that there are no blind forces worth speaking about in nature."[9] While Hoyle was vague about just who this "super intellect" is, he recognized that the fine-tuning of the universe requires intelligence.

Other atheists admit design but then claim there is no Designer. They say it all happened by chance. But how can they seriously suggest chance when there's virtually zero probability that all of the 100-plus constants would be as they are in the absence of intelligence? It's not easy. Atheists have had to resort to wild speculation to give chance more of a chance. Their speculation is called the Multiple Universe Theory.

According to the Multiple Universe Theory, there actually are an infinite number of universes in existence, and we just happen to be lucky enough to be in the universe with the right conditions. Given an infinite number of universes, these atheists say, every set of conditions will occur, including the life-supporting conditions of our universe.

There are multiple problems with this multiple-universe explanation. First, and most significantly, *there's no evidence for it!* The evidence shows that all of finite reality came into existence with the Big Bang. Finite reality is exactly what we call "the universe." If other finite realities exist, they're beyond our ability to detect. No one has ever observed any evidence that such universes may exist. That's why this multiple universe idea is nothing more than a metaphysical concoction—a fairy tale built on blind faith—as detached from reality as Stephen Hawking's "imaginary time."

Second, as we discussed in the last chapter, an infinite number of finite things—whether we're talking about days, books, bangs, or universes—is an actual impossibility. There can't be an unlimited number of limited universes.

Third, even if other universes could exist, they would need fine-tuning to get started just as our universe did (recall the extreme precision of the Big Bang we described in the last chapter). So positing multiple universes doesn't eliminate the need for a Designer—it *multiplies* the need for a Designer!

Fourth, the Multiple Universe Theory is so broad that *any event* can be explained away by it. For example, if we ask, "Why did the planes hit the World Trade Center and the Pentagon?" we need not blame

Muslim terrorists: the theory lets us say that we just happen to be in *the* universe where those planes—though they appeared to be flown deliberately into the buildings—actually hit the buildings by accident. With the Multiple Universe Theory we can even let Hitler off the hook. Perhaps we just happen to be in *the* universe where the Holocaust appeared to be murder, but actually the Jews secretly conspired with the Germans and sent themselves to the ovens. In fact, the Multiple Universe Theory is so broad that it can even be used to excuse the atheists who made it up. Perhaps we just happen to be in *the* universe where people are irrational enough to suggest that such nonsense is the truth!

In the end, the Multiple Universe Theory is simply a desperate attempt to avoid the implications of design. It doesn't multiply chances, it multiplies absurdities. It's akin to the *Apollo 13* astronauts denying the fact that NASA designed and built their spacecraft in favor of the unsupported theory that there are an infinite number of naturally occurring spacecraft out there and the astronauts are just lucky to be on one that happens to support life. Such a theory is, of course, nonsense, and its obvious absurdity reveals how strong the evidence for design really is. Extreme evidence calls for extreme theories to explain it away.

God? "Look to the Heavens"

On February 1, 2003, President George W. Bush solemnly peered into a TV camera to address the American people: "My fellow Americans, this day has brought terrible news and great sadness to our country. At 9:00 A.M. this morning, Mission Control in Houston lost contact with our Space Shuttle *Columbia*. A short time later, debris was seen falling from the skies above Texas. The *Columbia* is lost; there are no survivors."[10]

Traveling at 12,500 miles per hour, *Columbia* disintegrated as it attempted to reenter the earth's atmosphere. The second great shuttle tragedy left the nation shaken but not deterred. "The cause in which they died will continue," the president vowed. "Mankind is led into the darkness beyond our world by the inspiration of discovery and the longing to understand. Our journey into space will go on."

Yet any human journey into space will penetrate only a tiny fraction of it. There are 100 billion stars in our galaxy, and the average distance between those stars is 30 trillion miles. (By the way, this distance is another anthropic constant. If the stars were closer together or farther apart, planetary orbits would be affected.)

How far is 30 trillion miles? Let's put it this way: when the space shuttle is in orbit, it travels at about 17,000 miles an hour—*almost 5 miles per second.* If you could get in the Space Shuttle and speed through space at nearly five miles per second, it would take you 201,450 *years* to travel 30 trillion miles! In other words, if you had gotten into the Space Shuttle at the time of Christ and begun traveling from our sun toward another star an average distance away, you would be only *one-hundredth* of the way there right now. Incredible.

Now keep in mind that's just between *two* of the 100 billion stars in *our galaxy.* How many stars are there in the entire universe? *The number of stars in the universe is about equal to the number of sand grains on all the beaches on all the earth.* And at five miles per second it will take you over 200,000 years to go from one grain of sand to another! The heavens are *awesome.*

The Bible tells us to "look to the heavens" if we want to get an idea of what God is like. Expressing the Teleological Argument long before Newton and Paley, David wrote in Psalm 19, "The heavens declare the glory of God; the skies proclaim the work of his hands." A couple of centuries later the prophet Isaiah posed a question from God: "'To whom will you compare me? Or who is my equal?' says the Holy One" (40:25). The answer is in the next verse: "Lift your eyes and look to the heavens" (v. 26). Isaiah goes on to say that God knows all of heaven's stars by name!

Why does God tell us to compare him with the heavens? Because God has no limits, and from our perspective neither do the heavens. God is the unlimited limiter—the uncreated Creator—of all things. He's the self-existing, infinite Being who created this vast and beautiful universe out of nothing and who holds it all together today. There's only one entity in our experience that can provide an analogy to the infinity of God. An image intended to depict God won't do.[11] It merely limits his majesty. Only the heavens scream out infinity.

Infinity is what describes each of God's attributes including his power, knowledge, justice, and love. This is why the Bible uses the heavens to help us grasp the infinite height of God's love. Psalm 103:11 says, "For as high as the heavens are above the earth, so great is his love for those who revere him." How high are the heavens above the earth? When you consider that there are 30 trillion miles between stars as numerous as grains of beach sand, you might as well say, "the heavens are infinitely high." Indeed, and that's the height of God's love.

God's infinite love is perhaps what led President Bush to quote Isaiah in his tribute to *Columbia's* crew: "In the skies today we saw destruction and tragedy. Yet farther than we can see there is comfort and hope. In the words of the prophet Isaiah, 'Lift your eyes and look to the heavens. Who created all these? He who brings out the starry hosts one by one and calls them each by name. Because of his great power and mighty strength, not one of them is missing.' The same Creator who names the stars also knows the names of the seven souls we mourn today. The crew of the shuttle Columbia did not return safely to Earth; yet we can pray that all are safely home."[12]

CONCLUSION

Nearly 2,000 years ago, Paul wrote, near the beginning of his letter to the Romans, "For since the creation of the world God's invisible qualities—his eternal power and divine nature—have been clearly seen, being understood from what has been made, so that men are without excuse." The evidence for a Designer certainly is clear in creation, but we often take it for granted.

C. S. Lewis, in his classic book *The Screwtape Letters,* provides a great insight into this tendency we have to take for granted the amazing world all around us. The senior demon, Screwtape, writes some advice to his junior demon, Wormwood, on how to keep people from becoming Christians. Screwtape writes, "Keep pressing home on him the *ordinariness* of things. Above all, do not attempt to use science (I mean, the real sciences) as a defense against Christianity. They will positively encourage him to think about realities he can't touch and see. There have been sad cases among modern physicists."[13] The "sad cases" are, of course, physicists who have been honest with the evidence they've seen and have become Christians.

Lewis has hit on a tendency many of us have. In our fast-paced lives, we rarely stop and observe the world around us and, therefore, tend to consider every amazing facet of this beautiful universe as ordinary. But as we have seen, it is anything but ordinary. Now science is showing us like at no other time in history that this is a universe of incredible design and complexity. It's giving us a new perspective on a world that we too often take for granted.

Astronauts get a new perspective from their spaceships that helps them realize this universe is anything but ordinary. When the first astronauts passed over the surface of the moon and saw the *earth* rise—something no human being had ever seen before—they reverently read from the book of Genesis, "In the beginning God created the heavens and the earth." What else would fit the moment? A recitation of the Multiple Universe Theory certainly wouldn't have expressed the awe the astronauts were experiencing. They witnessed design from an angle no one had ever seen before and were overwhelmed with the realization that the amazing creation requires an amazing Creator. John Glenn echoed their convictions when, at seventy-seven years old, he looked out of the Space Shuttle *Discovery* and remarked, "To look out at this kind of creation and not believe in God is to me impossible."

The raw impact of their experiences reveals the intuitive nature of the Teleological Argument. You don't need anyone to tell you that something beautifully designed requires a designer. It's practically self-evident. Nevertheless, let's state the argument formally again, with emphasis on what we've discovered in this chapter:

1. Every design had a designer.
2. As verified by the Anthropic Principle, we know *beyond a reasonable doubt* that the universe is designed.
3. Therefore, the universe had a Designer.

There's no plausible explanation for the Anthropic Principle other than a Cosmic Designer. Atheists must take extreme measures to deny the obvious. When they dream up hypothetical theories that are not supported by any evidence—and in fact are actually impossible—they have left the realm of reason and rationality and entered into the realm of blind faith. Physicist Paul Davies writes, "one may find it easier to believe in an infinite array of universes than in an infinite Deity, but such a belief must rest on faith rather than observation."[14]

Believing without observation is exactly what atheists accuse "religious" people of doing. But, ironically, it's the atheists who are pushing a religion of blind faith. Christians have good reasons based on observation (such as the Big Bang and the Anthropic Principle) for believing what they believe. Atheists don't. *That's why we don't have enough faith to be atheists.*

This blind faith of the atheist reveals that the rejection of a Designer is not a *head* problem—it's not as if we lack evidence or intellectual justification for a Designer. On the contrary, the evidence is impressive. What we have here is a *will* problem—some people, despite the evidence, simply don't *want* to admit there's a Designer. In fact, one critic of the Anthropic Principle admitted to the *New York Times* that his real objection was "totally emotional" because "it smells of religion and intelligent design."[15] So much for scientific objectivity.

In chapter 6, we'll address more of these motivations for denying the strong evidence for the existence of God. But first, in chapter 5, we'll explore more persuasive evidence for a Designer—the evidence found in life itself.

The First Life: Natural Law or Divine Awe?

"God never performed a miracle to convince an atheist, because his ordinary works provide sufficient evidence."

—ARIEL ROTH

TAKE OUT THE GARBAGE—MOM

Sixteen-year-old Johnny came down from his bedroom and stumbled into the kitchen to get a bowl of his favorite cereal—Alpha-Bits. When he got to the table, he was surprised to see that the cereal box was knocked over, and the Alpha-Bit letters spelled "TAKE OUT THE GARBAGE—MOM" on the placemat.

Recalling a recent high school biology lesson, Johnny didn't attribute the message to his mom. After all, he'd just been taught that life itself is merely a product of mindless, natural laws. If that's the case, Johnny thought, why couldn't a simple message like "Take out the garbage—Mom" be the product of mindless natural laws as well? Maybe the cat knocked the box over, or an earthquake shook the house. No sense jumping to conclusions. Johnny didn't want to take out the garbage anyway. He didn't have time for house chores. This was summer vacation, and he wanted to get to the beach. Mary would be there.

Since Mary was the girl Scott liked too, Johnny wanted to get to the beach early to beat Scott there. But when Johnny arrived, he saw Mary and Scott walking hand-in-hand along the shore. As he followed them at a distance, he looked down and saw a heart drawn in the sand with the words "Mary loves Scott" scrawled inside. For a moment, Johnny felt his heart sink. But thoughts of his biology class rescued him from deep despair. "Maybe this is just another case of natural laws at work!" he thought. "Perhaps sand crabs or an unusual wave pattern just happened to produce this love note naturally." No sense accepting a conclusion he didn't like! Johnny would just have to ignore the corroborating evidence of the hand-holding.

Comforted by the fact that principles learned in his biology class could help him avoid conclusions he didn't like, Johnny decided to lie down for a few minutes to get a little sun. As he put his head back on his towel he noticed a message in the clouds: "Drink Coke," the white puffy letters revealed on the sky-blue background. "Unusual cloud formation?" Johnny thought. "Swirling winds, perhaps?"

No, Johnny couldn't play the game of denial any longer. "Drink Coke" was the real thing. A message like that was a sure sign of intelligence It couldn't be the result of natural forces because natural forces have never been observed to create messages. Even though he never saw a plane, Johnny knew there must have been a skywriter up there recently. Besides, he wanted to believe this message—the hot sun had left him parched, thirsting for a Coke.

SIMPLE LIFE? THERE'S NO SUCH THING!

One needs to be playing with only half a deck or be willfully blind to suggest that messages like "Take out the garbage—Mom" and "Mary loves Scott" are the work of natural laws. Yet these conclusions are perfectly consistent with principles taught in most high school and college biology classes today. That's where naturalistic biologists dogmatically assert that messages far more complicated are the mindless products of natural laws. They make this claim in trying to explain the origin of life.

Naturalistic biologists assert that life generated spontaneously from nonliving chemicals by natural laws without any intelligent intervention. Such a theory might have seemed plausible to a nineteenth-century scientist who didn't have the technology to investigate the cell and discover its amazing complexity. But today this naturalistic theory flies in the face of everything we know about natural laws and biological systems.

Since the 1950s, advancing technology has enabled scientists to discover a tiny world of awesome design and astonishing complexity. At the same time that our telescopes are seeing farther out into space, our microscopes are seeing deeper into the components of life. While our space observations have yielded the Anthropic Principle of physics (which we discussed in the last chapter), our life observations are yielding an equally impressive Anthropic Principle of biology.

To show you what we mean, let's consider so-called "simple" life—a one-celled animal known as an amoeba. Naturalistic evolutionists claim that this one-celled amoeba (or something like it) came together by spontaneous generation (i.e., without intelligent intervention) in a warm little pond somewhere on the very early earth. According to their theory, all biological life has evolved from that first amoeba without any intelligent guidance at all. This, of course, is the theory of macroevolution: from the infantile, to the reptile, to the Gentile; or, from the goo to you via the zoo.

Believers in this theory of origin are called by many names: naturalistic evolutionists, materialists, humanists, atheists, and Darwinists (in the remainder of this chapter and the next, we'll refer to believers in this atheistic evolutionary theory as Darwinists or atheists. This does not include those who believe in theistic evolution—i.e., that evolution was guided by God). Regardless of what we call the true believers in this theory, the key question for us is this: "Is their theory true?" It appears not.

Forget the Darwinist assertions about men descending from apes or birds evolving from reptiles. The supreme problem for Darwinists is not explaining how all life forms are related (although, as we'll see in the next chapter, that's still a major problem). The supreme problem for Darwinists is explaining the origin of the *first* life. For unguided, naturalistic macroevolution to be true, the first life must have generated spontaneously from nonliving chemicals. Unfortunately for Darwinists, the first life—indeed any form of life—is by no means "simple." This became abundantly clear in 1953 when James Watson and Francis Crick discovered DNA (deoxyribonucleic acid), the chemical that encodes instructions for building and replicating all living things.

DNA has a helical structure that looks like a twisted ladder. The sides of the ladder are formed by alternating deoxyribose and phosphate molecules, and the rungs of the ladder consist of a specific order of four nitrogen bases. These nitrogen bases are adenine, thymine, cytosine, and guanine, which commonly are represented by the letters A, T, C, and G. These letters comprise what is known as the four-letter genetic alphabet. This alphabet is identical to our English alphabet in terms of its ability to communicate a message, except that the genetic alphabet has only four letters instead of twenty-six.[1] Just as the specific order of the letters in this sentence communicates a unique message, the specific order of A, T, C, and G within a living cell determines the unique genetic makeup of that living entity. Another name for that message or information, whether it's in a sentence or in DNA, is "specified complexity." In other words, not only is it complex—it also contains a specific message.

The incredible specified complexity of life becomes obvious when one considers the message found in the DNA of a one-celled amoeba (a creature so small, several hundred could be lined up in an inch). Staunch Darwinist Richard Dawkins, professor of zoology at Oxford University, admits that the message found in just the cell *nucleus* of a tiny amoeba is more than all thirty volumes of the *Encyclopedia Britannica* combined, and the entire amoeba has as much information in its DNA as 1,000 complete sets of the *Encyclopedia Britannica*![2] In other words, if you were to spell out all of the A, T, C, and G in the "unjustly called 'primitive' amoeba" (as Dawkins describes it), the letters would fill 1,000 complete sets of an encyclopedia!

Now, we must emphasize that these 1,000 encyclopedias do not consist of random letters but of letters in a very specific order—just like real encyclopedias. So here's the key question for Darwinists like Dawkins: if simple messages such as "Take out the garbage—Mom," "Mary loves Scott," and "Drink Coke" require an intelligent being, then why doesn't a message 1,000 encyclopedias long require one?

Darwinists can't answer that question by showing how natural laws could do the job. Instead, they define the rules of science so narrowly that intelligence is ruled out in advance, leaving natural laws as the only game in town. Before we describe how and why Darwinists do this, let's take a look at the scientific principles that ought to be used in discovering how the first life began.

INVESTIGATING THE ORIGIN OF FIRST LIFE

Many evolutionists as well as many creationists speak as if they know, beyond any doubt, how the first life came into existence. Both, of course, cannot be right. If one is right, the other is wrong. So how can we discover who's right?

The following fact is obvious but often overlooked: no human *observed* the origin of the first life. The emergence of the first life on earth was a one-time, unrepeatable historical event. No one was present to see it—neither evolutionists nor creationists were there, and we certainly can't travel back in time and directly observe whether the first life was created by some kind of intelligence or arose by natural laws from nonliving materials.

That raises an important question: if we can't directly observe the past, then what scientific principles can we use to help us discover what caused the first life? We use the same principles that are utilized every day in our criminal justice system—forensic principles. In other words, the origin of life is a forensic question that requires us to piece together evidence much like detectives piece together evidence from a murder. Detectives can't go back in time and witness the murder again. Neither can they revive the victim and go into the laboratory to conduct some kind of experiment that will allow them to observe and repeat the crime over and over again. Instead, they must utilize the principles of forensic science to discover what really happened.

The central principle in forensic science is the Principle of Uniformity, which holds that causes in the past were like the causes we observe today. In other words, by the Principle of Uniformity, we assume that the world worked in the past just like it works today, especially when it comes to causes. If "Take out the garbage—Mom" requires an intelligent cause today, then any similar message from the past must also require an intelligent cause. Conversely, if natural laws can do the job today, then the Principle of Uniformity would lead us to conclude natural laws could do the job in the past.

Consider the Grand Canyon. What caused it? Did anyone see it form? No, but by the Principle of Uniformity, we can conclude that natural processes, particularly water erosion, were responsible for the Grand Canyon. We can conclude this confidently, even though we were not there to see it happen, because we can observe these natural processes creating canyons today. We see this in nature when we observe water's effect on a land mass. We can even go into the laboratory and repeatedly pour water in the middle of a mass of dirt, and we'll always get a canyon.

Now consider another geologic formation: Mount Rushmore. What caused it? Common sense tells us that we would never suggest that the presidential faces on Mount Rushmore were the result of natural laws. Erosion couldn't have done that. Our "common sense" is actually the Principle of Uniformity. Since we never observe natural laws chiseling a highly detailed sculpture of a president's head into stone at the present time, we rightly conclude that natural laws couldn't have done it in the past either. Today we see only intelligent beings creating detailed sculptures. As a result, we rightly conclude that, in the past, only an intelligent being (a sculptor) could have created the faces on Mount Rushmore.

In the same way, when we look at the first one-celled life, the Principle of Uniformity tells us that only an intelligent cause could assemble the equivalent of 1,000 encyclopedias. Natural laws never have been observed to create a simple message like "Drink Coke," much less a message 1,000 encyclopedias long.

Why then do Darwinists come to the conclusion that the first life generated spontaneously from nonliving chemicals without intelligent intervention? Spontaneous generation of life has never been observed. Ever since Pasteur sterilized his flask, one of the most fundamental observations in all of science has been that life arises only from similar existing life. Scientists have been unable to combine chemicals in a test tube and arrive at a DNA molecule, much less life.[3] In fact, all experiments *designed* to spontaneously generate life—including the now discredited Urey-Miller experiment—have not only failed but also suffer from the illegitimate application of intelligence.[4] In other words, scientists intelligently contrive experiments and they still cannot do what we are told mindless natural laws have done. Why should we believe that mindless processes can do what brilliant scientists cannot do? And even if scientists eventually did create life in the laboratory, it would prove creation. Why? Because their efforts would show that it takes a lot of intelligence to create life.

Do Darwinists insist on spontaneous generation because they just don't see the evidence for design? Not at all. In fact, exactly the opposite is true—they see the evidence clearly! For example, Richard Dawkins named his book *The Blind Watchmaker* in response to William Paley's design argument we cited in the last chapter. The appearance of design in life is admitted on the first page of *The Blind Watchmaker.* Dawkins writes, "Biology is the study of complicated things that give the appearance of having been designed for a purpose."[5] Two pages later, despite acknowledging "the intricate architecture and precision-engineering" in human life and in each of the trillions of cells within the human body, Dawkins flatly denies that human life or any other life has been designed. Apparently, Dawkins refuses to allow observation to interfere with his conclusions. This is very strange for a man who believes in the supremacy of science, which is supposed to be based on observation.

Francis Crick, codiscoverer of DNA and another ardent Darwinist, agrees with Dawkins about the appearance of design. In fact, the appearance of design is so clear he warns that "biologists must constantly keep in mind that what they see was not designed, but rather evolved."[6] Crick's little memo to biologists led Phillip Johnson, author and a leader in the Intelligent Design (ID) movement, to observe, "Darwinian biologists must keep repeating that reminder to themselves because otherwise they might become conscious of the reality that is staring them in the face and trying to get their attention."[7]

The complexity of DNA is not the only problem for Darwinists. Its origin is also a problem. A difficult chicken-egg dilemma exists because DNA relies on proteins for its production but proteins rely on DNA for *their* production. So which came first, proteins or DNA? One must already be in existence for the other to be made.

So why do Crick, Dawkins, and others in their camp ignore the plain implications of the evidence staring them in the face? Because their preconceived ideology—naturalism—prevents them from even considering an intelligent cause. As we're about to see, this is bad science, and it leads to wrong conclusions.

GOOD SCIENCE VS. BAD SCIENCE

It is commonly believed that the so-called creation-evolution debate (now often called the intelligent design vs. naturalism debate) entails a war between religion and science, the Bible and science, or faith and reason. This perception is perpetuated by the media, who consistently depict the debate in terms of the 1960 movie *Inherit the Wind*, which fictionalized the 1925 Scopes "monkey trial." You know that depiction. It basically goes like this: here come those crazy religious fundamentalists again, and they want to impose their dogmatic religion and ignore objective science.

Actually, nothing could be further from the truth. *The creation-evolution debate is not about religion versus science or the Bible versus science—it's about good science versus bad science.* Likewise, it's not about faith versus reason—it's about *reasonable* faith versus *unreasonable* faith. It may surprise you to see just who is practicing the bad science, and just who has the unreasonable faith.

As we've mentioned before, science is a search for causes. Logically, there are only two types of causes: intelligent and nonintelligent (i.e., natural). The Grand Canyon had a natural cause, and Mount Rushmore had an intelligent one (see fig. 5.1). Unfortunately, on the question of first life, Darwinists like Dawkins and Crick rule out intelligent causes before they even look at the evidence. In other words, their conclusions are preloaded into their assumptions. Spontaneous generation by natural laws *must* be the cause of life because they consider no other options.

Two Types of Causes

Intelligent   Natural

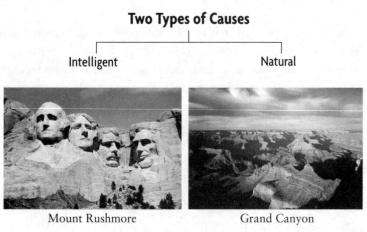

Mount Rushmore   Grand Canyon

Fig. 5.1

Spontaneous generation is what critics of evolution call a "just-so" story. Evolutionists provide no evidence to support spontaneous generation. It isn't supported by empirical observation or forensic science principles. It's "just-so" because life exists, and since *intelligent causes are ruled out in advance,* there can be no other possible explanation.

The problem for Darwinists is immense. Biochemist Klaus Dose admits that more than thirty years of research into the origin of life has led to "a better perception of the immensity of the problem of the origin of life on Earth rather than to its solution. At present all discussions on principal theories and experiments in the field either end in stalemate or in a confession of ignorance."[8] Francis Crick laments, "Every time I write a paper on the origin of life, I swear I will never write another one, because there is too much speculation running after too few facts."[9]

The evidence is so strong for intelligence and against naturalism that prominent evolutionists have actually suggested aliens deposited the first life here. Fred Hoyle (the same evolutionist who popularized the Steady State Theory we discussed in chapter 3) invented this far-out theory (called "panspermia," for "seeds everywhere") after calculating that the probability of life arising by spontaneous generation was effectively zero. (Of course panspermia doesn't solve the problem—it simply puts it off another step: who made the intelligent aliens?)

As crazy as the theory sounds, at least panspermia advocates recognize that some kind of intelligence must be behind the amazing wonder we call life. Still, when top evolutionists have to resort to aliens to explain the origin of life, you know the simplest life must be incredibly complex.

Another panspermia advocate, Chandra Wickramasinghe, admits that the Darwinists are acting on blind faith when it comes to spontaneous generation. He observes, "The emergence of life from a primordial soup on the Earth *is merely an article of faith* that scientists are finding difficult to shed. There is no experimental evidence to support this at the present time. Indeed all attempts to create life from non-life, starting from Pasteur, have been unsuccessful."[10] Microbiologist Michael Denton, though himself an atheist, adds, "The complexity of the simplest known type of cell is so great that it is impossible to accept that such an object could have been thrown together suddenly by some kind of freakish, vastly improbable event. Such an occurrence would be indistinguishable from a miracle."[11]

In light of "just-so" explanations such as spontaneous generation and panspermia, who do you think is practicing the bad science: the people derisively called "religious" (the theists/creationists) or the "enlightened" ones (the atheists/Darwinists) who are really just as religious as the "religious"? Physicist and information scientist Hubert Yockey realizes it's the Darwinists. He writes, "The belief that life on earth arose spontaneously from nonliving matter, *is simply a matter of faith* in strict reductionism and is based entirely on ideology."[12]

Yockey is right. Darwinists falsely believe they can reduce life to its nonliving chemical components. That's the ideology of reductionism. For Darwinists like Dawkins or Crick who must believe that only the material (and not the immaterial) exists, then life can be nothing more than chemicals. But life is clearly more than chemicals. Life contains a message—DNA—that is *expressed* in chemicals, but those chemicals cannot cause the message any more than the chemicals in ink and paper can cause the sentences on this page. A message points to something beyond chemicals. The message in life, just like the one on this page, points to an intelligence beyond its chemical elements. (We realize that life is certainly *more* than chemicals with a message, but the key point here is that it's certainly not *less*.)

So by blind allegiance to this naturalistic, reductionist ideology—which is against all observation and reason—Darwinists dogmatically assert that life arose spontaneously from its nonliving chemical components. Ironically, this is exactly what Darwinists have long accused creationists of doing—allowing their ideology to overrule observation and reason. In truth, it's the Darwinists who are allowing *their faith* to overrule observation and reason. Creationists and Intelligent Design proponents are simply making a rational inference from the evidence. They are following the evidence exactly where it leads—back to an intelligent cause.

Yockey is not the only one pointing out that Darwinists have a philosophical bias against intelligent causes. Phillip Johnson serves as the sharp edge of a steel wedge that is now splitting the petrified wood of naturalism in the scientific community. He correctly points out that "Darwinism is based on an *a priori* [prior] commitment to materialism, not on a philosophically neutral assessment of the evidence. Separate the philosophy from the science, and the proud tower collapses."[13]

And it's not just the critics of evolution who see this bias. Prominent

Darwinists admit it as well. In fact, Dawkins himself has acknowledged the bias in responding to an e-mail question from Phillip Johnson. "[Our] philosophical commitment to materialism and reductionism is true," Dawkins wrote, "but I would prefer to characterize it as philosophical commitment to a real explanation as opposed to a complete lack of an explanation, which is what you espouse."[14] (Dawkins may think he has a "real explanation," but, as we have seen, his explanation is against all of the observational and forensic evidence.)

If Richard Dawkins leaks out a half-hearted admission of bias, Darwinist Richard Lewontin of Harvard University gushes a complete written confession. Read how Lewontin acknowledges that Darwinists accept absurd "just-so" stories that are against common sense because of their prior commitment to materialism:

> Our willingness to accept scientific claims that are against common sense is the key to an understanding of the real struggle between science and the supernatural. We take the side of science in spite of the patent absurdity of some of its constructs, in spite of its failure to fulfill many of its extravagant promises of health and life, in spite of the tolerance of the scientific community for unsubstantiated just-so stories, because *we have a prior commitment to materialism*. It is not that the methods and institutions of science somehow compel us to accept a material explanation of the phenomenal world but, on the contrary, that *we are forced by our a priori adherence to material causes* to create an apparatus of investigation and a set of concepts that produce material explanations, no matter how counterintuitive, no matter how mystifying to the uninitiated. Moreover that materialism is absolute for *we cannot allow a divine foot in the door*.[15]

Now the real truth comes out. It's *not* that the evidence supports Darwinism—in fact, according to Lewontin and our own common sense, Darwinist explanations are "counterintuitive." The real truth is that the Darwinists have defined science in such a way that the only possible answer is Darwinism. Any other definition would, God forbid, allow God to get his "foot in the door"!

In the next chapter we'll investigate the possible motivations for keeping God out. For now, the bottom line is this: the event required to get the atheistic theory of macroevolution off the ground—the spontaneous generation of first life—is believed because of false philosophical assumptions disguised as science, not because there are legitimate scientific observations that support spontaneous generation. False science is bad science, and it's the Darwinists who are practicing it. Their belief in spontaneous generation results from their blind faith in naturalism. It takes tremendous faith to believe that the first one-celled creature came together by natural laws, because that's like believing 1,000 encyclopedias resulted from an explosion in a printing shop! Atheists can't even explain the origin of the printing shop, much less the 1,000 encyclopedias. *Therefore, we don't have enough faith to be atheists.*

GIVE TIME AND CHANCE A CHANCE!

"Not so fast!" say the Darwinists. "You've overlooked time and chance as plausible explanations for how life spontaneously generated."

Give Time More Time!

Darwinists dismiss the conclusion that intelligence was necessary for the first life by suggesting that more time would allow natural laws to do their work. Give it several billion years and eventually we'll get life. Is this plausible?

Let's go back to Mount Rushmore for a minute. Darwinists assert that science is built on observation and repetition. Okay, suppose we observe and repeat an experiment where we allow natural laws to work on rock for the next ten years. Will we ever get the faces on Mount Rushmore? Never.

You say, maybe natural laws would do it if we give them billions of years. No, they wouldn't. Why? Because nature disorders, it doesn't organize things (the fact that nature brings things toward disorder is another aspect of the Second Law of Thermodynamics). More time will make things worse for the Darwinist, not better. How so?

Let's suppose you throw red, white, and blue confetti out of an airplane 1,000 feet above your house. What's the chance it's going to form the American flag on your front lawn? Very low. Why? Because natural laws will mix up or randomize the confetti. You say, "Allow more time." Okay, let's take the plane up to 10,000 feet to give natural laws more time to work on the confetti. Does this improve the probability that the flag will form on your lawn? No, more time actually makes the flag less likely because natural laws have longer to do what they do—disorder and randomize.

What is different about the origin of the first life? Darwinists might say that the Second Law of Thermodynamics doesn't apply continuously to living systems. After all, living things do grow and can get more ordered. Yes, they grow and get more ordered, but they still lose energy in the process of growth. The food that goes into a living system is not processed at 100 percent efficiency. So the Second Law applies to living systems as well. But that's not even the point. The point is, we're *not* talking about what something can do once it's alive; *we're talking about getting a living thing in the first place.* How did life arise from nonliving chemicals, without intelligent intervention, when nonliving chemicals are susceptible to the Second Law? Darwinists have no answer, only faith.

Give Chance a Chance!

Can all the incredible specified complexity in life be explained by chance? Not a chance! Atheists and theists alike have calculated the probability that life could arise by chance from nonliving chemicals. The figures they calculate are astronomically small—virtually zero. For example, Michael Behe has said that the probability of getting *one protein molecule* (which has about 100 amino acids) by chance would be the same as a blindfolded man finding one marked grain of sand in the Sahara Desert three times in a row. And one protein molecule is not life. To get life, you would need to get about 200 of those protein molecules together![16]

That probability is virtually zero. But we believe the probability is *actually* zero. Why? Because "chance" is not a cause. Chance is a *word* that we use to describe mathematical possibilities. It has no power of its own. Chance is *nothing.* It's what rocks dream about.

If someone flips a fair coin, what's the chance it will come up heads? Fifty percent, we say. Yes, but what *causes* it to come up heads? Is it chance? No, the primary cause is an intelligent being who decided to flip the coin and apply so much force in doing so. Secondary causes, such as the physical forces of wind and gravity, also impact the result of the flip. If we knew all those variables, we could calculate how the flip would turn out beforehand. But since we don't know those variables, we use the word "chance" to cover our ignorance.

We shouldn't allow atheists to cover their ignorance with the word "chance." If they don't know a natural mechanism by which the first life could have come into existence, then they should admit they don't know rather than suggesting a powerless word that, of course, really isn't a cause at all. "Chance" is just another example of the bad science practiced by Darwinists.

Science Is a Slave to Philosophy

Unfortunately, Darwinists have been successful in convincing the public that the only bad science is that which disagrees with Darwinism (and that really isn't science at all, they say—it's just religion masquerading as science). In fact, the exact opposite is true. It's the Darwinists who are practicing the bad science, because their science is built on a false philosophy. In effect, it's *their* secular religion of naturalism that leads them to ignore the empirically detectable scientific evidence for design.

What lessons can we learn from the bad science of the Darwinists? To answer that, let's look at more of the debate we cited in chapter 3 between William Lane Craig, a Christian, and Darwinist Peter Atkins.[17] Recall that the debate was over the existence of God. At one point, Atkins argued that God wasn't necessary because science could explain everything.

"There is no need for God," declared Atkins. "Everything in the world can be understood without needing to evoke a God. You have to accept that's one possible view to take about the world."

"Sure, that's possible," Craig admitted. "But . . ."

[Interrupting] "Do you deny that science can account for everything?" challenged Atkins.

"Yes, I *do* deny that science can account for everything," said Craig.

"So what can't it account for?" demanded Atkins.

A veteran of many debates, Craig was ready with a multifaceted answer. "I think there are a good number of things that cannot be scientifically proven but we are all rational to accept," he said. Craig then cited these five examples of rational beliefs that cannot be proven by science:

1. mathematics and logic (science can't prove them because science presupposes them),
2. metaphysical truths (such as, there are minds that exist other than my own),

3. ethical judgments (you can't prove by science that the Nazis were evil, because morality is not subject to the scientific method),
4. aesthetic judgments (the beautiful, like the good, cannot be scientifically proven), and, ironically
5. science itself (the belief that the scientific method discovers truth can't be proven by the scientific method itself); (more on this below).

(Following this barrage of examples refuting Atkins's view, moderator William F. Buckley, Jr., could not hide his pleasure with Craig's answer. He peered over at Atkins and cracked, "So put that in your pipe and smoke it!")

Craig was right. The scientific method of searching for causes by observation and repetition is but *one* means of finding truth. It is not the *only* means of finding truth. As we saw in chapter 1, nonscientific (philosophical) laws, such as the laws of logic, help us discover truth as well. In fact, those laws are used by the scientific method!

Moreover, Atkins's claim that science can account for everything is not false only because of the five counterexamples Craig noted; it is also false because it is self-defeating. In effect, Atkins was saying, "Science is the only objective source of truth." If we test that statement by the Road Runner tactic from chapter 1, we see it is self-defeating and therefore false. The statement "science is the only source of objective truth" claims to be an objective truth, but it's not a scientific truth. The statement is philosophical in nature—it can't be proven by science—so it defeats itself.

This leads us to perhaps the greatest lesson we can learn from the bad science of the Darwinists: *science is built on philosophy. Indeed, science is a slave to philosophy.* Bad philosophy results in bad science, and good science requires good philosophy. Why? Because:

1. **Science cannot be done without philosophy.** Philosophical assumptions are utilized in the search for causes, and, therefore, cannot be the result of them. For example, scientists assume (by faith) that reason and the scientific method allow us to accurately understand the world around us. That cannot be proven by science itself. You can't prove the tools of science—the laws of logic, the Law of Causality, the Principle of Uniformity, or the reliability of observation—by running

some kind of experiment. You have to assume those things are true in order to *do* the experiment! So science is built on philosophy. Unfortunately, many so-called scientists are very poor philosophers.

2. **Philosophical assumptions can dramatically impact scientific conclusions.** If a scientist assumes beforehand that only natural causes are possible, then probably no amount of evidence will convince him that intelligence created the first one-celled amoeba or any other designed entity. When Darwinists *presuppose* that intelligent causes are impossible, then natural laws are the only game in town. Likewise, if a creationist rules out natural causes beforehand (and we don't know of any who do), then he also risks missing the right answer. But a scientist who is *open-minded* to both natural and intelligent causes can follow the evidence wherever it leads.

3. *Science* **doesn't really say anything**—*scientists* **do.** Data are always interpreted by scientists. When those scientists let their personal preferences or unproven philosophical assumptions dictate their interpretation of the evidence, they do exactly what they accuse religious people of doing—they let their ideology dictate their conclusions. When that's the case, their conclusions should be questioned, because they may be nothing more than philosophical presuppositions passed off as scientific facts.

MATERIALISM MAKES REASON IMPOSSIBLE

When you get down to the root of the problem, you find that the bad science of the Darwinists results from the false philosophy of naturalism or materialism at the foundation of their worldview. Why is materialism false? Here are five reasons why materialism is not reasonable:

First, as we've already pointed out, there is a message resident in life, technically called specified complexity, that cannot be explained materially. This message cannot be explained by nonintelligent natural laws any more than the message in this book can be explained by the nonintelligent laws of ink and paper.

Second, human thoughts and theories are not comprised only of materials. Chemicals are certainly involved in the human thought process, but they cannot explain all human thoughts. The *theory* of materialism isn't made of molecules. Likewise, someone's thoughts, whether they be of love or hate, are not chemicals. How much does love weigh? What's the chemical composition of hate? These are absurd questions because thoughts, convictions, and emotions are not completely materially based. Since they are not completely materially based, materialism is false.

Third, if life were nothing more than materials, then we'd be able to take all the materials of life—which are the same materials found in dirt—and make a living being. We cannot. There's clearly something beyond materials in life. What materialist can explain why one body is alive and another body is dead? Both contain the same chemicals. Why is a body alive one minute and dead the next? What combination of materials can account for consciousness? Even Atkins, in his debate with Craig, admitted that explaining consciousness is a great problem for atheists.

Fourth, if materialism is true, then everyone in all of human history who has ever had any kind of spiritual experience has been completely mistaken. While this is possible, given the vast number of spiritual experiences, it does not seem likely. It is difficult to believe that every great spiritual leader and thinker in the history of humanity—including some of the most rational, scientific, and critical minds ever—have all been completely wrong about their spiritual experience. This includes Abraham, Moses, Isaiah, Kepler, Newton, Pascal, and Jesus Christ himself. *If just one spiritual experience in the entire history of the world is true, then materialism is false.*

Finally, if materialism is true, then reason itself is impossible. For if mental processes are nothing but chemical reactions in the brain, then there is no reason to believe that *anything* is true (including the theory of materialism). Chemicals can't evaluate whether or not a theory is true. Chemicals don't reason, they react.

This is supremely ironic because Darwinists—who claim to champion truth and reason—have made truth and reason impossible by their theory of materialism. So even when Darwinists are right about something, their worldview gives us no reason to believe them—because reason itself is impossible in a world governed only by chemical and physical forces.

Not only is reason impossible in a Darwinian world, but the Darwinist's assertion that we should rely on reason alone cannot be justified. Why not? Because reason actually requires *faith*. As

J. Budziszewski points out, "The motto 'Reason Alone!' is nonsense any-way. Reason itself presupposes faith. Why? Because a defense of reason *by* reason is circular, therefore worthless. Our only guarantee that human reason works is God who made it."[18]

Let's unpack Budziszewski's point by considering the source of rea-son. Our ability to reason can come from one of only two places: either our ability to reason arose from preexisting intelligence, or it arose from mindless matter. The atheists/Darwinists/materialists believe, *by faith,* that our minds arose from mindless matter without intelligent interven-tion. We say it is by faith because it contradicts all scientific observation, which demonstrates that an effect cannot be greater than its cause. You can't give what you haven't got, yet materialists believe that dead, unin-telligent matter has produced intelligent life. This is like believing that the Library of Congress resulted from an explosion in a printing shop!

It makes much more sense to believe that the human mind is made in the image of the Great Mind—God. In other words, our minds can apprehend truth and can reason about reality because they were built by the Architect of truth, reality, and reason itself. Materialism cannot explain reason any more than it can explain life. Materialism is just not reasonable. *Therefore, we don't have enough faith to be materialists!*

The Atheist vs. the Critical Thinking Consultant

The very fact that Darwinists think they have reasons to be atheists actu-ally presupposes that God exists. How so? Because *reasons* require that this universe be a *reason*able one that presupposes there is order, logic, design, and truth. But order, logic, design, and truth can only exist and be known if there is an unchangeable objective source and standard of such things. To say something is *un*reasonable, Darwinists must know what *reasonable* is. To say something is *not* designed, Darwinists must know what *designed* is. To say something is *not* true, Darwinists must know what *truth* is, and so forth. Like all nontheistic worldviews, Darwinism borrows from the theistic worldview in order to make its own view intelligible.

This tendency of atheists to borrow unwittingly from the theistic worldview was beautifully exposed by author Pete Bocchino[19] during a curriculum meeting for the State of Georgia's Department of Education. Pete, who was working for an internationally known Christian ministry at the time, was slated to be on a subcommittee to review and improve the sixth- to twelfth-grade public school curriculum in subjects such as U.S. government, law, ethics, and character training.

The first of a week-long series of meetings was held in a large room where all the subcommittee members were given an opportunity to introduce themselves. Pete, who got held up in traffic, arrived late, missed the introductions, and started heading for his seat. When the subcommittee chairman noticed Pete walking in, he told him that they had already introduced themselves and asked Pete to do the same by giving his name, background, and occupation. Pete gave his name and said that he had a degree in mechanical engineering. Pete thought to himself, "I certainly don't want to bring Christianity into this by telling them that I work for an international Christian ministry." So he cryptically said, "I currently work for a not-for-profit organization as a critical thinking consultant."

The chairman said, "A what?!"

"A critical thinking consultant," Pete repeated.

"What exactly does a critical thinking consultant do?" the chairman persisted.

"Well, we're already running late, and I don't want to take up the committee's time," Pete reasoned, "but you'll find out during the week."

As the week progressed, the committee debated various topics, such as diversity, tolerance, human rights, and other controversial issues. At one point, when they were discussing psychology standards, Pete noted that the standards did not contain a definition of personhood. This was a gaping hole in the psychology curriculum; so Pete submitted the following definition based on a section of Mortimer Adler's book, *Haves Without Have-Nots*:[20]

Course: Psychology / Topic: Uniqueness

Standard: Evaluates the uniqueness of human nature and the concept of personhood.

1. intellect / conceptual thought
2. freedom to choose / free will
3. ethical responsibility (standards)
4. moral accountability (obligations), and
5. inalienable rights of personhood.

As soon as this standard was placed on the table, an educator sitting across from Pete—who had made it known that she was an atheist—was about to challenge this standard. Before she could do that, Pete stopped her and said to the group,

> If anyone were to disagree with this standard, they would be doing the following:
>
> 1. That person would be engaging me in conceptual thought (as in 1 above).
> 2. That person would be exercising his/her "freedom" to do so (as in 2 above).
> 3. That person must think that there is an ethical responsibility to teach what is right/true (as in 3 above).
> 4. That person is seeking to hold me morally accountable to teach the truth (as in 4 above).
> 5. That person has the right to disagree with my position (as in 5 above).
>
> So if one were to disagree with these criteria, that person would actually confirm the validity of each point of these criteria.

The group became rather quiet for a moment. Then the chairman spoke up and said, "Now we know what a critical thinking consultant does!" With that he told the committee secretary to include the standard in the recommendations.

With a little critical thinking, we see that the Darwinian worldview collapses not only from a lack of evidence but also because Darwinists must borrow from the theistic worldview as they attempt to make their case. Intellect, free will, objective morality, and human rights as well as reason, logic, design, and truth can exist only if God exists. Yet Darwinists assume some or all of these realities when they defend their atheistic worldview. They can't have it both ways.

DARWINISTS HAVE THE WRONG BOX TOP

In the introduction we said that a worldview is like a box top that allows you to place the many pieces of life's puzzle into a complete, cohesive picture. If you have the right box top, then the pieces make sense in light of the complete picture.

But what happens if you keep discovering pieces that don't fit the box top you have? Common sense would tell you that you've got the wrong box top, so you need to look for the right one. Unfortunately, the Darwinists won't do this. The evidence strongly indicates that they have the wrong box top, but they refuse to consider that's even possible (much less look for the right one). Their preconceived box top shows a picture without intelligent causes. Yet, as they themselves acknowledge, they've discovered many pieces to the puzzle that have the clear appearance of being intelligently designed. In effect, they're trying to fit theistic pieces into their atheistic/materialistic puzzle. How do they do this?

Instead of discarding the wrong box top and finding the right one, Darwinists simply insist that the pieces aren't really what they appear to be. They try to fit every piece—from the precisely designed universe to the information-rich single cell—into a puzzle that doesn't have those pieces in it. In doing so, they disregard observation, which is the very essence of the empirical science they claim to champion. As they themselves admit, Darwinists are philosophically committed to their box top regardless of what the puzzle pieces look like.

How do you find the right box top to the puzzle of life? Arriving at the right box top is not a matter of preference (you like atheism, I like theism). No, it's a matter of objective fact. By using the self-evident first principles of logic and the correct principles of scientific investigation, we discovered in chapters 3 and 4 that this is a theistic universe. If this is a theistic universe, then naturalism is false. If naturalism is false, then Darwinists may not be interpreting the evidence correctly.

Having the right box top is important because it provides the right context for interpreting the evidence. The context is the larger environment in which the evidence appears. If you have the wrong context, you may come to the wrong conclusion about evidence you are observing. For example, if I tell you that I just witnessed a man slashing open the stomach of a woman with a knife, you'd probably assume that man did something wrong. But look what happens when I reveal to you the context—the environment—in which this incident took place: we were in a hospital delivery room, the man was a doctor, and the baby's heart had just stopped. What do you think about the man now? Once you understand the environment, your entire view of the evidence has changed: you now consider the man a hero rather than a villain, because he was really trying to save the baby's life.

In the same way, the evidence from biology must be interpreted in light of the larger known environment. As we've already discovered, the larger known environment is that this is a theistic universe. There's actually an immaterial, powerful, and intelligent Being beyond the natural world who created the universe and designed it precisely to allow life on earth. In other words, we already know beyond a reasonable doubt that the Designer is part of the box top, because the evidence shows that he has already designed this awesome universe with amazing complexity and precision.

In light of the fact that this Designer exists, when we see biological systems that even Darwinists like Richard Dawkins recognize "give the appearance of having been designed for a purpose," maybe we ought to conclude that *they really were designed for a purpose*. As William Dembski points out, "If a creature looks like a dog, smells like a dog, barks like a dog, feels like a dog, and pants like a dog, the burden of evidence lies with the person insisting the creature isn't a dog."[21] Since the universe is created and designed, then we should expect life to be created and designed as well. (At least it's *possible* that life was created by intelligence. Ruling out that possibility beforehand is clearly illegitimate.)

So the conclusion that life is the product of an intelligent Designer makes sense because it's not a lone piece of evidence. It's consistent with other scientific findings. Or, to continue with our jigsaw puzzle metaphor, it's a piece that fits perfectly with the other pieces of the puzzle.

Summary and Conclusion

Since we've covered a lot of ground in this chapter, let's sum it up with a few short points:

1. Life does not consist merely of chemicals. If that were the case, mixing the chemicals of life in a test tube would produce life. Life clearly consists of more than chemicals; it also includes specified complexity (which comes only from a mind). Therefore, materialism is false. (There are numerous additional reasons why materialism is false, including the fact that reason itself would be impossible in a materialistic universe.)

2. There are no known natural laws that create specified complexity (information). Only intelligence has been observed creating specified complexity (e.g., "Take out the garbage—Mom, "Drink Coke," Mount Rushmore, etc.).

3. The simplest life consists of amazing specified complexity—equivalent to 1,000 complete sets of the *Encyclopedia Britannica*. Einstein said, "God doesn't play dice with the universe."[22] He was right. As Phillip Gold said, "God plays Scrabble!"[23]

4. Science is a search for causes that is built on philosophy. There are only two types of causes, intelligent and natural, but Darwinists philosophically rule out intelligent causes before they even look at the evidence. That's why when Darwinists look at those 1,000 encyclopedias—despite observing and recognizing their obvious design—they assert that their cause must be natural. But if "Take out the garbage—Mom" requires an intelligent cause, then so do 1,000 encyclopedias.

5. Spontaneous generation of life, which Darwinism requires to get the theory started, has never been observed. It is believed in by faith. And in light of the strong cosmological and teleological evidence that this is a theistic universe (and for many other reasons), the Darwinian belief in naturalism (or materialism) is also an article of faith. Hence, Darwinism is nothing more than a secular religion masquerading as science.

The skeptic may say, "Wait a minute! You're moving much too fast. What makes you think that Intelligent Design is scientific? Isn't ID just another case of the 'God-of-the-Gaps' fallacy—prematurely bringing God into the picture because you haven't found a natural cause yet? Why should we give up looking for a natural cause? In fact, it seems like ID is just that Bible-thumping, six-day creationism being smuggled into the public debate under a new name. And what about the evidence for the evolution of new life forms that you have yet to mention?"

Answers to these and other Darwinist claims are coming in the next chapter. Not only will we address those claims, but we will also provide more pieces to the puzzle that confirm that the Intelligent Design people, not the Darwinists, have the right box top.

6

New Life Forms: From the Goo to You via the Zoo?

"In grammar school they taught me that a frog turning into a prince was a fairy tale. In the university they taught me that a frog turning into a prince was a fact!"
—RON CARLSON

IN THE MOVIE *Contact*, Jodie Foster plays a scientist who is part of the Search for Extra-Terrestrial Intelligence (SETI) research team. SETI, which is a real organization, has scientists who scan space for unmistakable signs of intelligent life. What constitutes an unmistakable sign of intelligent life? A message. That's right, something like "Take out the garbage—Mom."

In the movie, Foster gets extremely excited when her antenna picks up radio waves that appear to have an intelligent pattern, "One, two, three, five, seven, eleven . . . those are primes!" she exclaims (meaning prime numbers). "That can't be natural phenomena!"

Indeed, random radio waves can be naturally produced, but those that contain a message always have an intelligent source. Prime numbers, from one to 101 in order, constitute a message that only comes from an intelligent being.

Foster is so confident that ET has been found, she goes public with her discovery. Government and military officials then converge on her facility. "If this is such an intelligent source, then why don't they just speak English?" one official asks with a hint of derision.

"Because math is the only universal language!" Foster fires back.

Of course she's right. In fact, alphabets, and thus language itself, can be ultimately reduced to numbers. This is why the English alphabet is mathematically identical to the genetic alphabet of DNA and why the comparison of cell information to encyclopedias is a one-to-one relationship rather than just an analogy.

While Foster and her colleagues later discover a more complicated message embedded in the radio waves, they are absolutely certain the prime numbers alone prove that the message came from intelligent life. Why are they so certain of this? Because repeated observation tells us that only intelligent beings create messages and that natural laws never do. When we see a sequence of prime numbers, we realize that it requires an intelligent cause just like the messages "Take out the garbage—Mom" and "Mary loves Scott" do.

Ironically, *Contact* was based on a novel by the late Carl Sagan, an ardent evolutionist who believed in spontaneous generation and who was instrumental in starting the real SETI program. The irony lies in the fact that Sagan was absolutely convinced that a simple string of prime numbers proves the existence of an intelligent being, but the equivalent of 1,000 encyclopedias in the first one-celled life does not. *It takes a lot of faith* not *to believe in God. More than we have!*

Moreover, it was Sagan who wrote this about the human brain:

> The information content of the human brain expressed in bits is probably comparable to the total number of connections among the neurons—about a hundred trillion bits. If written out in English, say, that information would fill some twenty million volumes, as many as in the world's largest libraries. The equivalent of twenty million books is inside the heads of every one of us. The brain is a very big place in a very small space. . . . The neurochemistry of the brain is astonishingly busy. The circuitry of a machine more wonderful than any devised by humans.[1]

Actually, Sagan probably *under*estimated the brain's information content at twenty million books. Nevertheless, the figure is still stunning. To conceptualize it, picture yourself at center court of Madison Square Garden several hours before a basketball game. You are the only one in the arena, and you are looking at almost 20,000 empty seats all around you. How many books would you have to stack on *each seat* in order to fit twenty million books in that arena?

You would need to stack 1,000 books *on each and every seat* to fit twenty million books in Madison Square Garden. Think about that. The roof is not high enough to allow that many books; you'd have to blow off the roof and keep stacking! That's how much specified and complex information is between your ears. Sagan was indeed right that the brain is a very big place in a very small space, and it's something immeasurably more sophisticated than anything humans have ever created.

Now let's review the facts: Sagan realized that the human brain has the information content of twenty million books. He also realized that's drastically more specified and complex than a string of prime numbers. Then why did he think the simpler message required an intelligent being but not the one twenty million books long? We might also ask Sagan and his fellow Darwinists a question of similar weight: If *intelligent* human beings can't create anything close to the human brain, why should we expect *nonintelligent* natural laws to do so?

The Darwinist response will usually involve "natural selection." Is this sufficient to account for new life forms? After all, it's a long way from one cell to the human brain.

What About New Life Forms?

Before discussing the origin of new life forms, we need to revisit the problem of the origin of first life. It certainly is a long way from one cell to the human brain, but the journey may be even longer from nonliving chemicals to the first cell. That's the most difficult problem for Darwinists. Where did the *first* life come from?

Do you see the magnitude of this problem for Darwinists? If Darwinists don't have an explanation for the first life, then what's the point of speaking about new life forms? The process of macroevolution, if it's possible at all, can't even begin unless there's preexisting life.

But as we saw in the last chapter, this doesn't stop the Darwinists. Against all empirical and forensic evidence, Darwinists make up a "just-so" story—spontaneous generation or panspermia—that magically gives them the first life they need. This isn't science—this is a joke. In fact it reminds us of a joke. Steve Martin used to say, "I know how you can be a millionaire and never pay taxes! First, get a million dollars, Okay, now . . ."

The Darwinists' position is even more problematic when you consider that they don't even have an explanation for the source of the non-living chemicals, much less an explanation for life. As we saw in chapter 3, one of the most profound questions to ask is, "If there is no God, why is there something rather than nothing at all?" We saw that the atheists have no plausible answer to this question. Suggesting a possibility is not enough—they have to present evidence if they are going to be scientific. It's obvious they don't know where the universe came from. A good box top (worldview) should be able to plausibly explain all of the data. If it can't answer the fundamental questions of the origin of the world or the origin of life, it's not a viable box top. It's time to look for a new one.

Even though we see that the Darwinist box top is fundamentally flawed, we need to look at a few of the claims the Darwinists make regarding the origin of new life forms. Their theory is macroevolution.

Microevolution vs. Macroevolution

You remember macroevolution—from the goo to you via the zoo. It's the belief that all life forms have descended from a common ancestor—the first one-celled creature—and all of this has happened by natural processes without any intelligent intervention. God was not involved. It has been a completely blind process.

Darwinists say this has happened by natural selection. But the term "natural selection" is a misnomer. Since the process of evolution is, by definition, without intelligence, there is no "selection" at all going on. It's a blind process. The term "natural selection" simply means that the fittest creatures survive. So what? That's true by definition—the fittest survive (this is called a tautology—a circular argument that doesn't prove anything). Logically, these are the creatures that are best equipped genetically or structurally to deal with changing environmental conditions (that's why they survive).

As an example of "natural selection," consider what happens to bacteria attacked by antibiotics. When bacteria survive a bout with antibiotics and multiply, that surviving group of bacteria may be resistant to that antibiotic. The surviving bacteria are resistant to that antibiotic because the parent bacteria possessed the genetic capacity to resist, or a rare biochemical mutation somehow helped it survive (we say "rare" because mutations are nearly always harmful). Since the sensitive bacteria die, the surviving bacteria multiply and now dominate.

Darwinists say that the surviving bacteria have evolved. Having adapted to the environment, the surviving bacteria provide us with an example of evolution. Fair enough, but what kind of evolution? The answer we're about to give is absolutely critical. In fact, outside of the philosophical presuppositions we've been exposing, defining "evolution" is perhaps the greatest point of confusion in the creation-evolution controversy. This is where Darwinian errors and false claims begin to multiply like bacteria if not checked by those who believe observation is important to science. Here's what observation tells us: *the surviving bacteria always stay bacteria.* They do not evolve into another type of organism. That would be macroevolution. Natural selection has never been observed to create new types.

But macroevolution is exactly what Darwinists claim from the data. They say that these observable *micro* changes can be extrapolated to prove that unobservable macroevolution has occurred. They make no distinction between *micro*evolution and *macro*evolution, and thus use the evidence for micro to prove macro. By failing to make this critical distinction, Darwinists can dupe the general public into thinking that any observable change in any organism proves that all life has evolved from the first one-celled creature.

This is why it is essential that the right distinctions be made and that all hidden assumptions be exposed when discussing the creation-evolution controversy. So if someone ever asks you, "Do you believe in evolution?" you should ask that person, "What do you mean by evolution? Do you mean micro- or macroevolution?" Microevolution has been observed; but it cannot be used as evidence for macroevolution, which has never been observed.

Darwinists are masters at defining the term "evolution" broadly enough so that evidence in one situation might be counted as evidence in another. Unfortunately for them, the public is beginning to catch on to this tactic, thanks largely to the popular works of Berkeley law professor Phillip Johnson. Johnson first exposed this Darwinistic sleight of hand with his groundbreaking book *Darwin on Trial.* That's where he points out that, "None of the 'proofs' [for natural selection] provides any persuasive reason for believing that natural selection can produce new species, new organs, or other major changes, or even minor changes that are permanent."[2] Biologist Jonathan Wells agrees when he writes, "Biochemical mutations cannot explain the large-scale changes in organisms that we see in the history of life."[3]

Why can't natural selection do the job? Here are five reasons it can't:

1. Genetic Limits—Darwinists say that microevolution within types proves that macroevolution has occurred. If these small changes can occur over a short period of time, think what natural selection can do over a long period of time.

Unfortunately for Darwinists, genetic limits seem to be built into the basic types. For example, dog breeders always encounter genetic limits when they intelligently attempt to create new breeds of dogs. Dogs may range in size from the Chihuahua to the Great Dane, but despite the best attempts of intelligent breeders, dogs always remain dogs. Likewise, despite the best efforts of intelligent scientists to manipulate fruit flies, their experiments have never turned out anything but more fruit flies (and usually crippled ones at that).[4] This is especially significant because the short life of fruit flies allows scientists to test many generations of genetic variation in a short period of time.

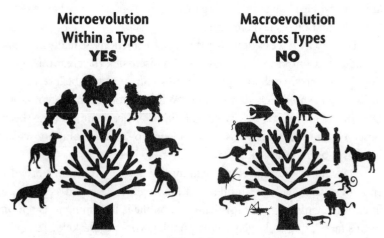

**Microevolution
Within a Type
YES**

**Macroevolution
Across Types
NO**

Fig. 6.1

Most importantly, the comparison between natural selection and the artificial selection that breeders do is completely invalid, as table 6.1

demonstrates. The biggest difference is the fact that artificial selection is intelligently guided while natural selection is not.

Crucial Differences:	ARTIFICIAL SELECTION	NATURAL SELECTION
Goal	Aim (end) in view	No aim (end) in view
Process	Intelligently guided process	Blind process
Choices	Intelligent choice of breeds	No intelligent choice of breeds
Protection	Breeds guarded from destructive processes	Breeds not guarded from destructive processes
Freaks	Preserves desired freaks	Eliminates most freaks
Interruptions	Continued interruptions to reach desired goal	No continued interruptions to reach any goal
Survival	Preferential survival	Non-preferential survival

Table 6.1

Confusing intelligent with nonintelligent processes is a common mistake of Darwinists. This was the case when I (Norm) debated humanist Paul Kurtz in 1986 on the topic of evolution. The debate, moderated by TV apologist John Ankerberg, produced this exchange regarding macroevolution:

> Geisler: [Chandra] Wickramasinghe [*who is an atheist*] said, "believing that life came by chance is like believing that a Boeing 747 resulted from a tornado going through a junk yard." You have to have a lot of faith to believe that!
>
> Kurtz: Well, the Boeing 747 evolved. We can go back to the Wright brothers and see that first kind of airplane they created . . .
>
> Geisler: Created?
>
> Kurtz: Yes, but . . .
>
> Ankerberg: By intelligence or by chance? [Laughter]
>
> Kurtz: There was a period of time in which these forms changed . . .
>
> Ankerberg: But didn't they create those airplanes using intelligence?
>
> Kurtz: I was using the analogy that Dr. Geisler was using.
>
> Geisler: Well, you're helping my argument! [Laughter] You ought to drop that one and find another one!

> Kurtz: No, no, I think the point I make is a good one because there have been changes from the simplest to the more complex airplanes.
>
> Geisler: Yes, but those changes were by intelligent intervention!

Indeed, directional change in airplanes *by intelligence* proves nothing about the possibility of directional change in living things *without intelligence*. As we'll see in the next section, directional change in living things by natural selection has not been observed. And directional change in living things *with intelligence* hits genetic limits. So even when it is intelligently guided, evolution hits walls. *In other words, even when scientists intelligently manipulate creatures with an end in mind—which is the antithesis of the blind Darwinian process—macroevolution still doesn't work!* If intelligent scientists cannot break genetic barriers, why should we expect nonintelligent natural selection to do so?

2. Cyclical Change—Not only are there genetic limits to change within types, but the change within types appears to be cyclical. In other words, changes are not directional toward the development of new life forms, as macroevolutionary theory requires, but they simply shift back and forth within a limited range. For example, Darwin's finches had varying beak sizes, which correlated with the weather.[5] Larger beaks helped crack larger, harder seeds during droughts, and smaller beaks worked fine when wetter weather brought an abundance of smaller, softer seeds. When the weather became drier, the proportion of finches with larger beaks grew relative to the smaller-beaked finches. The proportion reversed itself following a sustained period of wet weather. Notice that no new life forms came into existence (they always remained finches); only the relative proportion of existing large-beaked to small-beaked finches changed. Notice also that natural selection cannot explain how finches came into existence in the first place. In other words, natural selection may be able to explain the *survival* of a species, but it cannot explain the *arrival* of a species.

3. Irreducible Complexity—In 1859, Charles Darwin wrote, "If it could be demonstrated that any complex organ existed, which could not possibly have been formed by numerous, successive, slight modifications, my theory would absolutely break down."[6] We now know that there are many organs, systems, and processes in life that fit that description.

One of those is the cell. In Darwin's day the cell was a "black box"—a mysterious little part of life that no one could see into. But now that we have the ability to peer into the cell, we see that life at the molecular level is immeasurably more complex than Darwin ever dreamed. In fact, it is irreducibly complex. An irreducibly complex system is "composed of several well-matched, interacting parts that contribute to the basic function, wherein the removal of any one of the parts causes the system to effectively cease functioning."[7]

Those are the words of Michael Behe, professor of biochemistry at Lehigh University, who wrote the revolutionary book *Darwin's Black Box: The Biochemical Challenge to Evolution.* Behe's research verifies that living things are literally filled with molecular machines that perform the numerous functions of life. These molecular machines are irreducibly complex, meaning that all the parts of each machine must be completely formed, in the right places, in the right sizes, in operating order, at the same time, for the machine to function.

A car engine is an example of an irreducibly complex system. If a change is made in the size of the pistons, this would require simultaneous changes in the cam shaft, block, cooling system, engine compartment, and other systems, or the new engine would not function.

Behe shows that living things are irreducibly complex, just like a car engine. With painstaking detail, he shows that numerous functions in the body—such as blood clotting, cilia (cell propulsion organisms), and vision—require irreducibly complex systems that could not have developed in the gradual Darwinian fashion. Why? Because intermediates would be nonfunctional. As with a car engine, all the right parts must be in place in the right size at the same time for there to be any function at all. You can build an engine part by part (and that takes intelligence), but you can't drive to work with only a partial engine under the hood. Nor could you drive to work if one essential part of your engine were modified but others were not. In the same way, living systems quickly would become nonfunctional if they were modified piece by piece.

The degree of irreducible complexity in living things is mind-boggling. Recall that DNA's genetic alphabet consists of four letters: A, T, C, and G. Well, *within each human cell* there are about 3,000 *mil-*

lion pairs of those letters.[8] Not only does your body have *trillions* of cells and make millions of new cells every second, but each cell is irreducibly complex and contains irreducibly complex subsystems!

Behe's discoveries are fatal for Darwinism. Irreducible complexity means that new life cannot come into existence by the Darwinian method of slight, successive changes over a long period of time. Darwinism is akin to natural forces—without any intelligent help—producing a running car engine (i.e., an amoeba) and then modifying that irreducibly complex engine into successive intermediate engines until those natural forces finally produce the space shuttle (i.e., a human being). Darwinists can't explain the source of the materials to make an engine, much less how any irreducibly complex engine came to be in the first place. Nor can they demonstrate the *unintelligent* process by which any engine has evolved into the space shuttle while providing propulsion at every intermediate step. This is evident from the complete absence of explanations from Darwinists for how irreducibly complex systems could arise gradually. Behe exposes the empty claims of Darwinists when he writes,

> *The idea of Darwinian molecular evolution is not based on science.* There is no publication in the scientific literature—in journals or books—that describes how molecular evolution of any real, complex, biochemical system either did occur or even might have occurred. There are assertions that such evolution occurred, but absolutely none are supported by pertinent experiments or calculations. Since there is no authority on which to base claims of knowledge, *it can truly be said that the assertion of Darwinian molecular evolution is merely bluster.*[9]

The feeble attempts by Darwinists to deal with irreducible complexity reveal the magnitude of the problem for their theory. Darwinist Ken Miller has suggested that irreducible complexity isn't true because he can show that Behe's example of irreducible complexity—a mousetrap—isn't really irreducibly complex. According to Behe, all five parts of a traditional mousetrap need to be in place at the same time, in working order, for the mouse trap to work. You can't catch mice with just a platform and a spring, for example. But Miller thinks he can disprove Behe's point by building a similar mousetrap with only four parts. (Miller actually brought this up during a televised debate on *PBS* in the late nineties.)

But Miller's critique actually misses the mark. First, like a typical

Darwinist, Miller ignores the fact that his mousetrap requires intelligence to build. Second, Behe is not saying you need five parts for *any* mousetrap—just for the traditional mousetrap. It turns out that Miller's mousetrap is not a physical precursor to Behe's traditional mousetrap. In other words, transforming Miller's mousetrap into Behe's would require more than one random (i.e., Darwinian) step—it would require the addition of another very specific part and several very specific adjustments to existing parts (and that requires intelligence). Third, even if those changes could somehow be made by mindless processes, the mousetrap would be nonfunctional during the transition period. But for Darwinism to be true, functionality must be maintained at all times because living things cannot survive if, say, their vital organs do not perform their usual function during slow, trial-and-error Darwinian transitions.[10] Finally, a mousetrap is only an illustration. Living systems are immeasurably more complex than a mousetrap. So Behe's point clearly has not been refuted by Miller, nor has it been refuted by any other Darwinist.[11]

During an Intelligent Design conference in July 2002, at which both Behe and I (Frank) were speakers, one particular Darwinist was a bit militant during the question and answer period of the lectures. I wanted to turn the tables and ask him a few questions, so I made it a point to sit next to him during lunch.

"What do you do with Behe's irreducible complexity argument?" I asked between pizza slices.

He rolled his eyes and said, "Oh, that's no big deal. There are biochemical scaffolds that are built around the system to allow it to evolve gradually."

When I saw Behe later that day, I told him about the Darwinist's explanation. He rightly pointed out that: 1) there's no evidence for such "scaffolds," and 2) it actually complicates matters for Darwinists; namely, if these "scaffolds" do exist, then who keeps building them in just the right places? That would require intelligence.

Others have tried to find Darwinian paths around irreducible complexity, but all have failed. Behe confirms as much when he categorically states, "There is currently no experimental evidence to show that natural selection can get around irreducible complexity."[12]

Behe does not underestimate the implications of irreducible complexity and other discoveries regarding the complexity of life. He writes,

"The result of these cumulative efforts to investigate the cell—to investigate life at the molecular level—is a loud, clear, piercing cry of 'design!' The result is so unambiguous and so significant that it must be ranked as one of the greatest achievements in the history of science. The discovery rivals those of Newton and Einstein."[13]

4. Nonviability of Transitional Forms—Another problem that plagues the plausibility of natural selection creating new life forms is the fact that transitional forms could not survive. For example, consider the Darwinian assertion that birds evolved gradually from reptiles over long periods of time. This would necessitate a transition from scales to feathers. How could a creature survive that no longer has scales but does not quite have feathers? Feathers are irreducibly complex. A creature with the structure of half a feather has no ability to fly. It would be easy prey on land, in water, and from the air. And as a halfway house between reptiles and birds, it probably wouldn't be adept at finding food for itself either. So the problem for Darwinists is twofold: first, they have no viable mechanism for getting from reptiles to birds; and second, even if a viable mechanism were discovered, the transitional forms would be unlikely to survive anyway.

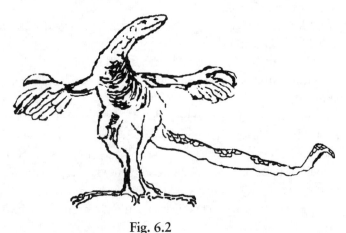

Fig. 6.2

5. Molecular Isolation—Darwinists often say that evidence of common descent lies in the fact that all living things contain DNA. For example, Richard Dawkins states, "The reason we know for certain we are all related, including bacteria, is the universality of the genetic code and other biochemical fundamentals."[14] Darwinists think the DNA similarity between apes and humans, for example, which some say is 85 to over 95 percent,[15] strongly implies an ancestral relationship.

But is this evidence for common *ancestry* or for a common *creator?* It could be interpreted either way. Perhaps the Darwinists are right—it is possible that we have a common genetic code because we've all descended from a common ancestor. But they could just as easily be wrong—*perhaps we a have a common genetic code because a common creator has designed us to live in the same biosphere.* After all, if every living creature were distinct biochemically, a food chain probably could not exist. Perhaps life with a different biochemical makeup is not possible. And even if it is, perhaps it couldn't survive in this biosphere.

Consider Fig. 6.3. Does similarity and progression prove that the kettle evolved from the teaspoon? No. Similarity and progression does not automatically imply common ancestry. In this case we know it means there is a common creator or designer. This is the same situation we have for real living things.

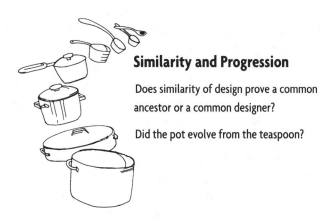

Similarity and Progression

Does similarity of design prove a common ancestor or a common designer?

Did the pot evolve from the teaspoon?

Fig. 6.3

As we said before, the capacity of the DNA genetic alphabet to contain a message is equivalent to the capacity of the English alphabet to contain a message (the only difference is that the DNA alphabet has only four letters versus twenty-six for the English alphabet). Since all living things have DNA with its four nitrogen-containing bases (represented by the letters A, T, C, and G), we would expect a high degree of similarity in the information among creatures whether or not they are ancestrally related.

Let's use an example from English to illustrate what we mean. Here are two sentences with exactly the same letters:

Charles Darwin was a scientific god.
Charles Darwin was a scientific dog.

While the letters in the two sentences are identical and the order is virtually the same (greater than 90 percent), the slight difference in order yields opposite meanings. In the same way, only a slight difference in the order of the letters (A, T, C, and G) in living things may yield creatures that are far apart on the hypothetical evolutionary tree. For example, while some studies show that the DNA similarity between humans and the most similar ape may be about 90 percent, other studies show the DNA similarity between humans and *mice* is also about 90 percent.[16] Such comparisons are controversial and are not completely understood. More research needs to be done in this field. But if mice genetically are as close to humans as apes, this would greatly complicate any Darwinian explanation.

But let's suppose that further studies someday show that ape DNA is indeed closer to humans than the DNA of any other creature. This would not prove the Darwinists' conclusion that there is an ancestral relationship. Again, the reason for the similarity could be a common creator rather than a common ancestor. We must find other evidence at the molecular level to help us discover whether the common genetic code is evidence of a common ancestor or of a common creator.

That other evidence *has* been found—by comparing protein sequences. Proteins are the building blocks of life. They are composed of long chains of chemical units called amino acids. Most proteins have in their structure more than 100 of these amino acids, which must be in a very specific order. It's the DNA that contains the instructions for ordering the amino acids in the proteins, and the order is critical because any variation usually renders the protein dysfunctional.

Here's where the problem arises for Darwinists. If all species share a common ancestor, we should expect to find protein sequences that are transitional from, say, fish to amphibian, or from reptile to mammal. But that's not what we find at all. Instead, we find that the basic types are molecularly isolated from one another, which seems to preclude any type of ancestral relationship. Michael Denton observes,

> At a molecular level there is no trace of the evolutionary transition from fish → amphibian → reptile → mammal. So amphibia, always traditionally considered intermediate between fish and the other terrestrial vertebrates, are in molecular terms as far from fish as any group of reptiles or mammals! To those well acquainted with the traditional picture of vertebrate evolution the result is truly astonishing.[17]

So even though all organisms share a common genetic code with varying degrees of closeness, that code has ordered the amino acids in proteins in such a way that the basic types are in molecular isolation from one another. There are no Darwinian transitions, only distinct molecular gaps. Darwinists cannot explain the presence of these molecular gaps by natural selection any more than they can explain the presence of huge gaps in the fossil record (which we'll talk about next).

What About the Fossil Record?

So let's quickly review what we've seen so far. These are the five lines of evidence which show that natural selection could not have produced new life forms:

1. Genetic limits
2. Cyclical change
3. Irreducible complexity
4. Nonviability of transitional forms
5. Molecular isolation

But doesn't the fossil record support the Darwinian theory? Let's take a look.

Without the benefit of today's technology, Charles Darwin could not recognize the problems his theory faced at the cellular level. However, he did recognize that the fossil record posed a big problem for his theory because it didn't show gradualism. That's why he wrote, "Why then is not every geological formation and every stratum full of such intermediate links? Geology assuredly does not reveal any such finely graduated organic chain, and this, perhaps, is the most obvious and gravest objection which can be urged against my theory."[18]

But Darwin thought that further fossil discoveries would reveal that his theory was true. Time has proven him wrong. Contrary to what you may hear in the general media, the fossil record has turned out to be a complete embarrassment for Darwinists. If Darwinism were true, we would have found thousands, if not millions, of transitional fossils by now. Instead, according to the late Harvard paleontologist Stephen Jay Gould (an evolutionist),

> The history of most fossil species includes two features particularly inconsistent with gradualism: 1). Stasis. Most species exhibit no directional change during their tenure on earth. They appear in the fossil record looking much the same as when they disappear; Morphological change is usually limited and directionless. 2). Sudden Appearance. In any local area, a species does not arise gradually by the steady transformation of its ancestors; it appears all at once and 'fully formed.'[19]

In other words, Gould is admitting that fossil types appear suddenly, fully formed, and remain the same until extinction without any directional change—exactly what one would expect to find if creation were true.

But instead of adopting creationism, Gould rejected the gradualism of Darwinism and formulated a theory he called "Punctuated Equilibria" (PE). PE suggests that species evolved faster over a shorter period of time, thereby explaining the huge fossil gaps. Gould had no natural mechanism by which this could have occurred, but since he was an atheist he had to explain the fossil record somehow. This is a classic case of allowing your prejudices to taint your observations.

But we digress. The main point here is that the fossil record actually lines up better with supernatural creation than with macroevolution. Indeed, there aren't missing links—there's a missing chain!

There is no chain because nearly all of the major groups of animals known to exist appear in the fossil record abruptly and fully formed in strata from the Cambrian period (which many scientists estimate to have occurred between 600 and 500 million years ago). Jonathan Wells writes, "The fossil evidence is so strong, and the event so dramatic, that it has become known as 'the Cambrian explosion,' or 'biology's big bang.'"[20]

This evidence, of course, is completely inconsistent with Darwinism. All animal groups appear separately, fully formed, and at the same time. That's not evidence of gradual evolution but of instantaneous creation. So the Darwinian tree we are so used to seeing doesn't properly illustrate the real fossil record. In fact, as Wells observes, "if any botanical analogy were appropriate, it would be a *lawn* rather than a tree."[21] And that lawn would have patches of different grasses or plants separated by large areas of nothing but dirt.

At this point you may be thinking, "But what about the skull progression we're so used to seeing? Doesn't it appear that man has evolved from apes?"

A number of years ago I (Norm) debated a Darwinist who lined up skulls on a table to illustrate that evolution had occurred. "Ladies and gentlemen, right here is the evidence for evolution," he declared.

Gee, how can you ignore the fossils? The skulls look like they're in a progression. They look as if they could be ancestrally related. Is this good evidence for Darwinism? No, it's not any better than the evidence that the large kettle evolved from the teaspoon.

The problem for the Darwinists is that the fossil record cannot establish ancestral relationships. Why not? Because, according to Michael Denton, "99 percent of the biology of any organism resides in its soft anatomy, which is inaccessible in a fossil."[22] In other words, it's extremely difficult to discover the biological makeup of a creature by looking at its fossil remains. Jonathan Wells observes, "The fossil evidence is open to many interpretations because individual specimens can be reconstructed in a variety of ways, and because the fossil record cannot establish ancestor-descendant relationships."[23]

But this doesn't stop the Darwinists. Since Darwinism *has* to be true because of their prior philosophical commitment, Darwinists *have* to find evidence supporting it. So instead of admitting that fossils can't establish ancestral relationships, Darwinists take the one percent that fossils tell them and then use the other 99 percent of leeway to depict their fossil discoveries as filling any gap they want. With such vast leeway and no facts to constrain them, Darwinists have been free to creatively build entire "missing links" from fossil remains as trivial as a single tooth. This is why many so-called "missing links" have later been exposed as frauds or mistakes.[24] Henry Gee, chief science writer for *Nature,* writes, "To take a line of fossils and claim that they represent a lineage is not a scientific hypothesis that can be tested, but an assertion that carries the same validity as a bedtime story—amusing, perhaps even instructive, but not scientific."[25]

Not only is the fossil record inadequate to establish ancestral relationships; in light of what we now know about the irreducibly complex nature of biological systems, *the fossil record is irrelevant to the question.* The similarity of structure or anatomy between types (sometimes called homology) also tells us nothing about common ancestry. Michael Behe writes,

> Anatomy is, quite simply, irrelevant to the question of whether evolution could take place on the molecular level. So is the fossil record. It no longer matters whether there are huge gaps in the fossil record or whether the record is as continuous as that of U.S. presidents. And if there are gaps, it does not matter whether they can be explained plausibly. The fossil record has nothing to tell us about whether the interactions of 11-cts-retinal with rhodopsin, transducin, and phosphodiesterase [irreducibly complex systems] could have developed step-by-step.[26]

So, according to Behe, biology dwarfs anatomy on the question of the plausibility of macroevolution. Just as the contents of a book provide far more information than its cover, the biology of a creature provides far more information than its skeletal structure. Nevertheless, Darwinists have long argued that similarity of structure between, say, apes and humans is evidence of common ancestry (or common descent). *Does it ever dawn on them that similarity of structure may be evidence of a common designer rather than a common ancestor?*[27] After all, in a world governed by certain physical and chemical laws, perhaps only a certain range of anatomical structures will be conducive to animals designed to walk on two legs. Since we all have to live in the same biosphere, we should expect some creatures to have similar designs.

Moreover, while apes may have a similar structure to humans, what is often overlooked is the fact that apes and humans bear almost no resemblance to snakes, fungus, and trees. But according to Darwinism, all living things have evolved from the same ancestor. To posit Darwinism, you must be able to explain the vast *dissimilarity* between living things. You must explain how the palm tree, the peacock, the octopus, the locust, the bat, the hippopotamus, the porcupine, the sea horse, the Venus flytrap, the human, and mildew, for example, have all descended from the first irreducibly complex life without intelligent intervention. You also have to explain how the first life and the universe came into existence as well. Without viable explanations, which Darwinists have failed to provide, it takes too much faith to be a Darwinist. *And that's why we don't have enough faith to be Darwinists.*

IS INTELLIGENT DESIGN AN INTELLIGENT ALTERNATIVE?

Much more could be said about macroevolution, but space does not permit us to go any further. Nevertheless, a reasonable conclusion can be drawn from the data we have investigated in this chapter. In light of the fossil record, molecular isolation, transitional difficulties, irreducible complexity, cyclical change, and genetic limits (and the fact that they can't explain the origin of the universe or of first life), you would think Darwinists might finally admit that their theory doesn't fit the observable evidence. Instead, Darwinists are still providing unsubstantiated "just-so" stories that actually contradict scientific observation. They continue to insist that evolution is a fact, fact, fact!

We agree that evolution is a fact, but not in the sense the Darwinists mean it. If you define evolution as "change," then certainly living beings have evolved. But this evolution is on the micro, not the macro level. As we have seen, there's not only a lack of evidence for macroevolution; *there's positive evidence that it has not occurred.*

If macroevolution isn't true, then what is? Well, if there's no natural explanation for the origin of new life forms, then there must be an intelligent explanation. It's the only other option. There's no halfway house between intelligence and nonintelligence. Either intelligence was involved or it wasn't. But Darwinists don't like this option. So once they exhaust their ability to adequately defend their own position with unbiased scientific evidence (which is very quickly), Darwinists typically turn their guns on the Intelligent Design people—those of us who believe there's intelligence behind the universe and life. Here are their typical objections and our responses:[28]

Objection: Intelligent Design is not science.

Answer: As we have seen, science is a search for causes, and there are only two types of causes: intelligent and nonintelligent (natural). The Darwinists' claim that Intelligent Design is not science is based on their biased definition of science. But that's arguing in a circle! If your definition of science rules out intelligent causes beforehand, then you'll never consider Intelligent Design science.

The irony for the Darwinists is this: if Intelligent Design is not science, then neither is Darwinism. Why? Because both Darwinists and Intelligent Design scientists are trying to discover what happened in the past. Origin questions are forensic questions, and thus require the use of the forensic science principles we already have discussed. In fact, for Darwinists to rule out Intelligent Design from the realm of science, in addition to ruling out themselves they would also have to rule out archaeology, cryptology, criminal and accident forensic investigations, and the Search for Extra Terrestrial Intelligence (SETI). These are all legitimate forensic sciences that look into the past for intelligent causes. Something must be wrong with the Darwinists' definition of science.

Table 6.2 shows the difference between empirical science and forensic science:

Empirical (Operation) Science	Forensic (Origin) Science
Studies present	Studies past
Studies regularities	Studies singularities
Studies repeatable	Studies unrepeatable
Re-creation possible	Re-creation impossible
Studies how things work	Studies how things began
Tested by repeatable experiment	Tested by uniformity
Asks how something operates	Asks what its origin is
Examples:	Examples:
How does water fall?	What's the origin of a hydroelectric plant?
How does rock erode?	What's the origin of Mount Rushmore?
How does an engine work?	What's the origin of an engine?
How does ink adhere to paper?	What's the origin of this book?
How does life function?	What's the origin of life?
How does the universe operate?	What's the origin of the universe?

Table 6.2

Objection: Intelligent Design commits the God-of-the-Gaps fallacy.
Answer: The God-of-the-Gaps fallacy occurs when someone falsely believes that God caused the event when it really was caused by undiscovered natural phenomena. For example, people used to believe that lightning was caused directly by God. There was a gap in our knowledge of nature, so we attributed the effect to God. Darwinists assert that theists are doing the same thing by claiming that God created the universe and life. Are they correct? No, for a number of reasons.

First, when we conclude that intelligence created the first cell or the human brain, it's not simply because we *lack* evidence of a natural explanation; it's also because we have positive, empirically detectable evidence *for* an intelligent cause. A message (specified complexity) is empirically detectable. When we detect a message—like "Take out the garbage—Mom" or 1,000 encyclopedias—we know that it must come from an intelligent being because all of our observational experience tells us that messages come only from intelligent beings. Every time we observe a message, it comes from an intelligent being. We couple this data with the fact that we never observe natural laws creating messages, and we know an intelligent being must be the cause. That's a valid scientific conclusion based on observation and repetition. It's not an argument from ignorance, nor is it based on any "gap" in our knowledge.

Second, Intelligent Design scientists are open to *both* natural and intelligent causes. They are not opposed to continued research into a natural explanation for the first life. They're simply observing that all known natural explanations fail, and all empirically detectable evidence points to an intelligent Designer.

Now, one can question the wisdom of continuing to look for a natural cause of life. William Dembski, who has published extensive research on Intelligent Design, asks, "When does determination [to find a natural cause] become pigheadedness? . . . How long are we to continue a search before we have the right to give up the search and declare not only that continuing the search is vain but also that the very object of the search is nonexistent?"[29]

Consider the implications of Dembski's question. Should we keep looking for a natural cause for phenomena like Mount Rushmore or messages like "Take out the garbage—Mom"? When is the case closed?

Walter Bradley, a coauthor of the seminal work *The Mystery of Life's Origin,* believes "there doesn't seem to be the potential of finding a [natural explanation]" for the origin of life. He added, "I think people who believe that life emerged naturalistically need to have a great deal more faith than people who reasonably infer that there's an Intelligent Designer."[30]

Regardless of whether or not you think we should keep looking for a natural explanation, the main point is that ID scientists are open to both natural and intelligent causes. It just so happens that an intelligent cause best fits the evidence.

Third, the Intelligent Design conclusion is falsifiable. In other words, ID could be disproven if natural laws were someday discovered to create specified complexity. However, the same *cannot* be said about the Darwinist position. Darwinists don't allow falsification of their "creation story" because, as we have described, they don't allow any other creation story to be considered. Their "science" is not tentative or open to correction; it's more closed-minded than the most dogmatic church doctrine the Darwinists are so apt to criticize.

Finally, it's actually the Darwinists who are committing a God-of-the-Gaps fallacy. Darwin himself was once accused of considering natural selection "an active power or Deity" (see chapter 4 of *Origin of Species*). But it seems that natural selection actually *is* the deity or "God of the Gaps" for the Darwinists of today. When they are totally at a loss for how irreducibly complex, information-rich biological systems came into existence, they simply cover their gap in knowledge by claiming that natural selection, time, and chance did it.

The ability of such a mechanism to create information-rich biological systems runs counter to the observational evidence. Mutations are nearly always harmful, and time and chance do the Darwinists no good, as we explained in chapter 5. At best, natural selection may be responsible for minor changes in living species, but it cannot explain the origin of the basic forms of life. You need a living thing to start with for any natural selection to take place. Yet, despite the obvious problems with their mechanism, Darwinists insist that it covers any gap in their knowledge. Moreover, they willfully ignore the positive, empirically detectable evidence for an intelligent being. This is not science but the dogma of a secular religion. Darwinists, like the opponents of Galileo, are letting their religion overrule scientific observations!

Objection: Intelligent Design is religiously motivated.
Answer: There are two aspects to this objection. The first is that some Intelligent Design people may be religiously motivated. So what? Does that make Intelligent Design false? Does the religious motivation of some Darwinists make Darwinism false? No, the truth doesn't lie in the motivation of the scientists, but in the quality of the evidence. A scientist's motivation or bias doesn't necessarily mean he's wrong. He could have a bias and still be right. Bias or motivation isn't the main issue—truth is.

Sometimes the objection is stated this way: "You can't believe anything he says about origins because he's a creationist!" Well, if the sword cuts at all, it cuts both ways. We could just as easily say, "You can't believe anything he says about origins because he's a Darwinist!"

Why are creationist conclusions immediately thought to be biased but Darwinist conclusions automatically considered objective? Because most people don't realize that atheists have a worldview just like creationists. As we are seeing, the atheist's worldview is not neutral and actually requires more faith than the creationist's.

Now, as we have said earlier, if philosophical or religious biases prevent someone from interpreting the evidence correctly, then we would have grounds for questioning that person's conclusions. In the current debate, that problem seems to afflict Darwinists more than anyone else. Yet, the main point is that even if someone is motivated by religion or philosophy, their conclusions can be corrected by an honest look at the evidence. Scientists on both sides of the fence may have a difficult time being neutral, but if they have integrity, they can be objective.

The second aspect of this objection is the charge that Intelligent Design people don't have any evidence for their view—they're simply parroting what the Bible says. This aspect of the objection doesn't work either. Intelligent Design beliefs may be *consistent* with the Bible, but they are not *based* on the Bible. As we have seen, Intelligent Design is a conclusion based on empirically detectable evidence, not sacred texts. As Michael Behe observes, "Life on earth at its most fundamental level, in its most critical components, is the product of intelligent activity. The conclusion of intelligent design flows naturally from the data itself—not from sacred books or sectarian beliefs."[31]

Intelligent Design is not "creation science" either. Intelligent Design scientists don't make claims that so-called "creation scientists" make. They don't say that the data unambiguously supports the six-twenty-four-hour-day view of Genesis, or a worldwide flood. Instead, they acknowledge that the data for Intelligent Design is not based on a specific age or geologic history of the earth. ID scientists study the same objects in nature that the Darwinists study—life and the universe itself—but they come to a more reasonable conclusion about the cause of those objects. In short, regardless of what the Bible may say on the topic, *Darwinism is rejected because it doesn't fit the scientific data,* and Intelligent Design is accepted because it does.

Objection: Intelligent Design is false because the so-called design isn't perfect.
Answer: Darwinists have long argued that if a designer existed, he would have designed his creatures better. Stephen Jay Gould pointed this out in his book *The Panda's Thumb,* where he cited the apparent sub-optimal design of a bony extrusion pandas have for a thumb.

The problem for the Darwinists is that this actually turns out to be an argument *for* a designer rather than an argument against one. First, the fact that Gould can identify something as sub-optimal design implies that he knows what optimal design is. You can't know something is imperfect unless you know what perfect is. So Gould's observation of even sub-optimal design implies an admission that design is detectable in the panda's thumb. (By the way, this is another reason the Darwinists are wrong when they assert that Intelligent Design is not science. When they claim something isn't designed correctly, they are implying they could tell if it *were* designed correctly. This proves what ID scientists have been saying all along—ID is science because design is empirically detectable.)

Second, sub-optimal design doesn't mean there's no design. In other words, even if you grant that something is not designed optimally, that doesn't mean it's not designed at all. Your car isn't designed optimally, yet it's still designed—it certainly wasn't put together by natural laws.

Third, in order to say that something is sub-optimal, you must know what the objectives or purpose of the designer are. If Gould doesn't know what the designer intended, then he can't say the design falls short of those intentions. How does Gould know the panda's thumb isn't exactly what the designer had in mind? Gould assumes the panda should have opposable thumbs like those of humans. But maybe the designer wanted the panda's thumbs to be just like they are. After all, the panda's thumb works just fine in allowing him to strip bamboo down to its edible interior. Maybe pandas don't need opposable thumbs because they don't need to write books like Gould; they simply need to strip bamboo. Gould can't fault the designer of that thumb if it wasn't intended to do more than strip bamboo.

Finally, in a world constrained by physical reality, all design requires trade-offs. Laptop computers must strike a balance between size, weight, and performance. Larger cars may be more safe and comfortable, but they also are more difficult to maneuver and consume more fuel. High ceilings make rooms more dramatic, but they also consume more energy. Because trade-offs cannot be avoided in this world, engineers must look for a compromise position that best achieves intended objectives. For example, you can't fault the design in a compact car because it doesn't carry fifteen passengers. The objective is to carry four not fifteen passengers. The carmaker traded size for fuel economy and achieved the intended objective. Likewise, it could be that the design of the panda's thumb is a trade-off that still achieves intended objectives. The thumb is just right for stripping bamboo. Perhaps, if the thumb had been designed any other way, it would have hindered the panda in some other area. We simply don't know without knowing the objectives of the designer. What we do know is that Gould's criticisms cannot succeed without knowing those objectives.

SO WHY ARE THERE STILL DARWINISTS?

If the evidence is so strong for Intelligent Design, then why are there still Darwinists? After all, these people are not dummies—their names are usually followed by the letters Ph.D.!

The first thing to note is that this is not just an intellectual issue where Darwinists take a dispassionate look at the evidence and then make a rational conclusion. Richard Dawkins has famously written, "It is absolutely safe to say that if you meet somebody who claims not to believe in evolution, that person is ignorant, stupid or insane (or wicked, but I'd rather not consider that)."[32] Of course, Dawkins's comment is simply false. There are brilliant Ph.D.s who believe in Intelligent Design. But the real question is, Why the invectives? Why the emotion? Why the hostility? I thought this was science. There must be something else at stake here.

There is. Let's go back to Richard Lewontin's quote from the last chapter. Recall his assertion that Darwinists believe in the absurdities they do because "materialism is absolute. For we cannot allow a divine foot in the door." Now, that's the real issue. Keeping God out. But why would Darwinists not want a "divine foot in the door"? We suggest four major reasons.

First, by admitting God, Darwinists would be admitting that they are not the highest authority when it comes to truth. Currently, in this technologically advanced world, scientists are viewed by the public as the revered authority figures—the new priests who make a better life possible and who comprise the sole source of objective truth. Allowing the possibility of God would be to relinquish their claim of superior authority.

Second, by admitting God, Darwinists would be admitting that they don't have absolute authority when it comes to explaining causes. In other words, if God exists, they couldn't explain every event as the result of predictable natural laws. Richard Lewontin put it this way: "To appeal to an omnipotent deity is to allow that at any moment the regularities of nature may be ruptured, that miracles may happen."[33] As Jastrow noted, when that happens, "the scientist has lost control," certainly to God, and perhaps to the theologian.[34]

Third, by admitting God, Darwinists would risk losing financial security and professional admiration. How so? Because there's tremendous pressure in the academic community to publish something that supports evolution. Find something important, and you may find yourself on the cover of National Geographic or the subject of a PBS special. Find nothing, and you may find yourself out of a job, out of grant money, or at least out of favor with your materialist colleagues. So there's a money, job security, and prestige motive to advance the Darwinian worldview.

Finally, and perhaps the most significantly, by admitting God,

Darwinists would be admitting that they don't have the authority to define right and wrong for themselves. By ruling out the supernatural, Darwinists can avoid the possibility that anything is morally prohibited. For if there is no God, everything is lawful, as a character in a Dostoevsky novel observed.[35] (We'll elaborate on the connection between God and morality in the next chapter.)

In fact, the late Julian Huxley, once a leader among Darwinists, admitted that sexual freedom is a popular motivation behind evolutionary dogma. When he was asked by talk show host Merv Griffin, "Why do people believe in evolution?" Huxley honestly answered, "The reason we accepted Darwinism even without proof, is because we didn't want God to interfere with our sexual mores."[36] Notice he didn't cite evidence for spontaneous generation or evidence from the fossil record. The motivation he observed to be prevalent among evolutionists was based on moral preferences, not scientific evidence.

Former atheist Lee Strobel reveals that he had the same motivation when he believed in Darwinism. He writes, "I was more than happy to latch onto Darwinism as an excuse to jettison the idea of God so I could unabashedly pursue my own agenda in life without moral constraints."[37]

Author and lecturer Ron Carlson has had Darwinists admit the same to him. On one such occasion, after lecturing at a major university on the problems with Darwinism and the evidence for Intelligent Design, Carlson had dinner with a biology professor who had attended his presentation.

"So what did you think of my lecture?" Carlson asked.

"Well, Ron," began the professor, "what you say is true and makes a lot of sense. But I'm gonna continue to teach Darwinism anyway."

Carlson was baffled. "Why would you do that?" he asked.

"Well, to be honest with you, Ron, it's because Darwinism is morally comfortable."

"Morally comfortable? What do you mean?" Carlson pressed.

"I mean if Darwinism is true—if there is no God and we all evolved from slimy green algae—then I can sleep with whomever I want," observed the professor. "In Darwinism, there's no moral accountability."[38]

Now that's a moment of complete candor. Of course, this is not to say that all Darwinists think this way or that all Darwinists are immoral—some undoubtedly live morally better lives than many so-called Christians. It simply reveals that some Darwinists are motivated not by the evidence but rather by a desire to remain free from the perceived moral restraints of God. This motivation may drive them to suppress the evidence for the Creator so they can continue to live the way they want to live. (In this sense, Darwinism is no different than many other world religions in that it provides a way to deal with the guilt that results from immoral behavior. The difference is that some Darwinists, instead of acknowledging guilt and offering ways to atone for it or rules to avoid it, attempt to avoid any implication of guilt by asserting that there's no such thing as immoral behavior to be guilty about!)

These four motivations that we've suggested should not surprise us. Sex and power are the motivators that underlie many of our most intense cultural debates, such as those about abortion and homosexuality. Too often people take positions in those debates that merely line up with their personal desires rather than taking the evidence into account.

In the same way, belief in Darwinism is often a matter of the will rather than the mind. Sometimes people refuse to accept what they know to be true because of the impact it will have on their personal lives. This explains why some Darwinists suggest such absurd "counterintuitive" explanations—explanations that are "against common sense." Despite the plain evidence for design, these Darwinists fear encroachment of God into their personal lives more than they fear being wrong about their scientific conclusions.

This is not to say that all Darwinists have such motivations for their beliefs. Some may truly believe that the scientific evidence supports their theory. We think they get this misconception because most Darwinists rarely study the research of those in other fields. As a result, very few get the big picture.

This is especially true of biologists. Molecular and cell biologist Jonathan Wells observes, "Most biologists are honest, hard-working scientists who insist on accurate presentation of the evidence, but who rarely venture outside their own fields."[39] In other words, although they do honest work, they only see their own piece of the puzzle. Since they've been taught that the Darwinian box top of the puzzle is generally true (it's just those pesky details that remain unresolved), most biologists interpret their piece of the puzzle with that box top in mind, giving the benefit of the doubt to the Darwinian view and assuming that the really strong evidence for Darwinism lies in another field of biology. So even if they can't see the evidence for spontaneous generation or macroevolution in their piece of the puzzle, the evidence must be somewhere else in biology because the Darwinian box top requires those things to be true. These circumstances leave the evolutionary paradigm unchallenged by the majority of biologists.

How Important Is the Age of the Universe?

We couldn't leave the discussion of evolution and creation without at least mentioning the age of the universe. Since there are several views on this topic, especially within Christian circles, we do not have space to treat them all here (they are discussed in detail in the *Baker Encyclopedia of Christian Apologetics* and *Systematic Theology, Volume 2*).[40]

However, we do want to point out that while the age of universe is certainly an interesting theological question, the more important point is not *when* the universe was created but *that* it was created. As we have seen, the universe exploded into being out of nothing, and it has been precisely tweaked to support life on earth. Since this universe—including the entire time-space continuum—had a beginning, it required a Beginner no matter how long ago that beginning was. Likewise, since this universe is designed, it required a Designer no matter how long ago it was designed.

We can debate how long the days in Genesis were, or whether the assumptions that are made in dating techniques are valid. But when we do, we must be sure not to obscure the larger point that this creation requires a Creator.[41]

Summary and Conclusion

Now, let's get to the bottom line. There are really only two possibilities: either God created us, or we created God. Either God really exists, or he's just a creation of our own minds. As we have seen, Darwinism—not God—is a creation of the human mind. You've got to have a lot of faith to be a Darwinist. You have to believe that, *without intelligent intervention:*

1. Something arose from nothing (the origin of the universe).

    2. Order arose from chaos (the design of the universe).

    3. Life arose from non-life (which means that intelligence arose from nonintelligence, and personality arose from non-personality).

    4. New life forms arose from existing life forms despite evidence to the contrary such as:

        (1) Genetic limits

        (2) Cyclical change

        (3) Irreducible complexity

        (4) Molecular isolation

        (5) Nonviability of transitional forms, and

        (6) The fossil record

Okay, so the evidence is not good for macroevolution. But what about theistic macroevolution? Perhaps what can't be explained naturally makes good sense if you add God to the picture.

Why suggest that? If there were evidence for God *and* for macroevolution, then there might be a reason to combine the two. But, as we have seen, there is no evidence that macroevolution has occurred. It's not like you have contradictory evidence: some evidence that points to macroevolution, and other evidence that disproves it. If you had, say, a fossil record with millions of transitional forms on one hand, but irreducibly complex creatures on another, then perhaps you could suggest that God guided evolution through those unbridgeable gaps. But since that is not the case, it seems that God wasn't needed to guide macroevolution because there's no evidence macroevolution has occurred!

Finally, let's look at the evidence with another question in mind: What would the evidence have to look like for creation (Intelligent Design) to be true? How about:

    1. A universe that has exploded into being out of nothing

    2. A universe with over 100 fine-tuned, life-enabling constants for this tiny, remote planet called Earth

    3. Life that:

        • has been observed to arise only from existing life (it has never been observed to arise spontaneously);

        • consists of thousands and even millions of volumes of empirically detectable specified complexity (and is, therefore, more than just the nonliving chemicals it contains);

- changes cyclically and only within a limited range;
- cannot be built or modified gradually (i.e., is irreducibly complex);
- is molecularly isolated between basic types (there's no ancestral progression at the molecular level);
- leaves a fossil record of fully formed creatures that appear suddenly, do not change, and then disappear suddenly.

An honest look at the facts suggests creation, not macroevolution, is true. As we have seen, atheists have to work really hard not to conclude the obvious. *That's why they need to have a lot more faith than we do.*

Finally, we have a proposal to help resolve the debate in this country over what should be taught in the public schools regarding creation and evolution. What would be wrong with teaching them what we've just covered in chapters 3 to 6? Notice we haven't been quoting Bible verses to make our points. We've been citing scientific evidence. So this isn't a battle of science versus religion; it's a battle of *good* science versus *bad* science. Right now, most of our children are being taught bad science because they're being taught evolution only. It doesn't have to be that way. What would be unconstitutional about teaching the SURGE evidence, showing them the complexity of the simplest life, making the distinctions between micro- and macroevolution and between forensic and empirical science, or exposing the problems with macroevolution? Nothing. So why do we continue to indoctrinate our children in a flawed and crumbling theory that is based more on philosophical presuppositions than on scientific observations? Why don't we give our children all the scientific evidence—pro and con—and let them make up their own minds? After all, shouldn't we be teaching them how to think critically on their own? Of course we should. But Darwinists will go to great lengths to ensure that that doesn't happen. Darwinists would rather suppress the evidence than allow it to be presented fairly. Why? Because this is the one area where Darwinists lack faith—*they lack the faith to believe that their theory will still be believed after our children see all the evidence.*

7

Mother Teresa
vs. Hitler

"We hold these Truths to be self-evident, that all Men are created equal, that they are endowed by their Creator with certain unalienable Rights, that among these are Life, Liberty and the Pursuit of Happiness."
—THE DECLARATION OF INDEPENDENCE

IS THERE A STANDARD?

My friend Dave and I were just finishing dinner at a dockside restaurant in Portland, Maine, when the conversation turned to religion. "I don't think one religion can be exclusively true," Dave said. "But it seems like you, Frank, have found a center. You have found something that's true for you, and I think that's great."

Playing along with his premise that something can be true for one person but not another, I asked, "Dave, what's true for you? What makes life meaningful for you?"

He said, "Making money and helping people!" Now Dave is a very successful businessman, so I pressed him a little bit more.

I said, "Dave, I know CEOs who have reached the pinnacle of business success. They've planned and achieved great things in their business life, but have planned nothing and achieved little in their personal lives. They're now facing retirement, and they're asking themselves, 'Now what?'"

Dave agreed and added, "Yeah, and I know that most of those CEOs have experienced nasty divorces, mostly because they ignored their families in pursuit of a buck. But I'm not like that. I will not sacrifice my family for money, and in my business I want to help people as well."

I commended him for his commitment to his family and his desire to help people, but questions still remained. Why should we be faithful to our families? Who said we should "help people?" Is "helping people" a universal moral obligation, or is it just true for you but not for me? And to what end should you help them: Financially? Emotionally? Physically? Spiritually?

I said, "Dave, if there's no objective standard, then life is nothing but a glorified Monopoly game. You can acquire lots of money and lots of property, but when the game is over, it's all going back in the box. Is that what life is all about?"

Uncomfortable with the direction of the conversation, Dave quickly changed the subject. But his sense that he ought to "help people" was correct; he just had no way of justifying it. Why did he think he should "help people"? Where did he get such an idea? And why do you and I, deep down, agree with him?

Stop and marinate on that point for a minute: Aren't you just like Dave? Don't you have this deep-seated sense of obligation that we all ought to "help people"? We all do. Why? And why do most human beings seem to have that same intuitive sense that they ought to do good and shun evil?

Behind the answers to those questions is more evidence for the theistic God. This evidence is not scientific—that's what we've seen in previous chapters—but moral in nature. Like the laws of logic and mathematics, this evidence is nonmaterial but it's just as real. The reason we believe we ought to do good rather than evil—the reason we, like Dave, believe we should "help people"—is because there's a Moral Law that has been written on our hearts. In other words, there is a "prescription" to do good that has been given to all of humanity.

Some call this moral prescription "conscience"; others call it "Natural Law"; still others (like our Founding Fathers) refer to it as "Nature's Law." We refer to it as "The Moral Law." But whatever you call it, the fact that a moral standard has been prescribed on the minds of all human beings points to a Moral Law Prescriber. Every prescription has a prescriber. The Moral Law is no different. Someone must have given us these moral obligations.

This Moral Law is our third argument for the existence of a theistic God (after the Cosmological and Teleological Arguments). It goes like this:

1. Every law has a law giver.
2. There is a Moral Law.
3. Therefore, there is a Moral Law Giver.

If the first and second premises are true, then the conclusion necessarily follows. Of course, every law has a law giver. There can be no legislation unless there's a legislature. Moreover, if there are moral obligations, there must be someone to be obligated to.

But is it really true that there is a Moral Law? Our Founding Fathers thought so. As Thomas Jefferson wrote in the Declaration of Independence, "Nature's Law" is "self-evident." You don't use reason to discover it, you just know it. Perhaps that's why my friend Dave hit a roadblock in his thinking. He knew "helping people" was the right thing to do, but he couldn't explain why without appealing to a standard outside himself. Without an objective standard of meaning and morality, then life is meaningless and there's nothing absolutely right or wrong. Everything is merely a matter of opinion.

When we say the Moral Law exists, we mean that all people are impressed with a fundamental sense of right and wrong. Everyone knows, for example, that love is superior to hate and that courage is better than cowardice. University of Texas at Austin professor J. Budziszewski writes, "Everyone knows certain principles. There is no land where murder is virtue and gratitude vice."[1] C. S. Lewis, who has written profoundly on this topic in his classic work *Mere Christianity,* put it this way: "Think of a country where people were admired for running away in battle, or where a man felt proud of double-crossing all the people who had been kindest to him. You might just as well try to imagine a country where two and two made five."[2]

In other words, everyone knows there are absolute moral obligations. An absolute moral obligation is something that is binding on all people, at all times, in all places. And an absolute Moral Law implies an absolute Moral Law Giver.

Now this does *not* mean that every moral issue has easily recognizable answers or that some people don't deny that absolute morality exists. There are difficult problems in morality, and people suppress and deny the Moral Law every day. It simply means that there are basic principles of right and wrong that everyone knows, whether they will admit them or not. Budziszewski calls this basic knowledge of right and wrong "what we can't *not* know," in his book by that title.[3]

We can't not know, for example, that it is wrong to kill innocent human beings for no reason. Some people may deny it and commit murder anyway, but deep in their hearts they know murder is wrong. Even serial killers *know* murder is wrong—they just may not *feel* remorse.[4] And like all absolute moral laws, murder is wrong for everyone, everywhere: in America, India, Zimbabwe, and in every other country, now and forever. That's what the Moral Law tells every human heart.

How Do We Know the Moral Law Exists?

There are many reasons we know the Moral Law exists, and we will present and discuss eight of them. Some of these reasons overlap one another, but we will discuss them in this order:

1. The Moral Law is undeniable.
2. We know it by our reactions.
3. It is the basis of human rights.
4. It is the unchanging standard of justice.
5. It defines a real difference between moral positions (e.g., Mother Teresa vs. Hitler).
6. Since we know what's absolutely wrong, there must be an absolute standard of rightness.
7. The Moral Law is the grounds for political and social dissent.
8. If there were no Moral Law, then we wouldn't make excuses for violating it.

1. The Moral Law Is Undeniable—Relativists usually make two primary truth claims: 1) there is no absolute truth; and 2) there are no absolute moral values. The Road Runner tactic will help you defuse their first claim: if there really is no absolute truth, then their absolute claim that "there is no absolute truth" can't be true. You can see that the relativist's statement is irrational because it affirms exactly what he's trying to deny.

Even Joseph Fletcher, the father of modern situation ethics, fell into this trap. In his book *Situation Ethics,* Fletcher insisted that "the situationist avoids words like 'never' and 'perfect' and 'always' . . . as he

avoids the plague, as he avoids 'absolutely.'"[5] Of course, this is tanta-
mount to claiming that "One should never say 'never,'" or "We should
always avoid using the word 'always.'" But those very statements do not
avoid what they say we must avoid. Relativists are *absolutely* sure that
there are no absolutes.

Like absolute truth, absolute values are also undeniable. While the
claim "There are no absolute values" is not self-defeating, the existence
of absolute values is practically undeniable. For the person who denies
all values, values his right to deny them. Further, he wants everyone to
value him as a person, even while he denies that there are values for all
persons. This was illustrated clearly a number of years ago when I
(Norm) was speaking to a group of affluent, well-educated Chicago sub-
urbanites. After I suggested there are such things as objective moral values to which we all have an obligation, one lady stood and protested
loudly, "There are no real values. It's all a matter of taste or opinion!"
I resisted the temptation to make my point by shouting, "Sit down and
shut up, you egghead. Who wants to hear your opinion?!" Of course, if
I had been so rude and discourteous, she would have rightly complained
that I had violated her right to her opinion and her right to express it.
To which I could have replied, "You have no such right—you just told
me such rights don't exist!"

Her complaint would have proved that she actually did believe in a
real absolute value—she valued her right to say that there are no absolute values. In other words, even those who deny all *values* nevertheless
value their right to make that denial. And therein lies the inconsistency.
Moral values are practically undeniable.

**2. Our Reactions Help Us Discover the Moral Law (Right from
Wrong)**—In the above scenario, the lady's reaction would have
reminded her that there are absolute moral values. A professor at a
major university in Indiana gave one of his relativistic students the same
experience not long ago. The professor, who was teaching a class in
ethics, assigned a term paper to his students. He told the students to
write on any ethical topic of their choice, requiring each student only to
properly back up his or her thesis with reasons and documentation.

One student, an atheist, wrote eloquently on the topic of moral relativism. He argued, "All morals are relative; there is no absolute stan-

dard of justice or rightness; it's all a matter of opinion; you like chocolate, I like vanilla," and so on. His paper provided both his reasons and
his documentation. It was the right length, on time, and stylishly presented in a handsome blue folder.

After the professor read the entire paper, he wrote on the front cover,
"F, I don't like blue folders!" When the student got the paper back he
was enraged. He stormed into the professor's office and protested, "'F!
I don't like blue folders!' That's not fair! That's not right! That's not just!
You didn't grade the paper on its merits!"

Raising his hand to quiet the bombastic student, the professor
calmly retorted, "Wait a minute. Hold on. I read a lot of papers. Let me
see . . . wasn't your paper the one that said there is no such thing as fair-
ness, rightness, and justice?"

"Yes," the student answered.

"Then what's this you say about me not being *fair, right,* and *just?*"
the professor asked. "Didn't your paper argue that it's all a matter of
taste? You like chocolate, I like vanilla?"

The student replied, "Yes, that's my view."

"Fine, then," the professor responded. "I don't like blue. You get
an F!"

Suddenly the lightbulb went on in the student's head. He realized
he really *did* believe in moral absolutes. He at least believed in justice.
After all, he was charging his professor with *injustice* for giving him an
F simply because of the color of the folder. That simple fact defeated his
entire case for relativism.

The moral of the story is that there are absolute morals. And if you
really want to get relativists to admit it, all you need to do is treat them
unfairly. Their reactions will reveal the Moral Law written on their
hearts and minds. Here, the student realized there is an objective standard of rightness by how he *reacted* to the professor's treatment of him.
In the same way, I may not think stealing is wrong when I steal from
you. But watch how morally outraged I get when you steal from me.

Our reactions also indicate that relativism is ultimately unlivable.
People may claim they are relativists, but they don't want their spouses,
for example, to live like sexual relativists. They don't want their spouses
to be only *relatively* faithful. Nearly every male relativist expects his wife
to live as if adultery were *absolutely* wrong, and would *react* quite neg-

atively if she lived out relativism by committing adultery. And even if there are a few relativists who wouldn't object to adultery, do you think they would accept the morality of murder or rape if someone wanted to kill or rape them? Of course not. Relativism contradicts our reactions and our common sense.

Reactions even help us identify right and wrong as a nation. When Muslim terrorists flew *our* planes into *our* buildings with *our* innocent loved ones in them, *our* emotional reaction fit the immensity of the crime. Our reaction reinforced the truth that the act was absolutely wrong. Some may say, "But Bin Laden and his fellow criminals thought the act was morally right." That's partially because they were not on the receiving end of the crime. How do you think Bin Laden would have *reacted* if we had flown *his* planes into *his* buildings with *his* innocent loved ones in them? He would have known immediately that such an act was undeniably wrong.

So the Moral Law is not always apparent from our actions, as evidenced by the terrible things human beings do to one another. But it is brightly revealed in our *reactions*—what we do when we personally are treated unfairly. In other words, *the Moral Law is not always the standard by which we treat others, but it is nearly always the standard by which we expect others to treat us.* It does not describe how we *actually* behave, but rather it prescribes how we *ought* to behave.

3. Without the Moral Law, There Would Be No Human Rights— The United States of America was established by the belief in the Moral Law and God-given human rights. Thomas Jefferson wrote, in the Declaration of Independence:

> We hold these Truths to be self-evident, that all Men are created equal, that they are endowed by their Creator with certain *unalienable Rights,* that among these are Life, Liberty and the pursuit of Happiness. That to secure *these rights,* Governments are instituted among Men, deriving their *just powers* from the consent of the governed (emphasis added).

Notice the phrase, "they are endowed by their Creator with certain unalienable Rights." In other words, the Founding Fathers believed that human rights are God-given, and, as such, they are universal and absolute—they are the rights of all people, in all places, at all times, regardless of their nationality or religion.

Jefferson and the other Founding Fathers recognized that there was a higher authority—the "Creator"—to whom they could appeal to establish objective moral grounds for their independence. Had they begun the Declaration with, "We hold these *opinions* as our own . . ." (rather than "self-evident" "truths"), they wouldn't have expressed an objective moral justification for their Declaration of Independence. It simply would have been their opinion against that of King George. So the Founders appealed to the "Creator" because they believed his Moral Law was the ultimate standard of right and wrong that would justify their cause. And their cause was to end the rule of King George in the American colonies. They were convinced that George's rule needed to be ended because he was violating the basic human rights of the colonists.

In a sense, the Founding Fathers were in the same position as were the Allied countries after World War II. When the Nazi war criminals were brought to trial in Nuremburg, they were convicted of violating basic human rights as defined by the Moral Law (which is manifested in international law). This is the law that all people inherently understand and to which all nations are subject. If there were no such international morality that transcended the laws of the secular German government, then the Allies would have had no grounds to condemn the Nazis. In other words, we couldn't have said that the Nazis were absolutely wrong unless we knew what was absolutely right. But we do know they were absolutely wrong, so the Moral Law must exist.

4. Without the Moral Law, We Couldn't Know Justice or Injustice— Perhaps the most popular argument against the existence of God is the presence and persistence of evil in the world. If there really is a good and just God, then why does he allow bad things to happen to good people? Atheists have long asserted that it would be more logical to believe that this God doesn't exist than to try and explain how evil and God can coexist.

C. S. Lewis was one such atheist. He believed that all of the injustice in the world confirmed his atheism. That is, until he thought about how he knew the world was unjust: He wrote, "[As an atheist] my argument against God was that the universe seemed so cruel and unjust. But how had I got this idea of just and unjust? A man does not call a line crooked unless he has some idea of a straight line. What was I comparing this universe with when I called it unjust?"[6] This realization led Lewis out of atheism and ultimately to Christianity.

Lewis, like you and me, can only detect *in*justice because there's an unchanging standard of justice written on our hearts. Indeed, you can't know what is evil unless you know what is good. And you can't know what is good unless there is an unchanging standard of good outside yourself. Without that objective standard, any objection to evil is nothing but your personal opinion.

I (Norm) love debating Jewish atheists. Why? Because I've never met a Jewish person who believes that the Holocaust was just a matter of opinion. They all believe it was really wrong, regardless of what anyone thinks about it. During one such debate with a Jewish atheist, I asked my opponent, "On what grounds do you say the Holocaust was wrong?" He said, "By my own benign moral feeling."

What else could he say? Unless he was going to admit that there was an objective Moral Law—but that would mean admitting God—he had no objective grounds to oppose the Holocaust. His opposition carried no more weight than his own personal opinion.

But we all know the moral status of the Holocaust is not just a matter of opinion. Your reaction to a comment on the Holocaust should give you a hint that there is something really wrong with murdering innocent people. After all, you don't have the same reaction to someone who says "that meal was wonderful!" when he also says "the Holocaust was wonderful!" You intuitively know that someone's taste for food is not the same as his taste for evil. There is a real moral difference between a meal and murder—one is a mere preference and the other is a true injustice. Your reactions to those comments help you realize that.

We'll discuss more about the coexistence of evil and God in appendix 1. For now the main point is this: if there were no Moral Law, then we wouldn't be able to detect evil or injustice of any kind. Without justice, injustice is meaningless. Likewise, unless there's an unchanging standard of good, there is no such thing as objective evil. But since we all know that evil exists, then so does the Moral Law.

5. Without the Moral Law, There Would Be No Way to Measure Moral Differences—Consider the two maps of Scotland in figure 7.1.

Which is the better map? How could you tell which is the better map? The only way to tell is to see what the real Scotland looks like. In other words, you would have to compare both maps to a real unchanging place called Scotland. If Scotland does not exist, then the maps are meaningless. But since it does, then we can see that Map A is the better map because it's closer to the unchanging standard—the real Scotland.

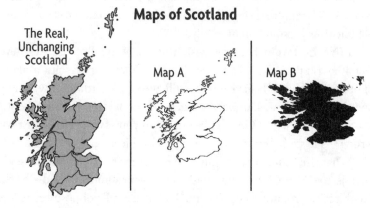

Fig. 7.1

This is exactly what we do when we evaluate the behavior of Mother Teresa against that of Hitler. We appeal to an absolute unchanging standard beyond both of them. That standard is the Moral Law. C. S. Lewis put it this way:

> The moment you say that one set of moral ideas can be better than another, you are, in fact, measuring them both by a standard, saying that one of them conforms to that standard more nearly than the other. But the standard that measures two things is something different from either. You are, in fact, comparing them both with some Real Morality, admitting that there is such a thing as a real Right, independent of what people think, and that some people's ideas get nearer to that real Right than others. Or put it this way. If your moral ideas can be truer, and those of the Nazis less true, there must be something—some Real Morality—for them to be true about.[7]

If the Moral Law doesn't exist, then there's no moral difference between the behavior of Mother Teresa and that of Hitler. Likewise, statements like "Murder is evil," "Racism is wrong," or "You shouldn't abuse children" have no objective meaning. They're just someone's opinion, on a par with "chocolate tastes better than vanilla." In fact, without the Moral Law, simple value-laden terms such as "good," "bad," "better," and "worse"would have no objective meaning when used in a moral sense. But we know they do have meaning. For example, when we say "society is getting better" or "society is getting worse," we are comparing society to some moral standard beyond ourselves. That standard is the Moral Law that's written on our hearts.

In short, to believe in moral relativism is to argue that there are no real moral differences between Mother Teresa and Hitler, freedom and slavery, equality and racism, care and abuse, love and hate, or life and murder. We all know that such conclusions are absurd. So moral relativism must be false. If moral relativism is false, then an objective Moral Law exists.

6. Without the Moral Law, You Couldn't Know What Was Right or Wrong—When Alan Dershowitz, a self-described agnostic, debated Alan Keyes, who is Roman Catholic, in September 2000 on the subject of religion in the public square, Dershowitz was asked by an audience member, "What makes something right?"

Dershowitz praised the question and then said, "We know what evil is. We have seen it," as he cited obvious examples of evil, such as the Holocaust and the Crusades. Then Dershowitz peered at the audience, raised his voice, and emphatically declared, "I DON'T KNOW WHAT'S RIGHT! I know what's WRONG!"

He then began to almost scold the audience: "But I have something else to tell you, folks. YOU don't know what's right! The minute you think you know what's right, the minute you think you have the answer to what's right, you have lost a very precious aspect of growing and developing. I don't expect ever to know precisely what's right, but I expect to devote the rest of my life trying to find it out."[8] With that, some in the audience applauded.

Keyes was not given the opportunity to respond to Dershowitz's answer. If he had, he could have unleashed the Road Runner tactic to expose the self-defeating nature of Dershowitz's argument—namely, by asking Dershowitz, "How do you know what's wrong unless you know what's right?" Indeed, you cannot know that 5 is the wrong answer to 2+2, unless you have some idea of what the right answer is! In the same way, Dershowitz can't know what's morally wrong unless he has some idea of what's morally right.

During the debate, Dershowitz had no problem railing against things he thought were morally wrong (i.e., anti-sodomy laws, anti-abortion laws, racism, slavery, the moral code of the Boy Scouts, mixing church and state, etc.). But in claiming certain things are wrong, he was, by default, affirming that certain things are right. Every negation implies an affirmation. To say that restricting abortion is wrong (the negation), Dershowitz must know that women have a moral right to abortion (the affirmation). But without the Moral Law, Dershowitz can't justify that or any other moral position. It's all just his own opinion.

It is also the height of error and arrogance to claim that no one in the audience knows what's right. Christians are often criticized for stating that they "have the truth," but here was Dershowitz stating that *he* has *the truth that no one has the truth*. In order to know that no one has the truth, *Dershowitz would have to know the truth himself*.

Some relativists are famous for this kind self-defeating arrogance. They claim there is no truth, but then make truth claims of their own. They claim they don't know what is right, but then claim their own political causes are right. They deny the Moral Law in one sentence and then assume it in the next.

7. Without the Moral Law, There Are No Moral Grounds for Political or Social Dissent—Political liberals like Alan Dershowitz and many in Hollywood are famous for their moral opposition to war, anti-abortion laws, anti-sodomy laws, tax cuts, and just about anything the "religious right" might support. The problem for them is that many of them are atheists who thereby have no objective moral grounds for the positions they vocally support. For if there is no Moral Law, then no position on any moral issue is objectively right or wrong—including the positions taken by atheists.

Without a Moral Law, there would be nothing objectively wrong with Christians or Muslims forcibly imposing their religion on atheists. There would be nothing wrong with outlawing atheism, confiscating the property of atheists, and giving it to Pat Robertson and Jerry Falwell. There would be nothing wrong with gay-bashing, racism, or imperialistic wars. Nor would there be anything wrong with prohibiting abortion, birth control, and even sex between consenting adults! In other words, without the Moral Law, atheists have no moral grounds to argue for their pet political causes. There is no *right* to an abortion, homosexual sex, or any of their other political sacraments because in a nontheistic world there are no rights. Unless atheists claim that there is a God and that his Moral Law condones or commands these activities, then their positions are nothing more than their own subjective preferences. And no one is under any moral obligation to agree with mere preferences or to allow atheists to legislatively impose them on the rest of us.[9]

So by rebelling against the Moral Law, atheists have, ironically, undermined their grounds for rebelling against anything. In fact, without the Moral Law, no one has any objective grounds for being for or against anything! But since we all know that issues involving life and liberty are more than mere preferences—that they involve real moral rights—then the Moral Law exists.

8. If There Were No Moral Law, Then We Wouldn't Make Excuses for Violating It—Did you ever notice that people make excuses for immoral behavior? Making excuses is a tacit admission that the Moral Law exists. Why make excuses if no behavior is actually immoral?

Even the number one virtue of our largely immoral culture—tolerance—reveals the Moral Law, because tolerance itself is a moral principle. If there is no Moral Law, then why should anyone be tolerant? Actually, the Moral Law calls us to go beyond tolerance to love. Tolerance is too weak—tolerance says, hold your nose and put up with them. Love says, reach out and help them. Tolerating evil is unloving, but that's what many in our culture want us to do.

Moreover, the plea to be tolerant is a tacit admission that the behavior to be tolerated is wrong. Why? Because you don't need to plead with people to tolerate good behavior, only bad. No one needs to be talked into tolerating the behavior of Mother Teresa, only the behavior of some relativists. Likewise, no one makes excuses for acting like Mother Teresa. We only make excuses when we act against the Moral Law. We wouldn't do so if it didn't exist.

ABSOLUTE VS. RELATIVE: WHY THE CONFUSION?

If there really is an absolute Moral Law as we have argued, then why do so many believe that morality is relative? And why do so many people appear to have different values? Rationally, the reason lies with the failure to make proper distinctions. Let's take a look at those distinctions to clear up the areas of confusion:

Confusion #1—Absolute Morals vs. Changing Behavior

A common mistake of relativists is to confuse behavior with value. That is, they confuse what *is* with what *ought* to be. What people *do* is subject to change, but what they *ought* to do is not. This is the difference between sociology and morality. Sociology is *descriptive;* morality is *prescriptive.*

In other words, relativists often confuse the changing behavioral situation with the unchanging moral duty. For example, when discussing a moral topic like premarital sex or cohabitation, you often hear people in support of it say something like, "Get with it, this is the twenty-first century!" as if current behaviors dictate what's right and wrong. To illustrate the absurdity of the relativist's reasoning, you need only to turn the discussion to a more serious moral issue like murder, which also occurs much more frequently in America today than it did fifty years ago. How many relativists would speak in support of murder by asking us to "Get with it, this is the twenty-first century!"? That's where their reasoning takes them when they confuse what people do with what they ought to do.

Another aspect of the *is–ought* fallacy manifests itself when people suggest that there is no Moral Law because people don't obey it. Of course everyone disobeys the Moral Law to some degree—from telling white lies to murder. But that doesn't mean there is no unchanging Moral Law; it simply means that we all violate it. Everyone makes mathematical mistakes too, but that doesn't mean there are no unchanging rules of mathematics.

Confusion #2—Absolute Morals vs. Changing Perceptions of the Facts

Another confusion is made between the existence of an absolute moral value itself and the understanding of the facts used in applying that value. For example, as C. S. Lewis has noted, in the late 1700s witches were sentenced as murderers, but now they are not.[10] A relativist might argue, "See! Our moral values have changed because we no longer seek to kill witches. Morality is relative to time and culture."

But the relativist's claim is incorrect. What has changed is not the moral principle that murder is wrong but the perception or factual understanding of whether "witches" can really murder people by their curses. People no longer believe they can. Hence, people no longer consider them murderers. In other words, *the perception of a moral situation is relative* (whether witches are really murderers), *but the moral values involved in the situation are not* (murder has always been and always will be wrong).

Failure to make this distinction also leads people to believe that cultural differences reflect essential differences in core moral values. For example, some believe that since Hindus revere cows and Americans eat them, there's an essential difference between the moral values of Americans and Hindus. But the reason people in India consider cows sacred has nothing to do with a core moral value—it has to do with their religious belief in reincarnation. Indians believe that cows may possess the souls of deceased human beings, so they won't eat them. In the United States, we do not believe that the souls of our deceased relatives may be in a cow, so we freely eat cows. In the final analysis, what appears to be a moral difference is actually an agreement—we both believe it's wrong to eat Grandma! The core moral value that it's wrong to eat Grandma is considered absolute by people in both cultures. They only disagree on whether Grandma's soul is in the cow![11] They have different *perceptions of the facts* pertaining to the moral value, but fundamentally agree that the moral value must be upheld.

Confusion #3—Absolute Morals vs. Applying Them to Particular Situations

As we have seen, people know right from wrong best by their reactions rather than by their actions. When people are the victims of bad behavior, they have no trouble understanding that the behavior is absolutely wrong. Yet even if two victims wind up disagreeing over the morality of a particular act, this does not mean morality is relative. An absolute Moral Law can exist even if people fail to know the right thing to do in a particular situation.

Consider the moral dilemma often used by university professors to get their students to believe in relativism: there are five people trying to survive on a life raft designed for only four. If one person isn't thrown overboard, then everyone will die. Students labor over the dilemma, come to different conclusions, and then conclude their disagreement proves that morality must be relative.

But the dilemma actually proves the opposite—that morality is absolute. How? Because *there would be no dilemma if morality were relative!* If morality were relative and there were no absolute right to life, you'd say, "It doesn't matter what happens! Throw everyone overboard! Who cares?" The very reason we struggle with the dilemma is because we know how valuable life is.

While people may get morality wrong in complicated situations, they don't get it wrong on the basics. For example, everyone knows murder is wrong. Hitler knew it. That's why he had to dehumanize the Jews in order to rationalize killing them. Even cannibals appear to know that it is wrong to kill innocent human beings. It may be that cannibals don't think that the people in other tribes are human. But chances are they do. Otherwise, as J. Budziszewski observes, why do cannibals "perform elaborate expiatory rituals before [they] take their lives?"[12] They wouldn't perform these rituals unless they thought there was something wrong with what they were about to do.

So the basics are clear, even if some difficult problems are not. Moreover, the fact that there are difficult problems in morality doesn't disprove the existence of objective moral laws any more than difficult problems in science disprove the existence of objective natural laws. Scientists don't deny that an objective world exists when they encounter a difficult problem in the natural world (i.e., when they have trouble knowing the answer). And we shouldn't deny that morality exists just because we have trouble knowing the answer in a few difficult situations.

There are easy and hard problems in morality just as there are in science. Answering a simple scientific problem such as "Why do objects fall to the ground?" proves that at least one natural law or force exists (i.e., gravity). Likewise, truthfully answering a simple moral question such as "Is murder justified?" proves that at least one law of morality exists (i.e., don't murder). If *just one* moral obligation exists (such as don't murder, or don't rape, or don't torture babies), then the Moral Law exists. If the Moral Law exists, then so does the Moral Law Giver.

Confusion #4—An Absolute Command (What) vs. a Relative Culture (How)

Another important difference, often overlooked by moral relativists, is between the absolute nature of the moral command and the relative way in which that command is manifested in different cultures. For example, all cultures have some form of greeting, which is an expression of love and respect. However, cultures differ widely on just what that greeting is. In some it is a kiss; in others it is a hug; and in still others it is a handshake or a bow. *What* should be done is common to all cultures, but *how* it should be done differs. Failure to make this distinction misleads many to believe that because people have different practices they have different values. The moral value is absolute, but how it is practiced is relative.

Confusion #5—Absolute Morals vs. Moral Disagreements

Relativists often point to the controversial issue of abortion to demonstrate that morality is relative. Some think abortion is acceptable while others think it's murder. But just because there are different opinions about abortion doesn't mean morality is relative.

In fact, instead of providing an example of relative moral values, the entire abortion controversy exists because each side defends what they think is an *absolute* moral value—protecting life and allowing liberty (i.e., allowing a woman to "control her own body"). The controversy is over *which* value applies (or takes precedence) in the issue of abortion.[13] If the unborn were not human beings, then the pro-liberty value should be applied in legislation. But since the unborn *are* human beings, the pro-life value should be applied in legislation because a person's right to life supersedes another person's right to individual liberty. (The baby is not just part of the woman's body; it has its own body with its own unique genetic code, its own blood type and gender.) Even if there were doubt as to when life begins, the benefit of the doubt should be given to protecting life—reasonable people don't shoot unless they're *absolutely* sure they won't kill an innocent human being.

Recall that our *reaction* to a particular practice reveals what we really think about its morality. Ronald Reagan once quipped, "I've noticed all those in favor of abortion are already born." Indeed, all pro-abortionists would become pro-life immediately if they found themselves back in the womb. Their *reaction* to the possibility of being killed would remind them that abortion really is wrong. Of course, most people deep in their hearts know an unborn child is a human being, and therefore know that abortion is wrong. Even some pro-abortion activists are finally admitting as much.[14] So in the end, this moral disagreement is not because morality is relative or because the Moral Law isn't clear. This moral disagreement exists because some people are suppressing the Moral Law in order justify what they want to do. In other words, support for abortion is more a matter of the will than of the mind. (For a more detailed discussion of this and other moral topics, see our book *Legislating Morality.*[15])

Confusion #6—Absolute Ends (Values) vs. Relative Means

Often moral relativists confuse the end (the value itself) with the means to attaining that end. Several political disputes are of this sort. On some issues (certainly not all), liberals and conservatives want the same things—the same *ends*. They just disagree on the best *means* to attain them.

For example, regarding the poor, liberals believe the best way to help is through government assistance. But since conservatives think such assistance creates dependency, they would rather stimulate economic opportunity so the poor can help themselves. Notice that the end is the same (assist the poor), but the means are different. Likewise, both militarists and pacifists desire peace (the end); they simply disagree as to whether a strong military is the best means to attain this peace. They both agree on the absolute *end*; they just disagree on the relative *means* to achieve it.

THE MORAL LAW: WHAT DO DARWINISTS SAY?

So the evidence for the Moral Law is sound, and objections to it miss the mark. How then do Darwinists deal with the question of morality? Actually, most Darwinists avoid the subject completely. Why? Because it's not easy to explain how there can be objective right and wrong (which even Darwinists know in their hearts) unless there exists a Moral Law Giver.

Darwinist Edward O. Wilson is a notable exception. He claims that our sense of morality has evolved in the same way we ourselves have evolved—by natural selection. While he admits that "very little progress has been made in the biological exploration of the moral sentiments," Wilson asserts that the biological process of people passing their genes on to their offspring "through thousands of generations inevitably gave rise to moral sentiments."[16] In other words, morality is materially and genetically determined. It's based on inherited feelings or instincts, not on an objective standard of right and wrong. We have already seen the inadequacy of natural selection to explain new life forms (chapter 6). As we're about to see, natural selection is also inadequate to explain "moral sentiments" within those new life forms.

First, Darwinism asserts that only materials exist, but materials don't have morality. How much does hate weigh? Is there an atom for love? What's the chemical composition of the murder molecule? These questions are meaningless because physical particles are not responsible for morality. If materials are solely responsible for morality, then Hitler had no real moral responsibility for what he did—he just had bad molecules. This is nonsense, and everyone knows it. Human thoughts and transcendent moral laws are not material things any more than the laws of logic and mathematics are material things. They are immaterial entities that cannot be weighed or physically measured. As a result, they can't be explained in material terms by natural selection or any other atheistic means.

Second, morality cannot be merely an instinct as Wilson suggests because: 1) we have competing instincts, and 2) something else often tells us to ignore the stronger instinct in order to do something more noble. For example, if you hear somebody who is being mugged calling for help, your stronger instinct may be to stay safe and not "get involved." Your weaker instinct (if we may call it that) might be to help. As C. S. Lewis puts it,

> But you will find inside you, in addition to these two impulses, a third thing which tells you that you ought to follow the impulse to help, and suppress the impulse to run away. Now this thing that judges between two instincts, that decides which should be encouraged, cannot itself

be either of them. You might as well say the sheet of music which tells you, at a given moment, to play one note on the piano and not another, is itself one of the notes on the keyboard. The Moral Law tells us the tune we have to play: our instincts are merely the keys.[17]

Third, Wilson says that social morals have evolved because those "cooperative" morals helped humans survive together. But this assumes an end—survival—for evolution, when Darwinism, by definition, has no end because it is a nonintelligent process. And even if survival is granted as the end, Darwinists cannot explain why people knowingly engage in self-destructive behavior (i.e., smoking, drinking, drugs, suicide, etc.). Nor can Darwinists explain why people often subvert their own survival instincts to help others, sometimes to the point of their own deaths.[18] We all know that there are nobler ends than mere survival: soldiers sacrifice themselves for their country, parents for their children, and, if Christianity is true, God sacrificed his Son for us.

Fourth, Wilson and other Darwinists assume that survival is a "good" thing, but there is no real good without the objective Moral Law. In fact, this is the problem with pragmatic and utilitarian ethical systems that say "do what works" or "do whatever brings the greatest good." Do what works toward whose ends—Mother Teresa's or Hitler's? Do whatever brings the greatest good by whose definition of good—Mother Teresa's or Hitler's? Such ethical systems must smuggle in the Moral Law to define what ends we *should* work toward and what really is the greatest "good."

Fifth, Darwinists confuse how one comes to *know* the Moral Law with the *existence of* the Moral Law. Even if we come to know some of our "moral sentiments" because of genetic and/or environmental factors, that doesn't mean there is no objective Moral Law outside ourselves.

This came up in the debate between Peter Atkins and William Lane Craig. Atkins claimed morality evolved from genetics and "our massive brains." Craig correctly responded, "At best that would show how moral values are *discovered,* but it would not show that those values are *invented.*" Indeed, I may inherit a capacity for math and learn the multiplication tables from my mother, but the laws of mathematics exist regardless of how I come to know them. Likewise, morality exists independently of how we come to know it.

Finally, Darwinists cannot explain why anyone *should* obey any biologically derived "moral sentiment." Why *shouldn't* people murder, rape, and steal to get what they want if there is nothing beyond this world? Why *should* the powerful "cooperate" with the weaker when the powerful can survive longer by exploiting the weaker? After all, history is replete with criminals and dictators who have lengthened their own survival precisely because they have *disobeyed* all "moral sentiments" in their repression and elimination of their opponents.

IDEAS HAVE CONSEQUENCES

If the Darwinists are right that morality has a natural source, then morality is not objective or absolute. For if there is no God and humans have evolved from the slime, then we have no higher moral status than slime because there is nothing beyond us to instill us with objective morality or dignity.

The implications of this have not been lost on Darwinists and their followers. In fact, Adolf Hitler used Darwin's theory as philosophical justification for the Holocaust. In his 1924 book *Mein Kampf* ("My Struggle"), he wrote:

> If nature does not wish that weaker individuals should mate with the stronger, she wishes even less that a superior race should intermingle with an inferior one; because in such cases all her efforts, throughout hundreds of thousands of years, to establish an evolutionary higher stage of being, may thus be rendered futile.
>
> But such a preservation goes hand-in-hand with the inexorable law that it is the strongest and the best who must triumph and that they have the right to endure. He who would live must fight. He who does not wish to fight in this world, where permanent struggle is the law of life, has not the right to exist.[19]

Hitler, like other Darwinists, illegitimately personifies nature by attributing will to it (i.e., "nature does not *wish*"). But his main point is that there are superior races and inferior races, and the Jews, being an inferior race, have no right to exist if they don't want to fight. In other words, racism and then genocide is the logical outworking of Darwinism. On the other hand, love and then self-sacrifice is the logical outworking of Christianity. Ideas have consequences.

The racism associated with evolution was exposed during the famous 1925 Scopes Trial. The high school biology textbook that occasioned the trial spoke of five races of man, and concluded that the "Caucasians" are the "highest type of all."[20] This, of course, directly contradicts biblical teaching (Gen. 1:27; Acts 17:26, 29; Gal. 3:28). It also contradicts what is affirmed by the Declaration of Independence ("all men are created equal").

In more recent times, Princeton professor and Darwinist Peter Singer has used Darwinism to assert that "the life of a newborn is of *less* value than the life of a pig, a dog, or a chimpanzee."[21] Yes, you read that correctly.

What are the consequences of Singer's outrageous Darwinian ideas? He believes that parents should be able to kill their newborn infants until they are 28 days of age! These beliefs are perfectly consistent with Darwinism. If we all came from slime, then we have no grounds to say that humans are morally any better than any other species. The only question is, why limit infanticide at 28 days, or, for that matter, 28 months or 28 years? If there is no Moral Law Giver, then there's nothing wrong with murder at any age! Of course, Darwinists such as Singer might reject this conclusion, but they have no objective grounds for disagreeing unless they can appeal to a standard beyond themselves—a Moral Law Giver.

James Rachels, author of *Created from Animals: The Moral Implications of Darwinism,* defends the Darwinian view that the human species has no more inherent value than any other species. Speaking of retarded people, Rachels writes:

> What are we to say about them? The natural conclusion, according to the doctrine we are considering [Darwinism], would be that their status is that of mere animals. And perhaps we should go on to conclude that they may be used as non-human animals are used—perhaps as laboratory subjects, or as food?[22]

As horrific as that would be—using retarded people as lab rats or for food—Darwinists can give no moral reason why we ought not use *any* human being in that fashion. Nazi-like experiments cannot be condemned by Darwinists, because there is no objective moral standard in a Darwinian world.

Two other Darwinists recently wrote a book asserting that rape is a natural consequence of evolution.[23] According to authors Randy Thornhill and Craig Palmer, rape is "a natural, biological phenomenon that is a product of the human evolutionary heritage," just like "the leopard's spots and the giraffe's elongated neck."[24]

Shocking as they are, these Darwinian conclusions about murder and rape should come as no surprise to anyone who understands the moral implications of Darwinism. Why? Because according to Darwinists, *all* behaviors are genetically determined. While some Darwinists might disagree with the implication that murder and rape are not wrong (precisely because the Moral Law speaks to them through their consciences), those conclusions are the inexorable result of their worldview. For if only material things exist, then murder and rape are nothing more than the results of chemical reactions in a criminal's brain brought about by natural selection. Moreover, murder and rape can't be objectively wrong (i.e., against the Moral Law) because there are no laws if only chemicals exist. Objective moral laws require a transcendent Law-Giver, but the Darwinian worldview has ruled him out in advance. So consistent Darwinists can only consider murder and rape as personal dislikes, not real moral wrongs.

To understand what's behind the Darwinist's explanation of morality, we need to distinguish between an assertion and an argument. An assertion merely states a conclusion; an argument, on the other hand, states the conclusion *and then supports it with evidence*. Darwinists make assertions, not arguments. There is no empirical or forensic evidence that natural selection can account for new life forms, much less morality. Darwinists simply assert that morals have evolved naturally because they believe man has evolved naturally. And they believe man has evolved naturally, not because they have evidence for such a belief, but because they've ruled out intelligent causes in advance. So the Darwinian explanation for morality turns out to be just another "just-so" story based on circular reasoning and false philosophical presuppositions.

SUMMARY AND CONCLUSION

When we conduct our seminar, "The Twelve Points That Show Christianity Is True," the following two statements about morality immediately capture the attention of the audience:

If there is no God, then what Hitler did was just a matter of opinion!

and

If at least one thing is really morally wrong—like it's wrong to torture babies, or it's wrong to intentionally fly planes into buildings with innocent people in them—then God exists.

These statements help people realize that, without an objective source of morality, all so-called moral issues are nothing but personal preference. Hitler liked killing people, and Mother Teresa liked helping them. Unless there's a standard beyond Hitler and Mother Teresa, then no one is really right or wrong—it's just one person's opinion against that of another.

Fortunately, as we have seen, there *is* a real moral standard beyond human beings. C. S. Lewis wrote, "Human beings, all over the earth, have this curious idea that they ought to behave in a certain way, and cannot really get rid of it. Secondly, that they do not in fact behave that way. They know the Law of Nature; they break it. These two facts are the foundation of all clear thinking about ourselves and the universe we live in."[25]

Hopefully we've done some clear thinking in this chapter. Here's a summary of what we've covered:

1. There is an absolute standard of right and wrong that is written on the hearts of every human being. People may deny it; they may suppress it; their actions may contradict it; but their *reactions* reveal that they know it.
2. Relativism is false. Human beings do not *determine* right and wrong; we *discover* right and wrong. If human beings determined right and wrong, then anyone would be "right" in asserting that rape, murder, the Holocaust, or any other evil is not really wrong. But we know those acts are wrong intuitively through our consciences, which are manifestations of the Moral Law.
3. This Moral Law must have a source higher than ourselves because it is a prescription that is on the hearts of all people. Since prescriptions always have prescribers—they don't arise from nothing—the Moral Law Prescriber (God) must exist.

4. This Moral Law is God's standard of rightness, and it helps us adjudicate between the different moral opinions people may have. Without God's standard, we're left with just that—human opinions. The Moral Law is the final standard by which everything is measured. (In Christian theology, the Moral Law is God's very nature. In other words, morality is not arbitrary—it's not "Do this and don't do that because I'm God and I said so." No, God doesn't make rules up on a whim. The standard of rightness *is* the very nature of God himself—infinite justice and infinite love.)

5. Although it is widely believed that all morality is relative, core moral values are absolute, and they transcend cultures. Confusion over this is often based on a misunderstanding or misapplication of moral absolutes, not on a real rejection of them. That is, moral values are absolute, even if our understanding of them or of the circumstances in which they should be applied are not absolute.

6. Atheists have no real basis for objective right and wrong. This does not mean that atheists are not moral or don't understand right from wrong. On the contrary, atheists can and do understand right from wrong because the Moral Law is written on their hearts just as on every other heart. But while they may *believe* in an objective right and wrong, they have no way to *justify* such a belief (unless they admit a Moral Law Giver, at which point they cease being atheists).

In the end, atheism cannot justify why anything is morally right or wrong. It cannot guarantee human rights or ultimate justice in the universe. To be an atheist—a consistent atheist—you have to believe that there is nothing really wrong with murder, rape, genocide, torture, or any other heinous act. By faith, you have to believe there is no moral difference between a murderer and a missionary, a teacher and a terrorist, or Mother Teresa and Hitler. Or, by faith, you have to believe that real moral principles arose from nothing. Since such beliefs are clearly unreasonable, *we don't have enough faith to be atheists.*

Chapter 8
will cover:

1. Truth about reality is knowable.
2. The opposite of true is false.
3. It is true that the theistic God exists. This is evidenced by the:
   a. Beginning of the universe (Cosmological Argument)
   b. Design of the universe (Teleological Argument/Anthropic Principle)
   c. Design of life (Teleological Argument)
   d. Moral Law (Moral Argument)
➤ **4. If God exists, then miracles are possible.**
   5. Miracles can be used to confirm a message from God (i.e., as acts of God to confirm a word from God).
6. The New Testament is historically reliable. This is evidenced by:
   a. Early testimony
   b. Eyewitness testimony
   c. Uninvented (authentic) testimony
   d. Eyewitnesses who were not deceived
7. The New Testament says Jesus claimed to be God.
8. Jesus' claim to be God was miraculously confirmed by:
   a. His fulfillment of many prophecies about himself;
   b. His sinless life and miraculous deeds;
   c. His prediction and accomplishment of his resurrection.
9. Therefore, Jesus is God.
10. Whatever Jesus (who is God) teaches is true.
11. Jesus taught that the Bible is the Word of God.
12. Therefore, it is true that the Bible is the Word of God (and anything opposed to it is false).

Miracles: Signs of God or Gullibility?

"If we admit God, must we admit Miracle? Indeed, indeed, you have no security against it. That is the bargain."

—C. S. LEWIS

WHO MADE THE CUT?

We need to pause for a moment and put together the pieces of the puzzle we've discovered so far. Remember, we're looking for unity in diversity. We're trying to put together the seemingly diverse pieces of life into a coherent picture. So far our coherent picture shows us that truth exists and it can be known. Any denial of truth presupposes truth, so the existence of truth is inescapable. And while we can't know most truth absolutely due to our human limitations, we can know many truths to a high degree of certainty (i.e., "beyond reasonable doubt"). One of these truths is the existence and nature of God. From the lines of evidence we have reviewed—the Cosmological, Teleological, and Moral Arguments—we are able to know beyond a reasonable doubt that a theistic God exists who has certain characteristics.

From the Cosmological Argument we know that God is:
1. Self-existent, timeless, nonspatial, immaterial (since he[1] created time, space, and matter, he must be outside of time, space, and matter). In other words, he is without limits. That is, he is infinite.
2. Unimaginably powerful, since he created the entire universe out of nothing.
3. Personal, since he chose to convert a state of nothingness into the time-space-material universe (an impersonal force has no ability to make choices).

From the Teleological Argument we know that God is:
1. Supremely intelligent, since he designed life and the universe with such incredible complexity and precision.
2. Purposeful, since he designed the many forms of life to live in this specific and ordered environment.

From the Moral Argument we know that God is:
Absolutely morally pure (He is the unchangeable standard of morality by which all actions are measured. This standard includes infinite justice and infinite love).

Theism is the proper term to describe such a God. Now here is the amazing truth about these findings: *the theistic God we have discovered is consistent with the God of the Bible, but we have discovered him without use of the Bible.* We have shown that through good reason, science, and philosophy much can be known about the God of the Bible. In fact, this is what the Bible itself says (e.g., Psalm 19; Rom. 1:18-20; 2:14-15). Theologians call this revelation of God *natural* or *general revelation* (that which is clearly seen independent of any type of scripture). The revelation of Scripture is called *special revelation.*

So we know through natural revelation that theism is true. This discovery helps us to see not only what the true box top looks like, but what it *cannot* look like. Since the opposite of true is false (chapter 2), we know that any nontheistic worldview must be false. Or, to put it another way, of the major world religions, only one of the theistic religions—Judaism, Christianity, or Islam—could be true. All other major world religions cannot be true, because they are nontheistic.

Could Be True (Theistic)	Could Not Be True (Nontheistic)
1. Judaism	1. Hinduism (pantheistic and polytheistic)
2. Christianity	2. Buddhism (pantheistic or atheistic)
3. Islam	3. New Age (pantheistic)
	4. Secular humanism (atheistic)
	5. Mormonism (polytheistic)
	6. Wicca (pantheistic or polytheistic)
	7. Taoism (pantheistic or atheistic)
	8. Confucianism (atheistic)
	9. Shinto (polytheistic)

Table 8.1

This may seem like a grandiose claim—to deny the truth of so many world religions at this stage. But by simple logic—using the Law of Noncontradiction—mutually exclusive religions cannot all be true. Just as certain football players are rightfully cut from the roster of possible players because they lack necessary abilities, certain world religions are rightfully cut from the roster of possible true religions because they lack necessary qualifications.

So, logically, if theism is true, then all nontheisms are false. Now this does not mean that every teaching of a nontheistic religion is false or that there is nothing good in those religions—there is certainly truth and goodness in most world religions. It simply means that as a way of looking at the world (i.e., a worldview), any nontheistic religion is built on a false foundation. While some details may be true, the core of any nontheistic religious system is false. They are systems of error, even though they have some truth in them.

For example, Hindus rightfully teach the truth that you reap what you sow, even though the worldview of Hinduism—that "you" don't really exist because everything is part of one indistinguishable reality called Brahman—is false. Secular humanists rightfully assert the reality of evil, even though the humanist worldview—which denies an objective standard by which we can detect evil—is false. Mormons rightfully teach that there are moral standards we ought to obey, even though the Mormon worldview that there are many gods is false.[2]

This last point about Mormonism raises a question. Namely, why does the existence of a theistic God disprove polytheism? It disproves polytheism because God is infinite, and there cannot be more than one infinite Being. To distinguish one being from another, they must differ in some way. If they differ in some way, then one lacks something that the other one has. If one being lacks something that the other one has, then the lacking being is not infinite because an infinite being, by definition, lacks nothing. So there can be only one infinite Being.

Now one could argue that finite beings (or "gods") exist that are more powerful than human beings. In fact, Judaism, Christianity, and Islam all teach the existence of angels and demons. But that's not polytheism, which denies that there is a supreme, infinite, eternal Being to whom all creatures owe their existence and to whom all creatures are ultimately accountable. Since theism is true, polytheism is just as false as atheism, pantheism, and all other nontheistic worldviews.

But we digress. The main point is that the right box top for the universe shows a theistic God. That means that only one of the three major theistic world religions can make the cut of truth: either Judaism, Christianity, or Islam. Now, logically, all of these theistic world religions cannot be true—because they make mutually exclusive claims. Moreover, it could be that none of these world religions is completely true. Maybe they have theism right but little else. That's possible. However, since we know beyond a reasonable doubt that God exists and that he has the characteristics we've listed above—characteristics that include design, purpose, justice, and love—then we should expect him to reveal more of himself and his purpose for our lives. This would require that he communicate with us. One of the three major theistic religions is likely to contain that communication.

How Does God Communicate?

As we have seen, God has already communicated to us through creation and conscience (natural or general revelation), which gives us basic ideas about his existence, power, and moral requirements. But how could God reveal himself so that we could get a more detailed understanding of what his ultimate purpose is for us?

Why couldn't he appear to each one of us? He could, but that might interfere with our free will. C. S. Lewis has some great insights on this topic. In his *Screwtape Letters*, Screwtape, the senior demon, writes the following to his disciple Wormwood:

> You must have wondered why the Enemy [God] does not make more use of His power to be sensibly present to human souls in any degree He chooses and at any moment. But you now see that the Irresistible and the Indisputable are the two weapons which the very nature of His scheme forbids Him to use. Merely to over-ride a human will (as His felt presence in any but the faintest and most mitigated degree would certainly do) would be for Him useless. He cannot ravish. He can only woo.[3]

If God has not chosen the overpowering option of face-to-face interactions with every person on the planet, then perhaps he has chosen a more subtle method of communication. (In fact, the Bible says God is not always as overt as we would like him to be [Isa. 45:15].) Perhaps God has manifested himself in some way to a select group of people over many centuries and inspired them to write down what they witnessed and heard from him. Written language is a precise medium of communication that can easily be duplicated and passed on to succeeding generations, yet it also can be easily ignored by those who freely decide that they don't want to be bothered with God.

So a book would work as a valid but not overpowering means of communication from God. But whose book? Has God communicated through the book of the Jews, the book of the Christians, or the book of the Muslims? How are we supposed to tell whose book, if any, is really a message from God?

THE KING'S SEAL

In the days before mass communications—when all long-distance messages were sent by hand—a king would place his seal on his message. This seal would be a sign to the recipient of the message that the message was authentic—it really came from the king and not from someone just posing as the king. Of course to make this system work, the seal needed to be unusual or unique, easily recognizable, and it had to be something only the king possessed.

God could use a similar system to authenticate his messages—specifically, he could use miracles. Miracles are unusual and unique, easily recognizable, and only God can do them. Even skeptics, by demanding a sign from God, are implicitly admitting that miracles would prove his existence.

What is a miracle? A miracle is a special act of God that interrupts the normal course of events. Atheist Antony Flew put it well: "A miracle is something which would never have happened had nature, as it were, been left to its own devices."[4] So we might say that natural laws describe what happens regularly, by natural causes; miracles, if they occur at all, describe what happens rarely, by supernatural causes.

Through miracles, God could tell the world which book or which person speaks for him. So, if God wanted to send a message through Moses, Elijah, Jesus, Paul, Muhammad, or anyone else, he could pour out miracles through that person.

If God actually works in this way, then a miracle confirms the message and the sign confirms the sermon. Or, to put it another way, a miracle is an act of God to confirm the word of God through a messenger of God.

The question is, does God work that way? Does the King of the universe use such signs? Are miracles even possible? Our secular world says no. As we're about to see, they are seriously mistaken.

IS THE BOX OPEN OR CLOSED?

On a recent trip to Russia to speak to Russian educators, seminary professor Ronald Nash had a big challenge. He wanted to talk to them about God, but knew he wouldn't get anywhere with them unless he could overcome their long-held biases against theism. For more than seventy years, Russians had been taught a worldview that ruled out God in advance. The official state religion was atheism, and the atheistic worldview asserts that only the natural, material world exists. According to atheists, miracles are impossible because there is no supernatural realm. To believe otherwise is to believe in fairy tales.

Nash began by showing them two small cardboard boxes. One was opened, and one was closed.

"Here is the difference between your worldview and mine," he began. Pointing to the closed box, he said, "You believe that the physical universe is closed; that the universe is all that exists, and there's nothing outside it."

Shifting to the open box he continued, "I believe that the physical universe exists as well; but I also believe the universe is open—that there's something outside the universe we call God." Nash paused and added, "And God created the box!"

He then reached into the open box and said, "Just like I can reach into this box to manipulate its contents, God can reach into our universe and perform what we call miracles."[5]

For some reason, this was a profound illustration to the Russians. Lightbulbs began coming on in the minds of educators all over the room. These educators had assumed their naturalistic worldview was correct and had considered no other alternatives. Nash helped them think that maybe another alternative, like theism, had better evidence.

As we have seen in chapters 3 through 7, theism does have better evidence. We know beyond a reasonable doubt that a theistic God exists. Since God exists, the universe represented by the closed box is false. The box is open and was created by God. So it *is* possible for God to intervene in the natural world by performing miracles. *In fact, miracles are not only possible; miracles are actual, because the greatest miracle of all—the creation of the universe out of nothing—has already occurred. So with regard to the Bible, if Genesis 1:1 is true—"In the beginning, God created the heavens and the earth"—then every other miracle in the Bible is easy to believe.*

Can a God who created the entire universe out of nothing part the Red Sea? Bring fire down from heaven? Keep a man safe in a great fish for three days?[6] Accurately predict future events? Turn water into wine? Heal diseases instantaneously? Raise the dead? Of course. All of those miraculous events are simple tasks for an infinitely powerful Being who created the universe in the first place.

Now this doesn't mean that God *has* performed those biblical miracles. That remains to be seen. It only means that he could have—that such miracles are possible. In light of the fact that we live in a theistic universe, ruling out miracles beforehand (as many atheists do) is clearly illegitimate. As C. S. Lewis put it, "If we admit God, must we admit Miracle? Indeed, indeed, you have no security against it. That is the bargain."[7]

So why do so many people today say that miracles are not possible or should not be believed? How can skeptics disbelieve in miracles when the whole universe appears to be one amazing miracle? We need to address those questions before we begin to investigate whether God has confirmed the truth of Judaism, Christianity, or Islam through miracles.

OBJECTIONS TO MIRACLES

Since the late 1600s, two major objections to miracles have arisen that we need to investigate. The first is from Benedict Spinoza, and the second is from David Hume. We'll start with Spinoza's objection.

Natural Laws Are Immutable—The argument that natural laws are immutable was first popularized in the 1670s by Benedict Spinoza, a Jewish pantheist. Spinoza's argument against miracles goes something like this:

1. Miracles are violations of natural laws.
2. Natural laws are immutable.
3. It is impossible to violate immutable laws.
4. Therefore, miracles are impossible.

If Spinoza is right—if there is no way natural laws can be overpowered, interrupted, or interfered with—then miracles are impossible.

The problem with this objection is that it begs the question. If you define natural laws as immutable, then of course miracles are impossible. But that's the very question! Who said natural laws are immutable?

Spinoza, in accord with his pantheistic worldview, illegitimately ruled out the theistic God, and thus miracles, in advance. But if God exists, miracles are possible. And as we have seen, the greatest miracle of all, the creation of the universe out of nothing, has already occurred.

Creation itself demonstrates that natural laws are not immutable. Something doesn't naturally come from nothing. But here we are.

We also know that natural laws are not immutable because they are *descriptions* of what happens, not *prescriptions* of what must happen. Natural *laws* don't really cause anything, they only describe what regularly happens in nature. They describe the effects of the four known natural *forces*—gravitation, magnetism, and the strong and weak nuclear forces. Once you introduce intelligent beings into the picture, natural forces can be overpowered. We know that those forces can be overpowered because we do so ourselves every day.

For example, when a baseball player catches a falling baseball, he is overpowering the force of gravity. We do the same whenever we fly planes or blast off into space. In such cases, gravity is not changed, it is simply overpowered. If finite beings like us can overpower natural forces, then certainly the infinite Being who created those forces can do so.[8]

Miracles Are Not Credible—A number of years ago, I (Norm) was invited to speak at Harvard University's divinity school, one of the most liberal divinity schools in the country. My topic was "Harvard's Premature Farewell to Evangelicalism." Believe it or not, Harvard, like most other schools of its day, was founded by evangelical Christians in order to train students to know Jesus Christ. Harvard's 1646 charter states its purpose clearly (original spelling and Scripture references retained):

Let every Student be plainly instructed, and earnestly pressed to consider well, the maine end of his life and studies is, to know God and
Jesus Christ which is eternal life (John 17:3) and therefore to lay Christ
in the bottome, as the only foundation of all sound knowledge and
Learning. And seeing the Lord only giveth wisedome, Let every one
seriously set himself by prayer in secret to seeke it of him (Prov. 2:3).[9]

How did Harvard get so far away from its charter? Because they
bought into one of the most powerful arguments against miracles ever
formulated. It wasn't Spinoza's argument. Due to the advances in modern science and our better understanding of the natural world, not many
today really believe that natural laws are immutable. The argument
against miracles that is accepted today—and has been accepted at
Harvard—was put forth by the great skeptic David Hume (1711–1776)
about a century after Spinoza.

You may remember Hume from chapter 2. He was the one who said
that any talk about God is meaningless because such talk does not
involve empirical observation or self-evident truths. We saw that his
claim is self-defeating.

But Hume's argument against miracles is a bit more sophisticated,
and not as easily refuted as his argument against God-talk. Perhaps
that's one reason it is still believed today. In fact, Hume's argument
against miracles is one of the pillars of the so-called Enlightenment
(that's where we supposedly became enlightened enough to abandon our
superstitious belief in miracles and put our faith in reason and the empirical truths found by the scientific method). Hume's argument helped
advance the naturalistic worldview, which later metastasized with
Darwin's theory of evolution.

What follows is basically the material I presented to the audience at
Harvard that day. I began by spelling out Hume's anti-miracle argument
and then moved on to critiquing it. Here is Hume's argument in syllo-
gistic form:

1. Natural law is by definition a description of a regular occurrence.
2. A miracle is by definition a rare occurrence.
3. The evidence for the regular is always greater than that for the
   rare.
4. A wise man always bases his belief on the greater evidence.
5. Therefore, a wise man should never believe in miracles.

If those four premises are true, then the conclusion necessarily fol-lows—the wise man should never believe in miracles. Unfortunately for Hume and for those over the years who have believed him, the argument has a false premise—premise 3 is not necessarily true. The evidence for the regular is *not* always greater than that for the rare.

At first glance this might not seem to be the case. In the age of instant replay, premise 3 seems to make sense. For example, a football referee sees a play from one angle at full speed, while we get to see it from several angles in slow motion. We have greater evidence seeing a play over and over again (the regular) than does the ref who only sees it once (the rare).

But what may be true for a videotaped football game is not neces-sarily true for every event in life. To disprove premise 3 we only need to come up with one counterexample. We actually have several, and they are from Hume's own naturalistic worldview:

1. **The origin of the universe happened only once.** It was a rare, unrepeatable event, yet virtually every naturalist believes that the Big Bang evidence proves that the universe exploded into being.
2. **The origin of life happened only once.** It too was a rare, unre-peatable event, yet every naturalist believes that life arose spontaneously from non-life somewhere on the earth or else-where in the universe.
3. **The origin of new life forms also happened only once.** Those rare, unrepeatable events are nevertheless dogmatically believed by most naturalists, who say it all happened by unob-served (i.e., rare) macroevolutionary processes.
4. **In fact, the entire history of the world is comprised of rare, unrepeatable events.** For example, David Hume's own birth happened only once, but he had no trouble believing it occurred!

In every one of these counterexamples from Hume's own naturalistic worldview, his third premise must be disregarded or considered false. If Hume really believed in that premise, he would not have believed in his own birth or his own naturalistic worldview!

So we know by some of these counterexamples that Hume's third premise, and thus his entire argument, cannot be true. But what are the specific problems with this naturalistic kind of thinking?

First, it confuses *believability* with *possibility*. Even if premise 3 were true, the argument would not disprove the *possibility* of miracles; it would only question their *believability*. So even if you personally witnessed, say, Jesus Christ rising from dead as he predicted—if you were in the tomb, verified the body was dead, and then saw him get up and walk out of the tomb—Hume's argument says that you (a "wise" person) shouldn't believe it. There's something wrong with an argument that tells you to disbelieve what you have verified to be true.

Second, Hume confuses *probability* with *evidence*. He doesn't *weigh* the evidence for each rare event; rather, he *adds* the evidence for all regular events and suggests that this somehow makes all rare events unworthy of belief. But this is flawed reasoning as well. There are many improbable (rare) events in life that we believe when we have good evidence for them. For example, a hole-in-one is a rare event, but when we witness one we have no trouble believing it. We certainly don't say to the golfer, "Since the evidence for the regular is always greater than that for the rare, I'm not going to believe your shot unless you can tee it up and do it five times in a row!" Likewise, we certainly don't tell a lottery winner who beat 76-million-to-one odds that he's not going to get his money until he can win it five times in a row! No, in these cases, the evidence for the rare is greater than that for the regular. Sober, sane eyewitnesses provide greater evidence for a rare hole-in-one no matter how regularly that golfer had missed the hole in the past. Likewise, a winning ticket provides greater evidence that a certain person improbably won the lottery no matter how regularly that person had failed to win in the past.[10]

So the issue is not whether an event is regular or rare—the issue is whether we have good evidence for the event. We must *weigh* evidence for the event in question, not *add* evidence for all previous events.

Third, Hume is actually arguing in a circle. Instead of evaluating the veracity of the evidence for each miracle claim, Hume rules out belief in miracles in advance because he believes there is uniform experience against them. As usual, C. S. Lewis has great insight:

> Now of course we must agree with Hume that if there is absolutely "uniform experience" against miracles, if in other words they have

never happened, why then they never have. Unfortunately we know
the experience against them to be uniform only if we know that all the
reports of them are false. And we can know all the reports to be false
only if we know already that miracles have never occurred. In fact, we
are arguing in a circle.[11]

So Hume commits the same error as the Darwinists—he hides his conclusion in the premise of his argument by way of a false philosophical
presupposition. His false presupposition is that all human experiences
have been against miracles. How can he know that? He can't, so he presupposes it. As we have seen, miracles are possible because God exists.
Therefore, human beings may have experienced true miracles. The only
way to know for sure is to investigate the evidence for each miracle
claim. Assuming that each and every miracle claim is false, as Hume
does, is clearly illegitimate.

Finally, although Hume correctly defines a miracle as a rare event,
he then punishes it for being a rare event! It's as if Hume is saying, "If
only miracles happened more often, then we could believe them." But
if miracles happened more often, say, regularly (to use Hume's terminology), then they would cease being miracles (rare events), and we
might consider them natural laws or part of unexplained natural phenomena. But as soon as we consider them natural in origin, then they
would no longer get our attention as special acts of God. Its rarity is one
of the characteristics that distinguishes a miracle from everything else!
To put it another way, the reason miracles get our attention is because
we know that such an event could not be produced by natural laws.

So by Hume's logic, even if there is a God who performs miracles,
we shouldn't believe any miracles he performs because they are not regular events. Again, there's something wrong with an argument that tells
you to disbelieve what has actually occurred. And there's something
wrong with an argument that requires that miracles not be miracles to
be believed.

The bottom line is that Hume, without justification, simply declares
that the only believable events are regular events, and since a miracle is
not a regular event, it fails to meet this artificial criteria. As we've mentioned above, if we can't believe in rare events then we can't believe anything from history, because history is comprised of succeeding rare,
unrepeatable events. Such a position is clearly unreasonable.

After presenting this information at Harvard University, I received no questions or challenges to my critique of Hume, just stunned silence. During this same time period (the 1980s) I was challenged by a professor at another Ivy League school, Princeton University, to a debate on this issue. The professor asked for a copy of my presentation before the debate, which is very unusual. The element of surprise at a debate is an advantage that most debaters will not relinquish. However, I was so confident that my critique of Hume was correct that I sent it to the professor in advance. After receiving my critique of Hume, the professor contacted me to say that he would prefer that I lecture to his class rather than debate him, but that he would be there to "lead the charge" during the question and answer period. I agreed.

When I arrived on campus on the appointed date and time, the professor was nowhere to be found. His assistant said that he had some "personal emergency" and that the meeting was canceled. I wound up presenting my critique to a group of students that Ravi Zacharias had brought down from Nyack College. The professor never responded to my subsequent attempts to contact him.

I received a similar response from Antony Flew, currently one of the foremost philosophical atheists. In the late 80s, I asked him to comment on my book *Miracles and Modern Thought*,[12] which critiqued numerous anti-miracle arguments including his own (which is very similar to Hume's). Flew agreed to provide a written critique in the next edition of a major humanist journal. But in that article, instead of attempting to refute the arguments I presented, Flew provided a back-handed compliment by suggesting that atheists need to come up with better arguments against miracles if they are going to answer contemporary theists.

The reluctance to deal directly with the flaws in Hume's argument tells us that disbelief in miracles is probably more a matter of the will than of the mind. It seems as though some people uncritically cling to David Hume's argument because they simply don't want to admit that God exists. *But since we know that God exists, miracles are possible. Any argument against miracles that can be concocted, including that of David Hume, is destroyed by that one fact.* For if there is a God who can act, there can be acts of God (miracles).

So in the end, it's not miracles that are hard to believe—David

Hume's argument is hard to believe! We might say it's a "miracle" so many people still believe it.

All That Glitters Is Not *God*—What Is and Isn't a Miracle?

So the box is open—miracles are possible. But how will we know a miracle if we see one? In order to answer this, it's important to define what a miracle is, and isn't, so that we know what we're looking for.

As shown in table 8.2, there are at least six different kinds of unusual events, only one of which is a miracle.

	Anomalies	Magic	Psychosomatic	Satanic Signs	Providence	Miracles
Description	Freaks of nature	Sleight of hand	Mind over matter	Evil power	Prearranged events	Divine act
Power	Physical	Human	Mental	Psychic	Divine	Supernatural
Traits	Natural event with pattern	Unnatural and man-controlled	Requires faith; fails for some sickness	Evil, falsehood, occult, limited	Naturally explained; spiritual context	Never fails, immediate, lasts, glory to God
Example	Bumblebee	Rabbit in hat	Psychosomatic cures	Demonic influence	Fog at Normandy	Raising the dead

There are at least six different categories of UNUSUAL EVENTS:

Table 8.2

Let's take a brief look at each of these unusual events. We'll start with miracles because if we know what those are, we can better understand why other unusual events are not miracles.

Miracle—For an act of God to be an unmistakable sign from God, the act would have to meet certain criteria—criteria that would distinguish God's acts from any other unusual event. Like a king's seal, God's sign must be unique, easily recognizable, and something only God can do. In other words, it has characteristics that cannot be explained by natural laws, natural forces, or anything else in the physical universe. What would these criteria look like?

As we saw from the Cosmological, Teleological, and Moral Arguments, God alone has infinite power (power beyond that in the natural world), supreme design and purpose, and complete moral purity.

Therefore, it seems reasonable to assume that his acts would display or contain elements of these attributes. So the criteria for true miracles include:

A. An instantaneous beginning of a powerful act, as evidenced by the Cosmological Argument (the beginning of the universe);
B. Intelligent design and purpose, as evidenced by the Teleological Argument (the precise design of the universe for the purpose of supporting life, and the specified and complex design of life itself);
C. The promotion of good or right behavior, as evidenced by the Moral Argument (the Moral Law pressing on us).

The power component of miracles (A) means that the sign could not be explained naturally. For if a natural cause is possible, then the sign cannot be definitely identified as a miracle. A miracle has an unmistakable supernatural cause—one that transcends nature.

The design component (B) means that any sign done without an obvious purpose—to confirm a truth or a messenger of truth or to bring glory to God—is probably not a sign from God. In other words, God is not likely to do miracles for mere entertainment purposes. Just like most earthly kings will not use their seals lightly, the King of the Universe is not likely to use his seal for frivolous reasons. After all, if he were to use miracles for mere entertainment, then we would be less likely to recognize his intent when he was trying to confirm a new truth or a new messenger. So as not to "cry wolf," miracles must be focused on promoting a truth claim and must be relatively rare if they are going to be effective.

The moral component of miracles (C) means that any sign connected with error or immorality cannot be a sign from God. Error and immorality are against God's nature because he is the unchanging standard of truth and morality. He cannot confirm error or immorality.

With these criteria—instantaneous power, intelligent design, and morality—we can identify what unusual events are true signs from God. Notice that we drew these criteria from what we've learned about God from the natural world and what we've learned about the limits of nature itself. The Bible agrees with our assessment by calling events that meet these same criteria miracles.[13] And both the Bible and the Qur'an teach that miracles have been used to confirm a word from God.[14]

So an event connected with a divine truth claim that had these characteristics would be a miracle—an act of God to confirm a word from God. For example, a miracle has occurred if Jesus—a man who predicted he would rise from the dead—actually rose from the dead. Such an event would display instantaneous power beyond natural capabilities, intelligent forethought and design, and a moral purpose by confirming that Jesus is from God (and we, therefore, ought to listen to what he has to say!). There is no natural force or other source of power that could explain such an event.

Moreover, if the Resurrection actually happened, it did not occur "out of the blue" but in context. In other words, the Resurrection was an event in the context of a theistic universe, where a man claiming to be from God and performing miracles along the way predicted it would happen. Such a context suggests it's a miracle and not just a yet-to-be-explained natural event. In short, if the Resurrection actually occurred (and we'll investigate that question later), it has God's "fingerprints" all over it.

Providence—Religious people, particularly Christians, throw the term "miracle" around rather loosely. Quite often they identify an event as a miracle when it could be more accurately described as providential.

Providential events are those caused by God indirectly, not directly. That is, God uses natural laws to accomplish them. Answered prayer and unlikely but beneficial happenings can be examples. These may be quite remarkable and may stimulate faith, but they are not supernatural. For example, the fog at Normandy was providential because it helped conceal the Allied attack against the evil Nazi regime. It wasn't a miracle, because it could be explained by natural laws, but God may have been behind it. By contrast, a miracle would require something like bullets bouncing off the chests of our young men as they assaulted the beach.

Satanic Signs—Another possible cause of an unusual event could be other spiritual beings. Since God exists, it is possible that other spiritual beings exist. But if Satan and demons do exist, they have limited powers. Why? Because, as we have mentioned earlier in this chapter, it is impossible for there to be two infinite beings. Since God is infinite, no other being can be infinite.

Moreover, pure dualism—an infinite Good power vs. an infinite Evil power—is impossible. There is no such thing as pure evil. Evil is a privation of or a parasite in good; it cannot exist on its own. Evil is like rust to a car. If you take away all the rust, you have a better car. If you take away all the car, you have nothing. So Satan cannot be the evil equivalent of God. In fact, Satan has good attributes such as power, free will, and rational thought, but he uses them for evil purposes.

The bottom line is that God has no equal. He is the one infinite Being who is supreme over all of creation. As a result, created spiritual beings, if they exist at all, are limited by God and cannot perform the kinds of supernatural acts that only God can perform.

So by natural revelation alone—without revelation from any religious book—we know that if other spiritual beings exist they are limited in their power. Incidentally, this is exactly what the Bible teaches.

But just how limited are these other spiritual beings? Now we need special revelation. While we haven't gotten to the point yet of proving beyond a reasonable doubt that the Bible is true, let's assume that such beings are real and can interact with the natural world as the Bible describes.

According to the Bible, only God can create life and raise the dead (Gen. 1:21; Deut. 32:39). Pharaoh's magicians, who had imitated the first two plagues, couldn't imitate the third, which created life (in the form of lice). These magicians acknowledged that the third plague was the "finger of God" (Ex. 8:19).

Satan can perform tricks better than the best magicians—and there are many examples of these in the Bible[15]—but those tricks fail to meet the characteristics of a true miracle. As we have seen, true miracles cause one to think more highly of God, tell the truth, and promote moral behavior. Counterfeit signs from Satan do not do this. They tend to glorify the person ostensibly performing the sign, and they are often associated with error and immoral behavior. They also may not be immediate, instantaneous, or permanent.

In short, only God performs true miracles; Satan does counterfeit miracles. This is precisely what the Bible calls them in 2 Thessalonians 2:9 when Paul writes that, "The coming of the lawless one will be in accordance with the work of Satan displayed in all kinds of *counterfeit* miracles, signs and wonders." Of course, unless one is discerning, such signs can be deceptive and may be mistaken for miracles (Matt. 24:24).

Table 8.3 summarizes the differences between a divine miracle and a Satanic sign:[16]

Divine Miracle	Satanic Sign
• actual supernatural act	• only a super*normal* act
• under Creator's control	• under creature's control
• never associated with the occult	• associated with the occult
• connected with the true God	• frequently connected with pantheistic or polytheistic gods
• associated with truth	• associated with error
• associated with good	• associated with evil
• involves true prophecies	• involves false prophecies
• glorifies the Creator	• glorifies the creature

Table 8.3

Psychosomatic—Many years ago, I (Norm) developed what I thought was an allergy to blooming flowers. I began taking a strong drug in the spring of that year to help alleviate the symptoms. One spring Sunday morning I was invited to preach at a local church and had arrived early to meet the elders. When I got near the pulpit I saw some flowers on a nearby table. Almost immediately, I began to sneeze and my eyes watered up.

I said to one of the elders, "I won't be able to preach with these flowers here because my allergy is acting up. So, would you please move them?"

He looked at me and said, "They're plastic!"

I said to myself, "Geisler, you just sneezed at plastic flowers. That allergy has got to be in your head!" So I threw away my prescription and have not had that problem to this day.

Now, perhaps not all allergies are purely psychosomatic. But certainly there are some illnesses and cures that are psychosomatic, and these are well documented. Norman Cousins, in his book *Anatomy of an Illness,* describes in detail how he literally laughed himself well from cancer. Indeed, mental stress can have a negative impact on our physical health, while having a positive mental attitude, faith, or happiness can have a positive, healing effect (see Prov. 17:22).

Yet there are some medical conditions—such as severed spinal cords or amputated limbs—that cannot be cured by mind over matter because they are not psychosomatic illnesses. A true miracle would have to occur for those conditions to be cured.

The bottom line is that psychosomatic cures are psychological, not supernatural, in nature. They are evidence that the mind can have a limited but significant impact on the body. They are not to be confused with miracles.

Magic—Perhaps the most familiar kind of unusual event is magic. Magic is based on human sleight of hand or misleading the mind. A good magician can make you think he has sliced a woman in half, pulled a rabbit out of a hat, or made an elephant disappear. But it's all an illusion, a clever trick. Once you're let in on it, you say, "Now, why didn't· I think of that?" Magic, being a trick under human control, is not a miracle. Only God can perform a miracle.

Anomalies—An anomaly is an unexplained freak of nature. For example, at one time scientists couldn't understand how a bumblebee could fly. Its wings were too small for its body. Scientists considered bumblebee flight an anomaly until they discovered a kind of "power pack" that made up for the small wings. They knew it wasn't a miracle because of the observable pattern—all bumblebees flew. So they kept looking for a natural explanation and they found one.

The skeptic might ask, "So why couldn't the resurrection of Jesus Christ be considered an anomaly?" Because the Resurrection was predicted. It had intelligent design behind it—God's fingerprints were all over it. Anomalies are not connected with intelligent truth claims, and they lack moral and theological dimensions. If the resurrection of Christ actually occurred, it was no anomaly.

WHY DON'T WE SEE BIBLICAL MIRACLES TODAY?

Many people today have a very provincial view of history and of human experience. "If I personally don't see certain events happening today," they think, "they probably never happened." The implication for miracles is obvious. Namely, "If there are no public, biblical-quality miracles happening today (and if they were, they'd be on the Fox News Channel), then why should I think they happened in the past?" It's a fair question.

However, there's a common misconception behind this question. It's the belief that the Bible is filled with miracles that occur continually throughout biblical history. That's only partially true. It is true that the Bible is filled with miracles, about 250 occasions of them.[17] But most of those miracles occur in very small windows of history, during three distinct time periods—during the lifetimes of Moses, Elijah and Elisha, and Jesus and the apostles. Why then? Because those were the times when God was confirming new truth (revelation) and new messengers with that truth.[18]

If most of the miracles are bunched there, what's happening miraculously during the other periods the Bible covers? Nothing. In fact, there are huge gaps of time in the Bible (even hundreds of years) where there are no recorded miracles from God. Why? Because there was no new word from God, and most miracles confirmed some new word from God.

So why don't we see biblical miracles today? Because if the Bible is true and complete, God is not confirming any new revelation and thus does not have this main purpose for performing miracles today. There is no new word from God that needs to be confirmed by God.

Now don't misunderstand us here. We are *not* saying that God cannot do miracles today, or that he never does. As the sovereign Creator and sustainer of the universe, he can do a miracle anytime he wants. It's just that he may not have a reason to publicly display his power the way he did during biblical times because all of the truths he wanted to reveal have already been revealed and confirmed. As with a house, the foundation only needs to be laid once. Biblical miracles were special acts of God that laid the foundation for his permanent revelation to mankind.

SUMMARY AND CONCLUSION

1. The essential characteristics of the biblical God can be discovered without the Bible by way of natural revelation—as manifested in the Cosmological, Teleological, and Moral Arguments. Those arguments, which are supported by very strong evidence, show us that this is a theistic universe. Since this is a theistic universe, only the theistic religions of Judaism, Christianity, and Islam have "made the cut" of truth to this point. All nontheisms are built on a false foundation because they are wrong about the existence and nature of God.

2. Since God exists, miracles are possible. In fact, the greatest miracle of all—the creation of the universe out of nothing—has already occurred, which means Genesis 1:1 and every other miracle in the Bible is believable. Arguments against miracles fail because they are based on false philosophical assumptions rather than observational evidence. As a result, they fail to disprove miracles. God can intervene in the universe he created despite what David Hume says.

3. A true miracle would be an act only God could perform, meaning it would include Godlike characteristics such as supernatural power, intelligent design, and the promotion of moral behavior. By these characteristics, miracles can be distinguished from other types of unusual events such as providence, Satanic signs, psychosomatic cures, magic, and anomalies.

4. Due to his moral nature, we would expect God to communicate his specific purpose to us in more detail (i.e., beyond natural revelation to special revelation). God could use miracles as his sign to confirm to us his special revelation. Used in this way, a miracle is an act of God to confirm a message from God.

Our only question now is, "Has God used miracles to confirm Judaism, Christianity, or Islam?" That's the question we'll begin to answer in the next chapter.

Chapters 9–12
will cover:

1. Truth about reality is knowable.
2. The opposite of true is false.
3. It is true that the theistic God exists. This is evidenced by the:
   a. Beginning of the universe (Cosmological Argument)
   b. Design of the universe (Teleological Argument/ Anthropic Principle)
   c. Design of life (Teleological Argument)
   d. Moral Law (Moral Argument)
4. If God exists, then miracles are possible.
5. Miracles can be used to confirm a message from God (i.e., as acts of God to confirm a word from God).
> **6. The New Testament is historically reliable. This is evidenced by:**
   a. Early testimony
   b. Eyewitness testimony
   c. Uninvented (authentic) testimony
   d. Eyewitnesses who were not deceived
7. The New Testament says Jesus claimed to be God.
8. Jesus' claim to be God was miraculously confirmed by:
   a. His fulfillment of many prophecies about himself;
   b. His sinless life and miraculous deeds;
   c. His prediction and accomplishment of his resurrection.
9. Therefore, Jesus is God.
10. Whatever Jesus (who is God) teaches is true.
11. Jesus taught that the Bible is the Word of God.
12. Therefore, it is true that the Bible is the Word of God (and anything opposed to it is false).

9

Do We Have Early Testimony About Jesus?

"Historical evidence moves us a long way towards demonstrating our belief; as a result, the faith that is necessary to fill in the remaining gap is reasonable."
—Craig Blomberg

The Gospel According to Non-Christians

In A.D. 66, Jews in Palestine initiated a revolt against Roman rule that—to put it mildly—the Romans did not appreciate. The emperor sent troops led by General Vespasian to squash the rebellion and regain control of rebel areas. In 67, Vespasian laid siege to the rebel town of Jotapata in Galilee. In the forty-seventh day of that siege, a young Jewish revolutionary chose to surrender to the superior Roman army rather than commit suicide—a fate many of his countrymen had chosen. That young man won favor with Vespasian and was later taken to Rome by General Titus, Vespasian's son, after Titus destroyed Jerusalem and the Jewish temple in 70.

That young man was Flavius Josephus (ca. 37—ca. 100), who ultimately became the greatest Jewish historian of his time. Josephus began his historical writings in Rome while serving as a historian for the Roman emperor Domitian. It was there that he authored his autobiography and two major historical works. One of those works is his now-famous *Antiquities of the Jews,* which he finished in about A.D. 93. In book 18, chapter 3, section 3 of that work, Josephus, who was not a Christian, wrote these words:

> At this time [the time of Pilate] there was a wise man who was called Jesus. His conduct was good and (he) was known to be virtuous. And

222 I DON'T HAVE ENOUGH FAITH TO BE AN ATHEIST

many people from among the Jews and the other nations became his disciples. Pilate condemned him to be crucified and to die. But those who had become his disciples did not abandon his discipleship. They reported that he had appeared to them three days after his crucifixion, and that he was alive; accordingly he was perhaps the Messiah, concerning whom the prophets have recounted wonders.[1]

That wasn't Josephus's only mention of Jesus.[2] In another passage from *Antiquities,* Josephus revealed how the new high priest of the Jews (Ananus the younger) took advantage of a gap in Roman rule to kill James, the brother of Jesus. It was A.D. 62, and the Roman governor Festus died suddenly in office. Three months elapsed before his successor, Albinus, could get to Judea, allowing ample time for Ananus to do his dirty work. Josephus describes the incident this way:

> Festus was now dead, and Albinus was but upon the road; so he [Ananus the high priest] assembled the Sanhedrin of the judges, and brought before them the brother of Jesus, who was called Christ, whose name was James, and some others, [or some of his companions], and when he had formed an accusation against them as breakers of the law, he delivered them to be stoned.[3]

So here we have not only another first-century reference to Jesus, but confirmation that he had a brother named James who, obviously, was not well liked by the Jewish authorities. Could it be that James was martyred because he was the leader of the Jerusalem church, as the New Testament implies?[4]

Just how many non-Christian sources are there that mention Jesus? Including Josephus, there are ten known non-Christian writers who mention Jesus within 150 years of his life.[5] By contrast, over the same 150 years, there are nine non-Christian sources who mention Tiberius Caesar, the Roman *emperor* at the time of Jesus.[6] So discounting all the Christian sources, Jesus is actually mentioned by one more source than the Roman emperor. If you include the Christian sources, authors mentioning Jesus outnumber those mentioning Tiberius 43 to 10![7]

Some of these non-Christian sources—such as Celsus, Tacitus, and the Jewish Talmud—could be considered *anti-Christian* sources. While these works do not have any eyewitness testimony that contradicts events described in the New Testament documents, they are works written by writers whose tone is decidedly anti-Christian. What can we learn from them and the more neutral non-Christian sources? We learn that they admit certain facts about early Christianity that help us piece together a storyline that is surprisingly congruent with the New Testament. Piecing together all ten non-Christian references, we see that:

1. Jesus lived during time of Tiberius Caesar.
2. He lived a virtuous life.
3. He was a wonder-worker.
4. He had a brother named James.
5. He was acclaimed to be the Messiah.
6. He was crucified under Pontius Pilate.
7. He was crucified on the eve of the Jewish Passover.
8. Darkness and an earthquake occurred when he died.
9. His disciples believed he rose from the dead.
10. His disciples were willing to die for their belief.
11. Christianity spread rapidly as far as Rome.
12. His disciples denied the Roman gods and worshiped Jesus as God.

In light of these non-Christian references, the theory that Jesus never existed is clearly unreasonable. How could non-Christian writers collectively reveal a storyline congruent with the New Testament if Jesus never existed?

But the implications run even deeper than that. What does this say about the New Testament? On the face of it, non-Christian sources affirm the New Testament. While the non-Christian authors don't say they believe in the Resurrection, they report that the disciples certainly believed it.

Since, as we have shown, the existence of God and the possibility of miracles is firmly established through natural revelation, and the general story of Christ and the early church is affirmed through non-Christian sources, did the miracles of Christ actually occur as the disciples claim? Do the New Testament documents record actual history? Could it be that they are not biased religious writings full of myths and fables as many in our modern world assume, but instead describe events that actually occurred about 2,000 years ago? If so, we'll be well on our way to discovering which theistic religion is true.

To see if the New Testament is a record of actual history, we need to answer two questions concerning the documents that comprise the New Testament:

1. Do we have accurate copies of the original documents that were written down in the first century?
2. Do those documents speak the truth?

In order to believe the New Testament message, both of those questions must be answered in the affirmative. It's not enough just to give evidence that we have an accurate copy of the original first-century documents (question 1) because those documents could be telling lies. We must have an accurate copy of the documents *and* have reason to believe that those documents describe what really happened nearly 2,000 years ago (question 2). Let's begin with question 1.

QUESTION 1: DO WE HAVE AN ACCURATE COPY?

We're sure you remember the child's game of "telephone." That's where one child is given a verbal message to pass to the next child, who passes what he's heard to the next child, and so on. By the time the message gets to the last child in the chain it barely resembles what the first kid was told. To the casual observer, it seems like that same type of distortion could infect documents that have been transmitted from generation to generation over 2,000 years.

Fortunately, the New Testament was not transmitted that way. Since it was not told to one person who told it to another and so on, the problem from the telephone game does not apply. Numerous people independently witnessed New Testament events, many of them committed it to memory, and nine of those eyewitnesses/contemporaries put their observations in writing.

At this point, we need to clear up a common misunderstanding about the New Testament. When we speak of the New Testament documents, we are not talking about one writing, but about 27 writings. The New Testament documents are 27 different documents that were written on 27 different scrolls by nine different writers over a 20- to 50-year period. These individual writings have since been collected into one book we now call the Bible. So the New Testament is not just one source, but a collection of sources.

There's only one problem: so far, none of the *original* written documents of the New Testament have been discovered. We have only *copies* of the original writings, called manuscripts. Will this prevent us from knowing what the originals said?

Not at all. In fact, all significant literature from the ancient world is reconstructed into its original form by comparing the manuscripts that survive. To reconstruct the original, it helps to have a large number of manuscripts that are written not long after the original. More manuscripts and earlier manuscripts usually provide more trustworthy testimony and enable a more accurate reconstruction.

How do the New Testament documents fare in this regard? Extremely well, and far better than anything else from the ancient world. In fact, the New Testament documents have more manuscripts, earlier manuscripts, and more abundantly supported manuscripts than the best ten pieces of classical literature *combined*. Here's what we mean:

More Manuscripts—At last count, there are nearly 5,700 hand-written Greek manuscripts of the New Testament. In addition, there are more than 9,000 manuscripts in other languages (e.g., Syriac, Coptic, Latin, Arabic). Some of these nearly 15,000 manuscripts are complete Bibles, others are books or pages, and a few are just fragments. As shown in fig. 9.1 on the next page, there is nothing from the ancient world that even comes close in terms of manuscript support. The next closest work is the *Iliad* by Homer, with 643 manuscripts. Most other ancient works survive on fewer than a dozen manuscripts,[8] yet few historians question the historicity of the events those works describe.

Earlier Manuscripts—Not only does the New Testament enjoy abundant manuscript support, but it also has manuscripts that were written soon after the originals. The earliest undisputed manuscript is a segment of John 18:31-33, 37-38 known as the John Rylands fragment (because it's housed in the John Rylands Library in Manchester, England). Scholars date it between A.D. 117–138, but some say it is even earlier. It was found in Egypt—across the Mediterranean from its probable place of composition in Asia Minor—demonstrating that John's Gospel was copied and had spread quite some distance by the early second century.

Even earlier than the John Rylands fragment are nine *disputed* fragments that date from A.D. 50 to 70, found with the Dead Sea Scrolls.[9]

Some scholars believe these fragments are parts of six New Testament books including Mark, Acts, Romans, 1 Timothy, 2 Peter, and James. While other scholars resist this conclusion (perhaps because its admission would undermine their liberal leanings that the New Testament was written later), they have not found any other non–New Testament texts that these fragments could be.[10]

Reliability of the New Testament Compared to Other Ancient Documents

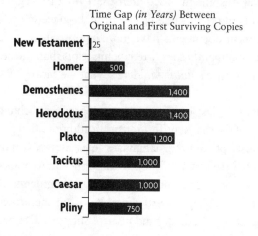

Time Gap *(in Years)* Between
Original and First Surviving Copies

New Testament 25
Homer 500
Demosthenes 1,400
Herodotus 1,400
Plato 1,200
Tacitus 1,000
Caesar 1,000
Pliny 750

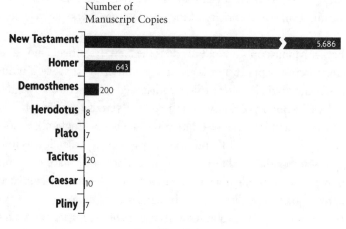

Number of
Manuscript Copies

New Testament 5,686
Homer 643
Demosthenes 200
Herodotus 8
Plato 7
Tacitus 20
Caesar 10
Pliny 7

Fig. 9.1

The fragments were found in a cave that had previously been identified as containing material from 50 B.C. to A.D. 50. The scholar who first identified these early fragments as New Testament books was Jose O'Callahan, a noted Spanish paleographer. The *New York Times* recognized the implications of O'Callahan's theory by admitting that if it is true "it would prove at least one of the Gospels—that of St. Mark—was written only a few years after the death of Jesus."[11]

But even if they are not true New Testament fragments and the John Rylands fragment really is the earliest, the time gap between the original and the first surviving copy is still vastly shorter than anything else from the ancient world.[12] The *Iliad* has the next shortest gap at about 500 years; most other ancient works are 1,000 years or more from the original. The New Testament gap is about 25 years and maybe less. (This does *not* mean there were no other manuscripts between the original and the first copy; there most certainly were. It simply means that those manuscripts have decayed, have been destroyed, or are still undiscovered.)

How old are the oldest surviving manuscripts of complete New Testament books? Manuscripts that are complete New Testament books survive from about A.D. 200. How about the oldest manuscripts of the entire New Testament? Most of the New Testament, including all of the Gospels, survives from 250, and a manuscript of the entire New Testament (including a Greek Old Testament) called Codex Vaticanus survives from about 325. Several other complete manuscripts survive from that century. And those manuscripts have spelling and punctuation characteristics that suggest that they are in a family of manuscripts that can be traced back to A.D. 100–150.

If these numerous and early manuscripts were all scholars had, they could reconstruct the original New Testament with great accuracy. But they also have abundant supporting evidence from the ancient world that makes New Testament reconstruction even more certain. Let's look at that next.

More Abundantly Supported Manuscripts—Beginning in February of A.D. 303, the Roman emperor Diocletian ordered three edicts of persecution upon Christians because he believed that the existence of Christianity was breaking the covenant between Rome and her gods.

The edicts called for the destruction of churches, manuscripts, and books and the killing of Christians.[13]

Hundreds if not thousands of manuscripts were destroyed across the Roman Empire during this persecution, which lasted until A.D. 311. But even if Diocletian had succeeded in wiping every biblical manuscript off the face of the earth, he could not have destroyed our ability to reconstruct the New Testament. Why? Because the early church fathers—men of the second and third centuries such as Justin Martyr, Irenaeus, Clement of Alexandria, Origen, Tertullian, and others—quoted the New Testament so much (36,289 times, to be exact) that all but eleven verses of the New Testament can be reconstructed just from their quotations.[14] In other words, you could go down to your local public library, check out the works of the early church fathers, and read nearly the entire New Testament just from their quotations of it! So we not only have thousands of manuscripts but thousands of quotations from those manuscripts. This makes reconstruction of the original text virtually certain.

But how certain? How are the originals reconstructed, and how accurate is this reconstructed New Testament?

How Is the Original Reconstructed?

These three facts—many, early, and supported manuscripts—help scholars reconstruct the original New Testament manuscripts rather easily. The process of comparing the many copies and quotations allows an extremely accurate reconstruction of the original even if errors were made during copying. How does this work? Consider the following example. Suppose we have four different manuscripts that have four different errors in the same verse, such as Philippians 4:13 ("I can do all things through Christ who gives me strength."). Here are the hypothetical copies:

1. I can do all t#ings through Christ who gives me strength.
2. I can do all th#ngs through Christ who gives me strength.
3. I can do all thi#gs through Christ who gives me strength.
4. I can do all thin#s through Christ who gives me strength.

Is there any mystery what the original said? None whatsoever. By the process of comparing and cross-checking, the original New Testament can be reconstructed with great accuracy. And the reconstruction of the New Testament is easier than this, because there are far fewer errors in the actual New Testament manuscripts than are represented by this example.

Let's assume for a minute that the New Testament really is the Word of God. Skeptics may ask, "Well, if the New Testament really is the Word of God, then why didn't God preserve the original?" We can only speculate here, but one possibility is because his Word might be better protected through copies than through original documents. How so? Because if the original were in someone's possession, that person could change it. But if there are copies spread all over the ancient world, there's no way one scribe or priest could alter the Word of God. As we have seen, the process of reconstruction allows variants and changes from copies to be identified and corrected rather easily. So, ironically, *not* having the originals may preserve God's Word better than having them.

How Accurate Is the Reconstruction?

In order to address the issue of accuracy, we need to clear up misunderstandings many critics have concerning "errors" in the biblical manuscripts. Some have estimated there are about 200,000 errors in the New Testament manuscripts. First of all, these are not "errors" but variant readings, the vast majority of which are strictly grammatical (i.e., punctuation and spelling). Second, these readings are spread throughout nearly 5,700 manuscripts, so that a variant spelling of *one* letter of *one* word in *one* verse in 2,000 manuscripts is counted as 2,000 "errors."

Textual scholars Westcott and Hort estimated that only *one in sixty* of these variants has significance. This would leave a text 98.33 percent pure.[15] Philip Schaff calculated that, of the 150,000 variants known in his day, only 400 changed the meaning of the passage, only fifty were of real significance, and *not even one* affected "an article of faith or a precept of duty which is not abundantly sustained by other and undoubted passages, or by the whole tenor of Scripture teaching."[16]

No other ancient book is so well authenticated. The great New Testament scholar and Princeton professor Bruce Metzger estimated that the *Mahabharata* of Hinduism is copied with only about 90 percent accuracy and Homer's *Iliad* with about 95 percent. By comparison, he estimated the New Testament is about 99.5 percent accurate.[17] Again, the 0.5 percent in question does not affect a single doctrine of the Christian faith.

Ancient manuscript authority Fredric Kenyon summed up well the status of the New Testament when he wrote:

> It cannot be too strongly asserted that in substance the text of the Bible is certain: Especially is this the case with the New Testament. The number of manuscripts of the New Testament, of early translations from it, and of quotations from it in the oldest writers of the Church, is so large that it is practically certain that the true reading of every doubtful passage is preserved in some one or other of these ancient authorities. This can be said of no other ancient book in the world.[18]

So we know we have the same New Testament that was written down nearly 2,000 years ago. But the next question is even more important: Do we have an accurate copy of the truth—or a lie? In other words, is the New Testament historically reliable?

QUESTION 2: IS THE NEW TESTAMENT HISTORICALLY RELIABLE?

When we ask the question "Is the New Testament historically reliable?" we are seeking to discover if the major events described in the New Testament documents really happened. Specifically, was there really a Jewish man nearly 2,000 years ago by the name of Jesus who taught profound truths, performed miracles, was crucified by Roman and Jewish authorities for claiming to be God, and who appeared to many witnesses after rising from the dead three days later?

It is important to keep in mind that, at this point, we are *not* seeking to discover if the New Testament is without error or is the "Word of God." We are simply trying to discover if the basic storyline is fact, not fiction. In order to discover this, we need to ascertain what kind of records comprise the New Testament. Are they documents written soon after the events by eyewitnesses (or by those who interviewed eyewitnesses), or are they documents written much later by biased followers who simply embellished details about the life of a real historical figure?

In order to find out, over the next few chapters we will test the New Testament documents by criteria historians often use to determine whether or not to believe a given historical document. We'll refer to these criteria as "historical tests." They include:

1. **Do we have early testimony?** Generally, the earlier the sources, the more accurate is the testimony.
2. **Do we have eyewitness testimony?** Eyewitness testimony is usually the best means of establishing what really happened.
3. **Do we have testimony from multiple, independent, eyewitness sources?** Multiple, independent eyewitnesses confirm that the events really occurred (they are not fiction), and provide additional details that a single source might miss. (True independent sources normally tell the same basic story but with differing details. Historians sometimes call this "coherence with dissimilarity.")
4. **Are the eyewitnesses trustworthy?** Should you believe them? Character matters.
5. **Do we have corroborating evidence from archaeology or other writers?** This adds further confirmation.
6. **Do we have any enemy attestation?** If opponents of the eyewitnesses admit certain facts the eyewitnesses say are true, then those facts probably are true (for example, if your mother says you are brave, that might be true; but it's probably more credible if your archenemy says the same thing).
7. **Does the testimony contain events or details that are embarrassing to the authors?** Since most people do not like to record negative information about themselves, any testimony that makes the author look bad is probably true.

In most cases, documents that meet most or all of these historical tests are considered trustworthy beyond a reasonable doubt. How do the New Testament documents fare? We'll find out over this chapter and the next three chapters. But before we start at historical test number 1 (early testimony), we need to clear away some objections that prevent many skeptics from even considering the reliability of the New Testament.

Common Objections to Reliability

History Cannot Be Known—The most recent argument generated against even considering the reliability of the New Testament documents is the assertion that history cannot be known. Ironically, this objection normally comes from the same people who say they *know* that the first life generated spontaneously from nonliving chemicals, and that all subsequent life evolved from that first life without intelligent intervention.

They are absolutely sure about *that history* despite the fact that there are no eyewitnesses or corroborating data for those events. Yet they assert that the resurrection of Jesus Christ—an event for which there are eyewitnesses and corroborating data—cannot be known!

The assertion that history cannot be known is against all common sense. Are we not sure that George Washington was the first president of the United States? That Lincoln was the sixteenth? That Japan attacked Pearl Harbor on December 7, 1941? That the New York Mets won the 1969 World Series? Of course we are. The skeptic is wrong. We can and do know history. In fact, if we can't know history, then we could never detect historical revisionism or historical propaganda, both of which assume there's an objective history that can be known.

Why can't someone have knowledge of a past event? The skeptic may say, "Because you don't have access to all the facts!" To which we respond, "Then scientists can't know anything either, because they don't have access to all the facts." This is obviously absurd. While we don't have access to all the facts, we may be able to gather enough of them to be reasonably certain about what happened.

Part of the confusion involves a failure to define what it means to "know." Since we can't go back in time and witness historical events again, our historical knowledge is based on probability. In other words, we use the same standard a jury uses to determine if a defendant committed a crime: beyond a reasonable doubt. If history cannot be known, then no jury could ever reach a verdict! After all, a jury makes a judgment about the guilt or innocence of someone based on *knowledge* of some *past* event. Historians must discover past events just like police and forensic scientists do—by piecing together evidence and interviewing eyewitnesses. And when they do, they often use the seven historical tests we've just identified above.

Finally, if we cannot know history, then skeptics cannot claim that Christianity is untrue. To say that Christianity is untrue, the skeptic must know history. Why? Because every negation implies an affirmation. To say that Jesus didn't rise from the dead (the negation), the skeptic must *know* what actually *did* happen to him (the affirmation).

In the end, skeptics are caught in a dilemma. If they say history cannot be known, then they lose the ability to say evolution is true and Christianity is false. If they admit history can be known, then they must deal with the multiple lines of historical evidence for creation and Christianity.

The New Testament Documents Contain Miracles—Skeptics usually charge, "The New Testament contains miracles, therefore much of it *has* to be legend!" We've already answered that objection. Since God exists, miracles are possible. And as we'll see in chapter 13, the events of the New Testament are in a context where miracles are not only possible but were predicted. So the inclusion of miracles does not negate the historicity of the New Testament documents but may actually strengthen their historicity (because they record predicted events).

The New Testament Writers Were Biased—The great skeptic David Hume said witnesses should be unbiased if we're going to consider them credible. So when skeptics look at the New Testament documents, they often ask, "How can you say they are reliable when they were written by the converted? These are biased accounts written by biased people."

It's true that the New Testament writers *were* biased and converted people. But that doesn't mean they lied or exaggerated. Indeed, their conversion and bias may have actually driven them to be *more* accurate. Let's see why.

A few years ago, a so-called documentary about Jesus on a cable TV channel led off with this comment from the narrator: "Most of what we think we know about Jesus comes from the New Testament Gospels: Matthew, Mark, Luke, and John. But we can't trust those books for accurate information because they were written by the converted."

Now, what's wrong with that logic? What's wrong with that logic is that it fails to ask the most important question: *Why were they converted?* Indeed, the first and most important question is *not*, "What were the beliefs of the New Testament writers?" The first and most important question is, "Why did they convert to these new beliefs?" In other words, why did the New Testament writers suddenly abandon their livelihoods and treasured religious traditions for these new beliefs?

I (Frank) posed that question to a couple of Black Muslims during a radio debate not long ago. Like traditional Muslims, Black Muslims do not believe that Jesus went to the cross, so there's no way he could have resurrected. With this in mind, I asked them, "Why did the New Testament writers suddenly convert from Judaism to believing that Jesus rose from the dead?"

One of them said, "Because they wanted power over the people!"

I said, "What power did the New Testament writers gain by asserting that Jesus rose from the dead? The answer is 'none.' In fact, instead of gaining power, they got exactly the opposite—submission, servitude, persecution, torture, and death." They had no answer.

I then asked them the question in a different way: "What possible motive did the New Testament writers have to make up the Resurrection story if it wasn't true?"

Again, they had no response. Why? Because they began to realize that the New Testament writers had every earthly motive to *deny* the Resurrection rather than proclaim it. There was no motive or incentive to make up the New Testament storyline. The last time we checked, the promise of submission, servitude, persecution, torture, and death would not motivate anyone to make up such a story.

The New Testament writers certainly had no reason to make up a new religion. We must remember that all of them (with the possible exception of Luke) were Jews who firmly believed they already had the one true religion. And that nearly 2,000-year-old religion asserted that they, the Jews, were the chosen people of God. Why would the Jews who converted to Christianity risk persecution, death, and perhaps eternal damnation to start something that 1) wasn't true and 2) elevated non-Jews into the exclusive relationship they claimed to have with the Creator of the Universe? And unless the Resurrection actually happened, why would they, almost immediately, stop observing the Sabbath, circumcision, the Law of Moses, the centrality of the temple, the priestly system, and other Old Testament teachings? The New Testament writers had to have witnessed some very strong evidence to turn away from those ancient beliefs and practices that had defined who they and their forebears were for nearly 2,000 years.

Converted People Are Not Objective—At this point, the skeptic might protest, "But since the New Testament writers were converted, they can't be objective." Nonsense. People can be objective even when they aren't neutral. A doctor can give an objective diagnosis even if he has strong feelings for the patient. That is, he can be objective even though he isn't neutral. In fact, his passion for the patient may cause him to be all the more diligent in diagnosing and then treating the disease properly.

In writing this book, while we certainly aren't neutral, we are presenting objective facts. Likewise, atheists are not neutral, but they too can present objective facts if they decide to. The New Testament writers could do the same.

The truth of the matter is that all books are written for a reason, and most authors believe what they are writing! But that doesn't mean what they write is wrong or has no objective element. As we mentioned in the preface, the survivors of the Holocaust who wrote down their experiences certainly were not neutral bystanders. They believed passionately in recording those events so that the world would never forget the Holocaust and, hopefully, never repeat it. While passion may cause some people to exaggerate, it may drive others to be all the more meticulous and accurate so as not to lose credibility and acceptance of the message they wish to communicate.

This distinction between the neutrality and the objectivity of the New Testament writers is an extremely important point. Too often the documents that make up the New Testament are automatically considered biased and untrustworthy. This is ironic, because those who hold this view are often biased themselves. They are biased because they have not first investigated the New Testament documents or the context in which they were written in order to make an educated assessment of their trustworthiness.

As we're about to see, the New Testament documents are not "church propaganda" or a monolith of writings designed to promote some church-manufactured theology. What are they, then? That's the question we'll address in the remainder of this chapter and the next three.

So let's get started. We know we have an accurate copy of what was written down by the New Testament writers. But are those documents trustworthy? Our first question deals with historical test #1: Are the New Testament documents early?

ARE THE NEW TESTAMENT DOCUMENTS EARLY?

Yes. How early?

All New Testament Books Were Written Before A.D. 100 (**About 70 Years After the Death of Jesus**)—As table 9.1 (on page 236) shows, in letters written between A.D. 95 and 110, three early church fathers—Clement, Ignatius, and Polycarp—quoted passages out of 25 of the 27

books in the New Testament.[19] Only the short books of Jude and 2 John
were not referenced, but they certainly had been written. (Jude had written his short letter by this time because, being Jesus' half brother, he was
almost certainly dead by A.D. 100; and 2 John had been written because
it came before 3 John, which was one of the 25 books quoted.)

NEW TESTAMENT DOCUMENTS CITED BY:		
Clement, writing from Rome (c. A.D. 95)	Ignatius, writing from Smyrna in Asia Minor (c. 107)	Polycarp, writing from Smyrna in Asia Minor (c. 110)
Matthew	Matthew	Matthew
Mark	Mark	Mark
Luke	Luke	Luke
Romans	John	John
1 Corinthians	Acts	Acts
Ephesians	Romans	Romans
1 Timothy	1 Corinthians	1 Corinthians
Titus	2 Corinthians	2 Corinthians
Hebrews	Galatians	Galatians
James	Ephesians	Ephesians
1 Peter	Philippians	Philippians
	Colossians	Colossians
	1 Thessalonians	2 Thessalonians
	1 Timothy	1 Timothy
	2 Timothy	2 Timothy
	Titus	Hebrews
	Philemon	1 Peter
	Hebrews	1 John
	James	
	1 Peter	
	2 Peter	
	1 John	
	3 John	
	Revelation	

Table 9.1

Since Clement was in Rome and Ignatius and Polycarp were hundreds of miles away in Smyrna, the original New Testament documents
had to have been written significantly earlier, otherwise they could not
have circulated across the ancient world by that time. Therefore, it's safe

to say that all of the New Testament was written by A.D. 100, and at least those in the left column several years before 95.

But that's just the *latest* they could have been written. Most were probably written much earlier. How much earlier? Most if not all before 70.

Most If Not All of These Books Were Written Before A.D. 70 (About 40 Years After the Death of Jesus)—Imagine this. You're a devout Jew in the first century. The center of your national, economic, and religious life is Jerusalem, and especially the temple. It has been that way in your nation, your family, and almost every Jew's family for a thousand years—ever since Solomon built the first temple. Most of the newest temple, constructed by King Herod, was completed when you were a child, but portions of it are still under construction and have been since 19 B.C. For your entire life you have attended services and brought sacrifices there to atone for the sins you've committed against God. Why? Because you and your countrymen consider this temple the earthly dwelling place of the God of the universe, the maker of heaven and earth, the very Deity whose name is so holy you dare not utter it.

As a young man, you begin following a Jew named Jesus who claims to be the long-awaited Messiah predicted in your Scriptures. He performs miracles, teaches profound truths, and scolds and befuddles the priests in charge of the temple. Incredibly, he predicts his own death and resurrection. He also predicts that the temple itself will be destroyed before your generation passes away (Mark 13:2, 30).

This is scandalous! Jesus is convicted of blasphemy by your temple priests and is crucified on the eve of the Passover, one of your holiest holidays. He's buried in a Jewish tomb, but three days later you and his other followers see Jesus alive just as he predicted. You touch him, eat with him, and he continues to perform miracles, the last being his ascension into heaven. Forty years later, your temple is destroyed just as Jesus had predicted, along with the entire city and thousands of your countrymen.

Question: If you and your fellow-followers write accounts of Jesus *after* the temple and city were destroyed in A.D. 70, aren't you going to at least mention that unprecedented national, human, economic, and religious tragedy somewhere in your writings, especially since this risen

Jesus had predicted it? Of course! Well, here's the problem for those who say the New Testament was written after 70—there's absolutely no mention of the fulfillment of this predicted tragedy anywhere in the New Testament documents. This means most, if not all, of the documents must have been written prior to 70.

Some may object, "That's an argument from silence, and that doesn't prove anything." But in fact it is not an argument from silence, for the New Testament documents speak of Jerusalem and the temple, or activities associated with them, as if they were still intact at the time of the writings.[20] But even if this were an argument from silence, that doesn't mean it's wrong. Consider these modern parallels. If a former sailor aboard the *USS Arizona* wrote a book related to the history of that ship, and the book ends with no mention of the ship being sunk and 1,177 of its sailors being killed at Pearl Harbor, do you have *any* doubt that the book must have been written prior to December 7, 1941? Or, if a former tenant of the World Trade Center wrote a book related to the history of those buildings, and the book ends with the towers still standing—there's absolutely no mention of the towers being destroyed and nearly 3,000 people being murdered by Muslim terrorists—do you have *any* doubt that the book must have been written prior to September 11, 2001? Of course not.

Well, the disaster in A.D. 70, in terms of lives, property, and national scope, was many magnitudes greater than Pearl Harbor and 9/11. It marked the end of such a terrible war that Josephus—who himself surrendered to the Romans in 67—called it the "greatest" war of all time.[21] The Jews didn't lose just one ship or a couple of prominent buildings—they lost their entire country, their capital city, and their temple, which had been the center of their religious, political, and economic life for the last thousand years. In addition, *tens of thousands* of their countrymen were dead and hundreds of their villages burned to the ground.

So if we would expect tragedies such as Pearl Harbor and 9/11 to be mentioned in the relevant writings of today, we certainly should expect the events of A.D. 70 to be cited somewhere in the New Testament (especially since the events were predicted by Jesus). But since the New Testament does not mention these events anywhere and suggests that Jerusalem and the temple are still intact, we can conclude reasonably that most, if not all, of the New Testament documents must have been written prior to 70.

How much earlier?

Many New Testament Books Were Composed Before A.D. 62 (About 30 Years After the Death of Jesus)—Imagine this: You are a first-century medical doctor who has embarked on a research project to record the events of the early church. This research will require you to interview eyewitnesses of the early church and to travel with the apostle Paul as he visits new churches across the ancient world. You record prominent events in the life of the church such as the early work of John and Peter, as well as the martyrdoms of Stephen and James (the brother of John). In Paul's life you record everything from sermons, beatings, and trials to shipwrecks and imprisonments. You also record his theological summit with Peter and James, who is Jesus' brother and the leader of the church in Jerusalem.

As you describe many of these events, your narrative is so filled with details that every informed reader will know that either you must have access to eyewitness testimony or you are an eyewitness yourself. For example, as you follow Paul on his travels you shift from using the pronoun "they" to "we," and you correctly record the names of local politicians, local slang, local weather patterns, local topography, local business practices; you even record the right depth of the water about a quarter mile off Malta as your ship is about to run aground in a storm! In fact, you record at least 84 such details in the last half of your narrative.

Question: Since you obviously find it important to record all of these minor details, if your main subject—the apostle Paul—was executed at the hands of the Roman emperor Nero, do you think you would record it? Or, if Jesus' brother, the leader of the church in Jerusalem, was killed at the hands of the Sanhedrin, the same Jewish body that sentenced Jesus to die, do you think you would record it? Of course! And if you failed to record such momentous events, we would rightly assume that you wrote your narrative *before* their deaths.

This is the situation we find in the New Testament. Luke, the medical doctor, meticulously records all kinds of details in Acts, which chronicles the early church (a listing of 84 historically confirmed details is in the next chapter). Luke records the deaths of two Christian martyrs (Stephen, and James the brother of John), but his account ends with two of its primary leaders (Paul, and James the brother of Jesus) still living. Acts ends abruptly with Paul under house arrest in Rome, and there's no mention of James having died. We know from Clement of Rome, writing in the late first century, and from other early church fathers, that Paul was executed sometime during the reign of Nero, which ended in A.D. 68.[22] And we know from Josephus that James was killed in 62. So we can conclude, beyond a reasonable doubt, that the book of Acts was written before 62.

If you're still not convinced, consider this modern parallel: suppose someone wrote a book recording the events surrounding the main figures of the Civil Rights movement in the 1960s. The book begins with the assassination of President John F. Kennedy and includes the Civil Rights legislation of 1964, the marches and protests of Martin Luther King, Jr., including his arrest and imprisonment, and his great "I have a dream" speech on the Mall in Washington, D.C. Question: If the book ends with Martin Luther King, Jr.—the very leader of the movement—still alive, when would you conclude that the book was written? Obviously before his assassination in April of 1968. This is the same situation we have with Luke's narrative. His book ends with the main leaders still alive, which means it was written no later than 62. (Classical scholar and historian Colin Hemer gives thirteen additional reasons why Acts was written by 62.[23])

If Acts was written by 62, then the Gospel of Luke was written before that. How do we know? Because Luke reminds the original recipient of Acts, Theophilus (who was probably an important Roman official), that he had written to him earlier. The first verse of Acts says, "In my former book, Theophilus, I wrote about all that Jesus began to do and to teach . . ." The "former book" must be the Gospel of Luke, because Luke addresses that to Theophilus as well (Luke 1:1-4, see citation below).

How much earlier is Luke? It would seem reasonable to place Luke at or before A.D. 60. Why? Because 62 is the *latest* Acts was written, and there had to have been some time between Luke's first writing to Theophilus and his second. If Acts is no later than 62 (and quite possibly earlier), then Luke is realistically 60 or before.

This date also makes sense in light of Paul's quotation of Luke's Gospel. Writing sometime between A.D. 62–65, Paul quotes from Luke 10:7 and calls it "Scripture" (1 Tim. 5:18). Therefore, Luke's Gospel must have been in circulation long enough before that time in order for both Paul and Timothy to know its contents and regard it as Scripture. (By the way, this was no minor claim for Paul to make. In effect, he was making the bold assertion that Luke's Gospel was just as inspired as the Holy Jewish Bible—the Old Testament he treasured so much!)

If Luke was written by A.D. 60, then Mark must have been written in the mid-to-late 50s if not earlier. Why? Because Luke says that he got his facts by checking with eyewitness sources:

> Many have undertaken to draw up an account of the things that have been fulfilled among us, just as they were handed down to us by those who from the first were eyewitnesses and servants of the word. Therefore, since I myself have carefully investigated everything from the beginning, it seemed good also to me to write an orderly account for you, most excellent Theophilus, so that you may know the certainty of the things you have been taught (Luke 1:1-4).

Most scholars believe Mark's Gospel was one of those eyewitness sources. And if those Dead Sea Scroll fragments we mentioned above are really from A.D. 50–70, then certainly Mark is earlier. But even if Mark is not before Luke, the very fact that we know beyond a reasonable doubt that Luke is before 62 and probably before 60 means that we have meticulously recorded eyewitness testimony written within 25 or 30 years of Jesus' death, burial, and resurrection. This is far too early to be legendary. It also means that the eyewitness sources go back even earlier. How much earlier?

Some New Testament Books Were Penned in the 40s and 50s A.D., with Sources from the 30s (Only a Few Years After the Death of Jesus)— As certain as we are about the date of Luke's records, there is no doubt from anyone—including the most liberal of scholars—that Paul wrote his first letter to the church at Corinth (which is in modern-day Greece) sometime between 55 and 56. In this letter, Paul speaks about moral problems in the church, and then proceeds to discuss controversies over tongues, prophecies, and the Lord's Supper. This, of course, demon-strates that the church in Corinth was experiencing some kind of mirac-ulous activity and was already observing the Lord's Supper within 25 years of the Resurrection.

But the most significant aspect of this letter is that it contains the earliest and most authenticated testimony of the Resurrection itself. In the fifteenth chapter of 1 Corinthians, Paul writes down the testimony he received from others and the testimony that was authenticated when Christ appeared to him:

> For I delivered to you as of first importance what I also received, that Christ died for our sins according to the Scriptures, and that He was buried, and that He was raised on the third day according to the Scriptures, and that He appeared to Cephas [Peter], then to the twelve. After that He appeared to more than five hundred brethren at one time, most of whom remain until now, but some have fallen asleep; then He appeared to James, then to all the apos-tles; and last of all, as it were to one untimely born, He appeared to me also (1 Cor. 15:3-8, NASB).

Where did Paul get what he "received"? He probably received it from Peter and James when he visited them in Jerusalem three years after his conversion (Gal. 1:18). Why is this important? Because, as Gary Habermas points out, most scholars (even liberals) believe that this tes-timony was part of an early creed that dates right back to the Resurrection itself—eighteen *months* to eight years after, but some say even earlier.[24] There's no possible way that such testimony could describe a legend, because it goes right back to the time and place of the event itself.[25] If there was ever a place that a legendary resurrection could *not* occur it was Jerusalem, because the Jews and the Romans were all too eager to squash Christianity and could have easily done so by parading Jesus' body around the city.

Moreover, notice that Paul cites fourteen eyewitnesses whose names are known: the twelve apostles, James, and Paul himself ("Cephas" is the Aramaic for Peter), and then references an appearance to more than 500 others at one time. Included in those groups was one skeptic, James, and one outright enemy, Paul himself. By naming so many people who could verify what Paul was saying, Paul was, in effect, challenging his

Corinthian readers to check him out. Bible scholar William Lillie puts it this way:

> What gives a special authority to the list as historical evidence is the reference to most of the five hundred brethren being still alive. St. Paul says in effect: "if you do not believe me, you can ask them." Such a statement in an admittedly genuine letter written within thirty years of the event is almost as strong evidence as one could hope to get for something that happened nearly two thousand years ago.[26]

If the Resurrection had not occurred, why would Paul give such a list of supposed eyewitnesses? He would have immediately lost all credibility with his Corinthian readers by lying so blatantly.

In addition to 1 Corinthians, there are numerous other New Testament documents that were written in the 50s or earlier. Galatians (A.D. 48), 1 Thessalonians (50–54), and Romans (57–58) are all in this category. In fact (and we know we may be going out on a limb here!) all of Paul's works had to have been written before he died, which was sometime in the mid-60s.

But it's not just conservative scholars who believe these early dates. Even some radical critics, such as atheist John A. T. Robinson, admit the New Testament documents were written early. Known for his role in launching the "Death of God" movement, Robinson wrote a revolutionary book titled *Redating the New Testament,* in which he posited that most New Testament books, including all four Gospels, were written sometime between A.D. 40 and 65.

The great and once-liberal archaeologist William F. Albright, after seeing how well the New Testament fit with the archaeological and historical data, wrote, "We can already say emphatically that there is no longer any solid basis for dating any book of the New Testament after about A.D. 80."[27] Elsewhere Albright said, "In my opinion, every book of the New Testament was written by a baptized Jew between the 40s and the 80s of the first century (very probably sometime between about A.D. 50 and 75)."[28]

So we know beyond a reasonable doubt that most if not all the New Testament documents are early. But skeptics still have a couple of objections.

SKEPTIC'S ADVOCATE

The Documents Are Not Early Enough

Some skeptics may think that a 15- to 40-year gap between the life of Christ and the writings about him is too wide for the testimony to be reliable. But they are mistaken.

Think about events that occurred 15 to 40 years ago. When historians write about those events, we don't say, "Oh, that's impossible! No one can remember events from that long ago!" Such skepticism is clearly unwarranted. Historians today write accurately about events in the 1970s, 80s, and 90s by consulting their own memories, those of other eyewitnesses, and any written sources from the time.

This process is the same one the New Testament writers used to record their documents. Like a good reporter, Luke interviewed eyewitnesses.[29] And as we'll see in the next chapter, some New Testament writers were eyewitnesses themselves. They could remember 15- to 40-year-old events quite easily, just as you can. Why can you remember certain events vividly from 15 to 40 years ago and (if you're old enough) even further back? You may be able to remember certain events because they made a great emotional impact on you. (In fact, those of us who are "over the hill" can remember some events from 30 years ago better than those from 30 minutes ago!)

Where were you and what were you doing when President Kennedy was assassinated? When the *Challenger* exploded? When the second plane hit the tower? Why can you remember those events so well? Because they made a deep emotional impact on you. Since an event like the Resurrection certainly would have made a deep emotional impact on the New Testament writers and the other eyewitnesses they may have consulted, it's easy to see why the history of Jesus could be easily recalled many years later, especially in a culture with an established reliance on oral testimony (more on this below).

Furthermore, if the major works of the New Testament are eyewitness accounts written within two generations of the events, then they are not likely to be legend. Why? Because historical research indicates that a myth cannot begin to crowd out historical facts while the eyewitnesses are still alive. For this reason, Roman historian A. N. Sherwin-White calls the mythological view of the New Testament "unbelievable."[30] William Lane Craig writes, "The tests show that even two generations is too short to allow legendary tendencies to wipe out the hard core of historical fact."[31] Inside of those two generations, eyewitnesses are still around to correct the errors of historical revisionists.

We are seeing this tendency right now with regard to the Holocaust. In the early twenty-first century, we've begun to see more people claim that the Holocaust never happened. Why are the revisionists trying this now? Because most of the eyewitnesses have now died. Fortunately, since we have written eyewitness testimony from the Holocaust, the revisionists are not successful in passing off their lies as the truth. The same holds true for the New Testament. If the New Testament was written within 60 years of the events it records, it is highly unlikely those events could be legendary. And as we have seen, all of the New Testament documents were written within 60 years of the events, and many much earlier.

Why Not Earlier?

At this point the skeptic might say, "Okay, fine. The New Testament is early, but it's not as early as I would expect. Why didn't they write down their testimony earlier? If I saw what they said they saw, I wouldn't wait 15 or 20 years to write it down."

There are a number of possible reasons for the wait.

First, since the New Testament writers were living in a culture where the vast majority of people were illiterate, there was no initial need or utility in writing it down. First-century people in Palestine, by necessity, developed strong memories in order to remember and pass on information. Craig writes,

> In an oral culture like that of first-century Palestine the ability to memorize and retain large tracts of oral tradition was a highly prized and highly developed skill. From the earliest age children in the home, elementary school, and the synagogue were taught to memorize faithfully sacred tradition. The disciples would have exercised similar care with the teachings of Jesus.[32]

In such an oral culture, facts about Jesus may have been put into a memorable form. There's good evidence for this. Gary Habermas has identified forty-one short sections of the New Testament that appear to be creeds—compact sayings that could easily be remembered and that were probably passed along orally before they were put into writing (one of these creeds we've already mentioned—1 Cor. 15:3-8).[33]

Second, since some of the New Testament writers may have had high hopes that Jesus was going to come back in their lifetime, they saw no immediate need to write it down. But as they aged, perhaps they thought it wise to put their observations down on papyrus.

Third, as Christianity spread all over the ancient world, writing became the most efficient means to communicate with the rapidly expanding church. In other words, time and distance forced the New Testament writers to write it down.

On the other hand, there may not have been a gap for at least one Gospel. If those fragments from the Dead Sea Scrolls are really from Mark (and they most likely are), then that Gospel might have been written in the 30s. Why? Because the fragments are of copies, not of the original. If we have copies from the 50s, then the original must have been earlier.[34]

Moreover, many scholars believe there actually were written sources that predate the Gospels. In fact, Luke, in the first four verses of his Gospel, says that he checked with other sources, though some of these may have been earlier Gospels (e.g., Matthew and Mark).[35] Was one of his sources Mark's Gospel? We don't know for sure. It certainly seems like Luke is speaking of *several* other *written* sources, because he says, "*Many* have undertaken to *draw up* an account of the things that have been fulfilled among us . . ." (Luke 1:1). Luke may have referenced Mark's Gospel and other written testimonies including public court records from Jesus' trial.

In the end, it doesn't really matter whether or not there were written sources that predate the New Testament. Nor does it matter if Mark was written in the 30s A.D. Why? Because the documents we do know about are early enough and contain early source material. As we'll see in the next chapter, many if not all of the New Testament documents were written by eyewitnesses or their contemporaries within 15 to 40 years of Jesus, and some contain oral or other written testimony that goes back to the Resurrection itself. In other words, *the real issue isn't so much the date of writings, but the date of the sources used in the writings.*

Why Not More?

Skeptics may ask, "If Jesus actually did rise from the dead, shouldn't there be more written about him than there is?" In response, we actually have *more* testimony than we might expect, and certainly more than enough to establish beyond a reasonable doubt what happened. As we have seen, Jesus is referenced by far more authors than the Roman *emperor* at the time (Jesus' 43 authors to Tiberius's 10 within 150 years of their lives). Nine of those authors were eyewitnesses or contemporaries of the events, and they wrote 27 documents, the majority of which mention or imply the Resurrection. That's more than enough to establish historicity.

For those who still think there should have been even more written about Jesus, New Testament scholar Craig Blomberg offers four reasons why that's not a reasonable expectation: 1) the humble beginnings of Christianity; 2) the remote location of Palestine on the eastern frontiers of the Roman Empire; 3) the small percentage of the works of ancient Graeco-Roman historians that have survived (this could be due to loss, decay, destruction, or all of the above); and 4) the lack of attention paid by surviving historical documents to Jewish figures in general.[36]

Nevertheless, some skeptics still think there should be testimony from some of the 500 people who allegedly saw the risen Christ. Skeptic Farrell Till is one of them. During a debate on the Resurrection that I (Norm) had with him in 1994, Till demanded, "Trot out one of those 500 witnesses or give us something that they wrote, and we will accept that as reliable proof or evidence."[37]

This is an unreasonable expectation, for a number of reasons. First, as we have already pointed out, first-century Palestine was an oral culture. Most people were illiterate and remembered and passed on information orally.

Second, how many of those predominately illiterate eyewitnesses would have written something even if they could write? Even today, with a much higher literacy rate and all the conveniences of modern writing and research tools, how many people do you know who have written a book or even an article on any subject? How many do you know who have written a book or article on a contemporary historical event, even a significant event like 9/11? Probably not many, and certainly fewer than one out of 500. (Has Farrell Till ever written an article on a major historical event he witnessed?)

Third, even if some of those 500 average people did write down what they saw, why would skeptics expect their testimony to survive for 2,000 years? The New Testament survives intact because of the thousands of manuscripts copied by scribes for a growing church over the centuries. Historical works from the major ancient historians such as Josephus, Tacitus, and Pliny survive on just a handful of copies, and those copies are hundreds of years from the originals. Why do the skeptics think anything is going to be written, much less survive, from an ancient group of illiterate Galilean peasants?[38]

Finally, we do know the names of many of the 500, and their testimony is written down in the New Testament. They include Matthew, Mark, Luke, John, Peter, Paul, and James—plus nine who are named elsewhere as apostles (Matthew 10 and Acts 1).

So we shouldn't expect more testimony than what we have about Jesus. And what we do have is more than enough to establish historicity.

SUMMARY AND CONCLUSION

We have much more to investigate regarding the historicity of the New Testament. But we can draw two major conclusions at this point:

1. We have an accurate copy of the original New Testament documents:
   a. While the original New Testament documents do not survive or have not yet been found, we have abundant and accurate copies of the original New Testament documents—many more than that for the ten best pieces of ancient literature combined. Moreover, nearly perfect reconstruction of the originals can be accomplished by comparing the thousands of manuscript copies that do survive. We have discovered manuscript fragments from the early second century and perhaps as early as the mid-first century. There are *no* works from the ancient world that even come close to the New Testament in terms of manuscript support.
   b. Reconstruction is further authenticated by the thousands of quotations from the early church fathers. In fact, the entire New Testament, except for eleven verses, can be reconstructed just from their quotations of it.

2. The New Testament documents are early and contain even earlier source material:
   a. Since the New Testament documents are referenced by other writers by about A.D. 100, they had to have been composed before then.
   b. Since the New Testament documents speak as if the temple and the city were still standing at the time of their writing—and there is no mention of the onset of the Jewish war or the destruction of the temple and Jerusalem—most of the New Testament documents are probably earlier than A.D. 70.
   c. We have very strong evidence that Acts was written by 62, which means Luke is even earlier.
   d. We have source material that goes back into the 30s. Nearly all scholars agree that the death, burial, and resurrection testimony found in 1 Corinthians 15 comes from the time of those events or within a few years of them. Furthermore, there are at least 40 other creeds in the New Testament that appear to be of very early origin.

So the documents are early and the sources are even earlier. But that's not enough to prove historicity beyond a reasonable doubt. To prove historicity, we need to be sure that these documents really contain *eyewitness* testimony. Do they? That's the question we'll investigate next.

10

Do We Have Eyewitness Testimony About Jesus?

"We did not follow cleverly invented stories when we told you about the power and coming of our Lord Jesus Christ, but we were eyewitnesses of his majesty."

—SIMON PETER

WE HAVE SEEN good evidence that the New Testament documents are early, so they meet historical test #1. But what about historical test #2? Do the New Testament documents contain eyewitness testimony? Let's begin by taking a look at the eyewitness claims of the New Testament writers.

If you accept the plain reading of the text, the New Testament certainly contains eyewitness testimony. Notice how many times various apostles claim to be eyewitnesses:

> God has raised this Jesus to life, and *we are all witnesses* of the fact (Acts 2:32).

> You killed the author of life, but God raised him from the dead. *We are witnesses* of this (Acts 3:15).

> Then [the rulers, elders, and teachers of the law] called them in again and commanded them not to speak or teach at all in the name of Jesus. But Peter and John replied, "Judge for yourselves whether it is right in God's sight to obey you rather than God. For we cannot help speaking about *what we have seen and heard*" (Acts 4:18-20).

The God of our fathers raised Jesus from the dead—whom you had killed by hanging him on a tree. God exalted him to his own right hand as Prince and Savior that he might give repentance and forgiveness of sins to Israel. *We are witnesses* of these things, and so is the Holy Spirit, whom God has given to those who obey him (Acts 5:30-32).

We are witnesses of everything he did in the country of the Jews and in Jerusalem. They killed him by hanging him on a tree, but God raised him from the dead on the third day and caused him to be seen (Acts 10:39-40).

. . . Christ died for our sins according to the Scriptures, that he was buried, that he was raised on the third day according to the Scriptures, and that he *appeared* to Peter, and then to the Twelve. After that, he *appeared* to more than five hundred of the brothers at the same time, most of whom are still living, though some have fallen asleep. Then he *appeared* to James, then to all the apostles, and last of all he *appeared* to me also, as to one abnormally born (1 Cor. 15:3-8).

To the elders among you, I appeal as a fellow elder, *a witness* of Christ's sufferings and one who also will share in the glory to be revealed (1 Pet. 5:1).

We did not follow cleverly invented stories when we told you about the power and coming of our Lord Jesus Christ, but *we were eyewitnesses* of his majesty (2 Pet. 1:16).

But when they came to Jesus and found that he was already dead, they did not break his legs. Instead, one of the soldiers pierced Jesus' side with a spear, bringing a sudden flow of blood and water. The man *who saw it* has given testimony, and his testimony is true (John 19:33-35).

Now Thomas (called Didymus), one of the Twelve, was not with the disciples when Jesus came. So the other disciples told him, *"We have seen the Lord!"* But he said to them, "Unless I see the nail marks in his hands and put my finger where the nails were, and put my hand into his side, I will not believe it." A week later his disciples were in the house again, and Thomas was with them. Though the doors were locked, Jesus came and stood among them and said, "Peace be with you!" Then he said to Thomas, *"Put your finger here; see my hands.*

Reach out your hand and put it into my side. Stop doubting and believe." Thomas said to him, "My Lord and my God!" Then Jesus told him, *"Because you have seen me,* you have believed; blessed are those who have not seen and yet have believed." *Jesus did many other miraculous signs in the presence of his disciples,* which are not recorded in this book (John 20:24-30).

That which was from the beginning, *which we have heard, which we have seen with our eyes, which we have looked at and our hands have touched*—this we proclaim concerning the Word of life. The life appeared; *we have seen it* and testify to it, and we proclaim to you the eternal life, which was with the Father and *has appeared to us* (1 John 1:1-2).

You get the impression that these folks wanted everyone to know they actually saw something, don't you? Furthermore, Luke and the writer of Hebrews claim to be informed by eyewitnesses:

Many have undertaken to draw up an account of the things that have been fulfilled among us, just as they were handed down to us by those who from the first *were eyewitnesses* and servants of the word (Luke 1:1-2).

This salvation, which was first announced by the Lord, *was confirmed to us by those who heard him.* God also testified to it by signs, wonders and various miracles, and gifts of the Holy Spirit distributed according to his will (Heb. 2:3-4).

In short, Peter, Paul, and John all claim to be eyewitnesses, and Luke and the writer of Hebrews claim to be informed by eyewitnesses. In addition, the New Testament writers name others who saw the Resurrection. Paul specifically lists 14 people whose names are known as eyewitnesses of the Resurrection (the 12 apostles, James, and himself) and claims that there were more than 500 others. Matthew and Luke confirm the appearances to the apostles. All four Gospels mention the women as witnesses, with Mark identifying them as Mary Magdalene, Mary the mother of James, and Salome. Luke adds Joanna. That's four more. Acts 1 also reveals that Joseph called Barsabbas was an eyewitness (Acts 1:23).

Not only do the apostles claim to be eyewitnesses, on several occasions they tell their audiences that everyone knows what they're saying is true. These are not offhanded comments but bold proclamations to powerful people.

Perhaps the boldest eyewitness claim comes from Paul as he stands trial before King Agrippa and Governor Festus. Paul has just begun to tell Agrippa and Festus why he has been converted to Christianity and how Christ rose from the dead as predicted by the Old Testament, when suddenly Festus interrupts and calls Paul insane! The dramatic exchange is recorded by Luke in Acts 26:24-28:

> At this point Festus interrupted Paul's defense. "You are out of your mind, Paul!" he shouted. "Your great learning is driving you insane."
>
> "I am not insane, most excellent Festus," Paul replied. "What I am saying is true and reasonable. The king is familiar with these things, and I can speak freely to him. I am convinced that none of this has escaped his notice, because it was not done in a corner. King Agrippa, do you believe the prophets? I know you do."
>
> Then Agrippa said to Paul, "Do you think that in such a short time you can persuade me to be a Christian?"

Do you see how brave, almost brash, Paul is? He not only boldly witnesses to the king and the governor, but he has the audacity to tell the king that he already knows Paul is telling the truth! Why is Paul so confident of this? Because the events of Christianity were "not done in a corner." They were common knowledge and surely had not "escaped [the king's] notice." Imagine a defendant challenging a ruler or judge in that way! Such a witness must know that the events he describes are well-known.

This provocative approach is taken by several New Testament characters, who are not shy about challenging their hearers to test the truth of their testimony. For example, the other apostles, led by Peter, are just as brash and confident when they are questioned by angry Jewish authorities. Luke records the incident in Acts 5:27-32:

> Having brought the apostles, they made them appear before the Sanhedrin to be questioned by the high priest. "We gave you strict

orders not to teach in this name," he said. "Yet you have filled Jerusalem with your teaching and are determined to make us guilty of this man's blood."

Peter and the other apostles replied: "We must obey God rather than men! The God of our fathers raised Jesus from the dead—whom you had killed by hanging him on a tree. God exalted him to his own right hand as Prince and Savior that he might give repentance and forgiveness of sins to Israel. We are witnesses of these things, and so is the Holy Spirit, whom God has given to those who obey him."

The account goes on to say that the Jewish authorities "were furious and wanted to put [the apostles] to death," but a well-respected Pharisee named Gamaliel talked them out of it.

The risk Paul, Peter, and the other apostles took to claim that they were providing eyewitness testimony certainly suggests that they were telling the truth. If these accounts are true, the apostles' unwavering testimony and provocative challenges demonstrate that they were eyewitnesses who really believed Jesus rose from the dead.

But are these accounts true? After all, why should we trust that Luke is telling us the truth about these events? It's one thing to claim that you're an eyewitness or have eyewitness testimony, and it's another thing to prove it. What evidence do we have that the New Testament writers were really eyewitnesses or had access to eyewitness testimony? Much more than you might think.

WERE THEY REALLY EYEWITNESSES?

Eyewitness Evidence: Luke

Suppose someone wrote a book in 1980 describing your hometown as it was that year. In the book, the author correctly describes: your town's politicians, its unique laws and penal codes, the local industry, local weather patterns, local slang, the town's roads and geography, its unusual topography, local houses of worship, area hotels, town statues and sculptures, the depth of the water in the town harbor, and numerous other unique details about your town that year. Question: If the author claimed he had visited your town that year—or said he had gotten good information from people who had been there—would you think he was telling the truth? Of course, because he provides details that only an eyewitness could provide. That's the type of testimony we have throughout much of the New Testament.

Luke includes the most eyewitness details. (While Luke may not have been an eyewitness to the Resurrection itself, he certainly was an eyewitness to many New Testament events.) In the second half of Acts, for example, Luke displays an incredible array of knowledge of local places, names, environmental conditions, customs, and circumstances that befit only an eyewitness contemporary of the time and events.

Classical scholar and historian Colin Hemer chronicles Luke's accuracy in the book of Acts verse by verse. With painstaking detail, Hemer identifies 84 facts in the last 16 chapters of Acts that have been confirmed by historical and archaeological research.[1] As you read the following list, keep in mind that Luke did not have access to modern-day maps or nautical charts. Luke accurately records:

1. the natural crossing between correctly named ports (Acts 13:4-5)
2. the proper port (Perga) along the direct destination of a ship crossing from Cyprus (13:13)
3. the proper location of Lycaonia (14:6)
4. the unusual but correct declension of the name Lystra (14:6)
5. the correct language spoken in Lystra—Lycaonian (14:11)
6. two gods known to be so associated—Zeus and Hermes (14:12)
7. the proper port, Attalia, which returning travelers would use (14:25)
8. the correct order of approach to Derbe and then Lystra from the Cilician Gates (16:1; cf. 15:41)
9. the proper form of the name Troas (16:8)
10. the place of a conspicuous sailors' landmark, Samothrace (16:11)
11. the proper description of Philippi as a Roman colony (16:12)
12. the right location for the river (Gangites) near Philippi (16:13)
13. the proper association of Thyatira as a center of dyeing (16:14)
14. correct designations for the magistrates of the colony (16:22)
15. the proper locations (Amphipolis and Apollonia) where travelers would spend successive nights on this journey (17:1)
16. the presence of a synagogue in Thessalonica (17:1)

17. the proper term ("politarchs") used of the magistrates there (17:6)
18. the correct implication that sea travel is the most convenient way of reaching Athens, with the favoring east winds of summer sailing (17:14-15)
19. the abundant presence of images in Athens (17:16)
20. the reference to a synagogue in Athens (17:17)
21. the depiction of the Athenian life of philosophical debate in the Agora (17:17)
22. the use of the correct Athenian slang word for Paul (*spermologos,* 17:18) as well as for the court (*Areios pagos,* 17:19)
23. the proper characterization of the Athenian character (17:21)
24. an altar to an "unknown god" (17:23)
25. the proper reaction of Greek philosophers, who denied the bodily resurrection (17:32)
26. *Areopagites* as the correct title for a member of the court (17:34)
27. a Corinthian synagogue (18:4)
28. the correct designation of Gallio as proconsul, resident in Corinth (18:12)
29. the *bema* (judgment seat), which overlooks Corinth's *forum* (18:16ff.)
30. the name Tyrannus as attested from Ephesus in first-century inscriptions (19:9)
31. well-known shrines and images of Artemis (19:24)
32. the well-attested "great goddess Artemis" (19:27)
33. that the Ephesian theater was the meeting place of the city (19:29)
34. the correct title *grammateus* for the chief executive magistrate in Ephesus (19:35)
35. the proper title of honor *neokoros,* authorized by the Romans (19:35)
36. the correct name to designate the goddess (19:37)
37. the proper term for those holding court (19:38)
38. use of plural *anthupatoi,* perhaps a remarkable reference to the fact that *two* men were conjointly exercising the functions of proconsul at this time (19:38)
39. the "regular" assembly, as the precise phrase is attested elsewhere (19:39)

40. use of precise ethnic designation, *beroiaios* (20:4)
41. employment of the ethnic term *Asianos* (20:4)
42. the implied recognition of the strategic importance assigned to this city of Troas (20:7ff.)
43. the danger of the coastal trip in this location (20:13)
44. the correct sequence of places (20:14-15)
45. the correct name of the city as a neuter plural (*Patara*) (21:1)
46. the appropriate route passing across the open sea south of Cyprus favored by persistent northwest winds (21:3)
47. the suitable distance between these cities (21:8)
48. a characteristically Jewish act of piety (21:24)
49. the Jewish law regarding Gentile use of the temple area (21:28) (Archaeological discoveries and quotations from Josephus confirm that Gentiles could be executed for entering the temple area. One inscription reads: "Let no Gentile enter within the balustrade and enclosure surrounding the sanctuary. Whoever is caught will be personally responsible for his consequent death."[2])
50. the permanent stationing of a Roman cohort (*chiliarch*) at Antonia to suppress any disturbance at festival times (21:31)
51. the flight of steps used by the guards (21:31, 35)
52. the common way to obtain Roman citizenship at this time (22:28)
53. the tribune being impressed with Roman rather than Tarsian citizenship (22:29)
54. Ananias being high priest at this time (23:2)
55. Felix being governor at this time (23:34)
56. the natural stopping point on the way to Caesarea (23:31)
57. whose jurisdiction Cilicia was in at the time (23:34)
58. the provincial penal procedure of the time (24:1-9)
59. the name Porcius Festus, which agrees precisely with that given by Josephus (24:27)
60. the right of appeal for Roman citizens (25:11)
61. the correct legal formula (25:18)
62. the characteristic form of reference to the emperor at the time (25:26)
63. the best shipping lanes at the time (27:5)
64. the common bonding of Cilicia and Pamphylia (27:4)
65. the principal port to find a ship sailing to Italy (27:5-6)

66. the slow passage to Cnidus, in the face of the typical north-west wind (27:7)
67. the right route to sail, in view of the winds (27:7)
68. the locations of Fair Havens and the neighboring site of Lasea (27:8)
69. Fair Havens as a poorly sheltered roadstead (27:12)
70. a noted tendency of a south wind in these climes to back suddenly to a violent northeaster, the well-known *gregale* (27:13)
71. the nature of a square-rigged ancient ship, having no option but to be driven before a gale (27:15)
72. the precise place and name of this island (27:16)
73. the appropriate maneuvers for the safety of the ship in its particular plight (27:16)
74. the fourteenth night—a remarkable calculation, based inevitably on a compounding of estimates and probabilities, confirmed in the judgment of experienced Mediterranean navigators (27:27)
75. the proper term of the time for the Adriatic (27:27)
76. the precise term (*Bolisantes*) for taking soundings, and the correct depth of the water near Malta (27:28)
77. a position that suits the probable line of approach of a ship released to run before an easterly wind (27:39)
78. the severe liability on guards who permitted a prisoner to escape (27:42)
79. the local people and superstitions of the day (28:4-6)
80. the proper title *protos tēs nēsou* (28:7)
81. Rhegium as a refuge to await a southerly wind to carry them through the strait (28:13)
82. Appii Forum and Tres Tabernae as correctly placed stopping places on the Appian Way (28:15)
83. appropriate means of custody with Roman soldiers (28:16)
84. the conditions of imprisonment, living "at his own expense" (28:30-31)

Is there any doubt that Luke was an eyewitness to these events or at least had access to reliable eyewitness testimony? What more could he have done to prove his authenticity as a historian?

Roman historian A. N. Sherwin-White says, "For Acts the confirmation of historicity is overwhelming. . . . Any attempt to reject its basic historicity must now appear absurd. Roman historians have long taken it for granted."[3] Classical scholar and archaeologist William M. Ramsay began his investigation into Acts with great skepticism, but his discoveries helped change his mind. He wrote:

> I began with a mind unfavorable to it [Acts]. . . . It did not lie then in my line of life to investigate the subject minutely; but more recently I found myself often brought into contact with the book of Acts as an authority for the topography, antiquities, and society of Asia Minor. It was gradually borne in upon me that in various details the narrative showed marvelous truth.[4]

Indeed, Luke's accuracy in Acts is truly amazing.

Now, here's where skeptics get very uncomfortable. Luke reports a total of 35 miracles in the same book in which he records all 84 of these historically confirmed details.[5] Several miracles of Paul are recorded in the second half of Acts. For example, Luke records that Paul: temporarily blinded a sorcerer (13:11); cured a man who was crippled from birth (14:8); exorcized an evil spirit from a possessed girl (16:18); "performed many miracles" that convinced many in the city of Ephesus to turn from sorcery to Jesus (19:11-20); raised a man from the dead who had died after falling out of a window during Paul's long-winded lecture (20:9-10); healed Publius's father of dysentery, and healed numerous others who were sick on Malta (28:8-9). All of these miracles are included in the same historical narrative that has been confirmed as authentic on 84 points. And the miracle accounts show no signs of embellishment or extravagance—they are told with the same level-headed efficiency as the rest of the historical narrative.

Now, why would Luke be so accurate with trivial details like wind directions, water depths, and peculiar town names, but not be accurate when it comes to important events like miracles? In light of the fact that Luke has proven accurate with so many trivial details, it is nothing but pure anti-supernatural bias to say he's not telling the truth about the miracles he records. As we have seen, such a bias is illegitimate. This is a theistic world where miracles are possible. So it makes much more sense to believe Luke's miracle accounts than to discount them. In other words, Luke's credentials as a historian have been proven on so many points that it takes more faith *not* to believe his miracle accounts than to believe them.

Is Luke's Gospel "Gospel?"

What about the Gospel of Luke? First, we need to recognize that Acts and the Gospel of Luke are closely related books. How do we know? First, both documents contain the same Greek vocabulary and literary style. But more important, Luke addresses both documents to "most excellent Theophilus." He was probably some kind of Roman official because "most excellent" is the same title Paul used to address the Roman governors Felix and Festus.[6]

Regardless of the true identity of Theophilus, the main point is that Luke reveals that Acts is a continuation of his Gospel. His opening says, "In my *former book,* Theophilus, I wrote about all that Jesus began to do and to teach until the day he was taken up to heaven . . ." (Acts 1:1). Luke uses the remainder of Acts to tell Theophilus what happened after Christ's ascension. And as we have seen, he did so with amazing precision.

Should we expect the same degree of accuracy from Luke's Gospel? Why not? In fact, Luke says as much when he writes, "Since I myself have *carefully* investigated everything from the beginning, it seemed good also to me to write an orderly account for you, most excellent Theophilus" (Luke 1:3). Judging from his meticulous work in Acts, Luke certainly is a careful historian who should be trusted. As New Testament scholar Craig Blomberg observes, "A historian who has been found trustworthy where he or she can be tested should be given the benefit of the doubt in cases where no tests are available."[7] Since Luke has been tested on 84 points and has earned a perfect score, there's every reason to believe his Gospel is "gospel" as well.

But we don't need to rely solely on his work in Acts to confirm Luke's Gospel. There are several details in Luke's Gospel that have been verified independently. For example, Luke names eleven historically confirmed leaders in the first three chapters of his Gospel alone (twelve if you include Jesus). These include Herod the Great, (1:5), Caesar Augustus (2:1), and Quirinius (2:2). He then writes this at the beginning of chapter 3:

> In the fifteenth year of the reign of Tiberius Caesar—when Pontius Pilate was governor of Judea, Herod tetrarch of Galilee, his brother Philip tetrarch of Iturea and Traconitis, and Lysanias tetrarch of

Abilene—during the high priesthood of Annas and Caiaphas, the word of God came to John son of Zechariah in the desert. He went into all the country around the Jordan, preaching a baptism of repentance for the forgiveness of sins.

Does this sound like Luke is making up a story? Of course not. If he were, there would be no way he would put historical crosshairs on the events he's describing by naming these prominent leaders and their dates. As Bible scholar F. F. Bruce observes, "A writer who thus relates his story to the wider context of world history is courting trouble if he is not careful; he affords his critical readers so many opportunities for testing his accuracy. Luke takes this risk, and stands the test admirably."[8] Indeed, all eleven of the historical figures Luke names in the first three chapters of his Gospel—including John the Baptist (son of Zechariah)—have been confirmed by non-Christian writers and/or archaeology. For example, John the Baptist is mentioned by Josephus (*Antiquities* 18:5.2), and an inscription dating from A.D. 14 to 29 bears the name of Lysanias.

Another historically accurate detail can be found in Luke 22:44. That's where Luke records that Jesus was in agony and sweat drops of blood the night before his crucifixion. Apparently, Jesus was experiencing a rare stress-induced condition we know today as hematohidrosis. That's when tiny blood vessels rupture due to extreme stress, thus allowing blood to mix with sweat. Since Luke probably didn't know of this medical condition 2,000 years ago, he could not have recorded it unless he had access to someone who saw it.

Details like this led William Ramsay (mentioned above) to say, "Luke's history is unsurpassed in respect of its trustworthiness," and "Luke is an historian of the first rank. . . . [He] should be placed along with the very greatest of historians."[9] The bottom line is that Luke can be trusted. Since he has been confirmed independently on so many testable points, there's every reason to believe he's telling the truth elsewhere.

Now here's the crucial point: *Since Luke is telling the truth, then so are Mark and Matthew because their Gospels tell the same basic story.* This is devastating to skeptics, but the logic is inescapable. *You need a lot of faith to ignore it.*

Eyewitness Evidence: John

Luke has proven reliable—and by implication Matthew and Mark—but what about John? The critics claim that John is a much later work that expresses an invented deity-of-Christ theology, so it cannot be trusted for accurate historical information. But if the critics are wrong and John is accurate, then we have another independent witness to conclude that the basic New Testament story is true. So how accurate is John? What does the evidence say?

On the face of it, John appears to be an eyewitness because he includes intimate details about numerous private conversations of Jesus (see John 3, 4, 8–10, and 13–17). But there's actually much more powerful evidence for John being an eyewitness—evidence of nearly the same character as what we have seen for Acts.

Like the work Colin Hemer did on Acts, Craig Blomberg has done a detailed study of the Gospel of John. Blomberg's *The Historical Reliability of John's Gospel*[10] examines John's Gospel verse by verse and identifies numerous historical details.

Since John describes events confined to the Holy Land, his Gospel doesn't contain quite as many geographical, topographical, and political items as does Acts. Nevertheless, as we're about to see, quite an impressive number of historically confirmed or historically probable details are contained in John's Gospel. Many of these details have been confirmed to be historical by archaeology and/or non-Christian writings, and some of them are historically probable because they would be unlikely inventions of a Christian writer. These details begin in John's second chapter and comprise the following list:

1. Archaeology confirms the use of stone water jars in New Testament times (John 2:6).
2. Given the early Christian tendency towards asceticism, the wine miracle is an unlikely invention (2:8).
3. Archaeology confirms the proper place of Jacob's Well (4:6).
4. Josephus (*Wars of the Jews* 2.232) confirms there was significant hostility between Jews and Samaritans during Jesus' time (4:9).
5. "Come down" accurately describes the topography of western Galilee. (There's a significant elevation drop from Cana to Capernaum.) (4:46, 49, 51).[11]

6. "Went up" accurately describes the ascent to Jerusalem (5:1).

7. Archaeology confirms the proper location and description of the five colonnades at the pool of Bethesda (5:2). (Excavations between 1914 and 1938 uncovered that pool and found it to be just as John described it. Since that structure did not exist after the Romans destroyed the city in A.D. 70, it's unlikely any later non-eyewitness could have described it in such vivid detail. Moreover, John says that this structure "*is* in Jerusalem," implying that he's writing before 70.)

8. Jesus' own testimony being invalid without the Father is an unlikely Christian invention (5:31); a later redactor would be eager to highlight Jesus' divinity and would probably make his witness self-authenticating.

9. The crowds wanting to make Jesus king reflects the well-known nationalist fervor of early first-century Israel (6:15).

10. Sudden and severe squalls are common on the Sea of Galilee (6:18).

11. Christ's command to eat his flesh and drink his blood would not be made up (6:53).

12. The rejection of Jesus by many of his disciples is also an unlikely invention (6:66).

13. The two predominant opinions of Jesus, one that Jesus was a "good man" and the other that he "deceives people," would not be the two choices John would have made up (7:12); a later Christian writer would have probably inserted the opinion that Jesus was God.

14. The charge of Jesus being demon-possessed is an unlikely invention (7:20).

15. The use of "Samaritan" to slander Jesus befits the hostility between Jews and Samaritans (8:48).

16. Jewish *believers* wanting to stone Jesus is an unlikely invention (8:31, 59).

17. Archaeology confirms the existence and location of the Pool of Siloam (9:7).

18. Expulsion from the synagogue by the Pharisees was a legitimate fear of the Jews; notice that the healed man professes his faith in Jesus only *after* he is expelled from the synagogue by the Pharisees (9:13-39), at which point he has nothing to lose. This rings of authenticity.

19. The healed man calling Jesus a "prophet" rather than anything more lofty suggests the incident is unembellished history (9:17).

20. During a winter feast, Jesus walked in Solomon's Colonnade, which was the only side of the temple area shielded from the cold winter east wind (10:22-23); this area is mentioned several times by Josephus.

21. Fifteen stadia (less than two miles) is precisely the distance from Bethany to Jerusalem (11:18).

22. Given the later animosity between Christians and Jews, the positive depiction of Jews comforting Martha and Mary is an unlikely invention (11:19).

23. The burial wrappings of Lazarus were common for first-century Jewish burials (11:44); it is unlikely that a fiction writer would have included this theologically irrelevant detail.

24. The precise description of the composition of the Sanhedrin (11:47): it was composed primarily of chief priests (largely Sadducees) and Pharisees during Jesus' ministry.

25. Caiaphas was indeed the high priest that year (11:49); we learn from Josephus that Caiaphas held the office from A.D. 18–37.

26. The obscure and tiny village of Ephraim (11:54) near Jerusalem is mentioned by Josephus.

27. Ceremonial cleansing was common in preparation for the Passover (11:55).

28. Anointing of a guest's feet with perfume or oil was sometimes performed for special guests in the Jewish culture (12:3); Mary's wiping of Jesus' feet with her hair is an unlikely invention (it easily could have been perceived as a sexual advance).

29. Waving of palm branches was a common Jewish practice for celebrating military victories and welcoming national rulers (12:13).

30. Foot washing in first-century Palestine was necessary because of dust and open footwear; Jesus performing this menial task is an unlikely invention (it was a task not even Jewish *slaves* were required to do) (13:4); Peter's insistence that he get a complete bath also fits with his impulsive personality (there's certainly no purpose for inventing this request).

31. Peter asks John to ask Jesus a question (13:24); there's no reason to insert this detail if this is fiction; Peter could have asked Jesus himself.

32. "The Father is greater than I" is an unlikely invention (14:28), especially if John wanted to make up the deity of Christ (as the critics claim he did).

33. Use of the vine as a metaphor makes good sense in Jerusalem (15:1); vineyards were in the vicinity of the temple, and, according to Josephus, the temple gates had a golden vine carved on them.

34. Use of the childbirth metaphor (16:21) is thoroughly Jewish; it has been found in the Dead Sea Scrolls (1QH 11:9-10).

35. The standard Jewish posture for prayers was looking "toward heaven" (17:1).

36. Jesus' admission that he has gotten his words from the Father (17:7-8) would not be included if John were inventing the idea that Christ was God.

37. No specific reference to fulfilled Scripture is given regarding the predicted betrayal by Judas; a fiction writer or later Christian redactor probably would have identified the Old Testament Scripture to which Jesus was referring (17:12).

38. The name of the high priest's servant (Malchus), who had his ear cut off, is an unlikely invention (18:10).

39. Proper identification of Caiaphas's father-in-law, Annas, who was the high priest from A.D. 6–15 (18:13)—the appearance before Annas is believable because of the family connection and the fact that former high priests maintained great influence.

40. John's claim that the high priest knew him (18:15) seems historical; invention of this claim serves no purpose and would expose John to being discredited by the Jewish authorities.

41. Annas's questions regarding Jesus' teachings and disciples make good historical sense; Annas would be concerned about potential civil unrest and the undermining of Jewish religious authority (18:19).

42. Identification of a relative of Malchus (the high priest's servant who had his ear cut off) is a detail that John would not have made up (18:26); it has no theological significance and could only hurt John's credibility if he were trying to pass off fiction as the truth.

43. There are good historical reasons to believe Pilate's reluctance to deal with Jesus (18:28ff.): Pilate had to walk a fine line between keeping the Jews happy and keeping Rome happy; any civil unrest could mean his job (the Jews knew of his competing concerns when they taunted him with, "If you let this man go, you are no friend of Caesar. Anyone who claims to be a king opposes Caesar," 19:12); the Jewish philosopher Philo records the Jews successfully pressuring Pilate in a similar way to get their demands met (*To Gaius* 38.301-302).

44. A surface similar to the Stone Pavement has been identified near the Antonia Fortress (19:13) with markings that may indicate soldiers played games there (as in the gambling for his clothes in 19:24).

45. The Jews exclaiming "We have no king but Caesar!" (19:15) would not be invented given the Jewish hatred for the Romans, especially if John had been written after A.D. 70. (This would be like New Yorkers today proclaiming "We have no king but Osama Bin Laden!")

46. The crucifixion of Jesus (19:17-30) is attested to by non-Christian sources such as Josephus, Tacitus, Lucian, and the Jewish Talmud.

47. Crucifixion victims normally carried their own crossbeams (19:17).

48. Josephus confirms that crucifixion was an execution technique employed by the Romans (*Wars of the Jews* 1.97; 2.305; 7.203); moreover, a nail-spiked anklebone of a crucified man was found in Jerusalem in 1968 (more on this in chapter 12).

49. The execution site was likely outside ancient Jerusalem, as John says (19:17); this would ensure that the sacred Jewish city would not be profaned by the presence of a dead body (Deut. 21:23).

50. After the spear was thrust into Jesus' side, out came what appeared to be blood and water (19:34). Today we know that a crucified person might have a watery fluid gather in the sac around the heart called the pericardium.[12] John would not have known of this medical condition, and could not have recorded this phenomenon unless he was an eyewitness or had access to eyewitness testimony.[13]

51. Joseph of Arimathea (19:38), a member of the Sanhedrin who buries Jesus, is an unlikely invention (more on this in the next chapter).

52. Josephus (*Antiquities* 17.199) confirms that spices (19:39) were used for royal burials; this detail shows that Nicodemus was not expecting Jesus to rise from the dead, and it also demonstrates that John was not inserting later Christian faith into the text.

53. Mary Magdalene (20:1), a formerly *demon-possessed* woman (Luke 8:2), would not be invented as the empty tomb's first witness; in fact, women in general would not be presented as witnesses in a made-up story (more on this later as well).

54. Mary mistaking Jesus for the gardener (20:15) is not a detail that a later writer would have made up (especially a writer seeking to exalt Jesus).

55. "Rabboni" (20:16), the Aramaic for "teacher," seems an authentic detail because it's another unlikely invention for a writer trying to exalt the risen Jesus.

56. Jesus stating that he is returning to "my God and your God" (20:17) does not fit with a later writer bent on creating the idea that Jesus was God.

57. One hundred fifty-three fish (21:11) is a theologically irrelevant detail, but perfectly consistent with the tendency of fisherman to want to record and then brag about large catches.

58. The fear of the disciples to ask Jesus who he was (21:12) is an unlikely concoction; it demonstrates natural human amazement at the risen Jesus and perhaps the fact that there was something different about the resurrection body.

59. The cryptic statement from Jesus about the fate of Peter is not clear enough to draw certain theological conclusions (21:18); so why would John make it up? It's another unlikely invention.

When we couple John's knowledge of Jesus' personal conversations with these nearly sixty historically confirmed/historically probable details, is there any doubt that John was an eyewitness or at least had access to eyewitness testimony? It certainly seems to us that it takes a lot more faith *not* to believe John's Gospel than to believe it.

HISTORICAL CROSSHAIRS

Let's review what we've found so far. By looking at just a few New Testament documents (John, Luke, and half of Acts), we have found more than 140 details that appear to be authentic, most of which have been historically confirmed and some of which are historically probable. If we investigated the other New Testament documents, we would probably find many more historical facts. Time and space does not permit us to embark on such an investigation. But what we have found just from John, Luke, and Acts is certainly enough to establish the historicity of the basic New Testament story (the life of Jesus and the early history of the church).

But there's even more evidence of historicity. The New Testament writers put historical crosshairs into their accounts by referencing real historical figures and their doings. All in all, *there are at least thirty characters in the New Testament who have been confirmed as historical by archaeology or non-Christian sources*[14] (see table 10.1 on the next page).

For example, Matthew mentions independently confirmed historical figures including Herod the Great (2:3) and his three sons: Herod Archelaus (2:22), Herod Philip (14:3), and Herod Antipas (14:1-11). Matthew also describes the man Herod Antipas killed, John the Baptist (chapter 14, introduced in chapter 3) along with the two women who instigated the killing, Herodias and her daughter. Mark tells the same story about Herod Antipas and John the Baptist (6:14ff.). And Luke extends the biblical citations of the Herodian bloodline by mentioning Herod the Great's grandson, Agrippa I, the king who killed James, John's brother (Acts 12); and his great-grandson, Agrippa II, the king before whom Paul testified (Acts 25:13–26:32).

Pilate is a prominent figure in all four Gospels and is cited by Paul.[15] This same Pilate appears on several occasions in two of Josephus's works (*Antiquities* and *The Wars of the Jews*), and is identified in an ancient inscription as the prefect (governor) of Judea. This archaeological discovery was made in the Israeli costal town of Caesarea in 1961.

In addition to Pilate, Matthew, Luke, and John specifically name another leader who figured prominently in Jesus' death—the high priest Caiaphas, who sentenced Jesus to die.[16] Caiaphas is not only mentioned by Josephus, but his actual bones were discovered in a fantastic archaeological discovery in 1990. This discovery was made possible by an ancient burial practice of the Jews.

New Testament Figures Cited by Non-Christian Writers and/or Confirmed Through Archaeology

Person	NT Citation	Non-Christian Source(s)*
Jesus	many citations	Josephus, Tacitus, Pliny the Younger, Phlegon, Thallus, Suetonius, Lucian, Celsus, Mara Bar-Serapion, The Jewish Talmud
Agrippa I	Acts 12:1-24	Philo, Josephus
Agrippa II	Acts 25:13–26:32	coins, Josephus
Ananias	Acts 23:2; 24:1	Josephus
Annas	Luke 3:2; John 18:13, 24; Acts 4:6	Josephus
Aretas	2 Cor. 11:32	Josephus
Bernice (wife of Agrippa II)	Acts 23:13	Josephus
Caesar Augustus	Luke 2:1	Josephus and others
Caiaphas	several citations	ossuary, Josephus
Claudius	Acts 11:28; 18:2	Josephus
Drusilla (wife of Felix)	Acts 24:24	Josephus
Egyptian false prophet	Acts 21:38	Josephus
Erastus	Acts 19:22	inscription
Felix	Acts 23:24–25:14	Tacitus, Josephus
Gallio	Acts 18:12-17	inscription
Gamaliel	Acts 5:34; 22:3	Josephus
Herod Antipas	Matt. 14:1-12; Mark 6:14-29; Luke 3:1; 23:7-12	Josephus
Herod Archelaus	Matt. 2:22	Josephus
Herod the Great	Matt. 2:1-19; Luke 1:5	Tacitus, Josephus,
Herod Philip I	Matt. 14:3; Mark 6:17	Josephus
Herod Philip II	Luke 3:1	Josephus
Herodias	Matt. 14:3; Mark 6:17	Josephus
Herodias's daughter (Salome)	Matt. 14:1-12; Mark 6:14-29	Josephus
James	several citations	Josephus
John the Baptist	several citations	Josephus
Judas the Galilean	Acts 5:37	Josephus
Lysanias	Luke 3:1	inscription, Josephus
Pilate	several citations	inscription, coins, Josephus, Philo, Tacitus
Quirinius	Luke 2:2	Josephus
Porcius Festus	Acts 24:27–26:32	Josephus
Sergius Paulus	Acts 13:6-12	inscription
Tiberius Caesar	Luke 3:1	Tacitus, Suetonius, Paterculus, Dio Cassius, Josephus

*Note: This is not an exhaustive compilation of non-Christian references. There may be additional citations of these New Testament figures in these and/or other non-Christian sources.

Table 10.1

From about 20 B.C. to A.D. 70 the Jews had a custom of exhuming the body of an important person about a year after his death and placing the remains in a small limestone box called an ossuary. In a tomb located to the south of Jerusalem, several of these ossuaries were discovered, one of which bore the Aramaic inscription "Yehosef bar Kayafa" (Joseph son of Caiaphas). Inside were bones of an entire family: four young people, an adult woman, and a sixty-year-old man. The man is very likely the former high priest Joseph Caiaphas—the same man whom Josephus identified as the high priest[17] and the same man the New Testament says sentenced Jesus to die.[18] So now we not only have non-Christian written references to the high priest at Jesus' trial; we also have his bones![19]

As table 10.1 illustrates, there are several other New Testament figures confirmed outside the New Testament. These include Quirinius, Sergius Paulus, Gallio, Felix, Festus, Augustus Caesar, Tiberius Caesar, and Claudius.[20] What else could the New Testament writers have done to prove that they were eyewitnesses who were not making up a story?

THE NEW TESTAMENT: A HISTORICAL NOVEL OR NOVEL HISTORY?

In spite of these 140-plus eyewitness details and 30-plus references to real people, a hardened skeptic might say, "But that doesn't necessarily mean that the New Testament is true. Suppose it's a historical novel—fiction set in a real historical context—something similar to a Tom Clancy novel?"

There are many problems with this theory. First, it can't explain why independent non-Christian writers collectively reveal a storyline similar to the New Testament. If the New Testament events are fictional, then why do the non-Christian writers record some of them as though they actually occurred?

Second, it can't explain why the New Testament writers endured persecution, torture, and death. Why would they have done so for a fictional story? (More on this in the next chapter.)

Third, historical novelists usually do not use the names of real people for the main characters in their stories. If they did, those real people—especially powerful government and religious officials—would deny the story, destroy the credibility of the authors, and maybe even take punitive action against them for doing so. As we have seen, the New Testament includes at least thirty actual historical figures who have been confirmed by non-Christian sources, and many of these are prominent and powerful leaders.

Finally, since the New Testament contains multiple independent accounts of these events by nine different authors, the historical novel theory would require a grand conspiracy over a 20- to 50-year period between those nine authors, who were spread all over the ancient world. This is not plausible either. In fact, the assertion that the New Testament events are part of a grand conspiracy exists only in novels. In the real world, such assertions are crushed by the weight of the evidence.

THE NEW TESTAMENT: ONE SOURCE OR MANY?

"Wait!" the skeptic might protest. "You might have eyewitness testimony, but you can't believe the New Testament because it's just from one source. They are not 'multiple independent accounts' as you say!" This is a common error skeptics make because they fail to distinguish between the Bible as a "religious book" and the historical documents that comprise the Bible.

When considering the historicity of the New Testament, we constantly must remind ourselves that the New Testament we see in the Bible is a *collection* of largely independent writings from the pens of nine different authors. It was not written or edited by one person or by the church. While the New Testament writers describe many of the same events and may even draw material from the same earlier sources, the evidence indicates that the New Testament documents contain several lines of independent eyewitness testimony.

How do we know we have independent eyewitness testimony? Because 1) each major author includes early and unique material that only eyewitnesses would know, and 2) their accounts describe the same basic events but include divergent details. Why are divergent details important? Because if the accounts were all from one source or a single editor, there would be harmonization, not divergence of details. When early accounts tell the same basic story but include divergent details, historians rightly conclude they have independent eyewitness accounts of actual historical events (historical test #3 from page 231). The story certainly cannot be made up, because independent sources could never invent the same fictional story.

By these criteria, we know that John and Mark are independent, and we know that Luke and Matthew differ enough from Mark and from one another to be the products of independent attestation as well. So there are at least four independent sources for the basic New Testament story, and, adding Paul (1 Cor. 15:8) and Peter (1 Pet. 1:21) to the mix, there are at least six independent sources for the Resurrection.

Six sane, sober eyewitnesses, who refuse to recant their testimony even under the threat of death, would convict anyone of anything in a court of law (even without the additional lines of corroborating evidence that support the New Testament story). Such eyewitness testimony yields a verdict that is certain beyond a reasonable doubt. Unless you saw the event yourself, you can't be any more certain that those historical events actually occurred.

SUMMARY AND CONCLUSION

1. We saw from chapter 9 that:
    a. The New Testament documents are early and contain even earlier source material.
    b. At least 10 ancient non-Christian writers within 150 years of his life give information about Jesus, and their collective references provide a storyline consistent with the New Testament.
2. From this chapter we conclude:
    a. The New Testament contains at least four to six lines of *early, independent eyewitness* written testimony. We conclude this because:
        i. The major New Testament writers record the same basic events with diverging details and some unique material.
        ii. They cite at least thirty real historical figures who have been confirmed by ancient non-Christian writers and various archaeological discoveries.
        iii. Luke peppers the second half of Acts with at least 84 historically confirmed eyewitness details and includes several others in his Gospel.

iv. Luke's proven trustworthiness affirms that of Matthew and Mark because they record the same basic story.

v. John includes at least 59 historically confirmed or historically probable eyewitness details in his Gospel.

vi. Paul and Peter provide the fifth and sixth written testimonies to the Resurrection.

b. Since this early, independent eyewitness testimony is within one generation of the events, the New Testament events cannot be considered legendary.

So there's no question that real historical events are at the core of the New Testament. *The bottom line is that a skeptic has to have a lot of faith to believe that the New Testament is fictional.*

However, there are more issues to investigate before concluding that the New Testament is definitely historically reliable. For example, how do we know that the eyewitness testimony is not exaggerated or embellished? That's the question we'll address in the next chapter.

The Top Ten Reasons
We Know the
New Testament Writers
Told the Truth

*"Why would the apostles lie? . . . If they lied, what was
their motive, what did they get out of it? What they got
out of it was misunderstanding, rejection, persecution,
torture, and martyrdom. Hardly a list of perks!"*

—PETER KREEFT

WE HAVE SEEN very powerful evidence that the major New Testament
documents were written by eyewitnesses and their contemporaries within
15 to 40 years of the death of Jesus. Add to that the confirmation from
non-Christian sources and archaeology, and we know beyond a reasonable doubt that the New Testament is based on historical fact. But how
do we know the authors did not exaggerate or embellish what they say
they saw? There are at least ten reasons we can be confident that the New
Testament writers did not play fast and loose with the facts.

1. THE NEW TESTAMENT WRITERS INCLUDED
EMBARRASSING DETAILS ABOUT THEMSELVES

One of the ways historians can tell whether an author is telling the truth
is to test what he says by "the principle of embarrassment" (historical
test #7 from page 231). This principle assumes that any details embarrassing to the author are probably true. Why? Because the tendency of
most authors is to leave out anything that makes them look bad.

How does the New Testament measure up to the principle of embarrassment? Let's put it this way: If you and your friends were concocting a story that you wanted to pass off as the truth, would you make yourselves look like dim-witted, uncaring, rebuked, doubting cowards? Of course not. But that's exactly what we find in the New Testament. The people who wrote down much of the New Testament are characters (or friends of characters) in the story, and often they depict themselves as complete morons:

- They are dim-witted—numerous times they fail to understand what Jesus is saying (Mark 9:32; Luke 18:34; John 12:16).
- They are uncaring—they fall asleep on Jesus twice when he asks them to pray (Mark 14:32-41). The New Testament writers later believe Jesus is the God-man, yet they admit they twice fell asleep on him in his hour of greatest need! Moreover, they make no effort to give their friend a proper burial, but record that Jesus was buried by Joseph of Arimathea, a member of the Jewish Sanhedrin—the very court that had sentenced Jesus to die.
- They are rebuked—Peter is called "Satan" by Jesus (Mark 8:33), and Paul rebukes Peter for being wrong about a theological issue. Paul writes, "When Peter came to Antioch, I opposed him to his face, because he was clearly in the wrong" (Gal. 2:11). Now keep in mind that Peter is one of the pillars of the early church, and here's Paul including in Scripture that he was wrong!
- They are cowards—all the disciples but one hide when Jesus goes to the cross. Peter even denies him three times after explicitly promising, "I will never disown you" (Matt. 26:33-35). Meanwhile, as the men are hiding for fear of the Jews, the brave women stand by Jesus and are the first to discover the empty tomb.
- They are doubters—despite being taught several times that Jesus would rise from the dead (John 2:18-22; 3:14-18; Matt. 12:39-41; 17:9, 22-23), the disciples are doubtful when they hear of his resurrection. Some are even doubtful *after* they see him risen (Matt. 28:17)!

Now think about this: If you were a New Testament writer, would you include these embarrassing details if you were making up a story? Would you write that one of your primary leaders was called "Satan" by Jesus, denied the Lord three times, hid during the crucifixion, and was later corrected on a theological issue? Would you depict yourselves as uncaring, bumbling cowards, and the women—whose testimony was not even admissible in court—as the brave ones who stood by Jesus and later discovered the empty tomb? Would you admit that some of you (the eleven remaining disciples) doubted the very Son of God *after* he had proven himself risen to all of you? Of course not.

What do you think the New Testament writers would have done if they were making up a story? You know perfectly well: they would have left out their ineptness, their cowardice, the rebuke, the three denials, and their theological problems, and depicted themselves as bold believers who stood by Jesus through it all and who confidently marched down to the tomb on Sunday morning right through the elite Roman guards to find the risen Jesus waiting to congratulate them on their great faith! The men who wrote it also would say that *they* declared the risen Jesus to the *women*, who were the ones hiding for fear of the Jews. And, of course, if the story was a concoction, no disciple, at any time, would have been portrayed as doubting (especially after Jesus had risen).

In short, *we don't have enough faith to believe that the New Testament writers included all of those embarrassing details in a made-up story.* The best explanation is that they were really telling the truth—warts and all.

2. THE NEW TESTAMENT WRITERS INCLUDED EMBARRASSING DETAILS AND DIFFICULT SAYINGS OF JESUS

The New Testament writers are also honest about Jesus. Not only do they record self-incriminating details about themselves, they also record embarrassing details about their leader, Jesus, that seem to place him in a bad light. Jesus:

- is considered "out of his mind" by his mother and brothers (his own family), who come to seize him in order to take him home (Mark 3:21, 31)
- is not believed by his own brothers (John 7:5)
- is thought to be a deceiver (John 7:12)
- is deserted by many of his followers (John 6:66)
- turns off "Jews who had believed in him" (John 8:30-31) to the point that they want to stone him (v. 59)

- is called a "drunkard" (Matt. 11:19)
- is called "demon-possessed" (Mark 3:22; John 7:20, 8:48)
- is called a "madman" (John 10:20)
- has his feet wiped with the hair of a prostitute (an event that had the potential to be perceived as a sexual advance—Luke 7:36-39)
- is crucified by the Jews and Romans, despite the fact that "anyone who is hung on a tree is under God's curse" (Deut. 21:23; cf. Gal. 3:13)

This is certainly not a list of events and qualities the New Testament writers would choose if they were trying to depict Jesus as the perfect, sinless God-man. Nor are these qualities congruent with the Jewish expectation that the Messiah would come to free them from political oppression. In fact, according to their own Bible at the time (the Old Testament), Jesus was cursed by God for being hanged on a tree! The best explanation for these embarrassing details is that they actually occurred, and the New Testament writers are telling the truth.

In addition to embarrassing details, there are several difficult sayings attributed to Jesus that the New Testament writers would not have included if they were making up a story about Jesus being God. For example, according to the New Testament, Jesus:

- declares, "The Father is greater than I" (John 14:28)
- seems to predict incorrectly that he's coming back to earth within a generation (Matt. 24:34)
- then says about his second coming, that no one knows the time, "not even the angels in heaven, nor the Son" (Matt. 24:36)
- seems to deny his deity by asking the rich young ruler, "Why do you call me good? . . . No one is good—except God alone" (Luke 18:19)
- is seen cursing a fig tree for not having figs when it wasn't even the season for figs (Matt. 21:18ff.)
- seems unable to do miracles in his hometown, except to heal a few sick people (Mark 6:5)

If the New Testament writers wanted to prove to everyone that Jesus was God, then why did they leave in these difficult sayings that seem to argue against his deity?

Moreover, Jesus makes what seems to be a completely morbid

claim: "I tell you the truth, unless you eat the flesh of the Son of Man and drink his blood, you have no life in you" (John 6:53). After this hard saying, John says, "From this time many of his disciples turned back and no longer followed him" (John 6:66). Since the New Testament writers certainly would not invent this strange saying and unfavorable reaction, it must be authentic.

While there are reasonable explanations for these difficult sayings,[1] it doesn't make sense that the New Testament writers would leave them in if they were trying to pass off a lie as the truth. (In fact, it doesn't make sense that they would make up a character anything like Jesus. A weak and dying Messiah—a sacrificial lamb—is the very antithesis of a man-made hero.) Again, the best explanation is that the New Testament writers were not playing fast and loose with the facts but were extremely accurate in recording exactly what Jesus said and did.

3. THE NEW TESTAMENT WRITERS LEFT IN DEMANDING SAYINGS OF JESUS

If the New Testament writers were making up a story, they certainly didn't make up a story that made life easier for them. This Jesus had some very demanding standards. The Sermon on the Mount, for instance, does not appear to be a human invention:

- "I tell you that anyone who looks at a woman lustfully has already committed adultery with her in his heart" (Matt. 5:28).
- "I tell you that anyone who divorces his wife, except for marital unfaithfulness, causes her to become an adulteress, and anyone who marries the divorced woman commits adultery" (Matt. 5:32).
- "I tell you, Do not resist an evil person. If someone strikes you on the right cheek, turn to him the other also. And if someone wants to sue you and take your tunic, let him have your cloak as well. If someone forces you to go one mile, go with him two miles. Give to the one who asks you, and do not turn away from the one who wants to borrow from you" (Matt. 5:39-42).
- "I tell you: Love your enemies and pray for those who persecute you, that you may be sons of your Father in heaven" (Matt. 5:44-45).
- "Be perfect . . . as your heavenly Father is perfect" (Matt. 5:48).
- "Do not store up for yourselves treasures on earth, where moth

and rust destroy, and where thieves break in and steal. But store up for yourselves treasures in heaven, where moth and rust do not destroy, and where thieves do not break in and steal. For where your treasure is, there your heart will be also" (Matt. 6:19-21).

• "Do not judge, or you too will be judged. For in the same way you judge others, you will be judged, and with the measure you use, it will be measured to you" (Matt. 7:1-2).

All of these commands are difficult or impossible for human beings to keep and seem to go against the natural best interests of the men who wrote them down. They certainly are contrary to the desires of many today who want a religion of spirituality that has no moral demands. Consider the extremity and undesirable implications of these commands:

• If thinking about a sin is sinful, then everyone—including the New Testament writers—is guilty.

• To set such stringent standards for divorce and remarriage does not appear to be in the earthly best interests of the men who recorded this saying.

• To not resist the insults of an evil person is to resist our basic human instincts; it also sets up an inconvenient standard of behavior for the apostles, who were undergoing persecution when this saying was written down.

• To pray for our enemies goes well beyond any ethic ever uttered and commands kindness where enmity is natural.

• To not accumulate financial wealth contradicts our deepest desires for temporal security.

• To be perfect is an unattainable request for fallible human beings.

• To not judge unless our own lives are in order counters our nat-ural tendency to point out faults in others.

These commands clearly are not the commands that people would impose on themselves. Who can live up to such standards? Only a per-fect person. Perhaps that's exactly the point.

4. The New Testament Writers Carefully Distinguished Jesus' Words from Their Own

Even though quotation marks did not exist in first-century Greek, the New Testament writers distinguished Jesus' words very clearly. Most red-letter editions of the Bibles are identical, illustrating how easy the New Testament writers made it to see what Jesus said and what he didn't say.

Why do we cite this as evidence of their trustworthiness? Because it would have been very easy for the New Testament writers to solve first-century theological disputes by putting words into Jesus' mouth. After all, if you were making up the "Christianity story" and trying to pass it off as the truth, wouldn't you simply make up more quotes from Jesus to convince stubborn people to see things your way? Think how convenient it would have been for them to end all debate on controversial issues such as circumcision, obeying the Law of Moses, speaking in tongues, women in the church, and so forth by merely making up quotes from Jesus!

Despite unending frustration with some early believers, the New Testament writers never do that. Instead of pulling rank in this way, the New Testament writers seem to stay true to what Jesus said and didn't say. Paul, the man who wrote nearly half of the New Testament books (at least 13 of the 27) and dealt with most of those controversial problems in the church, never pulls rank. He quotes Jesus just a few times. And on one of those occasions, he goes out of his way to explicitly distinguish his own words from those of Jesus (1 Cor. 7:10-12).

Why would Paul have been so careful if he were not telling the truth? Again, the best explanation for the accuracy of the New Testament writers is that they really were telling the truth.

5. THE NEW TESTAMENT WRITERS INCLUDE EVENTS RELATED TO THE RESURRECTION THAT THEY WOULD NOT HAVE INVENTED

In addition to the inclusion of embarrassing details regarding themselves and Jesus, the New Testament writers record events related to the Resurrection that they would not have inserted if they had invented the story. These include:

The Burial of Jesus—The New Testament writers record that Jesus was buried by Joseph of Arimathea, a member of the Sanhedrin, which was the Jewish ruling council that had sentenced Jesus to die for blasphemy. This is not an event they would have made up. Considering the bitterness some Christians harbored against the Jewish authorities, why would they put a member of the Sanhedrin in such a favorable light? And why would they put Jesus in the tomb of a Jewish authority? For if Joseph didn't really bury Jesus, the story would have been easily exposed as fraudulent by the Jewish enemies of Christianity. But the Jews never denied the story, and no alternative burial story has ever been found.

The First Witnesses—All four Gospels say women were the first witnesses of the empty tomb and the first to learn of the Resurrection. One of those women was Mary Magdalene, who Luke admits had been demon-possessed (Luke 8:2). This would never be inserted in a made-up story. Not only would a once-demon-possessed person make a questionable witness, but *women* in general were not considered reliable witnesses in that first-century culture. In fact, a woman's testimony carried no weight in a court of law. So if you were making up a resurrection story in the first century, you would avoid women witnesses and make yourselves—the brave men—the first ones to discover the empty tomb and the risen Jesus. Citing the testimony of women—especially demon-possessed women—would only hurt your attempt to pass off a lie as the truth.[2]

The Conversion of Priests—"Why didn't the risen Jesus appear to the Pharisees?" is a popular question asked by skeptics. The answer might be that it wasn't necessary. This is often overlooked, but many priests in Jerusalem became believers. Luke writes, "The number of disciples in Jerusalem increased rapidly, and *a large number of priests became obedient to the faith*" (Acts 6:7). These priests eventually initiated a controversy that took place later in the Jerusalem church. During a council meeting between Peter, Paul, James, and other elders, "some of the believers who belonged to the party of the *Pharisees* stood up and said, 'The Gentiles must be circumcised and required to obey the law of Moses'" (Acts 15:5).

The council resolved the issue, but our main point here is that Luke would not have included these details if they were fiction. Why not? Because everyone would have known Luke was a fraud if there were not significant converts from the ranks of the Pharisees. Theophilus and other first-century readers would have known—or could have easily found out—if such converts existed. Obviously, the Pharisees would have known too. Why would Luke give them an easy way of exposing his lies? After all, if you're trying to pass off a lie as the truth, you don't make it easy for your enemies to expose your story. Pharisee conversion and Joseph of Arimathea were two unnecessary details that—if untrue—would have completely blown Luke's cover. And the Joseph story would have blown the cover not only of Luke but of every other Gospel writer as well because they include the same burial story.

The Explanation of the Jews—The Jewish explanation for the empty tomb is recorded in the last chapter of Matthew:

> While the women were on their way, some of the guards went into the city and reported to the chief priests everything that had happened. When the chief priests had met with the elders and devised a plan, they gave the soldiers a large sum of money, telling them, "You are to say, 'His disciples came during the night and stole him away while we were asleep.' If this report gets to the governor, we will satisfy him and keep you out of trouble." So the soldiers took the money and did as they were instructed. And this story has been widely circulated among the Jews to this very day (Matt. 28:11-15).

Notice that Matthew makes it very clear that his readers already know about this Jewish explanation for the empty tomb because "this story has been widely circulated among the Jews to this very day." That means Matthew's readers (and certainly the Jews themselves) would know whether or not he was telling the truth. If Matthew were making up the empty tomb story, why would he give his readers such an easy way to expose his lies? The only plausible explanation is that the tomb must really have been empty, and the Jewish enemies of Christianity must really have been circulating that specific explanation for the empty tomb. (In fact, Justin Martyr and Tertullian, writing in A.D. 150 and 200 respectively, claim that the Jewish authorities continued to offer this theft story throughout the second century. We'll discuss the problems with this theory in the next chapter.[3])

6. THE NEW TESTAMENT WRITERS INCLUDE MORE THAN THIRTY HISTORICALLY CONFIRMED PEOPLE IN THEIR WRITINGS

This is a critical point that bears repeating. The New Testament documents cannot have been invented because they contain too many historically confirmed characters (see table 10.1, in chapter 10). The New

Testament writers would have blown their credibility with their contemporary audiences by implicating real people in a fictional story, especially people of great notoriety and power. There is no way the New Testament writers could have gotten away with writing outright lies about Pilate, Caiaphas, Festus, Felix, and the entire Herodian bloodline. Somebody would have exposed them for falsely implicating these people in events that never occurred. The New Testament writers knew this, and would not have included so many prominent real people in a fictional story that was intended to deceive. Again, the best explanation is that the New Testament writers accurately recorded what they saw.

7. The New Testament Writers Include Divergent Details

Critics are quick to cite the apparently contradictory Gospel accounts as evidence that the Gospels can't be trusted for accurate information. For example, Matthew says there was one angel at the tomb of Jesus while John mentions two. Isn't this a contradiction that blows the credibility of these accounts? No, exactly the opposite is true: divergent details actually strengthen the case that these are eyewitness accounts. How so?

First, let's point out that the angel accounts are not contradictory. Matthew does not say there was *only* one angel at the tomb. The critic has to add a word to Matthew's account to make it contradict John's.[4]

But why did Matthew mention only one if two angels were really there? For the same reason two different newspaper reporters covering the same event choose to include different details in their stories. Two independent eyewitnesses rarely see all the same details and will never describe an event in exactly the same words. They'll record the same major event (i.e., Jesus rose from the dead), but may differ on the details (i.e., how many angels were at his tomb). In fact, when a judge hears two witnesses giving exactly the same word-for-word testimony, what does that judge rightly assume? Collusion—the witnesses got together beforehand to make their stories agree.

So it's perfectly reasonable that Matthew and John differ—they are both recording eyewitness testimony. Maybe Matthew mentioned only the angel that spoke (Matt. 28:5) while John described how many angels Mary saw (John 20:12). Or maybe one angel was more prominent than the other. We don't know for sure. We just know that such differences are common among eyewitnesses.

In light of the numerous divergent details in the New Testament, it's clear that the New Testament writers didn't get together to smooth out their testimonies. This means they certainly were not trying to pass off a lie as the truth. For if they were making up the New Testament story, they would have gotten together to make sure they were consistent in every detail. Such harmonization clearly didn't happen, and this confirms the genuine eyewitness nature of the New Testament and the independence of each writer.

Ironically, it's not the New Testament that is contradictory, it's the critics. On one hand, the critics claim that the Synoptic Gospels (Matthew, Mark, and Luke) are too uniform to be independent sources. On the other hand, they claim that they are too divergent to be telling the truth. So which are they? Are they too uniform or too divergent?

Actually, we think they are a perfect blend of both. Namely, they are both sufficiently uniform and sufficiently divergent (but not too much so) precisely *because* they are independent eyewitness accounts of the same events. One would expect to see the same major facts and different minor details in three independent newspaper stories about the same event.

If you don't believe us, then log onto the Internet today and look at three independent stories about a particular event in the news. Pick one story from the AP, another from Reuters, and maybe another from UPI or an independent reporter. Each story will contain some of the same major facts but may include different minor details. In most cases, the accounts will be *complementary* rather than contradictory.

For example, if three news sources carry a story about a presidential visit to a foreign country, the stories will all properly identify the country, but they may emphasize different minor details. If one account says the president visited the prime minister of Great Britain, and if another account says the president visited the prime minister in a room with marble pillars, are those two accounts complementary or contradictory? They are complementary. The second account doesn't contradict the first, it just adds to it.

In the same way, all the Gospels agree on the same major fact—Jesus rose from the dead. They just have different complementary details. And even if one could find some minor details between the Gospels that are flatly contradictory, that wouldn't prove the Resurrection is fiction. It may present a problem for the doctrine that the Bible is without any minor error, but it wouldn't mean the major event didn't happen.

Simon Greenleaf, the Harvard law professor who wrote the standard study on what constitutes legal evidence, credited his own conversion to Christianity as having come from his careful examination of the Gospel witnesses. If anyone knew the characteristics of genuine eyewitness testimony, it was Greenleaf. He concluded that the four Gospels "would have been received in evidence in any court of justice, without the slightest hesitation."[5]

The bottom line is this: agreement on the major points and divergence on the minor details is the nature of eyewitness testimony, and this is the very nature of the New Testament documents.

8. THE NEW TESTAMENT WRITERS CHALLENGE THEIR READERS TO CHECK OUT VERIFIABLE FACTS, EVEN FACTS ABOUT MIRACLES

We've already seen some of the claims of accuracy the New Testament writers made to the recipients of their documents. These include Luke's overt assertion of accuracy to Theophilus (Luke 1:1-4); Peter's claim that they did not follow cleverly devised tales but were eyewitnesses to Christ's majesty (2 Pet. 1:16); Paul's bold declaration to Festus and King Agrippa about the resurrected Christ (Acts 26); and Paul's restatement of an early creed that identified more than 500 eyewitnesses of the risen Christ (1 Corinthians 15).

In addition, Paul makes another claim to the Corinthians that he wouldn't have made unless he was telling the truth. In his second letter to the Corinthians, Paul declares that he previously performed miracles for them. Speaking of his own qualifications as an apostle—someone who speaks for God—Paul reminds the Corinthians, "The things that mark an apostle—signs, wonders and miracles—were done among you with great perseverance" (2 Cor. 12:12).

Now why would Paul write this to the Corinthians unless he really had done miracles for them? He would have destroyed his credibility completely by asking them to remember miracles that he never did for them! The only plausible conclusion is that 1) Paul really was an apostle of God, 2) he therefore really had the ability to confirm his apostle-ship by performing miracles, and 3) he had displayed this ability openly to the Corinthians.

9. NEW TESTAMENT WRITERS DESCRIBE MIRACLES LIKE OTHER HISTORICAL EVENTS: WITH SIMPLE, UNEMBELLISHED ACCOUNTS

Embellished and extravagant details are strong signs that a historical account has legendary elements. For example, there's a legendary account of Christ's resurrection that was written more than 100 years after the actual event. It is from the apocryphal forgery known as the *Gospel of Peter,* and it goes like this:

> Early in the morning, as the Sabbath dawned, there came a large crowd from Jerusalem and the surrounding areas to see the sealed tomb. But during the night before the Lord's day dawned, as the soldiers were keeping guard two by two in every watch, there came a great sound in the sky, and they saw the heavens opened and two men descend shin-ing with a great light, and they drew near to the tomb. The stone which had been set on the door rolled away by itself and moved to one side, and the tomb was opened and both of the young men went in.
>
> Now when these soldiers saw that, they woke up the centurion and the elders (for they also were there keeping watch).While they were yet telling them the things which they had seen, they saw three men come out of the tomb, two of them sustaining the other one, and a cross following after them. The heads of the two they saw had heads that reached up to heaven, but the head of him that was led by them went beyond heaven. And they heard a voice out of the heavens say-ing, "Have you preached unto them that sleep?" The answer that was heard from the cross was, "Yes!"[6]

Wow! Now that's how I would have written it if I were making up or embellishing the Resurrection story! We see large crowds, moving stones, heads of men stretching to heaven and beyond. And we even see a walking and talking cross. How exciting! How embellished.

The New Testament resurrection accounts contain nothing like this. The Gospels give matter-of-fact, almost bland descriptions of the Resurrection.

Mark describes what the women saw this way:

> But when they looked up, they saw that the stone, which was very large, had been rolled away. As they entered the tomb, they saw a young man dressed in a white robe sitting on the right side, and they were alarmed.
>
> "Don't be alarmed," he said. "You are looking for Jesus the Nazarene, who was crucified. He has risen! He is not here. See the place where they laid him. But go, tell his disciples and Peter, 'He is going ahead of you into Galilee. There you will see him, just as he told you.'"
>
> Trembling and bewildered, the women went out and fled from the tomb. They said nothing to anyone, because they were afraid (Mark 16:4-8).

Luke's description is almost as stark:

> They found the stone rolled away from the tomb, but when they entered, they did not find the body of the Lord Jesus. While they were wondering about this, suddenly two men in clothes that gleamed like lightning stood beside them. In their fright the women bowed down with their faces to the ground, but the men said to them, "Why do you look for the living among the dead? He is not here; he has risen! Remember how he told you, while he was still with you in Galilee: 'The Son of Man must be delivered into the hands of sinful men, be crucified and on the third day be raised again.'" Then they remembered his words (Luke 24:2-8).

John's Gospel briefly mentions Mary Magdalene discovering the empty tomb, adds the experience of Peter and John, and then returns to Mary outside the tomb. Again, nothing appears embellished or extravagant in this account:

> Early on the first day of the week, while it was still dark, Mary Magdalene went to the tomb and saw that the stone had been removed from the entrance. So she came running to Simon Peter and the other disciple, the one Jesus loved, and said, "They have taken the Lord out of the tomb, and we don't know where they have put him!" So Peter and the other disciple started for the tomb. Both were running, but the other disciple outran Peter and reached the tomb first. He bent over and looked in at the strips of linen lying there but did not go in. Then

Simon Peter, who was behind him, arrived and went into the tomb. He saw the strips of linen lying there, as well as the burial cloth that had been around Jesus' head. The cloth was folded up by itself, separate from the linen. Finally the other disciple, who had reached the tomb first, also went inside. He saw and believed. (They still did not understand from Scripture that Jesus had to rise from the dead.) Then the disciples went back to their homes, but Mary stood outside the tomb crying. As she wept, she bent over to look into the tomb and saw two angels in white, seated where Jesus' body had been, one at the head and the other at the foot (John 20:1-12).

John's account then describes Jesus' appearance to Mary.

Matthew's account of the women's experience is more dramatic, but contains nothing as bizarre as the long heads or the walking and talking cross found in the legendary account of the *Gospel of Peter:*[7]

There was a violent earthquake, for an angel of the Lord came down from heaven and, going to the tomb, rolled back the stone and sat on it. His appearance was like lightning, and his clothes were white as snow. The guards were so afraid of him that they shook and became like dead men.

The angel said to the women, "Do not be afraid, for I know that you are looking for Jesus, who was crucified. He is not here; he has risen, just as he said. Come and see the place where he lay. Then go quickly and tell his disciples: 'He has risen from the dead and is going ahead of you into Galilee. There you will see him.' Now I have told you (Matt. 28:2-7).

The Resurrection is the central event in Christianity. As Paul wrote, "if Christ has not been raised, your faith is futile; you are still in your sins" (1 Cor. 15:17). If the Resurrection were a made-up story designed to convince skeptics, then the New Testament writers certainly would have made their accounts longer with more detail. Moreover, they probably would have said that they witnessed Jesus physically rising from the dead. Instead, they get to the tomb after he has risen, and they make no attempt to dress up their discovery with verbose descriptions or cartoonish talking crosses. Matthew, Mark, and Luke don't even say anything about the dramatic theological implications of the Resurrection, and John reports those implications in just one sentence (John 20:31).

This point about the theological restraint of the Gospel writers deserves amplification. It indicates that the Gospel writers were concerned about getting the history correct, not inventing some new kind of theology. New Testament scholar N. T. Wright makes the astute observation that "neither 'going to heaven when you die', 'life after death', 'eternal life', nor even 'the resurrection of all Christ's people', is so much as mentioned in the four canonical resurrection stories. If Matthew, Mark, Luke and John wanted to tell stories whose import was 'Jesus is risen, therefore you will be too', they have done a remarkably bad job of it."[8]

This is almost shocking when you think about it. If you go to most evangelical church services today, the constant emphasis is "come to Jesus to get saved." That is certainly taught in the whole of the New Testament, but it's hardly mentioned in the Gospels. Why? Because the Gospel writers were writing history, not mere theology. Of course New Testament history has dramatic implications on theology, but those implications are drawn out in other New Testament writings, namely the Epistles (letters). It would have been easy for the Gospel writers to interject the theological implications of every historical event, but they didn't. They were eyewitnesses who were writing history, not fiction writers or proselytizing theologians.

Their level-headedness is also on display with the other miracles they record. The thirty-five other miracles attributed to Jesus in the Gospels are described as if from reporters, not wild-eyed preachers. The Gospel writers don't offer flamboyant descriptions or fire and brimstone commentary—just the facts.

10. The New Testament Writers Abandoned Their Long-Held Sacred Beliefs and Practices, Adopted New Ones, and Did Not Deny Their Testimony Under Persecution or Threat of Death

The New Testament writers don't just say that Jesus performed miracles and rose from the dead—they actually back up that testimony with dramatic action. First, virtually overnight they abandon many of their long-held sacred beliefs and practices. Among the 1,500-year-old-plus institutions they give up are the following:

- The animal sacrifice system—they replace it forever by the one perfect sacrifice of Christ.

- The binding supremacy of the Law of Moses—they say it's powerless because of the sinless life of Christ.
- Strict monotheism—they now worship Jesus, the God-man, despite the fact that 1) their most cherished belief has been, "Hear, O Israel: The LORD our God, the LORD is one" (Deut. 6:4); and 2) man-worship has always been considered blasphemy and punishable by death.
- The Sabbath—they no longer observe it even though they've always believed that breaking the Sabbath was punishable by death (Ex. 31:14).
- Belief in a conquering Messiah—Jesus is the opposite of a conquering Messiah. He's a sacrificial lamb (at least on his first visit!).

And it's not just the New Testament writers who do this—thousands of Jerusalem Jews, including Pharisee priests, convert to Christianity and join the New Testament writers in abandoning these treasured beliefs and practices. J. P. Moreland helps us understand the magnitude of these devout Jews giving up their established institutions virtually overnight:

> [The Jewish people] believed that these institutions were entrusted to them by God. They believed that to abandon these institutions would be to risk their souls being damned to hell after death.
>
> Now a rabbi named Jesus appears from a lower-class region. He teaches for three years, gathers a following of lower- and middle-class people, gets in trouble with the authorities, and gets crucified along with thirty thousand other Jewish men who are executed during this time period.
>
> But five weeks after he's crucified, over ten thousand Jews are following him and claiming that he is the initiator of a new religion. And get this: they're willing to give up or alter all five of the social institutions that they have been taught since childhood have such importance both sociologically and theologically. . . . Something *very* big was going on.[9]

How do you explain these monumental shifts if the New Testament writers were making up a story? How do you explain them if the Resurrection did not occur?

Second, not only do these new believers abandon their long-held beliefs and practices, they also adopt some new radical ones. These include:

- Sunday, a work day, as the new day of worship
- Baptism as a new sign that one was a partaker of the new covenant (as circumcision was a sign of the old covenant)
- Communion as an act of remembrance of Christ's sacrifice for their sins[10]

Communion is especially inexplicable unless the Resurrection is true. Why would Jews make up a practice where they symbolically eat the body and drink the blood of Jesus?

Table 11.1 sums up the dramatic changes brought about by the Resurrection:

Pre-Resurrection Belief	Post-Resurrection Belief
Animal sacrifice	Unnecessary because of Christ's sacrifice
Binding Law of Moses	Nonbinding because it was fulfilled by Christ's life
Strict monotheism	Trinity (three persons in one divine essence)
The Sabbath	Replaced by Sunday worship
Conquering Messiah	Sacrificial Messiah (he'll conquer when he returns)
Circumcision	Replaced by baptism and Communion

Table 11.1

Finally, in addition to abandoning long-held sacred institutions and adopting new ones, the New Testament writers suffered persecution and death when they could have saved themselves by recanting. If they had made up the Resurrection story, they certainly would have said so when they were about to be crucified (Peter), stoned (James), or beheaded (Paul). But no one recanted—eleven out of the twelve were martyred for their faith (the only survivor was John, who was exiled to the Greek island of Patmos). Why would they die for a known lie?

Chuck Colson, former aide to President Nixon and founder of Prison Fellowship, went to prison over the Watergate scandal. Comparing his experience to that of the apostles, he writes,

> Watergate involved a conspiracy to cover up, perpetuated by the closest aides to the President of the United States—the most powerful men in America, who were intensely loyal to their president. But one of them, John Dean, turned state's evidence, that is, testified against Nixon, as he put it, "to save his own skin"—and he did so only two weeks after informing the president about what was really going on—

two weeks! The real cover-up, the lie, could only be held together for two weeks, and then everybody else jumped ship in order to save themselves. Now, the fact is that all that those around the president were facing was embarrassment, maybe prison. Nobody's life was at stake. But what about the disciples? Twelve powerless men, peasants really, were facing not just embarrassment or political disgrace, but beatings, stonings, execution. Every single one of the disciples insisted, to their dying breaths, that they had physically seen Jesus bodily raised from the dead. Don't you think that one of those apostles would have cracked before being beheaded or stoned? That one of them would have made a deal with the authorities? None did.[11]

Colson is right. The apostles surely would have cracked to save themselves. Peter had already denied Jesus three times before the Resurrection in order to "save his skin"! He surely would have denied him after the Resurrection if the story had turned out to be a hoax.

Supreme Court Justice Antonin Scalia pointed out the absurdity of those who doubt the historicity of the New Testament. In a remark biting with sarcasm against modern-day intellectuals, Scalia stated exactly what we've been saying regarding the motives of the New Testament writers. Namely, since the New Testament writers had nothing to gain and everything to lose, we ought to believe what they say about the Resurrection. Scalia declared, "It is not irrational to accept the testimony of eyewitnesses who had nothing to gain. . . . The [worldly] wise do not believe in the resurrection of the dead. So everything from Easter morning to the Ascension had to be made up by the groveling enthusiasts as part of their plan to get themselves martyred."[12]

Scalia and Colson are absolutely right. There's no reason to doubt, and every reason to believe, the New Testament accounts. While many people will die for a lie that they think is truth, no sane person will die for what they *know* is a lie. The New Testament writers and the other apostles knew for sure that Jesus had resurrected, and they demonstrated that knowledge with their own blood. What more could eyewitnesses do to prove that they are telling the truth!

WHAT ABOUT MUSLIM MARTYRS?

"Hold on!" the skeptic may object. "We see people dying for their faith every day! Do you ever watch the news? There's a suicide bomber nearly every week in the Middle East! Have you forgotten about 9/11 already? The hijackers were doing it for Allah! What does martyrdom prove? Does it prove Islam is true too?"

Not at all. There are some similarities, but there's one critical difference between the New Testament martyrs and those of today. One similarity shared by all martyrs is sincerity. Whether you're talking about Christians, Muslims, kamikaze pilots, or suicidal cult followers, everyone agrees that martyrs sincerely believe in their cause. But the critical difference is that the New Testament Christian martyrs had more than sincerity—they had evidence that the Resurrection was true. Why? Because *the New Testament martyrs were eyewitnesses of the resurrected Christ.* They knew the Resurrection was true and not a lie because they verified it with their own senses. They saw, touched, and ate with the risen Jesus on several occasions. And they had seen him do more than thirty miracles. In light of such strong empirical evidence, they needed very little faith to believe in the Resurrection. By commonsense observation standards, they had *proof* of it. So they willingly submitted themselves to persecution and death for what they had verified themselves.

This is unlike anything from Islam (or any other martyr-producing belief system). While the current martyrs for Islam are certainly sincere about Islam, they don't have miraculous eyewitness proof that Islam is true. They are not eyewitnesses to anything miraculous.

In fact, *the contemporaries of Muhammad weren't eyewitnesses to anything miraculous either.* When Muhammad was challenged to perform miracles to confirm that he was from God, he never took the challenge (Sura 3:181-184; 4:153; 6:8-9; 17:88-96). Instead, he said he was just a man (17:93) and implied that the Qur'an authenticated him as a prophet (17:88). But there are no clearly defined miracles recorded in the Qur'an.[13] Miracles were only attributed to Muhammad by Muslims who lived 100–200 years after his death because Christians kept asking them for proof that Muhammad was a prophet. These miracle claims are not based on eyewitness testimony, and give every indication of being legendary. Several speak of trees moving or saluting Muhammad as he passed by. Mountains and wolves allegedly salute Muhammad as well. And other miracle stories seem to be variations of the miracles Jesus performed (e.g., turning water into milk, feeding a thousand by multiplying a small meal).

These miracle stories are found in the *Hadith,* a later collection of Muhammad's saying and doings.

The most reliable author of the *Hadith,* Al Bukhari, and a majority of *Muslim* scholars admit that most of Muhammad's alleged miracles are not authentic.[14] Since Muhammad himself never claimed to do miracles, and since these miracle stories arise from sources well after contemporaries of Muhammad had died, we see no reason to believe *any* of the miracles attributed to Muhammad.

If Muhammad wasn't confirmed by miracles, then why did people follow him? They didn't at first. He and his few followers were kicked out of Mecca in A.D. 622, twelve years after he apparently got his first revelation. (Since Mecca was a polytheistic city filled with tributes to other gods, Muhammad's message of monotheism was not well received by the local merchants who made their living off of the commerce associated with polytheism.) It wasn't until Muhammad led several successful military conquests between 622 and 630 that he began to attract a large following. His popularity was greatly increased when he led raids on Meccan caravans and divided the booty from those raids with followers. He also took numerous wives, which helped solidify his base of support. In other words, Muhammad's popularity resulted from his lucrative military victories that he shared with his followers, his astute political dealings, and his personal charisma rather than from any miraculous confirmation.

The military aspect of Islam highlights another major difference between the origin of Christianity and the origin of Islam. Christianity began as a peaceful faith and was considered illegal for about the first 280 years of its existence (during which time it experienced its greatest growth). If you became a Christian in the Roman Empire before about 311, you might be killed for it.

By contrast, after a brief but unfruitful attempt to propagate his faith peacefully, Muhammad turned to military force to spread Islam. By 630, he had seized Mecca by force and had control of much of what is now the Saudi Arabian peninsula. Although Muhammad died in 632, his followers continued military campaigns in the name of Islam. By 638—only six years after Muhammad's death—the Muslims had seized the Holy Land by force. In the first 100 years of Islam—in addition to taking Jerusalem— the Muslims twice attempted to take over Constantinople (present-day Istanbul, Turkey), and they successfully swept across northern Africa, across the Straits of Gibralter, and into Europe. Had it not been for Charles Martel, mayor of the city of Tours, France, all of Europe would probably be speaking Arabic today. Martel (which means "hammer") drove the Muslims south out of Tours in 732, exactly 100 years after Muhammad's death. (The Muslims eventually retreated back over the Straits, but northern Africa remains predominantly Muslim to this day.)

So here's the contrast: in the early days of Christianity, you might be killed for becoming Christian; in the early days of Islam's growth, you might be killed for *not* becoming a Muslim! In other words, the spread of these two great monotheistic faiths couldn't have been more different: Islam spread by use of the sword on others; Christianity spread when others used the sword on it.

"What about the Crusades?" the skeptic will interject. Take a history course—the Crusades did not begin until nearly 1100, more than 1,000 years after the origin of Christianity. And the initial rationale for the Crusades was to take back the land the Muslims previously had seized by military conquest from the Christians. So it was Islam, not Christianity, that initially spread by military crusade.

Now, one can understand why a religion spreads when it takes over militarily. But why does a religion spread when its adherents are persecuted, tortured, and killed during its first 280 years? (Those are *not* good selling points.) Perhaps there's some very reliable testimony about miraculous events that proves the religion is true. How else can you explain why scared, scattered, skeptical cowards suddenly become the most dedicated, determined, self-sacrificing, and peaceful missionary force the world has ever known?

SUMMARY AND CONCLUSION

In the last two chapters we saw that we have an accurate copy of the early and eyewitness testimony found in the New Testament documents. Our central question in this chapter involves invention, embellishment, and exaggeration. Namely, did the New Testament writers make up, embellish, or exaggerate elements of the story? Did they play fast and loose with the facts?

No. As we have seen, there are at least ten good reasons to believe that they were honest men who meticulously and faithfully recorded what they saw. The New Testament writers:

1. include numerous embarrassing details about themselves
2. include numerous embarrassing details and difficult sayings of Jesus
3. include the demanding sayings of Jesus
4. carefully distinguish Jesus' words from their own
5. include events about the Resurrection that they would not have invented
6. include at least thirty historically confirmed public figures in their writings
7. include divergent details
8. challenge their readers to check out verifiable facts, even facts about miracles
9. describe miracles like other historical events: with simple, unembellished accounts
10. abandoned their long-held sacred beliefs and practices, adopted new ones, and did not deny their testimony under persecution or threat of death

So we have all these reasons to support the idea that the New Testament writers relentlessly stuck to the truth. And why wouldn't they? What would motivate them to lie, embellish, or exaggerate anyway? What did they possibly have to gain? They only gained persecution and death for testifying as they did. In other words, the New Testament writers had every motive to *deny* New Testament events, not to invent, embellish, or exaggerate them. Again, it wasn't as if they needed a new religion! When Jesus arrived, most of the New Testament writers were devout Jews who thought that Judaism was the one true religion and they were God's chosen people. Something dramatic must have happened to jolt them out of their dogmatic slumbers and into a new belief system that promised them nothing but earthly trouble. *In light of all this, we don't have enough faith to be skeptics concerning the New Testament.*

But despite all of this evidence against them, the skeptics still have faith. Since the evidence makes it virtually impossible to conclude that Jesus was a legend or that the New Testament writers were liars, some skeptics cling to their only remaining possibility: the New Testament writers were deceived. They sincerely thought Jesus had risen from the dead, but they were wrong. That's the possibility we'll address in the next chapter.

Did Jesus Really Rise from the Dead?

"Skeptics must provide more than alternative theories to the Resurrection; they must provide first-century evidence for those theories."

—GARY HABERMAS

THE RESURRECTION: WHAT DO SCHOLARS SAY?

Gary Habermas has completed the most comprehensive investigation to date on what scholars believe about the Resurrection. Habermas collected more than 1,400 of the most critical scholarly works on the Resurrection written from 1975 to 2003. In *The Risen Jesus and Future Hope*,[1] Habermas reports that virtually all scholars from across the ideological spectrum—from ultra-liberals to Bible-thumping conservatives—agree that the following points concerning Jesus and Christianity are actual historical facts:

1. Jesus died by Roman crucifixion.
2. He was buried, most likely in a private tomb.
3. Soon afterwards the disciples were discouraged, bereaved, and despondent, having lost hope.
4. Jesus' tomb was found empty very soon after his interment.[2]
5. The disciples had experiences that they believed were actual appearances of the risen Jesus.
6. Due to these experiences, the disciples' lives were thoroughly transformed. They were even willing to die for their belief.
7. The proclamation of the Resurrection took place very early, from the beginning of church history.
8. The disciples' public testimony and preaching of the Resurrection took place in the city of Jerusalem, where Jesus had been crucified and buried shortly before.

9. The gospel message centered on the preaching of the death and resurrection of Jesus.

10. Sunday was the primary day for gathering and worshiping.

11. James, the brother of Jesus and a skeptic before this time, was converted when he believed he also saw the risen Jesus.

12. Just a few years later, Saul of Tarsus (Paul) became a Christian believer, due to an experience that he also believed was an appearance of the risen Jesus.[3]

The acceptance of these facts makes sense in light of what we've seen so far. The evidence shows:

The New Testament Story Is Not a Legend—The New Testament documents were written well within two generations of the events by eyewitnesses or their contemporaries, and the New Testament storyline is corroborated by non-Christian writers. In addition, the New Testament mentions at least 30 historical figures who have been confirmed by sources outside the New Testament. Therefore, the New Testament story cannot be a legend.

The New Testament Story Is Not a Lie—The New Testament writers included divergent and embarrassing details, difficult and demanding sayings, and they carefully distinguished Jesus' words from their own. They also referenced facts and eyewitnesses that their readers either already knew or could verify. In fact, the New Testament writers provoked their readers and prominent first-century enemies to check out what they said. If that's not enough to confirm their truthfulness, then their martyrdom should remove any doubt. These eyewitnesses endured persecution and death for the empirical claim that they had seen, heard, and touched the risen Jesus, yet they could have saved themselves by simply denying their testimony.

The New Testament Story Is Not an Embellishment—The New Testament writers were meticulously accurate, as evidenced by well over 140 historically confirmed details. They recorded miracles in those same historically confirmed narratives, and they did so without apparent embellishment or significant theological comment.

So Is the New Testament True?—If most scholars agree with the twelve facts stated above because the evidence shows that the New Testament story is not a legend, a lie, or an embellishment, then we know beyond a reasonable doubt that the New Testament writers accurately recorded what they saw. Does this mean that all of the events of the New Testament are true? Not necessarily. The skeptic still has one last out.

The last possible out for the skeptic is that the New Testament writers were deceived. In other words, perhaps the New Testament writers simply were wrong about what they thought they saw.

Given the characteristics of the New Testament that we have already reviewed, it does not seem plausible that the New Testament writers were deceived about everyday, non-miraculous events. They have been proven right about so many historical details. Why doubt their observations about everyday events?

But were they deceived about miraculous events like the Resurrection? Perhaps they really believed that Jesus had risen from the dead—and that's why they paid with their lives—but they were mistaken or fooled. Perhaps there are natural explanations for all the miracles they think they saw.

Critical scholars leave themselves this out. Consider fact number 5 from the dozen facts that nearly all scholars believe: "The disciples had experiences *that they believed* were actual appearances of the risen Jesus." In other words, scholars are *not* necessarily saying that Jesus actually rose from the dead (although some think he did). The minimal consensus of nearly all scholars is that the disciples *believed* that Jesus rose from the dead.

For the eyewitnesses and contemporaries of the events to be wrong, there must be some other explanation for the Resurrection and the other miracles recorded in the New Testament. Since the Resurrection is the central event in Christianity, let's begin there. How do skeptics explain away the Resurrection?

SKEPTICAL ABOUT SKEPTICAL THEORIES

Here are the explanations for the Resurrection most frequently offered by skeptics:

Hallucination Theory—Were the disciples deceived by hallucinations? Perhaps they sincerely thought they had seen the risen Christ but instead were really experiencing hallucinations. This theory has a number of fatal flaws. We'll address two of them.

First, hallucinations are not experienced by groups but only by individuals. In that regard, they are a lot like dreams. That's why if a friend says to you one morning, "Wow! That was a great dream *we* had last night, eh?" You don't say, "Yeah, it was fabulous! Should we continue it tonight?" No, you think your friend has gone mad or is just cracking a joke. You don't take him seriously because dreams are not collective experiences. Individuals have dreams—groups do not. Hallucinations work the same way. If *rare* psychological conditions exist, an individual may have a hallucination, but his friends will not. And even if they do, they will not have the same hallucination.

The hallucination theory doesn't work because Jesus did not appear once to just one person—he appeared on a dozen separate occasions, in a variety of settings to different people over a *forty-day* period. He was seen by men and women. He was seen walking, talking, and eating. He was seen inside and outside. He was seen by many and by a few. A total of more than 500 people saw this risen Jesus. And they were not seeing a hallucination or a ghost because on six of the twelve appearances Jesus was physically touched and/or he ate real food (see table 12.1 on next page).

The existence of the empty tomb is the second fatal flaw with the hallucination theory. If the 500-plus eyewitnesses did have the unprecedented experience of seeing the same hallucination at twelve different times, then why didn't the Jewish or Roman authorities simply parade Jesus' body around the city? That would have ended Christianity once and forever. They would have loved to do so, but apparently they couldn't because the tomb really was empty.

The Witnesses Went to the Wrong Tomb—Maybe the disciples went to the wrong tomb and then assumed that Jesus had risen. This theory also has two fatal flaws.

First, if the disciples had gone to the wrong tomb, the Jewish or Roman authorities would have gone to the right one and paraded Jesus' body around the city. The tomb was known by the Jews because it was *their* tomb (it belonged to Joseph of Arimathea, a member of the Jewish Sanhedrin). And the tomb was known by the Romans because they placed guards there. As William Lane Craig notes, the wrong tomb theory assumes that the all of the Jews (and the Romans) had a permanent kind of "collective amnesia" about what they had done with the body of Jesus.[4]

THE ORDER OF THE TWELVE APPEARANCES OF CHRIST

	Persons	Saw	Heard	Touched	Other Evidence
1.	Mary Magdalene (John 20:10-18)	X	X	X	Empty tomb
2.	Mary Magdalene & other Mary (Matt. 28:1-10)	X	X	X	Empty tomb (empty tomb and grave clothes also in Luke 24:1-12)
3.	Peter (1 Cor. 15:5) & John (John 20:1-10)	X	X		Empty tomb, grave clothes
4.	Two disciples (Luke 24:13-35)	X	X		Ate with him
5.	Ten apostles (Luke 24:36-49; John 20:19-23)	X	X	X**	Saw wounds, ate food
6.	Eleven apostles (John 20:24-31)	X	X	X**	Saw wounds
7.	Seven apostles (John 21)	X	X		Ate food
8.	All apostles (Matt. 28:16-20; Mark 16:14-18)	X	X		
9.	500 brethren (1 Cor. 15:6)	X	X*		
10.	James (1Cor. 15:7)	X	X*		
11.	All apostles (Acts 1:4-8)	X	X		Ate with him
12.	Paul (Acts 9:1-9; 1 Cor. 15:8)	X	X		

*Implied   **Offered himself to be touched

Table 12.1

Second, even if the disciples did go to the wrong tomb, the theory does not explain how the risen Jesus appeared twelve different times. In other words, the appearances must be explained, not just the empty tomb.

Notice that the empty tomb did not convince most of the disciples (with the possible exception of John) that Jesus had risen from the dead. It was the *appearances* of Jesus that turned them from scared, scattered, skeptical cowards into the greatest peaceful missionary force in history. This is especially true of the devout enemy of Christianity, Saul (Paul). He was not only unconvinced by the empty tomb; he was persecuting Christians very soon after the Resurrection. It took an appearance of Jesus himself to turn Paul around. It seems that James, the skeptical brother of Jesus, also was converted after an appearance of Jesus. As we have seen, James's conversion was so dramatic that he became the leader of the Jerusalem church and was later martyred at the hands of the high priest.

The bottom line is this: even if one could explain the empty tomb naturally, this would not be enough to disprove the Resurrection. Any alternative theory of the Resurrection must also explain away the appearances of Jesus. The wrong tomb theory explains neither.

Swoon or Apparent Death Theory—Is it possible that Jesus didn't really die on the cross? Perhaps Jesus merely swooned. In other words, he was still alive when he was placed in the tomb, but he somehow escaped and convinced his disciples that he had risen from the dead. There are numerous fatal flaws with this theory as well.

First, enemies and friends alike believed Jesus was dead. The Romans, who were professional executioners, whipped and beat Jesus brutally to the point of his collapse. They then drove heavy, wrought-iron nails through his wrists and feet, and plunged a spear into his side. They didn't break his legs to speed death because they knew he was already dead. (Crucifixion victims often died by asphyxiation because they couldn't push themselves up to breathe. Breaking the legs would, therefore, speed death.) Moreover, Pilate checked to make sure Jesus was dead, and Jesus' death was the reason the disciples had lost all hope.

The brutal Roman crucifixion techniques have been verified through archaeology and non-Christian written sources (see chapter 15 for a vivid description of Jesus' crucifixion experience). In 1968, the remains of a first-century crucifixion victim were found in a Jerusalem cave; the heel bone of this man had a seven-inch nail driven through it, and his lower arms showed evidence of nails as well.[5] The spear in the heart has also been verified as a Roman crucifixion technique by the Roman author Quintilian (A.D. 35–95).[6] Given such treatment of Jesus, it's no wonder the eyewitnesses thought he was dead.

Not only did those in the first century believe Jesus was dead; modern medical doctors also believe Jesus actually died. Writing in the March 21, 1986, edition of the *Journal of the American Medical Association,* three medical doctors, including a pathologist from the Mayo Clinic, concluded:

> Clearly, the weight of historical and medical evidence indicates that Jesus was dead before the wound to his side was inflicted and supports the traditional view that the spear, thrust between his right rib, probably perforated not only the right lung but also the pericardium and heart and thereby ensured his death. Accordingly, interpretations based on the assumption that Jesus did not die on the cross appear to be at odds with modern medical knowledge.[7]

As we indicated in the last chapter, the blood and water from the spear wound appears to be another genuine eyewitness detail from the pen of John. That fact alone should end all doubt about the death of Jesus.

The second major flaw in the swoon theory is that Jesus was embalmed in seventy-five pounds of bandages and spices. It is highly unlikely that Joseph of Arimathea and Nicodemus (John 19:40) would have mistakenly embalmed a living Jesus.

Third, even if everyone was wrong about Jesus being dead when he went into the tomb, how would a badly injured and bleeding man still be alive thirty-six hours later? He would have bled to death in that cold, damp, dark tomb.

Fourth, even if he did survive the cold, damp, dark tomb, how could he unwrap himself, move the two-ton rock up and away from the inside of the tomb, get by the elite Roman guards (who would be killed for allowing the breach of security), and then convince the scared, scattered, skeptical cowards that he had triumphed over death? Even if he could get out of the tomb and past the Roman guards, Jesus would have been a battered, bleeding pulp of a man whom the disciples would pity, not worship. They'd say, "You may be alive, but you're certainly not risen. Let's get you to a doctor!"

Fifth, the swoon theory cannot explain Jesus' bright-light appearance to Paul on the road to Damascus. What turned around this avowed enemy of Christianity shortly after the crucifixion? It certainly wasn't a normal human being who had healed from his crucifixion experience.

Paul's description of his conversion is recorded twice in the historically authenticated book of Acts. In chapter 22, Paul tells a hostile Jewish crowd about Christ's appearance to him:

> "About noon as I came near Damascus, suddenly a bright light from heaven flashed around me. I fell to the ground and heard a voice say to me, 'Saul! Saul! Why do you persecute me?'
>
> "'Who are you, Lord?' I asked.
>
> "'I am Jesus of Nazareth, whom you are persecuting,' he replied" (vv. 6-8).

Paul was then blinded for three days and experienced a 180-degree attitude change. He went from Christianity's most eager enemy to its most ardent advocate.

Paul's conversion experience cannot be explained by a swooned Jesus wielding a torch and using his "God voice" from the bushes. This was a dramatic display of divine power in broad daylight that dramatically changed a man, and the world, forever.[8]

Sixth, several non-Christian writers affirmed that Jesus had died by crucifixion. These include Josephus, Tacitus, Thallus, and the Jewish Talmud. The Jewish Talmud, for example, says that Yeshua (Jesus) was hung on a tree on the eve of the Passover.[9] This is not a source considered friendly to Christianity, so there's no reason to doubt its authenticity.

For these reasons and others, very few scholars believe the swoon theory anymore. There's simply too much evidence against it.

The Disciples Stole the Body—The theory that the disciples stole Jesus' body cannot support the skeptic's last option—that the New Testament writers were all deceived. Why? Because the theory makes the New Testament writers the deceivers, not the deceived ones! This, of course, flies in the face of all the evidence we've seen so far. The theory takes the untenable position that the New Testament writers were all liars. For some inexplicable reason, they stole the body in order to get themselves beaten, tortured, and martyred! Adherents to this theory cannot explain why anyone would do this. Why would the disciples embark

on such a self-defeating conspiracy? And why did every one of them continue to say that Jesus had risen from the dead when they could have
saved themselves by recanting that testimony?

In addition to the disciples' severe conflict of interest, adherents of this
theory cannot explain other absurdities required by their theory. For
example, how did the disciples get past the elite Roman guards who were
trained to guard the tomb with their lives? If Jesus never rose from the
dead, then who appeared to Paul, James, and the other eyewitnesses? Did
the New Testament writers lie about their conversions too? Did Paul simply make up the evidence found in 1 Corinthians? And what about the
non-Christian writers? Did Josephus lie about James being martyred by
the Sanhedrin? Did the Roman writer Phlegon (born ca. A.D. 80) lie as well
when he wrote in his *Chronicles,* "Jesus, while alive, was of no assistance
to himself, but that he arose after death, and exhibited the marks of his
punishment, and showed how his hands had been pierced by nails"?[10] It
would take more of a "miracle" for all this to happen than for Jesus to
rise from the dead. *We don't have enough faith to believe all that!*

As we have seen, the notion that the disciples stole the body is
exactly the explanation the Jews offered to explain the empty tomb.
Beyond the fact that the disciples had no motive or ability to steal the
body, this ancient Jewish explanation was not a good lie for two other
reasons: 1) how would the sleeping guards have known that the disciples stole the body? and 2) no Roman guard would admit to the capital
crime of sleeping on the job. (Perhaps that's why, as Matthew records,
the Jewish authorities had to pay off the guards and promise to keep
them out of trouble with the governor.)

In 1878, a fascinating archaeological discovery was made that may
corroborate the Bible's claim that the Jews were circulating the theft
explanation. A marble slab measuring 15 by 24 inches was discovered
in Nazareth with this inscription:

> Ordinance of Caesar: It is my pleasure that graves and tombs remain
> perpetually undisturbed for those who have made them for the cult of
> their ancestors or children or members of their house. If, however, any-
> one charges that another has either demolished them, or has in any
> other way extracted the buried, or has maliciously transferred them to
> other places in order to wrong them, or has displaced the sealing on
> other stones, against such a one I order that a trial be instituted, as in

respect of the gods, so in regard to the cult of mortals. For it shall be much more obligatory to honor the buried. Let it be absolutely forbidden for anyone to disturb them. In case of violation I desire that the offender be sentenced to capital punishment on charge of violation of sepulchre.[11]

Scholars believe this edict was issued by Emperor Tiberius, who reigned from A.D. 14–37 (during most of Christ's life), or Emperor Claudius, who reigned from 41–54. The striking nature of this edict is that it raises the penalty for grave robbing from a mere fine to death!

Why would the Roman emperor bother to make such a severe edict at this time in such a remote area of his empire? While no one knows for sure the reason for the edict, there are a couple of likely possibilities, both of which point back to Jesus.

If the inscription is from Tiberius, then it's likely that Tiberius learned of Jesus through one of Pilate's annual reports to him. Justin Martyr claims that this was the case.[12] Included in that report may have been the Jewish explanation for the empty tomb (the disciples stole the body), prompting Tiberius to prevent any future "resurrections" with the edict.

If the inscription is from Claudius, then the edict may have been part of his response to the riots in Rome in A.D. 49. In Acts 18:2, Luke mentions that Claudius had expelled the Jews from Rome. This is confirmed by the Roman historian Seutonius, who tells us that, "Because the Jews at Rome caused continuous disturbances at the instigation of Chrestus, he [Claudius] expelled them from the city."[13] (Chrestus is a variant spelling of Christ.)

What did Christ have to do with Jewish riots in Rome? Perhaps Rome experienced the same course of events that took place in Thessalonica at roughly the same time. In Acts 17, Luke records that Thessalonica was thrown into "turmoil" when the Jews became "jealous" of Paul preaching that Jesus had risen from the dead. These Jews complained to the city officials, "These men [Paul and Luke] who have caused trouble all over the world have now come here. . . . They are all defying Caesar's decrees, saying that there is another king, one called Jesus" (vv. 6-7).

If this is what actually happened in Rome, then Claudius would not have been pleased with a group who was defying his decrees and following another king. Once he had learned that this new seditious sect originated with Jews who believed their leader had resurrected, he may have exiled all the Jews from Rome and made grave robbing a capital offense.

Either of these two possibilities would explain the timing, location, and severity of the edict. But even if the edict is *not* connected with Christ's empty tomb, we already have good evidence that the Jews put forth the theft hypothesis (see last chapter). The main point is that the theft hypothesis was a tacit admission that the tomb was really empty. *After all, why would the Jews concoct an explanation for the empty tomb if Jesus' body was still in there?*

A Substitute Took Jesus' Place on the Cross—This happens to be the explanation offered by many Muslims today—Jesus was not crucified, but someone like Judas was killed in his place.[14] The Qur'an claims of Jesus,

> They killed him not, nor crucified him, but so it was made to appear to them, and those who differ therein are full of doubts, with no (certain) knowledge, but only conjecture to follow, for of a surety they killed him not: Nay, Allah raised him up unto Himself; and Allah is Exalted in Power, Wise (Sura 4:157-158).

So according to the Qur'an, it only appeared that Jesus was crucified, and Allah took him directly to heaven.

There are a number of problems with this theory, not the least being that there's absolutely no evidence to back it up. This assertion from the Qur'an comes more than 600 years after the lifetime of Jesus. How can this be considered a more authoritative source for the life of Jesus than the accounts of the eyewitnesses? For this theory contradicts all the eyewitness testimony, and the testimony of the non-Christian sources.

Moreover, this theory raises more questions than it answers. Are we to believe that scores of people who witnessed some aspect of Jesus' death—the disciples, the Roman guards, Pilate, the Jews, Jesus' family and friends—were *all* mistaken about who was killed? How could so many people be wrong about a simple identification? This is like saying that Abraham Lincoln wasn't the one killed next to his wife on that April evening in 1865 at Ford's Theater. Was Mary Lincoln mistaken about the man sitting next to her? Was Lincoln's bodyguard wrong about whom he was guarding? Was everyone else mistaken about the identity of the president as well? This is not believable.

There are many other questions raised by this theory. If Jesus wasn't killed, then why was the tomb of the man who really *was* killed found empty? Are we to believe the *substitute* rose from the dead? If so, how did he do it? Are we to believe that all the non-Christian historians are wrong about the death of Jesus? And what are we to make about the Jewish admission of Jesus' death? Was the Talmud mistaken for saying that Jesus was hanged on a tree on the eve of the Passover? In short, are we to believe that everyone from the first century was wrong about everything?

One has to question a theory that comes more than 600 years after the events and asks you to believe that all the first-century evidence is wrong. In fact, this theory contradicts most of the twelve facts virtually all scholars believe (see the beginning of this chapter). Like other alternative theories, this one is built on mere speculation without a shred of evidence to support it. *Therefore, we don't have enough faith to believe it.*

The Disciples' Faith Led Their Belief in the Resurrection—John Dominic Crossan is cofounder of the far-left group of scholars and critics who call themselves "The Jesus Seminar." They have decided that only 18 percent of the sayings attributed to Jesus in the Gospels are authentic (for more on them see appendix 3). They don't give any real evidence for this skepticism, just speculative theories about how the faith of the disciples led to their belief in the Resurrection and just about everything else in the New Testament.

This theory was brought out well during the debate Crossan had with William Lane Craig over the Resurrection. Crossan offered the theory that the disciples made up the Resurrection story because they "searched the Scriptures" after his death and found that "persecution, if not execution, was almost like a job description of being God's elect."[15]

The entire two-hour debate turned on Craig's response. He said, "Right. And that came *after* they experienced the resurrection appearances. . . . *The faith of the disciples did not lead to the [resurrection] appearances, but it was the appearances which led to their faith*; they then searched the scriptures."[16]

Indeed, the scared, scattered, skeptical disciples were not of the mind to invent a resurrection story and then go out and die for it. They were of the mind to go and hide for fear of the Jews! It was the resurrection appearances that gave them bold faith, not the other way around. Crossan has it backwards.

In addition to the fact that there's no evidence for his theory, Crossan cannot account for the resurrection appearances to more than 500 people. Nor can he account for the empty tomb or the Jewish attempt to explain it. The Jews knew the disciples were claiming that the Resurrection was a real historical event, not a mere product of their faith. If, as Crossan says, the Resurrection didn't really occur, then why did Jewish authorities right through the second century continue to insist that the disciples had stolen the body? Crossan has no answer because his theory is false. *You have to have a lot of faith—and overlook a lot of evidence—to believe it.*

The New Testament Writers Copied Pagan Resurrection Myths— This theory asserts that the New Testament is not historical because New Testament writers merely copied pagan resurrection myths. Skeptics are quick to cite supposed resurrections of mythical characters like Marduk, Adonis, and Osiris. Is the New Testament just another myth? Could this theory be true? That's not likely, for a number of reasons.

First, as we have seen, the New Testament is anything but mythological. Unlike pagan myths, the New Testament is loaded with eyewitness evidence and real historical figures, and it is corroborated by several outside sources. C. S. Lewis, a writer of myths himself, has commented that the New Testament stories do not show signs of being mythological. "All I am in private life is a literary critic and historian, that's my job," said Lewis. "And I'm prepared to say on that basis if anyone thinks the Gospels are either legends or novels, then that person is simply showing his incompetence as a literary critic. I've read a great many novels and I know a fair amount about the legends that grew up among early people, and I know perfectly well the Gospels are not that kind of stuff."[17]

Second, the pagan-myth theory can't explain the empty tomb, the martyrdom of the eyewitnesses, or the testimony of the non-Christian writings. Nor can it explain the evidence that leads nearly all scholars to accept the other historical facts we listed at the beginning of this chapter.

Third, ancient non-Christian sources knew that the New Testament writers were not offering mythical accounts. As Craig Blomberg observes, "The earliest Jewish and pagan critics of the resurrection understood the Gospel writers to be making historical claims, not writing myth or legend. They merely disputed the plausibility of those claims."[18]

Fourth, no Greek or Roman myth spoke of the literal incarnation of a monotheistic God into human form (cf. John 1:1-3, 14), by way of a literal virgin birth (Matt. 1:18-25), followed by his death and physical resurrection. The Greeks were polytheists, not monotheists as New Testament Christians were. Moreover, the Greeks believed in reincarnation into a different mortal body; New Testament Christians believed in *resurrection* into the same physical body made immortal (cf. Luke 24:37; John 9:2; Heb. 9:27).

Fifth, the first real parallel of a dying and rising god does not appear until A.D. 150, more than 100 years *after* the origin of Christianity.[19] So if there was any influence of one on the other, it was the influence of the historical event of the New Testament on mythology, not the reverse.

The only known account of a god surviving death that predates Christianity is the Egyptian cult god Osiris. In this myth, Osiris is cut into fourteen pieces, scattered around Egypt, then reassembled and brought back to life by the goddess Isis. However, Osiris does not actually come back to physical life but becomes a member of a shadowy underworld. As Habermas and Licona observe, "This is far different than Jesus' resurrection account where he was the gloriously risen Prince of life who was seen by others on earth before his ascension into heaven."[20]

Finally, even if there are myths about dying and rising gods prior to Christianity, that doesn't mean the New Testament writers copied from them. The fictional TV show *Star Trek* preceded the U.S. Space Shuttle program, but that doesn't mean that newspaper reports of space shuttle missions are influenced by *Star Trek* episodes! One has to look at the evidence of each account to see whether it is historical or mythical. There's no eyewitness or corroborating evidence for the historicity of Osiris's resurrection or for that of any other pagan god. No one believes they are true historical figures. But, as we have seen, there is strong eyewitness and corroborating evidence to support the historicity of the death and resurrection of Jesus Christ.

Do You Have Any Evidence for That?

Christians are used to "counter-punching" alternative theories to the Resurrection. In fact, we've just done that by pointing out the numerous deficiencies in the alternative theories ourselves. But that's not enough. While skeptics rightfully put the burden of proof for the Resurrection on Christians (and, as we have seen, Christians can meet that burden with good evidence), *Christians need to put the burden of proof on skeptics for their alternative theories.* In light of all the positive evidence for the Resurrection, skeptics must offer positive, first-century evidence for their alternative views.

It's one thing to concoct an alternative theory to the Resurrection, but it's another thing to actually find first-century evidence for it. A theory is not evidence. Reasonable people demand evidence, not just theories. Anyone can concoct a theory to explain any historical event. For example, if someone were to claim that all of the video footage from the Holocaust concentration camps was staged and manufactured by Jews in order to garner sympathy and support for a Jewish state, would you believe that theory? Of course not, because it flies in the face of all the known evidence. To be taken seriously, those who offer such a theory must present credible, independent eyewitness reports and other corroborating evidence to counter the numerous reports that say the Holocaust was real and was actually carried out by the Nazis. But no such counterevidence exists.

This is the case with the Resurrection. While skeptics have formulated numerous alternative theories to explain away the Resurrection, there is no evidence from any first-century source supporting any of them.[21] The only alternative theory that's even mentioned in a first-century source (the disciples stole the body) is from Matthew, and it is clearly identified as a lie. No one from the ancient world—not even the enemies of Christianity—has offered a *plausible* alternative explanation for the Resurrection. Many alternative theories formulated over the past 200 years are rooted in anti-supernaturalism. Since modern scholars philosophically rule out miracles in advance, they concoct ad hoc explanations to explain away the Resurrection. As we have seen, their ad hoc explanations contain multiple absurdities or improbabilities.

Those who have alternative theories for the Resurrection should be asked, "What evidence do you have for your theory? Can you please name three or four first-century sources that support your theory?" When honest skeptics are presented with this question, they typically answer with silence or a stuttering admission that they have no such evidence because none exists.[22]

And it's not just the Resurrection that the skeptics have to explain. They also have to explain the other thirty-five miracles that eyewitnesses have associated with Jesus. Are we to believe that the four Gospel writers were all deceived about all of those miracles as well as the Resurrection?

This mass deception theory needs evidence. Do we have any other first-century sources that offer a different explanation for the works of Jesus? The only one discovered (and it's probably from the second century) is the Jewish Talmud, which admits that Jesus performed unusual acts by saying that he "practiced sorcery." But this explanation is just as weak as the Jewish explanation for the Resurrection (the disciples stole the body). Perhaps sorcery could explain *some* of Jesus' "miracles," but all thirty-five? Sorcerers and magicians cannot perform the kinds of acts that Jesus is said to have performed—raising the dead, giving sight to the blind, walking on water, and so forth.

So if there's no ancient evidence for deception, are we to take the New Testament miracles at face value? Why not? We live in a theistic universe where miracles are possible. And while it's true that we don't have independent attestation for all of the miracles in the New Testament (because some are mentioned by only one writer), we certainly have multiple attestation for many of them (including the Resurrection). The sheer number of Jesus' miracles cited by independent sources is too great to be explained away as a great deception. One person may be deceived once, but not numerous observers repeatedly.

German scholar Wolfgang Trilling writes, "We are convinced and hold it for historically certain that Jesus did in fact perform miracles. . . . The miracle reports occupy so much space in the Gospels that it is impossible that all could have been subsequently invented or transferred to Jesus."[23] William Lane Craig concludes, "The fact that miracle working belongs to the historical Jesus is no longer disputed."[24] That is, miracles are not disputed on historical grounds, only on philosophical grounds (more on this in a minute).

The bottom line is that there are too many miracles and too much testimony to believe that all of the eyewitnesses got it wrong every time. With regard to the Resurrection, all alternative theories have fatal flaws, and we have strong eyewitness and circumstantial evidence that Jesus actually rose from the dead. In other words, not only do we lack a natural explanation for the empty tomb, we have positive evidence *for* the Resurrection. The explanation that requires the *least* amount of faith is that Jesus really did perform miracles and really did rise from the dead as he predicted. *So we don't have enough faith to believe that the New Testament writers were all deceived.*

WHY DON'T ALL SCHOLARS BELIEVE?

If we have an accurate copy of early testimony (chapter 9); if that testimony is not only early but from eyewitnesses (chapter 10); if those eyewitnesses recorded what they saw accurately (chapter 11); and if those eyewitnesses were not deceived about what they recorded (this chapter), then why don't all scholars take the New Testament at face value? For the same reason Darwinists refuse to acknowledge the evidence that defeats their view: they have a philosophical bias against miracles.

This bias was admitted during the debate between Craig and Crossan. Craig believes, as we do, that the evidence for the historicity of the literal resurrection is strong. Crossan, on the other hand, does not believe that Jesus literally rose from the dead. Here is a very telling exchange between the two men:

> Craig: Would there be anything, Dr. Crossan, that could convince you that Jesus was risen from the dead as a historical fact?
>
> Crossan: I need to make certain of what we're talking about. Let's say we have a situation outside the empty tomb on Easter Sunday morning. If somebody had a videocam, would we have recorded something coming out of the tomb? Is that the type of question?
>
> Craig: I guess what I'm asking, and what I think Mr. Buckley [the moderator] is pushing for, is this: what evidence would it take to convince you? Or are your preconceived ideas about the impossibility of the miraculous and so forth so strong that, in fact, they skew your historical judgment so that such an event could never even be admitted into court?

Crossan: No. . . . A doctor at Lourdes might admit, "I have absolutely no medical way of explaining what has happened." That is a right statement. Then one has the right to say, "I by faith therefore believe that God has intervened here." *But it's a theological presupposition of mine that God does not operate that way.* . . . What would it take to prove to me what you ask? I don't know, unless God changes the universe. I could imagine discovering tomorrow morning that every tree outside my house has moved five feet. That needs some explanation. I don't know the explanation, but I won't immediately presume a miracle.[25]

Crossan's explicit statement of his theological presupposition against miracles is a candid admission on his part. Of course Crossan doesn't speak for all skeptical scholars. But certainly a majority of them deny the plain reading of the New Testament because they share his philosophical bias against miracles. It is not that the historical evidence for the New Testament is weak (it's very strong indeed). It's that they've ruled out miracles in advance. They arrive at the wrong conclusion because their bias makes it impossible for them to arrive at the right conclusion.

Context! Context! Context!

Let's take a look at Crossan's final comment about the trees in his yard moving five feet overnight. He says he wouldn't "immediately presume a miracle." Well, neither would we, because most events actually *do* have a natural explanation (which, incidentally, helps miracles stand out when they do occur). So it makes perfect sense to seek a natural explanation first.

But does that mean we should *never* conclude that any event (such as the trees moving) was a miracle? Crossan would not so conclude because of his theological presupposition that God does not "work that way." But since that presupposition is unjustified—because God exists—what would be the right conclusion? It depends on the context of the event. Recall from chapter 5 that evidence must be interpreted in light of the context in which it is found.[26]

So let's suppose that Crossan's tree moving event occurred in the following context: Two hundred years in advance, someone claiming to be a prophet of God writes down a prediction that all of the trees in one area of Jerusalem would indeed move five feet one night during a particular year. Two hundred years later, a man arrives to tell the towns-people that the tree moving miracle will occur shortly. This man claims to be God, teaches profound truths, and performs many other unusual acts that appear to be miracles.

Then one morning numerous eyewitnesses claim that the trees in Crossan's Jerusalem yard—including several deep-rooted, 100-foot oaks—actually moved five feet during the night, just as the God-man predicted. These eyewitnesses also say this is just one of more than thirty miracles performed by this God-man. They then suffer persecution and martyrdom for proclaiming these miracles and for refusing to recant their testimony. Opponents of the God-man don't deny the evidence about the trees or the other miracles, but offer natural explanations that have numerous fatal flaws. Many years later, after all the eyewitnesses are dead, skeptics offer additional natural explanations that prove to be fatally flawed as well. In fact, for the next 1,900 years skeptics try to explain the event naturally, but no one can.

Question: Given that context, wouldn't it be reasonable to assume that the movement of the trees was supernatural rather than natural in origin? Of course. The context makes all the difference.

This is the case we have with the Resurrection. It's not just that we lack a natural explanation for the empty tomb. It's that we have positive eyewitness and corroborating circumstantial evidence *for* the resurrection miracle. Here's the context in which we must evaluate the evidence:

I. The Theistic Nature of This Universe Makes Miracles *Possible*— We live in a theistic universe where miracles are possible. (Indeed, the greatest miracle of all—creation of the universe out of nothing—has already occurred.) So God can use prophets to announce his messages and miracles to confirm them. That is, a miracle can be used to confirm the word of God, through a man of God, to the people of God.

II. Ancient Documents Say Miracles Are to Be *Expected*—We have Old Testament documents, written hundreds of years in advance, that predict that the Messiah—a man who would actually be God—would come, be killed at a specific time as a sacrifice for sinful humanity, and rise from the dead (more on this in the next chapter).

III. Historically Confirmed Eyewitness Documents Say Miracles Are Actual—There are 27 documents written by nine eyewitnesses or their contemporaries that describe numerous miraculous events. Many of these documents contain historically confirmed eyewitness testimony that goes back to the time of the events, and the evidence demonstrates that the narrative is not invented, embellished, or the product of deception. We know this because the New Testament documents meet all seven tests of historicity identified in chapter 9. The New Testament documents:

1. are early (most written 15-40 years later, well within two generations of the events)
2. contain eyewitness testimony
3. contain independent eyewitness testimony from multiple sources
4. are written by trustworthy people who taught and lived by the highest standard of ethics, and who died for their testimony
5. describe events, locations, and individuals corroborated by archaeology and other writers
6. describe some events that enemies tacitly admit are true (enemy attestation)
7. describe events and details that are embarrassing to the authors and even to Jesus himself

These historically confirmed eyewitness documents tell the following story:

1. At the time and place, and in the manner predicted by the Old Testament, Jesus arrives in Jerusalem and claims to be the Messiah. He teaches profound truths and, according to numerous independent eyewitnesses, performs thirty-five miracles (some on groups of people) and rises from the dead.
2. Once-cowardly and unbelieving eyewitnesses suddenly begin to boldly proclaim Jesus' resurrection in the face of persecution and death. (Misguided people may die for a lie they think is true, but they will not die for a lie they know is a lie. The New Testament writers were in a position to know the real truth about the Resurrection.)

3. In the very city of Jesus' death and tomb, a new movement (the church) is born and quickly spreads by peaceful means on the belief that Jesus has risen from the dead. (This is difficult to explain if there was no Resurrection. How could Christianity begin in a hostile city like Jerusalem if Jesus' body was still in the tomb? The hostile religious and government authorities would have exposed Christianity as fraudulent by exposing the body.)

4. Thousands of Jerusalem Jews, including Pharisee priests, abandon five of their most treasured beliefs and practices and adopt strange new ones after converting to Christianity.

5. Saul, the most ardent enemy of the new church, is suddenly converted and becomes its most prolific proponent. He travels the ancient world to proclaim the Resurrection, suffering persecution and martyrdom. (If there was no Resurrection, then why did the greatest enemy of Christianity suddenly become its greatest leader? Why did he willingly suffer persecution and death?)

6. James, the skeptical brother of Jesus, suddenly becomes convinced that his brother is the Son of God, and then becomes the leader of the church in Jerusalem. He later suffers martyrdom at the hands of the high priest. (We all know that family members can be the most difficult people to convince to our religious viewpoint. James began as the unconvinced brother of Jesus [John 7:5]. If there was no Resurrection, then why did James—who was called "the Just" by second-century historians Clement and Hegesippus[27]—suddenly come to believe that his brother really was the Messiah? Unless he saw the resurrected Christ, why would James become the leader of the church in Jerusalem and suffer a martyr's death?)

7. The Jewish enemies of Christianity don't deny the evidence but offer faulty naturalistic explanations to account for it.

IV. Additional Confirmation—The collective references of other ancient historians and writers confirm this basic storyline of the New Testament documents, and several archaeological discoveries affirm the details those documents describe.

When you put the evidence in proper context, you can see why *we don't have enough faith to be skeptical about it.* It's a lot more reasonable to be skeptical about skepticism!

Skeptics who look at points II-IV above (including the subpoints) may conclude that Jesus did not rise from the dead. But if they do, they've got to provide evidence for an alternative theory that can account for *all* of these points. As we have seen, they have failed, and failed miserably. The Resurrection best explains *all* of the evidence.

Since there's a God who can act, there can be acts of God. When God's intention is announced in advance, and you then have good eyewitness testimony and corroborating evidence that such events actually occurred, *it takes a lot more faith to deny those events than to believe them.*

Extraordinary Claims and Self-Canceling Evidence

There are two more objections that skeptics often bring up against the Resurrection and miracles. The first one is a demand for extraordinary evidence.

Extraordinary Evidence—Some skeptics might admit that the Resurrection is possible, but they say it would require extraordinary evidence to believe it. That is, since the New Testament makes extraordinary claims—such as miracles—we must have extraordinary evidence in order to believe those claims. This objection seems reasonable until you ask, "What does 'extraordinary' mean?"

If it means *beyond the natural,* then the skeptic is asking the Resurrection to be confirmed by another miracle. How could that work? In order to believe in the first miracle (the Resurrection), the skeptic would then need a second miracle to support it. He would then demand a third miracle to support the second, and this would go on to infinity. So by this criteria, the skeptic would never believe in the Resurrection even if it really happened. There's something wrong with a standard of proof that makes it impossible for you to believe what actually has occurred.

If "extraordinary" means *repeatable* as in a laboratory, then no event from history can be believed because historical events cannot be repeated. The believability of historical events can only be confirmed by looking at the quality of the eyewitness evidence and the nature of the forensic evidence in the light of the principles of uniformity and causality (we covered those principles in chapter 5). Besides, atheists who demand repeatability for biblical miracles are inconsistent because they do not demand repeatability of the historical "miracles" in which they believe—the Big Bang, spontaneous generation of first life, and macroevolution of subsequent life forms.

If "extraordinary" means *more than usual,* then that's exactly what we have to support the Resurrection. We have *more* eyewitness documents and *earlier* eyewitness documents for the Resurrection than for anything else from the ancient world. Moreover, these documents include *more* historical details and figures that have been corroborated by *more* independent and external sources than anything else from the ancient world. And as we've just reviewed, we also have *more* than usual circumstantial evidence supporting the Resurrection.

Finally, the skeptic's presupposition can be challenged. We don't need "extraordinary" evidence to believe something. Atheists affirm that from their own worldview. They believe in the Big Bang not because they have "extraordinary" evidence for it but because there is good evidence that the universe exploded into being out of nothing. Good evidence is all you need to believe something. However, atheists don't have even good evidence for some of their own precious beliefs. For example, atheists believe in spontaneous generation and macroevolution on faith alone. We say faith alone because, as we saw in chapters 5 and 6, there's not only little or no evidence for spontaneous generation and macroevolution, but there's strong evidence *against* those possibilities.

Furthermore, skeptics don't demand "extraordinary" evidence for other "extraordinary" events from history. For example, few events from ancient history are more "extraordinary" than the accomplishments of Alexander the Great (356–323 B.C.). Despite living only 33 years, Alexander achieved unparalleled success. He conquered much of the civilized world at the time, from Greece, east to India and south to Egypt. Yet how do we know this about Alexander? We have no sources from his lifetime or soon after his death. And we have only fragments of two works from about 100 years after his death. The truth is, *we base virtually everything we know about the "extraordinary" life of Alexander the Great from historians who wrote 300 to 500 years after his death!* In light of the robust evidence for the life of Christ, anyone who doubts Christ's historicity should also doubt the historicity of Alexander the Great. In fact, to be consistent, such a skeptic would have to doubt *all* of ancient history.[28]

Why do skeptics demand "extraordinary" evidence for the life of Christ but not the life of Alexander the Great? Because they're hung up on miracles again. Despite the fact that miracles are possible because God exists—and despite the fact that miracles were predicted and then witnessed—skeptics can't bear to admit that miracles have actually occurred. So they set the bar for believability too high. It's as if some skeptics are saying, "I won't believe in miracles because I haven't seen one. If the resurrected Jesus were to appear to me, then I would believe in him." Now that would be extraordinary evidence.

It certainly would be extraordinary, but is it really necessary? Does Jesus have to appear to every person in the world to make his claims credible? Why would he? We don't have to witness every event firsthand in order to believe the event actually occurred. In fact, it would be physically impossible to do so. We believe the testimony of others if they are trustworthy individuals, and especially if their testimony is corroborated by other data. This is exactly the case with the testimony of the New Testament writers.

Furthermore, as we pointed out in chapter 8, if God were too overt because of frequent miraculous displays, then he might, in some cases, infringe on our free will. If the purpose of this life is to allow us to freely make choices that will prepare us for eternity, then God will give us convincing evidence but not compelling evidence of his existence and purposes. Therefore, those who want to follow God can do so with confidence, and those who do not can suppress or ignore the evidence and live as if he didn't exist.

Self-Canceling Miracles—The great skeptic David Hume argued that miracles cannot affirm any one religion because miracles are based on poor testimony and all religions have them. In other words, miracle claims are self-canceling. Unfortunately for Hume, his objection does not describe the actual state of affairs.

First, Hume makes a hasty generalization by saying that alleged miracles from all religions are alike. As we've seen since chapter 9, the miracles associated with Christianity are not based on poor testimony. They are based on early, eyewitness, multiple-source testimony that is unrivaled in any other world religion. That is, no other world religion has verified miracles like those in the New Testament.

Second, Hume's objection is prior to the discoveries of modern science that confirm that this is a theistic universe (chapters 3–6). Since this is a theistic universe, Judaism and Islam are the only other major world religions that possibly could be true. Miracles confirming the Old Testament of Judaism also confirm Christianity. So we are left with Islam as the only possible alternative to "cancel" the miracles of Christianity. But as we saw in chapter 10, there are no verifiable miracles confirming Islam. All alleged miracles of Muhammad come long after his death and were not based on eyewitness testimony.

Finally, the uniqueness, number, and quality of New Testament miracles cannot be explained by anything other than a supernatural cause. Jesus performed more than thirty miracles that were instantaneous, always successful, and unique. Some were even predicted. So-called miracle workers who claim partial success effect only psychosomatic cures, engage in trickery, perform satanic signs, or rely on naturally explainable events. In fact, no contemporary healer even claims to be able to heal all diseases (including "incurable" ones) instantaneously, with 100 percent success. But Jesus and his apostles did. This demonstrates the unique, God-authenticating nature of the New Testament miracles against all other supernatural claims of any other religion. In short, nothing "cancels" the miracles of the New Testament.

CONCLUSION: ONE SOLITARY LIFE

In the beginning of chapter 9, we said there are two questions we needed to answer to see if the New Testament is truly historical:

1. Do we have accurate copies of the original documents that were written down in the first century?
2. Do those documents speak the truth?

As we've seen in the last four chapters, the evidence is strong that the answer to both of those questions is yes. In other words, we can be sure beyond a reasonable doubt that the New Testament is historically reliable.

At this point, we are *not* saying that the New Testament is without error. We'll investigate that question later. Right now, we can only conclude that the major events of the New Testament really occurred nearly 2,000 years ago. Jesus really lived, taught, performed miracles, died by crucifixion, and then rose from the dead.

If you're still not convinced, consider one more piece of corroborating evidence: the incredible impact of Christ's life as expressed in a short sermon excerpt that is often titled "One Solitary Life":

> He was born in an obscure village, the child of a peasant. He grew up in another village, where he worked in a carpenter shop until he was 30. Then, for three years, he was an itinerant preacher.
>
> He never wrote a book. He never held an office. He never had a family or owned a home. He didn't go to college. He never lived in a big city. He never traveled 200 miles from the place where he was born. He did none of the things that usually accompany greatness. He had no credentials but himself.
>
> He was only 33 when the tide of public opinion turned against him. His friends ran away. One of them denied him. He was turned over to his enemies and went through the mockery of a trial. He was nailed to a cross between two thieves. While he was dying, his executioners gambled for his garments, the only property he had on earth. When he was dead, he was laid in a borrowed grave, through the pity of a friend.
>
> [Twenty] centuries have come and gone, and today he is the central figure of the human race. I am well within the mark when I say that all the armies that ever marched, all the navies that ever sailed, all the parliaments that ever sat, all the kings that ever reigned—put together—have not affected the life of man on this earth as much as that one, solitary life.[29]

If there was no resurrection, how could this life be the most influential life of all time? We don't have enough faith to believe that this one solitary life from a remote, ancient village could be the most influential life of all time . . . *unless the Resurrection is true.*

Chapters 13–14 will cover:

1. Truth about reality is knowable.
2. The opposite of true is false.
3. It is true that the theistic God exists. This is evidenced by the:
   a. Beginning of the universe (Cosmological Argument)
   b. Design of the universe (Teleological Argument/ Anthropic Principle)
   c. Design of life (Teleological Argument)
   d. Moral Law (Moral Argument)
4. If God exists, then miracles are possible.
5. Miracles can be used to confirm a message from God (i.e., as acts of God to confirm a word from God).
6. The New Testament is historically reliable. This is evidenced by:
   a. Early testimony
   b. Eyewitness testimony
   c. Uninvented (authentic) testimony
   d. Eyewitnesses who were not deceived
➤ **7. The New Testament says Jesus claimed to be God.**
   8. Jesus' claim to be God was miraculously confirmed by:
   a. His fulfillment of many prophecies about himself;
   b. His sinless life and miraculous deeds;
   c. His prediction and accomplishment of his resurrection.
   9. Therefore, Jesus is God.
   10. Whatever Jesus (who is God) teaches is true.
   11. Jesus taught that the Bible is the Word of God.
   12. Therefore, it is true that the Bible is the Word of God (and anything opposed to it is false).

13

Who Is Jesus: God?
Or Just a Great Moral
Teacher?

"There are none who are as deaf as those who do not want to hear."

—Barry Leventhal

WE'VE ESTABLISHED THAT the New Testament documents are historically reliable. That is, we can be reasonably certain that Jesus said and did what those documents say he said and did, including his resurrection from the dead. So who is this Jesus? What did he say about himself? Is he really God as Christians claim?

Before we investigate the claims of Christ, we need to take a look at the messianic predictions we've been alluding to in recent chapters. This will help us discover Jesus' true identity, and it also will provide further evidence relating to the authenticity of the New Testament. We start on the campus of UCLA in the mid-60s.

THE MESSIAH AND THE "TRICK" BIBLE

In early 1966, Barry Leventhal was a young Jewish man on top of the world. As offensive captain of the UCLA football team, Barry had just led UCLA—a team predicted to finish last that year—to its first ever Rose Bowl championship.

"My life was great!" he remembers. "I was a hero. People loved me. My Jewish fraternity chose me as the national athlete of the year. And I basked in the glory of it all."[1]

Soon after the Rose Bowl victory, Barry's best friend, Kent, said that he had come to know Jesus Christ in a personal way.

"I had no idea what Kent was talking about," Barry said. "I thought he had always been a Christian. After all, he had been born into a Christian home, just as I had been born into a Jewish home. Isn't that how a person got his particular religion? You inherited it from your parents."

But Barry was intrigued by the change in Kent's life, especially when Kent said to him, "Barry, I want you to know that I thank God every day for the Jews."

"Why in the world would you do that?" Barry asked.

Kent's answer utterly surprised him. "I thank God every day for the Jews for two reasons," Kent began. "First, God used them to give me my Bible. And second, and most important, God used the Jews to bring his Messiah into the world, the One who died for the sins of the whole world and especially for all of my sins."

"To this day I remember the impact of those few simple but true statements," Barry recalls. "*Genuine* Christians don't hate the Jews after all. In fact, they truly love us and are grateful and honored that God has included them by faith into his forever family."

A few weeks later, Kent introduced Barry to Hal, the Campus Crusade for Christ leader on the UCLA campus. One day Barry and Hal were sitting in the crowded student lounge, when things got very tense. As Hal was showing Barry that predictions of the Messiah from the Old Testament were fulfilled by Jesus, Barry blurted out loudly, "How could you do this?!"

"Do what?" Hal asked.

"Use a trick Bible!" Barry charged. "You've got a trick Bible to fool the Jews!"

"What do you mean by a 'trick Bible?'" Hal asked.

Barry responded, "You Christians took those so-called messianic predictions from your own New Testament and then rewrote them into your edition of the Old Testament in order to fool the Jews. But I guarantee you, those messianic prophecies are not in our Jewish Bible!"

"No, Barry. That's not it at all," said Hal.

"No, that's a trick Bible!" Barry shouted as he jumped up.

"No, it isn't!" Hal said again, amazed at the charge. "I've never had anyone say this before. Please sit down."

People began to stare.

"No, Hal. This relationship is over!"

"Barry, Barry, wait a minute. Do you have your own Tanach [a Jewish Bible]?"

"Yes, I've got one from my Bar Mitzvah. So what?"

"Why don't you write down these verses and go read them in your own Tanach?"

"Because that'll be a waste of time!" Barry blasted. "Those verses aren't in the Tanach!"

"Please," Hal persisted, "just write them down and check them out for yourself."

The two men volleyed back and forth until Barry—wanting to get Hal off his back—agreed to check them out. "Alright," he said as he scribbled the references down, "I'll check them out. But don't call me, I'll call you!"

Barry left, never expecting to see Hal again. He didn't check the verses for several days, and then guilt began to gnaw at him. "I told Hal I'd check them out," Barry recalled, "so I should at least do that and put this Christianity thing to rest once and for all!"

That night Barry dusted off his old Tanach—the one he hadn't even opened since he was thirteen—and was shocked at what he found. Every prediction Hal had referenced was indeed in the Tanach!

Barry's initial reaction was, "I'm in deep trouble! Jesus really is the Messiah!"

But at this point, Barry's acceptance was only intellectual. He immediately began to worry about the implications if he made his discovery public. "If I accept Jesus as the Messiah, what will my parents think? What will my Jewish fraternity friends do? What will my rabbi say?"

More study was needed before Barry was ready to go public, especially on one passage that Hal had referenced several times: Isaiah 53. Before we reveal the conclusion of Barry's search, let's take a look at Isaiah 53 and some of the other messianic prophecies he was investigating.

THE SUFFERING SERVANT

In March of 1947 a young Arab shepherd boy (Muhammad adh-Dhib) was watching his sheep seven-and-a-half miles south of Jericho and one mile west of the Dead Sea. After tossing a rock at a stray goat, he heard the sound of breaking pottery. What ensued was one of the greatest archaeological discoveries of all time—the Dead Sea Scrolls.

In excavations of area caves through 1956, numerous scrolls and thousands of manuscript fragments were found in pottery that had been placed there about 2,000 years ago by a Jewish religious sect known as the Essenes. The Essenes existed as a group from 167 B.C. to A.D. 68. They had broken away from the temple authorities and established their own monastic community in the Judean desert near Qumran.

One of their scrolls found in Qumran is now known as the Great Isaiah Scroll. Dated from 100 B.C., this twenty-four-foot scroll is the complete book of Isaiah (all sixty-six chapters) and is the oldest biblical scroll in existence.[2] It is currently protected in a vault somewhere in Jerusalem, but a copy of it is on display at the Shrine of the Book museum in Jerusalem.

The importance of this discovery is not just that the scroll predates Christ and is in good condition, but that it contains perhaps the clearest and most complete prophecy about the coming Messiah. Isaiah calls the Messiah the "Servant of the Lord," and he begins to refer to the Servant in chapter 42 in what is known as the first "Servant Song." However, the Servant is most often referred to as the "Suffering Servant," because of the vivid description of his sacrificial death found in Isaiah 53.

As you read the passage (52:13–53:12), ask yourself, "To whom is this referring?"

> (52:13) See, my servant will act wisely;
>   he will be raised and lifted up and highly exalted.
> (14) Just as there were many who were appalled at him—
>   his appearance was so disfigured beyond that of any man
>   and his form marred beyond human likeness—
> (15) so will he sprinkle many nations,
>   and kings will shut their mouths because of him.
> For what they were not told, they will see,
>   and what they have not heard, they will understand.
>
> (53:1) Who has believed our message
>   and to whom has the arm of the LORD been revealed?
> (2) He grew up before him like a tender shoot,
>   and like a root out of dry ground.
> He had no beauty or majesty to attract us to him,
>   nothing in his appearance that we should desire him.
> (3) He was despised and rejected by men,
>   a man of sorrows, and familiar with suffering.

Like one from whom men hide their faces
  he was despised, and we esteemed him not.

(4) Surely he took up our infirmities
  and carried our sorrows,
yet we considered him stricken by God,
  smitten by him, and afflicted.
(5) But he was pierced for our transgressions,
  he was crushed for our iniquities;
the punishment that brought us peace was upon him,
  and by his wounds we are healed.
(6) We all, like sheep, have gone astray,
  each of us has turned to his own way;
and the LORD has laid on him
  the iniquity of us all.

(7) He was oppressed and afflicted,
  yet he did not open his mouth;
he was led like a lamb to the slaughter,
  and as a sheep before her shearers is silent,
  so he did not open his mouth.
(8) By oppression and judgment he was taken away.
  And who can speak of his descendants?
For he was cut off from the land of the living;
  for the transgression of my people he was stricken.
(9) He was assigned a grave with the wicked,
  and with the rich in his death,
though he had done no violence,
  nor was any deceit in his mouth.

(10) Yet it was the LORD's will to crush him and cause him to suffer,
  and though the LORD makes his life a guilt offering,
he will see his offspring and prolong his days,
  and the will of the LORD will prosper in his hand.
(11) After the suffering of his soul,
  he will see the light of life and be satisfied;
by his knowledge my righteous servant will justify many,
  and he will bear their iniquities.
(12) Therefore I will give him a portion among the great,
  and he will divide the spoils with the strong,

because he poured out his life unto death,
   and was numbered with the transgressors.
For he bore the sin of many,
   and made intercession for the transgressors.

To whom do you think this is referring? Barry had a good idea who. Reading out of his own Tanach, he was startled at the parallels to Jesus, but he was still a bit confused. He wanted to give his rabbi a chance to explain it.

"I vividly remember the first time I seriously confronted Isaiah 53, or better still, the first time it seriously confronted me," Barry explains. "Being rather confused over the identity of the Servant in Isaiah 53, I went to my local rabbi and said to him, 'Rabbi, I have met some people at school who claim that the so-called Servant in Isaiah 53 is none other than Jesus of Nazareth. But I would like to know from you, who is this Servant in Isaiah 53?'"

Barry was astonished at his response. The rabbi said, "Barry, I must admit that as I read Isaiah 53 it does seem to be talking about Jesus, but since we Jews do not believe in Jesus, it can't be speaking about Jesus."

Barry didn't know a lot about formal logic at that point, but he knew enough to say to himself, "That just doesn't sound kosher to me! Not only does the rabbi's so-called reasoning sound circular, it also sounds evasive and even fearful." Today Barry observes, "There are none who are as deaf as those who do not want to hear."

For those who do want to hear, Larry Helyer does a fine job of summarizing the characteristics and accomplishments of Isaiah's Servant. Beginning with the first Servant Song in chapter 42, Helyer makes the following observations of the Servant:

1. He is elected by the Lord, anointed by the Spirit, and promised success in his endeavor (42:1, 4).
2. Justice is a prime concern of his ministry (42:1, 4).
3. His ministry has an international scope (42:1, 6).
4. God predestined him to his calling (49:1).
5. He is a gifted teacher (49:2).
6. He experiences discouragement in his ministry (49:4).
7. His ministry extends to the Gentiles (49:6).
8. The Servant encounters strong opposition and resistance to his teaching, even of a physically violent nature (50:4-6).

9. He is determined to finish what God called him to do (50:7).
10. The Servant has humble origins with little outward prospects for success (53:1-2).
11. He experiences suffering and affliction (53:3).
12. The Servant accepts vicarious and substitutionary suffering on behalf of his people (53:4-6, 12).
13. He is put to death after being condemned (53:7-9).
14. Incredibly, he comes back to life and is exalted above all rulers (53:10-12; 52:13-15).[3]

In addition to Helyer's observations, we note that the servant is also sinless (53:9).

Just a casual reading of the passage should leave little doubt that the Suffering Servant is Jesus. In fact, the traditional *Jewish* interpretation of the Servant passages was that they predicted the coming Messiah.[4] That is, until Jews began having more contact with Christian apologists about a thousand years ago, at which point they reinterpreted the Suffering Servant to be the nation of Israel. The first Jew to claim that the Suffering Servant was Israel rather than the Messiah was Shlomo Yitzchaki, better known as Rashi (c. 1040–1105). Today Rashi's view dominates Jewish and rabbinical theology.

Unfortunately for Rashi and many present-day Jewish theologians, there are at least three fatal flaws with the assertion that Israel is the Suffering Servant. First, unlike Israel, the Servant is sinless (53:9). To say that Israel is sinless is to contradict and negate virtually the entire Old Testament. The recurrent theme of the Old Testament is that Israel has sinned by breaking God's commandments and by chasing after other gods instead of the one true God. If Israel is sinless, then why did God give the Jews a sacrificial system? Why did they have a Day of Atonement? Why did they constantly need prophets to warn them to stop sinning and to come back to God?

Second, unlike Israel, the Suffering Servant is a lamb who submits without any resistance whatsoever (53:7). History shows us that Israel certainly is not a lamb—she lies down for no one.

Third, unlike Israel, the Suffering Servant dies as a substitutionary atonement for the sins of others (53:4-6, 8, 10-12). But Israel has not died, nor is she paying for the sins of others. No one is redeemed on account of what the nation of Israel does. Nations, and the individuals that comprise them, are punished for their own sins.

This Johnny-come-lately interpretation of Isaiah 53 appears to be motivated by the desire to avoid the conclusion that Jesus is indeed the Messiah who was predicted hundreds of years beforehand. But there's no legitimate way to avoid the obvious. Remember, the Great Isaiah Scroll was written some 100 years before Christ, and we know that the material it contains is even older. The Septuagint, which is the translation of the Hebrew Old Testament (including all of Isaiah) into Greek, is dated about 250 B.C. So the Hebrew original must be even older. Furthermore, manuscripts or manuscript fragments of all the Old Testament books except Esther were found with the Dead Sea Scrolls. So there's no doubt that the Old Testament, including the Suffering Servant passage, predates Christ by several hundred years.

Hitting the Bull's-eye

If Isaiah 53 were the only prophetic passage in the Old Testament, it would be enough to demonstrate the divine nature of at least the book of Isaiah. But there are several other passages in the Old Testament that predict the coming of Jesus Christ or are ultimately fulfilled by him. These include (table 13.1):

Messianic Passage	Messianic Prediction
Genesis 3:15 [God speaking to Satan] "And I will put enmity between you and the woman, and between your offspring and hers; he will crush your head, and you will strike his heel."	Seed of a Woman: The offspring of Eve (literally the "seed" of Eve) will ultimately crush Satan. But this human being, unlike other human beings, will be from the seed of a woman rather than from the seed of a man (cf. Matt. 1:23).
Genesis 12:3, 7 [God speaking to Abraham] I will bless those who bless you, and whoever curses you I will curse; and all peoples on earth will be blessed through you. . . . The LORD appeared to Abram and said, "To your offspring I will give this land."	Seed of Abraham: The offspring of Abraham spoken of here literally means "seed" (not "seeds"). It refers to only one person—a messiah—who will ultimately bless all peoples on the earth and rule over the land (cf. Gal. 3:16).

Messianic Passage	Messianic Prediction
Genesis 49:10 The scepter will not depart from Judah, nor the ruler's staff from between his feet, until he comes to whom it belongs and the obedience of the nations is his.	**Tribe of Judah:** The scepter (the king's ceremonial staff) will not depart from the tribe of Judah until the ultimate king, the Messiah, comes. In other words, Messiah will come from the tribe of Judah (one of Israel's twelve tribes).
Jeremiah 23:5-6: "The days are coming," declares the LORD, "when I will raise up to David a righteous Branch, a King who will reign wisely and do what is just and right in the land. In his days Judah will be saved and Israel will live in safety. This is the name by which he will be called: The LORD Our Righteousness." (See also Jer. 33:15-16; Isa. 11:1)	**Son of David:** Messiah will be a son of David, and he will be called God.
Isaiah 9:6-7 (NASB): For a child will be born to us, a son will be given to us; and the government will rest on His shoulders; and His name will be called Wonderful Counselor, Mighty God, Eternal Father, Prince of Peace. There will be no end to the increase of His government or of peace, on the throne of David and over his kingdom, to establish it and to uphold it with justice and righteousness from then on and forevermore.	**He will be God:** Messiah will be born as a child, but he will also be God. He will rule from the throne of David.
Micah 5:2 (NASB): But as for you, Bethlehem Ephrathah, too little to be among the clans of Judah, from you One will go forth for Me to be ruler in Israel. His goings forth are from long ago, from the days of eternity.	**Born in Bethlehem:** Messiah, who is eternal, will be born in Bethlehem.
Malachi 3:1 (NASB): Behold, I am going to send My messenger, and he will clear the way before Me. And the Lord, whom you seek, will suddenly come to His temple; and the messenger of the covenant, in whom you delight, behold, He is coming," says the LORD of hosts.	**He will come to the temple:** Messiah, who will be preceded by a messenger, will suddenly come to the temple.
Daniel 9:25-26: Know and understand this: From the issuing of the decree to restore and rebuild Jerusalem until the Anointed One [Messiah], the ruler, comes, there will be seven "sevens," and sixty-two "sevens." It will be rebuilt with streets and a trench, but in times of trouble. After the sixty-two "sevens," the Anointed One will be cut off and will have nothing. The people of the ruler who will come will destroy the city and the sanctuary.	**He will die in A.D. 33:** Messiah will die (be "cut off") 483 years (69 x 7) after the decree to rebuild Jerusalem (that works out to A.D. 33).[5] The city and the temple will then be destroyed. (This occurred in 70.)

Table 13.1

Question: Who, in all the history of the world,

1. is from the seed of a woman;
2. from the seed of Abraham;
3. from the tribe of Judah;

4. from the line of David;
5. was both God and man;
6. was born in Bethlehem;
7. was preceded by a messenger, and visited the Jerusalem temple before it was destroyed in A.D. 70;
8. died in A.D. 33; and
9. rose from the dead (Isa. 53:11)?

Jesus Christ of Nazareth is the only possible candidate. Only he hits the bull's-eye. Of course, the case is strengthened further when you consider the other aspects of Isaiah 53. Jesus meets all of those criteria as well.

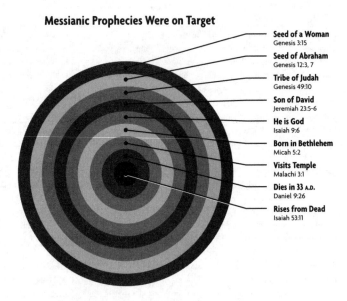

Messianic Prophecies Were on Target

Seed of a Woman
Genesis 3:15

Seed of Abraham
Genesis 12:3, 7

Tribe of Judah
Genesis 49:10

Son of David
Jeremiah 23:5-6

He is God
Isaiah 9:6

Born in Bethlehem
Micah 5:2

Visits Temple
Malachi 3:1

Dies in 33 A.D.
Daniel 9:26

Rises from Dead
Isaiah 53:11

Fig. 13.1

The prophetic case for Christ is strengthened even further when you realize that the Old Testament predicted that God himself would be pierced, as happened when Jesus was crucified. As recorded by the Old Testament prophet Zechariah (also written well before Christ), *God says*, "I will pour out on the house of David and the inhabitants of Jerusalem a spirit of grace and supplication. They will look on *me, the one they have pierced,* and they will mourn for him as one mourns for an only child, and grieve bitterly for him as one grieves for a firstborn son" (Zech.

12:10). Later, Zechariah predicts that the Lord's "feet will stand on the Mount of Olives, east of Jerusalem" (Zech. 14:4). These predictions refer to Christ's second coming, but the reference to God having been "pierced" (i.e., crucified) by the "house of David and the inhabitants of Jerusalem" obviously refers to his first coming. In fact, the apostle John quotes Zechariah 12:10 as prophetic of the crucifixion (John 19:37).

You can see why Barry realized he was "in trouble." These messianic prophecies are beyond coincidental. These are far beyond predictions any psychic could make.[6] Something truly supernatural is going on here, but many of his fellow Jews didn't see it. Barry realized that while the Jews have been waiting for a political messiah, they failed to recognize that the Messiah would first have to come as a lamb to be slaughtered for the sins of the world (Isa. 53:7, 11-12; John 1:29).

With a sense of intrigue, Barry contacted Hal once more. They reviewed the messianic prophecies again, particularly Isaiah 53. Hal then offered Barry a small booklet.

"This is an account of Jesus' life by a young man who knew him and followed him," Hal said. "Why don't you read it and tell me what you think?"

Once Barry picked it up, he couldn't put it down. The story had many Jewish elements, from priests to Passover. And this Jesus was an amazing figure—a miracle worker who had great insights, and spoke with authority but with kindness as well.

Barry didn't know it at the time, but he was reading the Gospel of John. He was particularly struck with the free gift of eternal salvation that Jesus offers to anyone who will receive him. "Everything I ever wanted out of life I had to earn myself," Barry remembers. "And yet, here was Jesus offering himself and all his best gifts for time and eternity as a free gift of his love. Who wouldn't want to embrace such an offer?"

It was April now, more than three months after that glorious Rose Bowl victory. "I suddenly realized that I had nothing that withstood the test of time, let alone the test of eternity," Barry recalls. "This was most graphically demonstrated to me by the Rose Bowl victory itself. Just a few mere months after the most significant event in my life, and perhaps in my *entire* life, all the glory, everything involved, was now slowly fading away into a distant memory."

"Is that all there is to life?" Barry thought. And then he remembered that Jesus the Messiah was offering *eternal* life! Barry knew *intellectually* that Jesus was the Messiah weeks earlier when he found those messianic prophecies in his own Tanach. But believing *that* Jesus was the Messiah wasn't enough (after all, even the demons know *that* Jesus is the Messiah—James 2:19). Barry needed to believe *in* Jesus as the Messiah. In order to accept the free gift of eternal salvation from the punishment he deserved, Barry needed to take a step of the will, not just of the mind. After all, it would be unloving of God to force Barry into heaven against his will.

On the afternoon of April 24, 1966, Barry was ready to act on what the evidence told him was true. He knelt by his bed and prayed, "Jesus, I believe that you are the promised Messiah for the Jewish people and for the whole world, and so, for me as well, and that you died for my sins and that you are alive from the dead forevermore. So I now receive you into my life as my own personal Lord and Savior. Thank you for dying in my place." Barry says, "There was no lightning or thunder— only his personal presence and peace as he promised, which has not left me to this very day."

Since his remarkable discovery, Barry has been reaching the Jewish people with the truth that the Messiah has come. The evidence for this truth is in their own Scriptures! And the examining of the evidence for those Scriptures is a focus of Southern Evangelical Seminary near Charlotte, North Carolina, where Barry currently serves as academic dean and professor.

The Box Top to Prophecy

We have seen several Old Testament passages that are clear predictions of the Messiah. These have been fulfilled only by Jesus Christ. However, skeptics are quick to point out that some other prophecies quoted as messianic are taken out of context or do not really predict the future. For example, Psalm 22 says, "they have pierced my hands and my feet." Many Christians claim that this verse is a reference to Christ's crucifixion, which was not even a method of punishment in the days of David (the author of the psalm). But skeptics charge that David is speaking only about himself, not Christ, so any messianic application is illegitimate. There are three possibilities here.

First, some Christian scholars agree with the skeptics on verses like this. They say that Psalm 22 is not intended to be predictive. (Of course, even if they are correct, there are plenty of verses that clearly *are* predictive, as we have already seen.)

Second, other Christian scholars point out that some biblical prophecies may apply to two different people at two different times. Both David and Jesus certainly had enemies and difficulties in their lives as expressed in Psalm 22. So why couldn't the psalm be true of David *and* Jesus?

The third option—which is the one that seems most plausible to us—is that Psalm 22 is solely predictive of Jesus. After all, the psalm contains several direct references to Christ's crucifixion experience. It begins with his cry from the cross—"My God, my God, why have you forsaken me?" (Ps. 22:1, cf. Matt. 27:46)—and then describes other events associated with the crucifixion, including: the scorn, mocking, and insults of his accusers (vv. 6-7); his thirst (v. 15); his pierced hands and feet (v. 16); his unbroken bones (v. 17); his divided garments (v. 18); the fact that his enemies cast lots for his garments (v. 18); his ultimate rescue by the Lord (v. 19), and even his public praise of God to his fellow Israelites after his rescue (v. 22). This goes beyond coincidence, and leads us to believe that Christ is actually the one speaking in the entire psalm. In other words, while David wrote the psalm, Christ is the one speaking. This is not unprecedented. In Psalm 110, God the Father is actually having a conversation with God the Son.

The skeptic may say, "But you're only interpreting Psalm 22 that way because you now know what happened to Christ. It probably wouldn't have been apparent to someone living in Old Testament times that Psalm 22 was about Christ."

To which we reply: even if that is true, so what? It may be true that certain messianic prophecies in the Old Testament become clear only in light of Christ's life. But that doesn't mean those prophecies are any less amazing. Look at it this way: If you can't make sense of the pieces of a jigsaw puzzle without the box top, does that mean that no one made the puzzle? No. Does it mean there's no design to the puzzle? No. In fact, once you see the box top, you suddenly realize not only how the pieces fit together but how much forethought it took to design the pieces that way. In the same way, Jesus' life serves as the box top for many pieces of the prophetic puzzle found throughout the Old Testament. In fact, one

Bible scholar has identified 71 Old Testament messianic prophecies fulfilled by Christ, some of which are illuminated by the light of Christ's life.[7]

Some have summarized it this way: in the Old Testament Christ is concealed; in the New Testament he is revealed. While many prophecies are clear beforehand, some can be seen only in the light of Christ's life. Those that become clear *after* Christ are no less a product of supernatural design than those that were clear *before* Christ.

Is Jesus God?

As we have seen, the Old Testament predicts the coming of a Messiah who would be born a man but somehow be God as well (Isa. 9:6). Jesus is the only known person who meets the predicted qualifications of the Messiah. But did he claim to be God?

Certainly the New Testament writers claimed on several occasions that Jesus was God. For example, in the opening chapter of his Gospel, John says "the Word was God" and "the Word became flesh" (John 1:1, 14). Paul says that Christ is "God over all" (Rom. 9:5), and "in Christ all the fullness of the Deity lives in bodily form" (Col. 2:9). Peter declares that believers receive righteousness from "our God and Savior Jesus Christ" (2 Pet. 1:1). Matthew applies deity to Jesus when he quotes Isaiah 7:14: "The virgin will be with child and will give birth to a son, and they will call him Immanuel"—which means, "God with us" (Matt. 1:23). The writer of Hebrews says, "The Son is the radiance of God's glory and the exact representation of his being, sustaining all things by his powerful word" (Heb. 1:3). He also quotes Psalm 45:6 in claiming that God says of the Son, *"Your* throne, O God, will last for ever and ever" (Heb. 1:8). These are clear claims of Christ's deity by the apostles. Even the demons acknowledged that Jesus was God (Matt. 8:29; Luke 4:34, 41)! But did Jesus himself claim to be God?

Direct Claims to Be God

Perhaps no claim is more direct than Jesus' response to Caiaphas's point-blank interrogation:

> "Are you the Christ, the Son of the Blessed One?"
> "I am," said Jesus. "And you will see the Son of Man sitting at the right hand of the Mighty One and coming on the clouds of heaven."

The high priest tore his clothes. "Why do we need any more witnesses?" he asked. "You have heard the blasphemy. What do you think?" They all condemned him as worthy of death (Mark 14:61-64).

Notice that Jesus responded to the direct question with a direct answer: "I am." Referring to himself as the "Son of Man," Jesus then added that he would be coming back on the clouds of heaven. Caiaphas and his onlookers knew the implication. This was a reference to the vision the Old Testament prophet Daniel had of the end times: the Messiah—the Son of Man—will come to earth to judge the world on the authority given to him by God the Father ("the Ancient of Days"), and all the world's people will worship him (Dan. 7:13). Of course, no one is to be worshiped but God himself. Yet here was Christ claiming that he would be the one to judge the world and receive worship from its people. He was claiming to be God, and everyone knew it.

While Matthew, Mark, and Luke all record the "I am" response to Caiaphas, John tells of another occasion where Jesus claims deity by answering, "I am." This occurs during a tense exchange with some Jews. After several volleys back and forth about the true identity of Jesus, the conversation culminates with Jesus declaring,

"Your father Abraham rejoiced at the thought of seeing my day; he saw it and was glad."

"You are not yet fifty years old," the Jews said to him, "and you have seen Abraham!"

"I tell you the truth," Jesus answered, "before Abraham was born, I am!" At this, they picked up stones to stone him, but Jesus hid himself, slipping away from the temple grounds (John 8:56-59).

Skeptics may say, "'Before Abraham was born, I am!' is not even good English! It's the wrong tense." Exactly. Jesus isn't worried about grammar because he's quoting the very name God gave to Moses at the burning bush.

Do you remember the movie *The Ten Commandments?* What did Moses (played by Charlton Heston) do when he encountered the burning bush? He asked God, "Suppose I go to the Israelites and say to them, 'The God of your fathers has sent me to you,' and they ask me, 'What is his name?' Then what shall I tell them?"

God then said to Moses, "I AM WHO I AM. This is what you are to say to the Israelites: 'I AM has sent me to you'" (Ex. 3:13-14).

I AM is the self-existent One. He has no past or future because he is eternal. He's not in time. Jesus was claiming to be that eternal, self-existent One, and that's why the Jews picked up stones to stone him.

For those who continue to say, "No, Jesus never claimed to be God," we have a question: If Jesus didn't claim to be God, then why was he killed? Jesus' crucifixion, which is probably the most well-attested fact from all of ancient history, is difficult to explain unless he claimed to be God.

The unbelieving Jews certainly knew he claimed to be God. On several occasions they picked up stones to stone him for blasphemy. Why was it obvious to first-century people that Jesus claimed to be God, but it's not obvious to some present-day skeptics?

Indirect Claims to Be God

In addition to these direct claims to be God, Jesus made several other statements that clearly implied he was God:

- Jesus prayed, "And now, O Father, glorify thou me with thine own self with the glory which I had with thee before the world was" (John 17:5, KJV). But the Old Testament says there is only one God (Deut. 6:4; Isa. 45:5ff.), and God says, "my glory will I not give to another" (Isa. 42:8).
- He declared, "I am the first and the last" (Rev. 1:17)—precisely the words used by God of himself in Isaiah 44:6.
- He said, "I am the good shepherd" (John 10:11); but the Old Testament says, "The LORD is my shepherd" (Ps. 23:1). Moreover, God says, "As a shepherd looks after his scattered flock when he is with them, so will I look after my sheep" (Ezek. 34:12).
- Jesus claimed to be the judge of all people (Matt. 25:31ff.; John 5:27); but Joel quotes God as saying, "for there I will sit to judge all the nations on every side" (Joel 3:12).
- Jesus said, "I am the light of the world. Whoever follows me will never walk in darkness, but will have the light of life" (John 8:12). But the psalmist declares, "The LORD is my light" (Ps. 27:1).
- Jesus declared, "For just as the Father raises the dead and gives them life, even so the Son gives life to whom he is pleased to

give it" (John 5:21). But the Old Testament clearly taught that only God was the giver of life (Deut. 32:39; 1 Sam. 2:6) and the one to raise the dead (Isa. 16:19; Dan. 12:2; Job 19:25), and the only judge (Deut. 32:35; Joel 3:12).

• Jesus insisted, "No one comes to the Father except through me" (John 14:6).

God in OT	Claim	Jesus in NT
Ps. 23:1	Shepherd	John 10:11
Isa. 44:6	First and Last	Rev. 1:17
Joel 3:12	Judge	Matt. 25:31ff.
Isa. 62:5	Bridegroom	Matt. 25:1
Ps. 27:1	Light	John 8:12
Isa. 43:11	Savior	John 4:42
Isa. 42:8	God's Glory	John 17:5
1 Sam. 2:6	Giver of Life	John 5:21

Table 13.2

Jesus also declared his deity implicitly through parables. In several of his parables, Jesus depicts himself in the role of God. For example:

• In responding to the Pharisees' complaint that Jesus is receiving and dining with sinners (Luke 15:2), Jesus tells three parables—the lost sheep, the lost coin, and the prodigal son (Luke 15:4-32). The implication is that Jesus is doing what the Old Testament says God does: he is a shepherd who goes and finds what is lost, and a forgiving father who welcomes home repentant sinners (Ezek. 34:11; Ps. 103:8-13). (Incidentally, the Pharisees are represented by the complaining older son in the parable of the prodigal son. The Pharisees, like the older son, mistakenly think they *deserve* the father's gifts because of their good works. So this parable not only affirms the deity of Christ but also teaches that salvation is a free gift that cannot be earned, only accepted.)

• In Matthew 19:28-30, Jesus declares that he—the "Son of Man"—will rule on the glorious throne of Israel at the renewal of all things, and that his followers will rule with him. He then immediately teaches the parable of the workers and the vineyard (Matt. 20:1-16). That's where the kingdom of God is represented by a vineyard owned by an employer. The employer pays all workers equally, regardless of time worked, thereby communicating that God's grace is not based on any kind of merit such as length of service ("the first will be last and the last will be first"). Jesus is represented by the employer who owns the vineyard and dispenses grace freely. This equates him with God because, in the Old Testament, God owns the vineyard (Isa. 5:1-7). (As we have seen, his use of "Son of Man" is also a claim to deity.)

- Jesus refers to himself as the "bridegroom" on several occasions (Mark 2:19; Matt. 9:15; 25:1; Luke 5:34) including in the parable of the ten virgins (Matt. 25:1-13). Since the Old Testament identifies God as the bridegroom (Isa. 62:5; Hos. 2:16), Jesus is equating himself with God.

There are several other instances of Jesus implicitly claiming deity through parables. While we don't have space to treat them all here, Philip Payne concludes, "Out of Jesus' fifty-two recorded narrative parables, twenty depict him in imagery which the Old Testament typically refers to God."[8]

Divine Actions

In addition to making statements that affirmed his deity (and in addition to performing miracles), Jesus *acted* as if he was God:

- He said to a paralytic, "Son, your sins are forgiven" (Mark 2:5-11). The scribes correctly responded, "Who can forgive sins but God alone?"
- Jesus declared, "All authority in heaven and on earth has been given to me" and then immediately gave a new commandment, "Therefore go and make disciples of all nations . . ." (Matt. 28:18-19).
- God had given the Ten Commandments to Moses, but Jesus said, "A new commandment I give you: Love one another" (John 13:34).
- He requested prayer in his name: "And I will do whatever you ask in my name. . . . You may ask me for anything in my name, and I will do it" (John 14:13-14); "If you remain in me and my words remain in you, ask whatever you wish, and it will be given you" (John 15:7).
- Despite the fact that both the Old and New Testaments forbid

worshiping anyone other than God (Ex. 20:1-4; Deut. 5:6-9; Acts 14:15; Rev. 22:8-9), Jesus accepted worship on at least nine occasions. These include worship from:

1. a healed leper (Matt. 8:2)
2. a ruler whose son Jesus had healed (Matt. 9:18)
3. the disciples after a storm (Matt. 14:33)
4. a Canaanite woman (Matt. 15:25)
5. the mother of James and John (Matt. 20:20)
6. a Gerasene demoniac (Mark 5:6)
7. a healed blind man (John 9:38)
8. all the disciples (Matt. 28:17)
9. Thomas, who said, "My Lord and my God" (John 20:28)

All of these people worshiped Jesus without one word of rebuke from him. Not only did Jesus accept this worship, he even commended those who acknowledged his deity (John 20:29; Matt. 16:17). This could only be done by a person who seriously considered himself to be God.

Now let's put all of this into perspective. No one did that better than C. S. Lewis, who wrote:

> Among these Jews there suddenly turns up a man who goes about talking as if He was God. He claims to forgive sins. He says He has always existed. He says He is coming to judge the world at the end of time. Now let us get this clear. Among Pantheists, like the Indians, anyone might say that he was a part of God, or one with God: there would be nothing very odd about it. But this man, since He was a Jew, could not mean that kind of God. God, in their language, meant the Being outside the world Who had made it and was infinitely different from anything else. And when you have grasped that, you will see that what this man said was, quite simply, the most shocking thing that has ever been uttered by human lips.[9]

Imagine your neighbor making these kinds of claims: "I am the first and the last—the self-existing One. Do you need your sins forgiven? I can do it. Do you want to know how to live? I am the light of the world—whoever follows me will never walk in darkness, but will have the light of life. Do you want to know whom you can trust? All authority in heaven and on earth has been given to me. Do you have any worries or requests? Pray in my name. If you remain in me and my words remain in you, ask whatever you wish, and it will be given you. Do you need access to God the Father? No one comes to the Father except through me. The Father and I are one."

What would you think about your neighbor if he seriously said those things? You certainly wouldn't say, "Gee, I think he's a great moral teacher!" No, you'd say this guy is nuts, because he's definitely claiming to be God. Again, no one has articulated this point better than C. S. Lewis, who wrote:

> I am trying here to prevent anyone saying the really foolish things that people often say about Him: "I'm ready to accept Jesus as a great moral teacher, but I don't accept His claim to be God." That is the one thing we must not say. A man who was merely a man and said the sort of things Jesus said would not be a great moral teacher. He would rather be a lunatic—on a level with the man who says he is a poached egg—or else he would be the Devil of Hell. You must make your choice. Either this man was, and is, the Son of God: or else a madman or something worse. You can shut Him up for a fool, you can spit at Him and kill Him as a demon; or you can fall at His feet and call Him Lord and God. But let us not come with any patronizing nonsense about His being a great human teacher. He has not left that open to us. He did not intend to.[10]

Lewis is absolutely right. Since Jesus clearly claimed to be God, he couldn't be just a great moral teacher. Great moral teachers don't deceive people by falsely claiming to be God. Since Jesus claimed to be God, one of only three possibilities could be true: he was either a liar, a lunatic, or the Lord.

Liar doesn't fit the facts. Jesus lived and taught the highest standard of ethics. And it's unlikely he would have laid down his life unless he really thought he was telling the truth.

If Jesus thought he was God but really wasn't, then he would have been a *lunatic*. But lunatic doesn't fit either. Jesus uttered some of the most profound sayings ever recorded. And everyone—even his enemies—claimed that Jesus was a man of integrity who taught the truth (Mark 12:14).

That leaves us with *Lord*. Peter Kreeft puts the argument very simply:

> There are only two possible interpretations: Jesus is God, or Jesus is not God. The argument in its simplest form looks like this: Jesus was either (1) God, if his claim about himself was true, or (2) a bad man, if what he said was not true, for good men do not claim to be God. But he was not a bad man. (If anyone in history was not a bad man, Jesus was not a bad man.) Therefore, he was (and is) God.[11]

This seems logical. But is *Lord* really the right conclusion? After all, it's one thing to claim to be God—anyone can do that—but it's another thing to prove it.

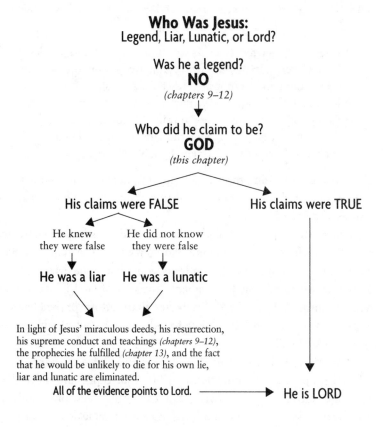

Fig. 13.2

Proofs That Jesus Is God

As we have seen, Jesus clearly claimed to be God and often acted the part. But he didn't just claim it or act it, he proved it! He did so with three unparalleled proofs:

1. He fulfilled numerous messianic prophecies written hundreds of years in advance.
2. He lived a sinless life and performed miraculous deeds.
3. He predicted and then accomplished his own resurrection from the dead.

We've already given evidence regarding the messianic prophecies, Jesus' miracles, and his resurrection. But what about this idea of Jesus being sinless? Jesus himself said, "Which one of you convicts Me of sin" (John 8:46, NASB)? Moreover, his disciples, who spent *three years* with him day and night, claimed that Jesus was sinless:

- Peter characterized Jesus as an "unblemished and spotless" lamb (1 Pet. 1:19, NASB) "who committed no sin, nor was any deceit found in His mouth" (1 Pet. 2:22, NASB).
- John said of Christ, "in Him there is no sin" (1 John 3:5, NASB).
- Paul wrote that Jesus "knew no sin" (2 Cor. 5:21, NASB).
- The writer of Hebrews made the same point by claiming that Jesus was "without sin" (Heb. 4:15, NASB).

Now, you try spending three *days* with any human being—much less three *years*—and you definitely will find faults. The New Testament writers said Jesus had none.

But it wasn't just his friends who affirmed his supreme character. Christ's enemies couldn't find fault with him either. The Pharisees, who were actively searching for dirt on Jesus, could find none (Mark 14:55). They even admitted that Jesus taught "the way of God in accordance with the truth" (Mark 12:14). Even after all the efforts of the Pharisees to pin some charge on Jesus, Pilate found him innocent of any wrongdoing (Luke 23:22).

But proof of Christ's deity does not depend on his sinlessness. The fulfilled prophecies, his miracles, and his resurrection are more than enough to prove that Jesus was God. Yet there are a few objections we need to address before concluding beyond a reasonable doubt that Jesus was (and is) the one true God.

OBJECTIONS TO THE DEITY OF CHRIST

Why Wasn't Jesus More Overt?—Despite some very clear claims to be God, skeptics point out that Jesus could have been a lot more overt more often if he really was God. Certainly that's true. He could have made many more direct claims if he thought it was necessary. However, there are several possible reasons he did not.

First, Jesus didn't want interference from the Jews, who had the misconception that the Messiah would come and free them from Roman oppression. This actually became a problem despite Jesus' careful approach: at one point after performing miracles, Jesus had to escape from the Jews who wanted to make him king (John 6:15)!

Second, Jesus could not be our supreme human example if he pulled rank every time he got into any earthly trouble. His conduct provides us with a perfect example of humility and servitude, and how we ought to glorify the Father rather than ourselves.

Third, Jesus had to be very careful about when and where he revealed his deity so that he could accomplish his mission of sacrificial atonement. If he had been too overt with his claims and miraculous proof, they might not have killed him. But if he had been too reserved, there would have been little proof that he was really God, and he may not have attracted a large enough following to spread his message.

Finally, we must understand the religious context in which Jesus lived and taught. He introduced the idea that he personally fulfilled the entire Old Testament law (Matt. 5:17)—the law that had been revered and followed for centuries and was the foundation of all of the political and religious practices of the Jews. As N. T. Wright says, "[This] would be like announcing in a Muslim country that one was fulfilling the will of Allah while apparently vilifying Muhammad and burning a copy of the Qur'an!"[12] It's no wonder Jesus used parables to teach and made more indirect than direct references to his deity. He gave enough evidence to convince the open-minded, but not enough to overwhelm the free will of those wishing to cling to their own traditions.

So there are good reasons why Jesus didn't directly proclaim his deity more often. However, we must not lose sight of the fact that he did so often enough. Before the Jews (John 8:58) and while under oath before the high priest when he knew his mission of sacrificial atonement was going to be completed (Matt. 26:64; Mark 14:62; Luke 22:70), Jesus clearly claimed to be God.

Indirect Denials of Deity—Critics often cite three specific occasions in the New Testament where the deity of Christ can be called into question. The first is recorded in Matthew 19:17, where the rich young ruler calls Jesus "good." Jesus appears to deny his deity by responding, "No one is good but One, that is, God."

But the critics are mistaken. Jesus is not denying his deity. He is *affirming* his deity by prompting the man to consider the implications of his statement. In effect, Jesus is asking, "Do you realize what you are saying when you call me good? Are you saying I am God?" This is apparent from the context, because just a few verses later Jesus refers to himself as the "Son of Man" who "sits on his glorious throne" and will enable the disciples to rule with him (Matt. 19:28).

The second and third objections to Christ's deity have to do with Jesus being subordinate to the Father and limited in knowledge. In John 14:28, Jesus clearly subordinates himself to God by admitting, "The Father is greater than I." And in Matthew 24:36, Jesus claims he doesn't know the date of his own return when he declares, "No one knows about that day or hour, not even the angels in heaven, nor the Son, but only the Father." Now how can Jesus be God if he is subordinate to the Father and is limited in knowledge?

The answer to both of these objections lies in a proper understanding of the Trinity. First, let's state clearly what the Trinity is *not*: the Trinity is not three Gods, three modes of one God, or three divine essences. *The Trinity is three persons in one divine essence.* In other words, there are three persons—Father, Son, and Holy Spirit—who share one divine nature. The Trinity is like a triangle: a triangle has three corners but it is still one triangle (figs. 13.3a and 13.3b).

Jesus shares in the one divine nature, but he also has a distinct human nature. Jesus is one "who" with two "what's" (a divine "what" and a human "what"); God is three "who's" (Father "who," Son "who," and Holy Spirit "who") in one "what," that is, three persons in one divine nature. Athanasius, one of the early church fathers, said the Incarnation was not the subtraction of deity; it was the addition of humanity. Indeed, when Jesus was conceived, he did not cease being God. He simply added a human nature.

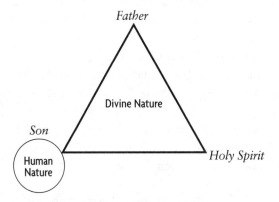

The Trinity: Three Persons in One Nature
Jesus: One Person with Two Natures

Fig. 13.3a

The Trinity: Three Persons in One Nature
Jesus: One Person with Two Natures

Fig. 13.3b

How does this help us deal with objections two and three? Well, since Jesus has two natures, whenever you ask a question about him you really have to ask two questions. For example, did Jesus know the time of his second coming? As God, yes; as man, no. Did Jesus know all things? As God, yes; as man, no. (In fact, Luke 2:52 admits that Jesus increased in wisdom.) Did Jesus get hungry? As God, no; as man, yes. Did Jesus get tired? As God, no; as man, yes.

The Trinity also helps us understand the sense in which Jesus declared, "the Father is greater than I." The Father and Son are equal *in essence* but different *in function*. This is analogous to human relationships. For example, an earthly father is equally human with his son, but the father holds a higher office. Likewise, Jesus and the Father have different offices but are both equally God (John 1:1; 8:58; 10:30). When Jesus added humanity, he voluntarily subordinated himself to the Father and accepted the limitations inherent with humanity (this is exactly what Paul explains in his letter to the Philippians [2:5-11]). But Jesus never lost his divine nature or ceased being God. Table 13:3 summarizes the differences between Jesus and the Father:

JESUS AND THE FATHER AS GOD	
Jesus Is Equal to the Father	**Jesus Is Subordinate to the Father**
in his divine nature	in his human nature
in his divine essence	in his human function
in his divine attributes	in his human office
in his divine character	in his human position

Table 13.3

Objections to the Trinity—Despite what some skeptics may say, the Trinity is not illogical or against reason. Saying that there is one God and three Gods would be illogical. But saying that there is one God who has three persons is not illogical. It may be *beyond* reason, but it's not *against* reason.

That doesn't mean the Trinity can be completely understood. After all, no finite being can completely comprehend an infinite God. But we can *apprehend* the Trinity, just like we apprehend but do not completely *comprehend* the ocean. When we're standing on the beach, we can apprehend that there's an ocean in front of us, even though we can't completely comprehend its vast magnitude.

Some Muslims charge that the Trinity is too complex. But who said that truth must always be simple? As C. S. Lewis aptly puts it, "If

Christianity was something we were making up, of course we could make it easier. But it is not. We cannot compete, in simplicity, with people who are inventing religions. How could we? We are dealing with fact. Of course anyone can be simple if he has no facts to bother about."[13]

Some critics and cult leaders have suggested that the Trinity is a later invention of the church. But this simply isn't true. The Father, the Son and the Holy Spirit[14] are all referred to as God in the Scriptures. Besides, even if the Trinity was not accepted by all the early church fathers, that doesn't mean it's false. Truth is not determined by majority vote. The doctrine of the Trinity is sound scripturally as well as philosophically.

In fact, instead of creating theological problems, the Trinity actually solves theological problems. For example, the Trinity helps us understand how love has existed from all eternity. The New Testament says God is love (1 John 4:16). But how can love exist in a rigid monotheistic being? There's no one else to love! Tri-unity in the Godhead solves the problem. After all, to have love, there must be a lover (the Father), a loved one (the Son), and a spirit of love (the Holy Spirit). Because of this triune nature, God has existed eternally in a perfect fellowship of love. He is the perfect being who lacks nothing, not even love. Since he lacks nothing, God didn't *need* to create human beings for any reason (he wasn't lonely, as some preachers have been known to say). He simply *chose* to create us, and loves us in accordance with his loving nature. In fact, his love is why he sent his Son—the second person of the Trinity—to take the punishment for our sins. His infinite justice condemns us, but his infinite love saves those who want to be saved.

SUMMARY AND CONCLUSION

Jesus Christ of Nazareth claimed and proved to be the Messiah-God predicted by the Old Testament. His claims come in many forms: from direct "I am" statements to those that strongly imply his deity. His actions—including forgiving sins, assuming the authority of God to issue commands, and accepting worship due only to God—also reveal that Jesus really believed he was God. He then proved he was God by:

1. fulfilling numerous specific messianic prophecies written hundreds of years in advance (Jesus is the only person in history who fulfills all of these prophecies);

2. living a sinless life and performing miraculous deeds;
3. predicting and then accomplishing his own resurrection from the dead.

We believe these facts have been established beyond a reasonable doubt. Therefore, we conclude that Jesus is God.

Since we have already established that God is a morally perfect being (from the Moral Argument in chapter 7), then anything Jesus (who is God) teaches is true. What did Jesus teach? More specifically, what did he teach about the Bible? That's the subject of the next chapter.

14

What Did Jesus Teach About the Bible?

"My high school science teacher once told me that much of Genesis is false. But since my high school science teacher did not prove he was God by rising from the dead, I'm going to believe Jesus instead."

—ANDY STANLEY

WOE TO YOU, HYPOCRITES!

The United States Congress was in a rare joint session. All 435 representatives and 100 senators were in attendance, and the C-SPAN-TV cameras were rolling. The members were gathered together to hear a speech by a descendant of George Washington. But what they thought would be a polite speech of patriotic historical reflections quickly turned into a televised tongue-lashing. With a wagging finger and stern looks, Washington's seventh-generation grandson declared,

> Woe to you, egotistical hypocrites! You are full of greed and self-indulgence. Everything you do is done for appearances: You make pompous speeches and grandstand before these TV cameras. You demand the place of honor at banquets and the most important seats wherever you go. You love to be greeted in your districts and have everyone call you "Senator" or "Congressman." On the outside you appear to people as righteous, but on the inside you are full of hypocrisy and wickedness! You say you want to clean up Washington, but as soon as you get here you become twice as much a son of hell as the one you replaced!
>
> Woe to you, makers of the law, you hypocrites! You do not practice what you preach. You put heavy burdens on the citizens, but then opt out of your own laws!
>
> Woe to you, federal fools! You take an oath to support and

defend the Constitution, but then you nullify the Constitution by allowing judges to make up their own laws.

Woe to you, blind hypocrites! You say that if you had lived in the days of the Founding Fathers, you never would have taken part with them in slavery. You say you never would have agreed that slaves were the property of their masters but would have insisted that they were human beings with unalienable rights. But you testify against yourselves because today you say that unborn children are the property of their mothers and have no rights at all! Upon you will come all the righteous blood that has been shed in this country. You snakes! You brood of vipers! You have left this great chamber desolate! How will you escape being condemned to hell!

Of course such an address never really took place (if it had, you certainly would have heard about it!). Who would be so blunt and rude to address the nation's leaders that way? Certainly no one claiming to be a Christian! Are you sure?

While we're not sure that Jesus would make such comments to today's political leaders, he actually did make similar comments to the religious leaders of his day. What!? Sweet and gentle Jesus? Absolutely. If you read the twenty-third chapter of Matthew you'll see that much of our fictitious speech is adapted from the real speech Jesus made to the crowds and the Pharisees. Contrary to the spineless Jesus invented today by those who want to be spineless themselves, the real Jesus taught with authority and did not tolerate error. When religious people were wrong, he made righteous judgments and let everyone know what those judgments were. And who could be better at correcting error than God himself? Since Jesus is God, whatever he teaches is true.

The historically reliable Gospels record Jesus' teachings on many subjects. But no teaching of Jesus has more far-reaching impact than what he taught about the Bible. If Jesus taught that the Bible is the Word of God, then the Bible is our primary source of divine truth. So what did Jesus teach about the Bible?

What Did Jesus Teach About the Bible?
The Old Testament

Jesus taught that the Old Testament was the Word of God in seven ways. He said it:

1. Is Divinely Authoritative—When tempted by Satan, Jesus corrected him by quoting from the Old Testament. He said, "'It is written, "Man does not live on bread alone, but on every word that comes from the mouth of God.'" . . . Jesus answered him, 'It is also written: "Do not put the Lord your God to the test.'" . . . Then Jesus said to him, 'Away from me, Satan! For it is written: "Worship the Lord your God, and serve him only'"'" (Matt. 4:4, 7, 10). Why would Jesus so confidently quote from the Old Testament if the Old Testament was not authoritative? He must have considered the Old Testament to be a source of truth in order to dismiss his most powerful enemy with it.

In fact, on ninety-two occasions Jesus and his apostles supported their position by saying "it is written" (or the equivalent) and then quoting the Old Testament. Why? Because Jesus and his apostles considered the Old Testament Scriptures to be the written Word of God, and thus the ultimate authority for life.

2. Is Imperishable—In the Sermon on the Mount, a passage loved by conservatives and liberals alike, Jesus claimed that not even the smallest little mark in the Scriptures—the equivalent of a dot on an "i" or a cross on a "t"—will ever perish: "Do not think that I came to destroy the Law or the Prophets," he declared. "I did not come to destroy but to fulfill. For assuredly, I say to you, till heaven and earth pass away, one jot or one tittle will by no means pass from the law till all is fulfilled" (Matt. 5:17, NKJV). Jesus could not express the imperishability of the Scriptures more forcefully.

3. Is Infallible—In John 10, Jesus was about to be stoned for blasphemy. To get himself out of this jam, Jesus cited the Old Testament and declared, "the Scripture cannot be broken" (John 10:35, NKJV). In other words, when his life was on the line, Jesus referred to an infallible authority that cannot be broken—the Scripture. Furthermore, he later affirmed the truth of the Scriptures when he prayed for the disciples, "Sanctify them by the truth; your word is truth" (John 17:17).

4. Is Inerrant—When the Sadducees tried to trap Jesus with a question, Jesus said to them, "You are in error because you do not know the Scriptures or the power of God" (Matt. 22:29). The implication, of course, is that the Scriptures are inerrant. It wouldn't make any sense for Jesus to say, "You are in error because you don't know the Scriptures, which also err!"

5. Is Historically Reliable—In addition to declaring that the Old Testament is divinely authoritative, imperishable, infallible, and inerrant, Jesus affirmed two of the most historically disputed stories in the Old Testament: Noah (Matt. 24:37-38) and Jonah (Matt. 12:40). Jesus spoke of those stories as being historically true. And why wouldn't they be true? The miracles associated with Noah and Jonah are child's play for the all-powerful God who created the universe. With our limited intelligence, we build great ships and keep people alive for months underwater. Why couldn't God do the same?

Jesus also affirmed other aspects of the Old Testament that the critics deny. Jesus taught that Daniel was a prophet (Matt. 24:15) while many critics say Daniel was merely a historian. (The critics claim a later date for Daniel, because surely he couldn't have made all those predictions. Their anti-supernatural bias is revealed again.) Furthermore, Jesus specifically quoted different sections of the book of Isaiah (e.g., Matt. 7:6-7; 13:14-15; Luke 4:17-19), never once suggesting that there were two or three Isaiahs as many critics claim.

6. Is Scientifically Accurate—Jesus made other claims that contradict those of today's critics. When asked if divorce was acceptable, Jesus cited a scientific fact out of Genesis. He said, "Haven't you read that at the beginning the Creator 'made them male and female,' and said, 'For this reason a man will leave his father and mother and be united to his wife, and the two will become one flesh'? So they are no longer two, but one. Therefore what God has joined together, let man not separate" (Matt. 19:4-6). In other words, the nature of marriage is bound up in the scientific fact that Adam and Eve were created for a purpose.

Moreover, Jesus did not accept the false idea that the Bible could tell you how to "go to heaven" but not "how the heavens go." He told Nicodemus, "If I told you earthly things and you do not believe, how will you believe if I tell you heavenly things?" (John 3:12, NASB). In other words, Jesus taught that if the Bible does not speak truthfully about the physical world that you can see, then it cannot be trusted when it speaks about the spiritual world that you cannot see. Indeed, Christianity is built on historical events—such as Creation and the Resurrection—that can be tested through scientific and historical investigation. While adherents of other religions may accept a complete separation from science, Christians do not. Truth about the universe cannot be contradictory. Since all truth is God's truth, religious beliefs must agree with scientific facts. If they do not, then either there is an error in our scientific understanding, or our religious beliefs are wrong. As we have seen, many of the claims of Christianity are affirmed by scientific investigation. Christ knew it would be this way.

7. Has Ultimate Supremacy—Since Jesus taught that the Old Testament is divinely authoritative, imperishable, infallible, inerrant, historically reliable, and scientifically accurate, you would expect him to assert that it has ultimate supremacy over any teaching of man. This is exactly what Jesus said. He corrected the Pharisees and the teachers of the law by claiming that they should be obeying the Old Testament Scriptures instead of their own man-made traditions. He said, "Why do you break the command of God for the sake of your tradition? . . . . You nullify the word of God for the sake of your tradition" (Matt. 15:3, 6). He then blasted them for failing to live up to the Scriptures by quoting from the Old Testament: "You hypocrites! Isaiah was right when he prophesied about you: 'These people honor me with their lips, but their hearts are far from me. They worship me in vain; their teachings are but rules taught by men'" (Matt. 15:7-9). Why would Jesus correct the religious leaders of Israel with the Old Testament unless the Old Testament had ultimate supremacy over their own ideas?

In light of Jesus' teaching, there's no question he considered the entire Old Testament to be the inerrant, written Word of God. He said he came to fulfill the entire Jewish Old Testament (Matt. 5:17), which he referred to as "the Law and the Prophets" (Matt. 5:17; Luke 24:26-27). And he told the Jews, "You diligently study the Scriptures because you think that by them you possess eternal life. These are the Scriptures that testify about me, yet you refuse to come to me to have life" (John 5:39-40).

So Jesus came to fulfill the Scriptures that testify of him. But what did that Old Testament comprise? To what books was Jesus referring when he spoke of "the Scriptures"? In his rebuke of the Pharisees in Matthew 23, Jesus covered every book in the Jewish Old Testament, first to last, when he declared, "Upon you will come all the righteous blood that has been shed on earth, from the blood of righteous Abel to the blood of Zechariah son of Berekiah, whom you murdered between the temple and the altar" (v. 35). Abel was killed in the first book of the Jewish Old Testament (Genesis), and Zechariah was killed in the last (Chronicles).

Old Testament Event	New Testament Affirmation(s)
1. Creation of the universe (Gen. 1)	John 1:3; Col. 1:16
2. Creation of Adam and Eve (Gen. 1–2)	1 Tim. 2:13, 14
3. Marriage of Adam and Eve (Gen. 1–2)	Matt. 19:4-5
4. Temptation of the woman (Gen. 3)	1 Tim. 2:14
5. Disobedience and sin of Adam (Gen. 3)	Rom. 5:12; 1 Cor. 15:22
6. Sacrifices of Abel and Cain (Gen. 4)	Heb. 11:4
7. Murder of Abel by Cain (Gen. 4)	1 John 3:12
8. Birth of Seth (Gen. 4)	Luke 3:38
9. Translation of Enoch (Gen. 5)	Heb. 11:5
10. Marriage before the Flood (Gen. 6)	Luke 17:27
11. The Flood and destruction of man (Gen. 7)	Matt. 24:39
12. Preservation of Noah and his family (Gen. 8–9)	2 Pet. 2:5
13. Genealogy of Shem (Gen. 10)	Luke 3:35, 36
14. Birth of Abraham (Gen. 11)	Luke 3:34
15. Call of Abraham (Gen. 12–13)	Heb. 11:8
16. Tithes to Melchizedek (Gen. 14)	Heb. 7:1-3
17. Justification of Abraham (Gen. 15)	Rom. 4:3
18. Ishmael (Gen. 16)	Gal. 4:21-24
19. Promise of Isaac (Gen. 17)	Heb. 11:18
20. Lot and Sodom (Gen. 18–19)	Luke 17:29
21. Birth of Isaac (Gen. 21)	Acts 7:8
22. Offering of Isaac (Gen. 22)	Heb. 11:17
23. The burning bush (Ex. 3:6)	Luke 20:37
24. Exodus through the Red Sea (Ex. 14:22)	1 Cor. 10:1, 2
25. Provision of water and manna (Ex. 16:4; 17:6)	1 Cor. 10:3-5
26. Lifting up serpent in wilderness (Num. 21:9)	John 3:14
27. Fall of Jericho (Josh. 6:22-25)	Heb. 11:30
28. Miracles of Elijah (1 Kings 17:1; 18:1)	James 5:17
29. Jonah and the great fish (Jonah 2)	Matt. 12:40
30. Three Hebrew youths in furnace (Dan. 3)	Heb. 11:34
31. Daniel in lions' den (Dan. 6)	Heb. 11:33
32. Slaying of Zechariah (2 Chron. 24:20-22)	Matt. 23:35

Table 14.1

In fact, Jesus and the New Testament writers cited every section of the Old Testament as authoritative as they referenced events in 18 of the 22 books of the Jewish Old Testament.[1] The historicity of many of the events listed in table 14.1[2] have been disputed by critics. But Jesus and the apostles reference them as if they are historically true. In addition to Noah and Jonah, Jesus himself affirms the historicity of Creation (Mark 13:19), Adam and Eve (Matt. 19:4-5), Sodom and Gomorrah (Luke 10:12), and Moses and the burning bush (Luke 20:37). This shows that Jesus linked the historical reality of the Old Testament with the truth of his own spiritual message.

But Could Jesus Have Been Wrong?—So Jesus declared that the entire Old Testament is the inerrant Word of God, and he and his apostles affirmed Old Testament events that many critics deny. But could Jesus have been wrong? Perhaps he wasn't saying that those events in the Old Testament really happened, but just that the Jews believed they did. In other words, maybe he was just accommodating to the beliefs of the Jews, in effect saying, "just as you believe in Jonah, you ought to believe in my resurrection."

This accommodation theory doesn't work. As we have seen, Jesus did not tolerate error. He wasn't accommodating to the beliefs of the Jews, as some skeptics have suggested. He rebuked and corrected them repeatedly, from scathing public tongue-lashings (like Matthew 23) to correcting their false interpretations of the Old Testament (Matt. 5:21-43), to overturning tables in the temple (Matthew 21; Mark 11; John 2). Jesus didn't back down on anything, and he certainly didn't back down on the truth of the Old Testament.

The skeptic may say, "But couldn't Jesus have erred because of his human limitations? After all, if he didn't know when he was coming back, maybe he didn't know about errors in the Old Testament." No, this limitation theory doesn't work either. Limits on understanding are different from misunderstanding. As a man, there were some things Jesus didn't know. But that doesn't mean he was wrong on what he *did* know. What Jesus *did know* was true because he only taught what the Father told him to teach (John 8:28; 17:8, 14). So to charge Jesus with an error is to charge God the Father with an error. But God can't err because he is the unchangeable standard and source of truth.[3]

Furthermore, Jesus affirmed the truth of his teaching when he declared, "Heaven and earth will pass away, but My words will not pass away" (Matt. 24:35, NASB), and "All authority in heaven and on earth has been given to me" (Matt. 28:18).

So where does that leave us? We need to ask only one question: Who knew more about the Old Testament, Christ or the critics? If Jesus is God, then whatever he teaches is true. If he teaches that the Old Testament is divinely authoritative, imperishable, infallible, inerrant, historically reliable, scientifically accurate, and has ultimate supremacy, then those things are true. His credentials trump those of any fallible critic (especially those whose criticisms are not grounded in evidence but in an illegitimate anti-supernatural bias).

Other Evidence Supporting the Old Testament—In addition to the claims of Jesus, there are many other reasons to support the truthfulness of the Old Testament documents. For example, the Old Testament has many of the same characteristics that make the New Testament believable: strong manuscript support, confirmation by archaeology, and a storyline that its authors would not invent.

Let's consider that last point for just a minute. Who would invent the Old Testament storyline? A story invented by Hebrews probably would depict the Israelites as noble and upright people. But the Old Testament writers don't say this. Instead they depict their own people as sinful and fickle slaves who, time after time, are miraculously rescued by God, but who abandon him every chance they get. The history they record is filled with bone-headed disobedience, distrust, and selfishness. Their leaders are all Olympic-quality sinners, including Moses (a murderer), Saul (a paranoid egomaniac), David (an adulterer, liar, and murderer), and Solomon (a serial polygamist). These are the people who are supposed to be leading the nation through which God has chosen to bring the Savior of the world. Yet the Old Testament writers admit that the ancestors of this Messiah include sinful characters such as David and Solomon and even a prostitute named Rahab. This is clearly not an invented storyline!

While the Old Testament tells of one embarrassing gaffe after another, most other ancient historians avoid even mentioning unflattering historical events. For example, there's been nothing found in the records of Egypt about the Exodus, leading some critics to suggest the event never occurred. But what do the critics expect? Writer Peter Fineman imagines what a press release from Pharaoh might say:

> A spokesman for Rameses the great, Pharaoh of Pharaohs, supreme ruler of Egypt, son of Ra, before whom all tremble in awe blinded by his brilliance, today announced that the man Moses had kicked his royal [rear end] for all the world to see, thus proving that God is Yahweh and the 2,000-year-old-culture of Egypt is a lie. Film at 11:00.[4]

Of course no press secretary for Pharaoh would admit such an event! The Egyptian silence on the Exodus is understandable. However, by contrast, when the Egyptians scored a military victory, they went to press and exaggerated greatly. This is apparent from the oldest known reference to the Israel outside the Bible. It comes from a granite monument found in the funerary temple of Pharaoh Merneptah in Thebes. The monument boasts about the military victory of the Pharaoh in the highlands of Canaan, claiming that "Israel is laid waste, his seed is not."[5] Historians date the battle to 1207 B.C., which confirms that Israel was in the land by that time.

There are several other archaeological findings corroborating the Old Testament. And recall from chapter 3 that there's even evidence from astronomy (the Big Bang) that supports Genesis. (For more evidence supporting the Old Testament, see *The Baker Encyclopedia of Christian Apologetics*).[6] But in the end, the strongest argument for the Old Testament comes from Jesus himself. As God, he holds the trump card. If the New Testament documents are reliable, then the Old Testament is without error because Jesus said it is.

Our friend Andy Stanley put it well: "My high school science teacher once told me that much of Genesis is false. But since my high school science teacher did not prove he was God by rising from the dead, I'm going to believe Jesus instead."[7] Wise move.

What About the New Testament?

Jesus taught that the Old Testament is inerrant, but what could he say about the New Testament? After all, it was not written until after the end of Christ's earthly life.

While Jesus *confirmed* the Old Testament, he *promised* the New

Testament. He said the New Testament would come through his apostles because the Holy Spirit would remind them what Jesus had said and would lead them into "all truth." This is recorded in two passages of John's Gospel. Jesus declared:

> "All this I have spoken while still with you. But the Counselor, the Holy Spirit, whom the Father will send in my name, *will teach you all things and will remind you of everything I have said to you*" (John 14:25-26).

And,

> "I have much more to say to you, more than you can now bear. But when he, the Spirit of truth, comes, *he will guide you into all truth*. He will not speak on his own; he will speak only what he hears, and he will tell you what is yet to come" (John 16:12-13).

In other words, Jesus is promising his apostles that the Holy Spirit would lead them to author what we now know as the New Testament. Paul would later echo this teaching of Jesus by asserting that the church is "built on the foundation of the apostles and prophets, with Christ Jesus himself as the chief cornerstone" (Eph. 2:20). The early church recognized this as well because they "devoted themselves to the apostles' teaching" (Acts 2:42).

But did the apostles really get the message from the Holy Spirit as Jesus promised? They certainly claim as much. John writes that the apostles *"are from God"* (1 John 4:6), and begins the book of Revelation with, "The revelation of Jesus Christ, *which God gave him*" (Rev. 1:1). Paul claims that his words are *"taught by the Spirit"* (1 Cor 2:10, 13; 7:40), and that his writings are *"the Lord's command"* (1 Cor. 14:37). In the opening of his letter to the Galatians, Paul declares, "I want you to know, brothers, that the gospel I preached is not something that man made up. I did not receive it from any man, nor was I taught it; rather, *I received it by revelation from Jesus Christ"* (Gal. 1:11-12). In fact, in his first letter to the Thessalonians, Paul affirms that he is providing them with the word of God: "And we also thank God continually because, *when you received the word of God, which you heard from us, you accepted it not as the word of men, but as it actually is, the word of God,* which is at work in you who believe" (1 Thess. 2:13). In addition to affirming the inspired nature of his own works, Paul quotes the Gospels of Luke and Matthew as "Scripture," putting them on the same level as Deuteronomy (1 Tim. 5:18; Luke 10:7; Matt. 10:10).

Referring to Paul's letters (there are thirteen of them), Peter agrees they are inspired when he writes, "His letters contain some things that are hard to understand, which ignorant and unstable people distort, as they do *the other Scriptures,* to their own destruction" (2 Pet. 3:15-16; cf. 2 Tim. 3:15-16). Peter also affirms the divine source of his own words and those of the other apostles when he declares, *"We* did not follow cleverly invented stories when we told you about the power and coming of our Lord Jesus Christ, but we were eyewitnesses of his majesty . . . . *we have the word of the prophets made more certain,* and you will do well to pay attention to it. . . . you must understand that no prophecy of Scripture came about by the prophet's own interpretation. For prophecy never had its origin in the will of man, but men spoke from God as they were carried along by the Holy Spirit" (2 Pet. 1:16-21).

But the apostles didn't just *claim* to be getting messages from God. Anyone can do that. They gave evidence that their words were inspired by performing miraculous signs. In fact, one of the two qualifications of an apostle was the ability to perform such signs; the other qualification was being an eyewitness to the Resurrection (Acts 1:22; 1 Cor 9:1). Paul affirmed that he was an apostle when he declared to his Corinthian readers, "The things that mark an apostle—signs, wonders and miracles— were done among you with great perseverance" (2 Cor. 12:12). Paul must have been telling the truth about having done miracles in their presence, or he would have lost all credibility with his readers.

In addition to Paul claiming to do miracles, Luke records thirty-five miracles in the book of Acts alone—the well-authenticated book we've already investigated that chronicles the propagation of the church from the Resurrection to about A.D. 60. Most of these miracles are performed by the apostles (a few were performed by angels or by God).[8] Furthermore, the writer of Hebrews, speaking of the salvation announced by the Lord, declares, *"God also testified to it by signs, wonders and various miracles,* and gifts of the Holy Spirit distributed according to his will" (Heb. 2:3-4).

Recall from chapter 8 that this is the way God authenticates his prophets—through miracles. The miracle confirms the message. The sign confirms the sermon. Acts of God confirm the Word of God to the people of God (Exodus 4; 1 Kings 18; John 3:2; Acts 2:22). It's God's way of telling us that a message really comes from him. And the New Testament apostles confirmed that their message came from God by performing miracles.

The skeptic may say, "Oh, they were just making up the miracle stories." Nonsense. We've already seen in chapters 10, 11, and 12 that they were incredibly accurate historians and had no motive to make up miracle stories. In fact, they had every motive *not* to make up such stories because they were tortured, beaten, and killed for affirming them.

Moreover, the ability to perform miracles was not ultimately in their control, but resided with God himself. How do we know? For two reasons. First, the apostles appear to have lost the ability to perform miracles sometime in the mid-60s A.D. The writer of Hebrews, writing in the late 60s, referred to these special sign gifts of an apostle in the past tense (Heb. 2:3-4). And later in his ministry, Paul apparently could not heal some of his own trusted helpers (Phil. 2:26; 2 Tim. 4:20). If he still possessed the power to perform miracles, then why was he asking for prayer and recommending that his helpers take medicine (1 Tim. 5:23)?

Second, even *while Paul was doing miracles* he was unable to heal his own physical infirmity (Gal. 4:13). In fact, there's no instance in Scripture of anyone performing a miracle for his own benefit or for entertainment. This demonstrates that the ability to perform miracles was limited by the will of God (cf. Heb. 2:4). Miracles were done for a specific purpose, which was usually to confirm some new messenger or new revelation.

This is probably why there is no record of apostolic miracles in Paul's letters after about A.D. 62—the latest date Acts could have been composed.[9] By this time, Paul and the other apostles had been proven as true messengers of God, and there was no need for further confirmation.

The Spirit of the Lord Is on Jesus—There is one additional line of evidence regarding the fact that Jesus and the Holy Spirit would provide the New Testament. The Old Testament predicted that the Messiah would come and "preach good news." Jesus declared that he fulfilled that prediction. As recorded in Luke 4, Jesus goes into the synagogue in his hometown of Nazareth and makes that amazing claim. Luke says,

> [Jesus] stood up to read. The scroll of the prophet Isaiah was handed to him. Unrolling it, he found the place where it is written:

"The Spirit of the Lord is on me,
    because he has anointed me
    to preach good news to the poor.
He has sent me to proclaim freedom for the prisoners
    and recovery of sight for the blind,
to release the oppressed,
    to proclaim the year of the Lord's favor."

Then he rolled up the scroll, gave it back to the attendant and sat down. The eyes of everyone in the synagogue were fastened on him, and he began by saying to them, "Today this scripture is fulfilled in your hearing" (Luke 4:14-21).

What was fulfilled that day? The first coming of the Messiah. Quoting from Isaiah 61:1-2, Jesus stopped in mid-verse to indicate that he was the Messiah who had come to "preach good news to the poor," "proclaim freedom for the prisoners," offer "recovery of sight for the blind," and so forth. He stopped halfway through verse 2 because the second half of the verse declares the "day of vengeance of our God," which refers to Christ's second coming. The Jews in his hometown, who knew Jesus was the son of Joseph, also knew that he was claiming to be the Messiah. In fact, after Jesus made one more messianic claim, the crowd in the synagogue became "furious" and drove him out of town to push him off a cliff. But Jesus escaped by walking right through the crowd (4:22-30).

Isaiah 61 predicts that the Messiah will perform healing miracles and preach "good news. . . . to release the oppressed" by the "Spirit of the Lord." In other words, the Messiah will do exactly what Jesus did—provide new revelation and back it up with miracles. Of course, since the Messiah is to provide new revelation, someone has to write it down. That's why Jesus promised his apostles that the Holy Spirit would bring to their remembrance all of his words and guide them into "all truth" (John 14:26; 16:13).

Discovering the Canon—What does all of this mean for the New Testament? It means that, according to Jesus, the only books that should be in the New Testament are those that are authored and/or confirmed by his apostles. Which books specifically are those?

First, we need to clear up a common misunderstanding about what we call "the canon." It is this: It's wrong to say that "the church" or the early church fathers *determined* what would be in the New Testament. They didn't *determine* what would be in the New Testament—they *discovered* what *God intended* to be in the New Testament. Bruce Metzger of Princeton University put it well. He said, "The canon is a list of authoritative books more than it is an authoritative list of books. These documents didn't derive their authority from being selected; each one was authoritative before anyone gathered them together."[10] In other words, the only books that should be part of the New Testament are those that God has inspired. Since Jesus said that his apostles would produce those books, our only questions are historical: 1) Who were the apostles? and 2) What did they write?

The early church fathers can help us answer those questions because they were much closer to the events than we are. The fact is they had no trouble *discovering* the divine nature of the major New Testament books. While there was some initial controversy over some of the minor books (such as Philemon, 3 John, and James), the early church fathers immediately recognized the Gospels and major Epistles as divinely inspired. Why? Because they knew the books were written by apostles (or by those confirmed by apostles), and those apostles had been confirmed by miracles. How did they know that? Because there is an unbroken chain of testimony from the apostles to the early church fathers regarding the authorship and authenticity of the New Testament books.

John, who obviously knew all of the apostles, had a disciple named Polycarp (A.D. 69–155), and Polycarp had a disciple named Irenaeus (130–202). Polycarp and Irenaeus collectively quote 23 of the 27 New Testament books as if they are authentic—and in some cases they specifically say they are authentic.[11] Irenaeus explicitly affirms the authorship of all four Gospels.[12] Furthermore, through the historian Eusebius, we know that Papias (60–120) affirmed the authorship of Matthew and Mark. And no one doubts the authorship of the major works of Paul.

While the major works of the New Testament were immediately seen as authentic by these early church fathers, most of the New Testament was accepted before A.D. 200, and all of it was officially and finally recognized as authentic by the Council of Hippo in 393. See table 14.2.[13]

The New Testament Canon During the First Four Centuries

	Matthew	Mark	Luke	John	Acts	Romans	1 Corinthians	2 Corinthians	Galatians	Ephesians	Philippians	Colossians	1 Thessalonians	2 Thessalonians	1 Timothy	2 Timothy	Titus	Philemon	Hebrews	James	1 Peter	2 Peter	1 John	2 John	3 John	Jude	Revelation
INDIVIDUALS																											
Pseudo-Barnabas (c. 70-130)	X	X	X							X					X	X			X		X	X					
Clement of Rome (c. 95-97)	X		X			X	O			X					X		X		X	X	X						
Ignatius (c. 110)										X	X	X	X	X				X									
Polycarp (c. 115-150)	X	X	X	X	X	X	X	X	X	X	X	X	X	X	X						X		X	X			
Hermas (c. 115-140)	X	X		X			X	X			X			X	X					X	X	X		X			X
Didache (c. 120-150)	X		X		X		X					X			X												X
Papias (c. 130-140)				X																							O
Irenaeus (c. 130-202)	O	O	O	O	O	O	O	O	O	O	O	O	O	O	X	X	X		X		O		O	X		X	O
Diognetus (c. 150)							X	X				X					X										
Justin Martyr (c. 150-155)	X	X	X	O	X	X	X	X	X	X					X	X	X				X						X
Clement of Alexandria (c. 150-215)	X	X	X	X	X	O	O	O	O	X	O	O	X	X	O		O		O		O		O			O	O
Tertullian (c. 150-220)	X	X	X	X	X	X	X	X	X	X	X	X	X	X	X	X	X		X		X		X			X	X
Origen (c. 185-254)	X	X	X	X	X	X	X	X	X	X	X	X	X	X	X	X	X		?		O	?		?	?		O
Cyril of Jerusalem (c. 315-386)	O	O	O	O	O	O	O	O	O	O	O	O	O	O	O	O	O	O	O	O	O	O	O	O	O	O	
Eusebius (c. 325-340)	O	O	O	O	O	O	O	O	O	O	O	O	O	O	O	O	O	O	O	?	O	?	O	?	?	?	O
Jerome (c. 340-420)	O	O	O	O	O	O	O	O	O	O	O	O	O	O	O	O	O	O	O	O	O	O	O	O	O	O	O
Augustine (c. 400)	O	O	O	O	O	O	O	O	O	O	O	O	O	O	O	O	O	O	O	O	O	O	O	O	O	O	O
CANONS																											
Marcion (c. 140)			O			O	O	O	O	O	O	O	O	O				O									
Muratorian (c. 170)	O	O	O	O	O	O	O	O	O	O	O	O	O	O	O	O	O	O					O	O		O	O
Apostolic (c. 300)	O	O	O	O	O	O	O	O	O	O	O	O	O	O	O	O	O	O	O	O	O	O	O	O	O	O	
Cheltenham (c. 360)	O	O	O	O	O	O	O	O	O	O	O	O	O	O	O	O	O	O			O	?	O	?	?		O
Athanasius (367)	O	O	O	O	O	O	O	O	O	O	O	O	O	O	O	O	O	O	O	O	O	O	O	O	O	O	O
TRANSLATIONS																											
Tatian Diatessaron (c. 170)	O	O	O	O																							
Old Latin (c. 200)	O	O	O	O	O	O	O	O	O	O	O	O	O	O	O	O	O	O					O	O	O	O	O
Old Syriac (c. 400)	O	O	O	O	O	O	O	O	O	O	O	O	O	O	O	O	O	O	O	O	O		O				
COUNCILS																											
Nicea (c. 325-340)	O	O	O	O	O	O	O	O	O	O	O	O	O	O	O	O	O	O	O	?	O	?	O	?	?	?	O
Hippo (393)	O	O	O	O	O	O	O	O	O	O	O	O	O	O	O	O	O	O	O	O	O	O	O	O	O	O	O
Carthage (397)	O	O	O	O	O	O	O	O	O	O	O	O	O	O	O	O	O	O	O	O	O	O	O	O	O	O	O
Carthage (419)	O	O	O	O	O	O	O	O	O	O	O	O	O	O	O	O	O	O	O	O	O	O	O	O	O	O	O

X = Citation or allusion   O = Named as authentic   ? = Named as disputed

Table 14.2

"Why did the recognition of these books take so long?" the skeptic may ask. Perhaps because Christianity was generally illegal in the Roman Empire until 313. It wasn't as if the early church fathers could go down to the local Hilton and convene a Bible conference to examine the evidence together and come to a conclusion. They often feared for their lives in their own homes! The important point is that once all the evidence was on the table, all 27 New Testament books, and only those 27 books, were recognized as authentic.

Those 27 books comprise the only authentic record of apostolic teaching we have. As we have seen, all of those were written in the first century by eyewitnesses or by those who interviewed eyewitnesses. In other words, they meet the criteria of Jesus—they are books that are either written by the apostles or confirmed by the apostles.[14] Since there are no other authentic apostolic works known to exist—and since it's unlikely that God would allow an authentic work to go undiscovered for so long—we can rest assured that the New Testament canon is complete.

How Can the Bible Be Inerrant?

If Jesus confirmed that the Old Testament was the inerrant Word of God, then his promised New Testament must be part of the inerrant Word of God too. Of course. But how can this be? Aren't there scores if not hundreds of errors in the Bible?

No. The Bible does not have errors, but it certainly has *alleged* errors or difficulties. In fact, I (Norm) and another professor at Southern Evangelical Seminary, Thomas Howe, have written a book titled *When Critics Ask,* which addresses more than 800 difficulties critics have identified in the Bible (there is also more on inerrancy in *Systematic Theology, Volume One*).[15] While we certainly can't include the contents of those books in this one, here are a few points worth mentioning.

First, let's spell out logically why the Bible can't have errors:

1. God cannot err.
2. The Bible is the word of God.
3. Therefore, the Bible cannot err.

Since this is a valid syllogism (form of reasoning), if the premises are true, then the conclusion is true. The Bible clearly declares itself to be the Word of God, and we've seen the strong evidence that it is. The Bible also informs us several times that God cannot err, and we know this from general revelation as well. So the conclusion is inevitable. The Bible cannot err. If the Bible erred in anything it affirms, then God would be mistaken. But God cannot make mistakes.

So what happens when we think we've found an error in the Bible? Augustine had the answer. "If we are perplexed by any apparent contradiction in Scripture," he wisely noted, "it is not allowable to say, 'The author of this book is mistaken'; but either the manuscript is faulty, or the translation is wrong, or you have not understood."[16] In other words, it's more likely that *we've* made an error than the Bible. In *When Critics Ask,* we identify seventeen errors typically made by critics. Here is a summary of just four of them:

- **Assuming That Divergent Accounts Are Contradictory**—As we have seen, it's not a contradiction if one Gospel writer says he saw one angel at the tomb and another says he saw two. Matthew doesn't say there was *only* one. And if there were two, there certainly was (at least) one! So divergence doesn't always mean contradiction. Instead, it often suggests genuine eyewitness testimony.
- **Failing to Understand the Context of the Passage**—Sometimes we may think we've found a contradiction in the Bible, but instead we've simply taken a passage out of context. An obvious example would be Psalm 14:1b, which says, "there is no God." However, the proper context is revealed when the full verse is read: *"The fool has said in his heart,* 'There is no God.'"
- **Presuming That the Bible Approves of All That It Records**— Critics may site the polygamy of Solomon (1 Kings 11:3) as an example of a contradiction. Doesn't the Bible teach monogamy, not polygamy? Of course. But God certainly does not approve of every act recorded in the Bible. It records Satan's lies as well, but God doesn't approve of them either. God's standards are found in what the Bible *reveals,* not in everything it *records.* (As we have seen, instead of this being an argument that the Bible has errors, it's actually an argument for the Bible's historicity. The fact that the Bible records all of the sins and faults of its people suggests that it is true—no one would make up such a self-condemning story.)

- **Forgetting That the Bible Is a Human Book with Human Characteristics**—Critics have been known to falsely impugn the integrity of the Bible by expecting a level of expression higher than that which is customary for a human document. However, this is illegitimate because most of the Bible was not verbally dictated but written by human authors (an exception is the Ten Commandments, which were "written with the finger of God" [Ex. 31:18]). The writers were human composers who employed their own literary styles and idiosyncrasies. They wrote historical narratives (e.g., Acts), poetry (e.g., Song of Solomon), prayers (e.g., many Psalms), prophecy (e.g., Isaiah), personal letters (e.g., 1 Timothy), theological treatises (e.g., Romans), and other types of literature. These writers speak from a *human standpoint* when they write of the sun rising or setting (Josh. 1:15). They also reveal *human thought patterns,* including memory lapses (1 Cor. 1:14-16), as well as *human emotions* (Gal. 4:14). In short, since God used the styles of about 40 authors over nearly 1,500 years to get his message across, it's wrong to expect the level of expression to be greater than that of other human documents. However, as with Christ's human nature, the Bible's distinct human nature is without error.

OBJECTIONS TO INERRANCY

Critics may say, "Humans err, so the Bible must err." But again it's the critic who is in error. True, humans err, but humans don't *always* err. Fallible people write books all the time that have no errors. So fallible people who are guided by the Holy Spirit certainly can write a book without any errors.

"But aren't you just arguing in a circle," the critic might ask, "by using the Bible to prove the Bible?" No, we're not arguing in a circle, because we're not starting with the assumption that the Bible is an inspired book. We're starting with several separate documents that have proven beyond a reasonable doubt to be historically reliable. Since those documents reveal that Jesus is God, then we know his teaching on the Old Testament must be true. On several occasions, Jesus said that not only is the Old Testament the Word of God—it is also inerrant. He also promised that the rest of God's truth ("all truth") would come to the apostles from the Holy Spirit. The apostles then wrote the New Testament and proved their authority through miracles. Therefore, on the authority of Jesus, who is God, the New Testament is inerrant as well. That's not arguing in a circle; it is arguing inductively, collecting evidence and following that evidence where it leads.

Critics may also charge, "But your position on inerrancy is not falsifiable. You will not accept an error in the Bible because you've decided in advance that there can't be any!" Actually, our position *is* falsifiable, but the critics' position is not. Let us explain.

First, because Jesus' authority is well established by the evidence, we reasonably give the benefit of the doubt to the Bible when we come across a difficulty or question in the text. In other words, when we run across something inexplicable, we assume that we, not the infinite God, are making an error. It's more likely that Geisler and Turek are ignorant than that the Bible is wrong.

However, that doesn't mean we believe there's absolutely no possibility for Bible errors. After all, there's always a chance that our conclusions about inerrancy are wrong—for *we* are certainly not inerrant. In fact, our conclusion on inerrancy would be falsified if someone could trace a real error back to an original scroll.[17] But to this day, after nearly 2,000 years of looking, no one has found such an irreconcilable problem. (This is truly amazing when you consider that the Bible is really a collection of documents written by about 40 authors over a 1,500-year period. Where could you find such agreement on a variety of issues from 40 authors who all live today, much less over a 1,500-year period?)

Second, even if inerrancy is falsified someday, that wouldn't falsify the central truths of Christianity. As we have seen, the historical evidence that Jesus taught profound truths, performed miracles, and died and rose from the dead for sinful humanity is very strong indeed. Even if the Scriptures are found to contain a false detail or two, the historical truth of Christianity will not be diminished. We hasten to add, we don't think inerrancy will ever be falsified, but if it is, Christianity will still be true beyond a reasonable doubt.

Is there any discovery that would cause us to disbelieve Christianity? Yes. If someone could find the body of Jesus, Christianity would be proven false and we'd give it up. In effect, we agree with Paul, who said that our Christian faith is in vain if Jesus did not actually rise from the dead (1 Cor. 15:14-18).

This is unique about Christianity. Unlike most other religious worldviews, Christianity is built on historical events and can therefore be either proven or falsified by historical investigation. The problem for skeptics and critics is that all the historical evidence points to the Resurrection. The people who lived in Jerusalem at the time—some of whom would have loved to have found Jesus' body and paraded it around the city—couldn't find his body and actually admitted that his tomb was empty. And nothing has been found since. If, after 2,000 years of looking, no one can find the remains of Jesus or real errors in the Bible, isn't it quite possible that neither exist? When can a question be confidently closed? If not after 2,000 years, when?

Third, after many years of continual and careful study of the Bible, we can only conclude that those who have "discovered a mistake" in the Bible do not know too much about the Bible—they know too little. This doesn't mean that we understand how to resolve all the difficulties in the Scriptures, but it means we keep doing research. We are really no different than scientists who can't resolve all the difficulties or mysteries of the natural world. They don't deny the integrity of the natural world just because they can't explain something. Like a scientist of the natural world, a scientist of theology keeps looking for answers. As we do, the list of difficulties keeps getting shorter.[18] (Meanwhile, for those of you who can't get past Bible difficulties, Mark Twain had a point when he concluded that it was not the parts of the Bible he did not understand that bothered him—but the parts he did understand!)

Finally, it's the critics who actually maintain an unfalsifiable position. What would convince them that their view is wrong? In other words, what would convince them that Jesus actually rose from the dead or that inerrancy is true? Maybe they ought to consider the evidence we've presented in this book. Unfortunately, many critics will not do this. They will not allow facts to interfere with their desire to maintain control over their own lives. After all, if a critic were to admit that the Bible is true, he'd have to admit that he no longer calls all the shots. There would be an Authority in the universe greater than himself, and that Authority might not approve of the life the critic wants to live.

CONCLUSION AND SUMMARY

Jesus taught that the Jewish Old Testament is the inerrant Word of God, and he promised that the rest of God's Word would come through his apostles. The apostles, who were authenticated by miracles, wrote or confirmed 27 books. All major books were immediately recognized as part of God's Word by those connected with the apostles themselves. And all of the 27 books were later recognized as authentic by the early church councils. In other words, the Bible we have today is the true, inerrant Word of God.

Since the Bible is our established standard for truth, anything that contradicts a teaching in the Bible is false. This *does not* mean there is no truth in other religions. It simply means that any specific teaching that contradicts a teaching of the Bible is false.

Now, let's review the conclusions we've drawn since chapter 1:

1. Truth about reality is knowable.
2. The opposite of true is false.
3. It is true that the theistic God exists. This is evidenced by the:
   a. Beginning of the universe (Cosmological Argument)
   b. Design of the universe (Teleological Argument/ Anthropic Principle)
   c. Design of life (Teleological Argument)
   d. Moral Law (Moral Argument)
4. If God exists, then miracles are possible.
5. Miracles can be used to confirm a message from God (i.e., as acts of God to confirm a word from God).
6. The New Testament is historically reliable. This is evidenced by:
   a. Early testimony
   b. Eyewitness testimony
   c. Uninvented (authentic) testimony
   d. Eyewitnesses who were not deceived
7. The New Testament says Jesus claimed to be God.
8. Jesus' claim to be God was miraculously confirmed by:
   a. His fulfillment of many prophecies about himself;
   b. His sinless life and miraculous deeds;
   c. His prediction and accomplishment of his resurrection.
9. Therefore, Jesus is God.
10. Whatever Jesus (who is God) teaches is true.

11. Jesus taught that the Bible is the Word of God.
12. Therefore, it is true that the Bible is the Word of God (and anything opposed to it is false).

Let's go back to chapter 8 to unpack the implications of this. The evidence we had gathered up to chapter 8 (points 1–3 above) helped us conclude that all nontheistic worldviews and religions are false. This left us to consider the three major theistic world religions: Judaism, Christianity, and Islam. Which one of them is true? The evidence presented in chapters 9 through 14 (points 4-12 above) now yield their verdict:

- The revelation of Judaism is true, but it is incomplete. It lacks the New Testament.
- The revelation of Islam has some truth, but it errs on some fundamental teachings, including its denial of the deity and resurrection of Christ (Suras 5:75; 4:157-159).
- Only the revelation of Christianity is the complete, inerrant Word of God.

Could we be wrong about all this? It's possible. *But in light of the evidence, critics, skeptics, and those of other faiths need to have a lot more faith than we do.*

15

Conclusion: The Judge, the Servant King, and the Box Top

"There are only two kinds of people in the end: those who say to God, 'Thy will be done,' and those to whom God says, in the end, 'Thy will be done.'"

—C. S. LEWIS

THE JUDGE

A young man is brought before a judge for drunk driving. When his name is announced by the bailiff, there's a gasp in the courtroom—the defendant is the judge's son! The judge hopes his son is innocent, but the evidence is irrefutable. He's guilty.

What can the judge do? He's caught in a dilemma between justice and love. Since his son is guilty, he deserves punishment. But the judge doesn't want to punish his son because of his great love for him.

He reluctantly announces the sentence: "Son, you can either pay a $5,000 fine or go to jail."

The son looks up at the judge and says, "But, Dad, I promise to be good from now on! I'll volunteer at soup kitchens. I'll visit the elderly. I'll even open a home to care for abused children. And I'll never do anything wrong again! Please let me go!"

At this point, the judge asks, "Are you still drunk? You can't do all of that. But even if you could, your future good deeds can't change the fact that you're already guilty of drunk driving." Indeed, the judge realizes that *good works cannot cancel bad works!* Perfect justice demands that his son be punished for what he has done.

So the judge repeats, "I'm sorry, Son. As much as I'd like to allow you to go, I'm bound by the law. The punishment for this crime is $5,000 or you go to jail."

The son pleads with his father, "But, Dad, you know I don't have $5,000. There has to be another way to avoid jail!"

The judge stands up and takes off his robe. He walks down from his raised bench and gets down to his son's level. Standing eye to eye next to his son, he reaches into his pocket, pulls out $5,000, and holds it out. The son is startled, but he understands there's only one thing he can do to be free—take the money. There's nothing else he can do. Good works or promises of good works cannot set him free. Only the acceptance of his father's free gift can save the son from certain punishment.

God is in a situation similar to that of the judge—he's caught in a dilemma between his justice and his love. Since we've all sinned at one time in our lives, God's infinite justice demands that he punish that sin. But because of his infinite love, God wants to find a way to avoid punishing us.

What's the *only way* God can remain just but not punish us for our sins? He must punish a sinless substitute who voluntarily takes our punishment for us (sinless because the substitute must pay for our sins, not his own; and voluntary because it would be unjust to punish the substitute against his will). Where can God find a sinless substitute? Not from sinful humanity, but only from himself. Indeed, God *himself* is the substitute. Just as the judge came down from his bench to save his child, God came down from heaven to save you and me from punishment. And we all deserve punishment. I do. You do.

"But I'm a good person!" you say. Perhaps you are "good" compared to Hitler or even the man next door. But God's standard isn't Hitler or the man next door. His standard is moral perfection because his unchanging nature is moral perfection.

In fact, the greatest myth believed today when it comes to religion is that "being good" will get you to heaven. According to this view, it doesn't matter what you believe as long as you're a "good person" and your good deeds outweigh your bad. But this is false, because a perfectly just God must punish bad deeds regardless of how many good ones someone has performed. Once we've sinned against an eternal Being—and we all have—we deserve eternal punishment, and no good deed can change that fact.

Jesus came to offer us a way out of that punishment and to offer us eternal life. Paradise lost in Genesis becomes paradise regained in Revelation. So when Jesus said, "I am the way and the truth and the life. No one comes to the Father except through me" (John 14:6), he was not making an arbitrary claim but a statement that reflected the reality of the universe. Jesus is the only way because there is only one way God can reconcile his infinite justice and his infinite love (Rom. 3:26). If there were any other way, then God allowed Christ to die for nothing (Gal. 2:21).

Like the father did for his drunkard son, God satisfies his justice by punishing himself for our sins and holding out that payment for each one of us. All we need to do in order to be set free is to accept the gift. There's only one problem: *just as the father can't force his son to accept the gift, God can't force you to accept his gift either.* God loves you so much that he even respects your decision to reject him.

THE SERVANT KING

You can reject Christ because he has left your free will truly free.[1] Author Philip Yancey adapts a parable by Christian philosopher Søren Kierkegaard that helps us understand how God attempts to save us while respecting our freedom. It's a parable of a king who loves a humble maiden:

> The king was like no other king. Statesmen trembled before his power. No one dared breathe a word against him, for he had the strength to crush all opponents. And yet this mighty king was melted by love for a humble maiden.
>
> How could he declare his love for her? In an odd sort of way, his very kingliness tied his hands. If he brought her to the palace and crowned her head with jewels and clothed her body in royal robes, she would surely not resist—no one dared resist him. But would she love him?
>
> She would say she loved him, of course, but would she truly? Or would she live with him in fear, nursing a private grief for the life she had left behind. Would she be happy at his side? How could he know?
>
> If he rode up to her forest cottage in his royal carriage, with an armed escort waving bright banners, that too would overwhelm her. He did not want a cringing subject. He wanted a lover, an equal. He

wanted her to forget that he was a king and she a humble maiden and to let shared love cross over the gulf between them. "For it is only in love that the unequal can be made equal," concluded Kierkegaard.[2]

This is exactly the problem God has in his pursuit of you and me—if he overwhelms us with his power we may not be free to love him (love and power are often inversely related). And even if we retain our freedom, we may not love *him* but merely love what he gives us. What can God do? Here's what the king did:

> The king, convinced he could not elevate the maiden without crushing her freedom, resolved to *descend*. He clothed himself as a beggar and approached her cottage incognito, with a worn cloak fluttering loosely about him. It was no mere disguise, but a new identity he took on. He renounced the throne to win her hand.[3]

This is exactly what God did to win you and me! He descended to the human level—in fact to one of the lowest social levels possible—to that of a servant. Paul describes Christ's sacrifice this way in his letter to the Philippians (2:5-8):

> Your attitude should be the same as that of Christ Jesus:
>
> > Who, being in very nature God,
> >   did not consider equality with God something to be grasped,
> > but made himself nothing,
> >   taking the very nature of a servant,
> >   being made in human likeness.
> > And being found in appearance as a man,
> >   he humbled himself
> >   and became obedient to death—even death on a cross!

Imagine, the Creator of the universe humbling himself by coming to serve, suffer, and die at the hands of the very creatures he created! Why would he do this? Because his infinite love compels him to offer salvation to those made in his image. And taking the form of a human servant was the only way he could offer us that salvation without negating our ability to accept it.

It's one thing to acknowledge that Christ took "the very nature of a servant" in order to save us from our sins—it's quite another to fathom the magnitude of his suffering. Most of us take it for granted. C. Truman Davis, M.D., wrote a vivid description of Christ's suffering and crucifixion, which we have adapted into the following account.[4]

THE SUFFERING OF THE SERVANT KING

The whip the Roman soldiers use on Jesus has small iron balls and sharp pieces of sheep bones tied to it. Jesus is stripped of his clothing, and his hands are tied to an upright post. His back, buttocks, and legs are whipped either by one soldier or by two who alternate positions. The soldiers taunt their victim. As they repeatedly strike Jesus' back with full force, the iron balls cause deep contusions, and the sheep bones cut into the skin and tissues. As the whipping continues, the lacerations tear into the underlying skeletal muscles and produce quivering ribbons of bleeding flesh. Pain and blood loss set the stage for circulatory shock.

When it is determined by the centurion in charge that Jesus is near death, the beating is finally stopped. The half-fainting Jesus is then untied and allowed to slump to the stone pavement, wet with his own blood. The Roman soldiers see a great joke in this provincial Jew claiming to be a king. They throw a robe across his shoulders and place a stick in his hand for a scepter. They still need a crown to make their travesty complete. A small bundle of flexible branches covered with long thorns are plaited into the shape of a crown, and this is pressed into his scalp. Again there is copious bleeding (the scalp being one of the most vascular areas of the body). After mocking him and striking him across the face, the soldiers take the stick from his hand and strike him across the head, driving the thorns deeper into his scalp.

Finally, when they tire of their sadistic sport, the robe is torn from his back. The robe had already become adherent to the clots of blood and serum in the wounds, and its removal—just as in the careless removal of a surgical bandage—causes excruciating pain, almost as though he were being whipped again. The wounds again begin to bleed. In deference to Jewish custom, the Romans return his garments. The heavy horizontal beam of the cross is tied across his shoulders, and the procession of the condemned Christ, two thieves, and the execution party walk along the Via Dolorosa. In spite of his efforts to walk erect, the weight of the heavy wooden beam, together with the shock produced by copious blood loss, is too much. He stumbles and falls. The rough wood of the beam gouges into the lacerated skin and muscles of the shoulders. He tries to rise, but human muscles have been pushed beyond their endurance. The centurion, anxious to get on with the crucifixion, selects a stalwart North African onlooker, Simon of Cyrene, to carry the cross. Jesus follows, still bleeding and sweating the cold, clammy sweat of shock.

The 650-yard journey from the fortress Antonia to Golgotha is finally completed. Jesus is again stripped of his clothes except for a loin-cloth which is allowed the Jews. The crucifixion begins. Jesus is offered wine mixed with myrrh, a mild pain-killing mixture. He refuses to drink. Simon is ordered to place the cross beam on the ground, and Jesus is quickly thrown backward with his shoulders against the wood. The legionnaire feels for the depression at the front of the wrist. He drives a heavy, square, wrought-iron nail through the wrist and deep into the wood. Quickly, he moves to the other side and repeats the action, being careful not to pull the arms too tight, but to allow some flexibility and movement. The beam is then lifted, and the title reading "Jesus of Nazareth, King of the Jews" is nailed in place.

The victim Jesus is now crucified. As he slowly sags down with more weight on the nails in the wrists, excruciating, fiery pain shoots along the fingers and up the arms to explode in the brain—the nails in the wrists are putting pressure on the median nerves. As he pushes himself upward to avoid this stretching torment, he places his full weight on the nail through his feet. Again, there is the searing agony of the nail tearing through the nerves between the metatarsal bones of the feet. At this point, another phenomenon occurs. As the arms fatigue, great waves of cramps sweep over the muscles, knotting them in deep, relentless, throbbing pain. With these cramps comes the inability to push himself upward. Hanging by his arms, the pectoral muscles are paralyzed, and the intercostal muscles are unable to act. Air can be drawn into the lungs but it cannot be exhaled. Jesus fights to raise himself in order to get even one short breath. Finally, carbon dioxide builds up in the lungs and in the bloodstream, and the cramps partially subside. Spasmodically, he is able to push himself upward to exhale and bring in the life-giving oxygen. It is undoubtedly during these periods that he utters the seven short sentences that are recorded.

Now begin hours of this limitless pain, cycles of cramping and twisting, partial asphyxiation, searing pain as tissue is torn from his lacerated back as he moves up and down against the rough timber. Then another agony begins. A deep, crushing pain in the chest as the pericardium slowly fills with serum and begins to compress the heart. It is now almost over—the loss of tissue fluids has reached a critical level; the compressed heart is struggling to pump heavy, thick, sluggish blood into the tissues; the tortured lungs are making a frantic effort to gasp in small gulps of air. The markedly dehydrated tissues send their flood of stimuli to the brain. His mission of atonement has been completed. Finally he can allow his body to die. With one last surge of strength, he once again presses his torn feet against the nail, straightens his legs, takes a deeper breath, and utters his seventh and last cry: "Father, into your hands I commit my spirit."

Jesus went through all of that so you and I could be reconciled to him, so you and I could be saved from our sins by affirming, *Father, into your hands I commit my life.*

THE BOX TOP

We began this book by seeking the "box top" to this puzzle we call life. We said that if we could find the box top, we'd be able to answer the five greatest questions that confront every human being. Since we now know beyond a reasonable doubt that the box top is the Bible, the answers to those five questions are:

1. **Origin: Where did we come from?**—We are created beings, wonderfully made in the image and likeness of God (Gen. 1:27; Ps. 139:14).
2. **Identity: Who are we?**—Since we are made in the image and likeness of God, we are creatures of supreme worth. We are loved by God and endowed with certain God-given rights and responsibilities (John 3:16-18; 1:12; Gal. 4:5).
3. **Meaning: Why are we here?**—Adam and Eve were created in a state of innocence, but their choice to disobey condemned the human race to punishment in accordance with the infinite justice of God (Gen. 3:6-19). Since that time, each of us has confirmed the choice of Adam and Eve through our own disobedience (Rom. 3:10-12; 5:12). We remain in this fallen state so that we can make free choices that will have implications in eternity. This temporal life is the choosing ground for the

eternal one. Choices we can make that will bring glory to God (Isa. 43:7; John 15:8), and may bring us eternal rewards, include:

    a. *accepting* the ransom Jesus paid in order to free us from eternal punishment and welcome us into his eternal presence (Mark 10:45; 1 Tim. 2:6; Heb. 9:15; Luke 16:9; John 14:2)

    b. *serving* as ambassadors for Christ to help others make that same choice (2 Cor 5:17-21; Matt. 28:19); and

    c. *learning* from our own sufferings to comfort others who suffer (2 Cor. 1:3-4), and realizing that our sufferings enhance our own capacity to enjoy eternity (2 Cor. 4:15–5:1; 2 Pet. 1:5-11)

4. **Morality: How should we live?**—Since God first loved us, we should love him and others (Rom 5:8; 1 John 4:19-21). In fact, the "whole duty of man" is to "fear God and keep his commandments" (Eccles. 12:13-14). This includes making disciples of all nations (Matt. 28:19) and enjoying the good things God gives us (1 Tim. 6:17).

5. **Destiny: Where are we going?**—God's infinite justice demands that he punish our sins, but because of his infinite love he has taken the punishment on himself (Isa. 53:4, 10, 12; Rom. 3:26; 2 Cor. 5:21; 1 Pet. 2:24). This is the only way he could remain just and still justify sinners (John 14:6; Rom. 3:26). His gift of salvation from eternal punishment is free to all the world (John 3:16; Eph. 2:8-9; Rev. 22:17). It cannot be earned through good works or any kind of merit. And God wants everyone to be saved from the eternal punishment we all deserve (1 Tim. 2:4; 2 Pet. 3:9). But since he cannot force us to love him (forced love is a contradiction), each one of us must choose for ourselves whom we will serve (Josh. 24:15; John 3:18).

Your Destiny

Whom will you serve? God leaves that choice in your hands. Love knows no other way. In order to respect your free choice, God has made the evidence for Christianity convincing but not compelling. If you want to suppress or ignore the evidence all around you (Rom. 1:18-20)—

including that which is presented in this book—then you are free to do so. But that would be a volitional act, not a rational one. *You can reject Christ, but you cannot honestly say there's not enough evidence to believe in him.*

C. S. Lewis said it best when he wrote, "There are only two kinds of people in the end: those who say to God, 'Thy will be done,' and those to whom God says, in the end, '*Thy* will be done.' All that are in Hell, choose it. Without that self-choice there would be no Hell. No soul that seriously and constantly desires joy will ever miss it. Those who seek find. To those who knock it is opened."[5]

The door is being held open by Jesus Christ. How can you walk through it? Paul wrote, "If you confess with your mouth, 'Jesus is Lord,' and believe in your heart that God raised him from the dead, you will be saved. For it is with your heart that you believe and are justified, and it is with your mouth that you confess and are saved" (Rom. 10:9).

You say, "I believe that Jesus rose from the dead." Good. But merely believing *that* Jesus rose from the dead is not enough. You need to put your trust *in* him. You can believe *that* a certain person would make a great spouse, but that's not enough to make that person your husband or wife. You must go beyond the intellectual to volitional—you must put your trust *in* that person by saying "I do." The same is true concerning your relationship with God. Trusting him is not just a decision of the head but one of the heart. As someone once said, "The distance between heaven and hell is about eighteen inches—the distance between the head and the heart."

What happens if you freely choose *not* to walk through the door Jesus is holding open? Jesus said you will remain in your condemned state: "For God did not send his Son into the world to condemn the world, but to save the world through him. Whoever believes in him is not condemned, *but whoever does not believe stands condemned already* because he has not believed in the name of God's one and only Son" (John 3:18). In other words, you'll remain condemned and separated from God forever. God will respect your choice by saying to you, "*Thy* will be done."

You say, "God doesn't send anyone to hell!" You're right. If you reject Christ, you'll send yourself there.

You say, "God will just annihilate those who don't believe." No, he won't. Hell is real. In fact, Jesus spoke more of hell then he did of heaven. God will not annihilate unbelievers because he will not destroy creatures made in his own image. That would be an attack on himself. (What would you think of an earthly father who killed his son just because his son chose not to do what his father wanted him to do?) God is too loving to destroy those who don't want to be in his presence. His only choice is to quarantine those who reject him. That's what hell does—it quarantines evil, which is contagious.

You say, "God will save everybody!" How? Against their will? Some people would rather be ruined than changed. They'd rather continue their rebellion than be reformed. So God says, "Have it your way. You may continue your rebellion, but you'll be quarantined so that you can't pollute the rest of my creation." Besides, it would be unloving of God to send people who can't bear to spend an hour on Sunday praising him to a place where they will be praising him for eternity. That would be "hell" to them!

You say, "I can't believe there is only one way to God." Why not? Do you need more than one way to get into a building? Do you bring this charge against Muslims for saying that Islam is the only way? How about Hindus? They say reincarnation is the only way to salvation. We have shown philosophically and biblically that Jesus is the only way to reconcile infinite justice and infinite love. If that's not true, then God sent Jesus to die a brutal death for nothing.

You say, "But what about those who have never heard?" Why should that affect *your* decision? You *have* heard!

"Because I can't believe in a God who would torture people in hell just because they haven't heard of Jesus." Who said God does this? First, God doesn't torture anyone. Hell is not a place of externally inflicted torture, but a place of self-inflicted *torment* (Luke 16:23, 28). Those in hell certainly don't want it, but they *will* it. Hell is a terrible place, but its doors are locked on the *inside*. Second, people may choose hell whether or not they've heard of Jesus. Everyone knows of God because of the starry heavens above and the Moral Law within (Rom 1:18-20; 2:14-15). Those who reject that natural revelation will reject Jesus too. However, those that truly seek God will be rewarded (Heb. 11:6). Since God wants everyone to be saved (even more than you do—2 Pet. 3:9), he will ensure that seekers get the information they need. And since God is just (Gen. 18:25; Ps. 9:8; Rom. 3:26), no one will go to hell who should go to heaven, and vice versa. "In the meantime," as C. S. Lewis said, "if you are worried about people on the outside, the most unreasonable thing you can do is to remain outside yourself. Christians are Christ's body, the organism through which he works. Every addition to that body enables Him to do more. If you want to help those outside, you must add your own little cell to the body of Christ who alone can help them. Cutting off a man's fingers would be an odd way of getting him to do more work."[6]

You say, "You Christians just want to scare people with hell!" No, we just want people to know the truth. If that scares them, maybe it should. We certainly don't like what the Bible says about hell. We wish it weren't true. But Jesus, who is God, taught it, and for good reason. It seems to be necessary. Without a hell, injustices in this world would never be righted, the free choices of people would not be respected, and the greater good of a redemption could never be accomplished. If there is no heaven to seek and no hell to shun, then nothing in this universe has any ultimate meaning: your choices, your pleasures, your sufferings, the lives of you and your loved ones ultimately mean nothing. We struggle through this life for no ultimate reason, and Christ died for nothing. Without heaven and hell, this incredibly designed universe is a stairway to nowhere.

"So what?" says the atheist. "Maybe this universe *is* a stairway to nowhere. Just because you want life to have meaning doesn't mean it does." True. But we don't just *want* life to have meaning—we have *evidence* that it has meaning.[7]

We end with the greatest news anyone could ever hear. Your choices do matter. Your life does have ultimate meaning. And thanks to Christ, no one has to experience hell. Every human being can accept his free gift of eternal salvation. It takes no effort at all. Does it take some faith? Yes, but every choice—even the choice to reject Christ—requires faith. Since the evidence shows beyond a reasonable doubt that the Bible is true, accepting Christ is the choice that requires the *least* amount of faith. The choice is up to you. Do you have enough faith to believe anything else?

You say, "I still have doubts and questions." So what? We do too. Everyone has doubts and questions. And why shouldn't we? As finite creatures, we shouldn't expect to understand everything about an infinite God and how he does things. Paul certainly didn't (Rom. 11:33-36), and many of the Old Testament writers expressed doubts and even questioned God.[8] But since we are finite creatures who must make our decisions based on probability, there has to be a point where we realize that the weight of the evidence comes down on one side or the other. We'll never have *all* the answers. But as we have seen throughout this book, there are more than enough answers to give God the benefit of our doubts.

Finally, have you ever thought about questioning your doubts? Just ask yourself, "Is it reasonable to doubt that Christianity is true in light of all the evidence?" Probably not. In fact, *in light of the evidence, you ought to have a lot more doubts about atheism and every other non-Christian belief system.* They are not reasonable. Christianity is. So start doubting your doubts and accept Christ. *It takes too much faith to believe anything else!*

Appendix 1:

If God, Why Evil?

Atheist: If there really is an all-good, all-powerful, theistic God, then why does he allow evil?

Christian: How do you know what evil is unless you know what good is? And how do you know what good is unless there is an objective standard of good beyond yourself?

Atheist: Don't try to avoid the question.

Christian: I'm not trying to avoid the question. I'm simply showing you that your complaint presupposes that God exists. In fact, the existence of evil doesn't disprove God. It may prove that there is a devil, but it doesn't prove that there's no God.

Atheist: Interesting move, but I'm not convinced.

Christian: You may not be convinced, but your complaint still presupposes God.

Atheist: For the sake of argument, suppose I grant you that God exists. Will you then answer the question?

Christian: Sure. It's good to see you're making progress.

Atheist: Remember, it's just for the sake of argument. So why doesn't your so-called "all-powerful" God stop evil?

Christian: Do you really want him to?

Atheist: Of course!

Christian: Suppose he starts with you?

Atheist: Be serious.

Christian: No, really. We always talk about God stopping evil, but we forget that if he did, he would have to stop us too. We all do evil.

Atheist: Oh, come on! We're not talking about the minor sins of you and me—but we're talking about real evil, like what Hitler did!

Christian: My point is not the degree of evil, but the source of evil. The source of evil is our free choice. If God were to do away with evil, then he would have to do away with free choice. And if he did away with our free choice, we would no longer have the ability to love or do good. This would no longer be a moral world.

Atheist: But not all evil is due to free choice. Why do babies die? Why do natural disasters occur?

Christian: The Bible traces it all back to the fall of man. No one is really innocent because we all sinned in Adam (Rom. 5:12) and as a consequence deserve death (Rom. 6:23). Natural disasters and premature deaths are a direct result of the curse on creation because of the fall of humankind (Genesis 3; Romans 8). This fallen world will not be righted until Christ returns (Revelation 21–22). So no one is guaranteed a trouble-free life, or a full life of seventy years.

Atheist: Oh, isn't that convenient—dust off the Bible and tell us that God will make it right in the end! I'm not interested in the future. I want pain and suffering to end now! Why won't God end it?

Christian: He will end it, but just not on your timetable. Just because God hasn't ended evil *yet* doesn't mean that he never will end it.

Atheist: But why doesn't Christ return right now to end all this pain? The sum of human pain is enormous!

Christian: First, no one is experiencing the "sum of human pain." If it's 80 degrees in Manhattan, 85 degrees in Brooklyn, and 80 degrees in Queens, does any New Yorker experience a heat of 245 degrees?

Atheist: No.

Christian: That's right. Each person experiences his own pain.

Atheist: But that still doesn't tell me why God doesn't end it all now. Why is he waiting?

Christian: If God wanted to end evil now, he could. But have you thought that maybe God has other goals that he would like to accomplish while evil exists?

Atheist: Like what?

Christian: For starters, he would like to have more people choose heaven before he closes the curtain on this world. Paul seems to indicate that Jesus will come back after "the full number" of people become believers (Rom. 11:25).

Atheist: Well, while God is waiting for the "full number" of people to be saved, other people are hurting!

Christian: Yes, they are. And that means Christians have a job to do. We have the privilege of helping those who are hurting. We are ambassadors for Christ here on earth.

Atheist: That's nice, but if I were suffering I'd rather have *God* help me than you!

Christian: If God prevented pain every time we got into trouble, then we would become the most reckless, self-centered creatures in the universe. And we would never learn from suffering.

Atheist: Learn from suffering! What are you talking about?

Christian: Ah, you've just hit on another reason why God doesn't end evil right now. Can you name me one enduring lesson that you ever learned from pleasure?

Atheist: Give me a minute.

Christian: I could give you an hour; I doubt that you would come up with much. If you think about it, you'll find that virtually every valuable lesson you've ever learned resulted from some hardship in your life. In most cases, bad fortune teaches while good fortune deceives. In fact, you not only learn lessons from suffering, but it's practically the only way you can develop virtues.

Atheist: What do you mean?

Christian: You can't develop courage unless there is danger. You can't develop perseverance unless you have obstacles in your way. You won't learn how to be a servant unless there's someone to serve. And compassion would never be summoned if there were never anyone in pain or in need. It's the old adage: "no pain, no gain."

Atheist: But I wouldn't need all those virtues if God would just quarantine evil right now!

Christian: But since God has reasons for not quarantining evil right now, you need to develop virtues for this life and the life hereafter. This earth is an uncomfortable home, but it's a great gymnasium for the hereafter.

Atheist: You Christians always punt to the hereafter. You're so heavenly minded that you're no earthly good!

Christian: We may be heavenly minded, but we know that what we do on earth matters in eternity. Virtues that a believer develops through suffering will enhance his capacity to enjoy eternity. Paul says that "our light and momentary troubles are achieving for us an eternal glory that far outweighs them all" (2 Cor. 4:17; cf. Rom. 8:18).

Atheist: How is hardship here going to help me feel better in a place where there's not going to be any pain anyway?

Christian: You like football, don't you?

Atheist: I've watched a few games.

Christian: How does every player on the Super Bowl–winning team feel after the game?

Atheist: Great, of course!

Christian: Does the captain of the winning team—who also won the MVP trophy—enjoy the victory more than the third-string quarterback who didn't play a down all year?

Atheist: I suppose so.

Christian: Of course he does. While the third-string quarterback is happy to be on the winning team, the victory is much sweeter for the captain who won the MVP trophy because he contributed to the win and persevered through the entire year to get there. By persisting through all the hardships and pains of playing, he actually enhanced his capacity to enjoy the victory. And it's made even sweeter by the MVP trophy.

Atheist: What does football have to do with heaven?

Christian: Heaven will be like the winning locker room (but without the smell!). We'll all be happy to be there, but some will have a greater ability to enjoy it and have more rewards than others.

After all, God's justice demands that there will be degrees of rewards in heaven just like there will be degrees of punishment in hell.

Atheist: So you're saying life is like a Super Bowl?

Christian: To a certain extent, yes. Like a Super Bowl, life has rules, a referee, and rewards. But in life there are no spectators—everyone is in the game—and we already know who will win. Christ will win, and anyone, regardless of ability, can be a winner simply by joining the team. While everyone on the team will enjoy the victory parade, some will appreciate it even more because of the hardships they experienced during the game and the rewards they receive for playing it well. In other words, the feeling of victory is greater the more intense the battle is.

Atheist: So you're saying that evil has a purpose that has implications in eternity.

Christian: Yes.

Atheist: Why do you insist on putting everything in light of eternity?

Christian: Because we're all going to be dead a lot longer than we're going to be alive! Furthermore, the Bible teaches us to look to the eternal, and life makes sense only in light of eternity. If there is no eternity, then there is no ultimate purpose for anything, pleasures or pains.

Atheist: Suppose there is no eternity. Suppose we live, we die, and that's it.

Christian: It's possible, but *I don't have enough faith to believe it.*

Atheist: Why not?

Christian: Haven't you read this book?

Atheist: No, I jumped right to this appendix.

Christian: That's just like you, isn't it? You don't want to play the game; you just want to see the final score.

Atheist: I suppose I suffer from the American disease of instant gratification.

Christian: That's probably why you're having trouble realizing the value of suffering and "no pain, no gain!"

Atheist: You're right, reading this book is too painful. It's too long.

Christian: It could be shorter if we didn't have to address all those crazy arguments you atheists bring up. Besides, you've got time to read. Sunday mornings are free for you.

Atheist: There are a lot less painful things I could do on Sunday mornings.

Christian: Look, I know this book may be painful to read, but it's more painful to reject its conclusion. You've got to read this book from beginning to end if you want to see the whole argument for Christianity. The case is laid out in logical order. Each chapter builds on the previous one.

Atheist: Alright, I'll read the book. But in the meantime, let's get back to the question of evil. If there is an eternity, then some evils in this world may have an eternal purpose. But there are certainly some evil acts in this world that have absolutely no purpose.

Christian: How do you know?

Atheist: It's obvious! What good purpose could there be in, say, the terrorist attacks on 9/11?

Christian: While I wish it had never happened, there were some good things that we know about that came out of those terrible events. For example, we came together as a country; we helped those in need; and we resolved to fight the evil of terrorism. We also were shocked into pondering the ultimate questions about life, and some people came to Christ as result of it. As C. S. Lewis said, pain is God's "megaphone to rouse a deaf world."[1] 9/11 certainly woke us up!

Atheist: Yes, you can find a silver lining in just about anything, but there's no way your "silver lining" outweighs the pain and suffering.

Christian: How do you know? Unless you are all-knowing and have an eternal perspective, how do you know the events of 9/11 will not work together for good in the end? Perhaps there are many good things that will come out of that tragedy in the individual lives we will never hear about. In fact, good results may even come generations from now unbeknownst to those who will experience them.

Atheist: Come on! That's a cop-out!

Christian: No, it's simply recognizing our limits and acknowledging the limitless knowledge and unseen purposes of God (Rom. 11:33-36). We can't see the future on earth, much less what eternity in heaven will be like. So how can we say that the ultimate eternal outcome of 9/11 won't work out for good? We already know some good things that have resulted from it. Just because we can't think of an ultimate good reason or purpose for it, that doesn't mean an infinite God doesn't have one.

Atheist: If God would tell me his reasons, then maybe I could believe you.

Christian: Job already tried that tactic. After he questioned God about why he suffered, God baffled Job with questions about the wonders of creation (Job 38–41). It's as if God were saying to him, "Job, you can't even understand how I run the physical world that you *can* see, so how are you going to understand the vastly more complex moral world that you *cannot* see—a world where the results of billions of free choices made by human beings every day interact with one another?" Indeed, it would be impossible for us to comprehend such complexity. By the way, have you ever seen the movie *It's a Wonderful Life*?

Atheist: Do you mean the one with Jimmy Stewart that's shown every Christm . . . I mean, winter solstice?

Christian: Yeah, that's the one. Jimmy Stewart plays George Bailey, a character who is despondent because his business dealings have gone bad and his life seems to be falling apart. He is averted from suicide at the last minute by an angel who shows him what life would have been like for others if George had never been born. It turns out that life would have been terrible for many people throughout his hometown. But George never knew this. He never realized the amazing impact his life had on others. Hence the title, *It's a Wonderful Life*.

Atheist: Bah! Humbug!

Christian: Come on. You get the point, don't you?

Atheist: Yeah, I get the point: we don't know what impact any person or event might have in the long run, especially since there are so many interacting choices being made.

Christian: Yes, and even choices meant for evil can turn out for good (Gen. 50:20). Perhaps many people now or generations from now will come to Christ because of the direct or indirect effects of evil events.

Atheist: But it seems like that's an argument from ignorance.

Christian: No. It's not like we have *no* information about why bad things happen. We know that we live in a fallen world, and we know that good things can come from bad. So we know it's possible that God can have a good reason for bad things even if we don't know what those reasons are. And we know that he can bring good from bad. So it's not an argument from ignorance, but a reasonable conclusion from what we do know. And while we don't know the reason for every *specific* bad thing that happens, we know why we don't know: we don't know because of our human limitations.

Atheist: What do you think of Rabbi Kushner's answer to the question? You know, he wrote the book *When Bad Things Happen to Good People*.

Christian: I think his answer is wrong.

Atheist: Wrong? Why?

Christian: Because his answer is that God isn't powerful enough to defeat evil on earth. So we need to forgive God for allowing evil.

Atheist: What's wrong with that?

Christian: Because there's strong evidence that God is infinitely powerful. Fifty-six times in the Bible God is referred to as "almighty," and in several other ways he is described as all-powerful. We also know from scientific evidence that he created this universe out of nothing (take a look at chapter 3 of this book). So Rabbi Kushner's finite god doesn't square with the facts.

Atheist: If God is infinitely powerful as you say, then why does he allow bad things to happen to good people?

Christian: We've already pointed out that there are good outcomes for pain and suffering. But we also need to point out that the question makes an assumption that isn't true.

Atheist: What's that?

Christian: There are no *good* people!

Atheist: Oh, come on!

Christian: No, really. Some people are better than others, but no one is really good. We all have a natural bent toward selfishness. And we all commit sins routinely.

Atheist: I do more good things than bad.

Christian: By whose standard?

Atheist: By society's standard. I'm a law-abiding citizen. I'm not a murderer or a thief.

Christian: That's the problem. We consider ourselves good people only by the standards of bad people. We judge ourselves against others rather than against an absolute standard of good. By the way, have you ever stolen anything?

Atheist: Well, yes.

Christian: Have you ever lied about anything?

Atheist: No.

Christian: You're lying.

Atheist: I can't fool you.

Christian: So you're a lying thief, then!

Atheist: That doesn't mean I'm all bad.

Christian: No, but it means you're not all good either. Think about it: it's much easier to be bad than good; it's much more natural to you to be selfish rather than generous. We all have that depraved human nature. As Augustine said, "We're all born with a propensity to sin and a necessity to die."[2] That propensity is inborn. That's why young children naturally grab things and yell, "Mine!" It's also why James Madison said, "If men were angels, no government would be necessary."[3]

Atheist: So Kushner makes incorrect assumptions about the nature of man and the nature of God.

Christian: Exactly. The question is not "Why do bad things happen to good people?" but "Why do good things happen to bad people?"

Atheist: If God really is all-powerful as you say, I still don't understand why he didn't stop 9/11. If you knew it was going to happen and had the power to stop it, wouldn't you have stopped it?

Christian: Yes.

Atheist: So you are better than God!

Christian: No, by stopping 9/11, I would be preventing evil. But God, who has an unlimited, eternal perspective, allows evil choices knowing that he can redeem them in the end. We can't redeem such choices, so we try to stop every one.

Atheist: Yes, but by your own Christian doctrine, God doesn't redeem all evil choices in the end. After all, some people go to hell!

Christian: Yes, but that's because God can bring eternal good only to those who will accept it. Some people ignore the facts or simply choose to play the game in a way that brings them defeat. Since God cannot force them to *freely choose* to play the game the right way, ultimate good only comes to those who choose it. That's why Paul says, "And we know that in all things God works for the good of those who love him, who have been called according to his purpose" (Rom. 8:28). Notice he doesn't say, "all things are good." He says all things work together *for* the good *of those who love him.*

Atheist: So how did "all things work together for good" for those who died in 9/11?

Christian: Those who loved God and accepted the free gift of salvation are with God in eternity. Those who did not, are having their free choice of eternal separation respected as well.

Atheist: And the rest of us?

Christian: Those of us who remain here still have time to make our decision. And those who already were Christians at the time may have had their character strengthened through 9/11.

Atheist: But if God is all-good and all-knowing, why would he create creatures who he knew would go to hell?

Christian: Good question. There are only five options God had. He could have: 1) not created at all; 2) created a non-free world of robots; 3) created a free world where we would not sin; 4) created a free world where we would sin, but everyone would accept God's salvation; or 5) created the world we have now—a world where we would sin, and some would be saved but the rest would be lost.

Atheist: Yes, and it seems like God picked the worst of those five options! So God is not all-good!

Christian: Not so fast. The first option can't even be compared to the other four because something and nothing have nothing in common. Comparing a real world and a non-world is not even like comparing apples and oranges, since they both are fruit. It is like comparing apples and non-apples, insisting that non-apples taste better. In logic, this is called a category mistake. It's like asking, "What color is math?" Math is not a color, so the question is meaningless.

Atheist: If comparing existence to nonexistence is a category mistake, then Jesus made a category mistake when he said it would have been better if Judas had never been born (Matt. 26:24).

Christian: No, Jesus was not talking about the supremacy of non-being over being. He was simply making a forceful point about the severity of Judas's sin.

Atheist: Okay, so why didn't God make his second option—a robot world?

Christian: He could have, but that wouldn't have been a moral world. It would have been a world with no evil, but with no moral good either.

Atheist: So why didn't he make worlds three or four? Those worlds would allow love, and they certainly would be better worlds than this one.

Christian: Yes, but not everything *conceivable* is actually *achievable* with free creatures. For example, it is conceivable that I could have been robbing a bank instead of talking to you. But that is not achievable because I freely chose to talk to you. Likewise, God can't force free creatures *not* to sin. Forced freedom is a contradiction.

Atheist: But this world could be better if there were one less murder or one less rape. So God failed because he didn't create the best possible world.

Christian: Hold on. While I will admit that this world is not the best possible world, it may *be the best way to get to* the best possible world.

Atheist: What kind of theistic psychobabble is that?

Christian: God may have permitted evil in order to defeat it. As I've already said, if evil is not allowed, then the higher virtues cannot be attained. People who are redeemed have stronger character than people who have not been tested. Soul-building requires some pain. The Job of chapter 42 is a deeper and more joyful man than the Job of chapter 1. So evil in this world actually serves a good purpose in the end. It creates an eternal world that's the best possible world.

Atheist: But why would God create people knowing that they would choose hell?

Christian: Do you have children?

Atheist: Yes. In fact I'm a former child myself!

Christian: Why did you have them, knowing that someday they would disobey you?

Atheist: My wife asks me that question a lot!

Christian: I know why I did. Because love takes risks. I was willing to take the risk of loss in order to experience the joy of love. The same is true of every Super Bowl. Both teams know that one will lose, yet both are willing to play the game despite that risk.

Atheist: I must admit that your intellectual answers make some sense, but evil still bothers me.[4]

Christian: It bothers me too, and it should. We all know that this world just isn't right, and we all long for heaven. Perhaps our longing for heaven is another clue that it's really there (some of the other clues being the evidence we've presented in this book).

Atheist: Perhaps, but I don't think your intellectual answers will sustain a person through evil.

Christian: You may be right. But you don't have to withstand evil with just answers. You can have access to the Divine Comforter—the Holy Spirit—to help you through this soul-building life of pain and suffering.

Atheist: I'd rather not suffer at all than to have a comforter.

Christian: Maybe that's why God doesn't put pain and suffering in our control. If he did, who would choose to go through it?

Atheist: No one.

Christian: Well, that's not exactly true. One man certainly chose to suffer. Jesus Christ volunteered to suffer so that you and I could be reconciled to God. It has been the only real case of a bad thing happening to a truly good person. So we can complain to God about pain and suffering, but we have to admit that he did not exempt himself from it. As for you and me, sometimes God saves us *from* evil, but sometimes he comforts us *through* evil. In either event, whether we know his reasons or not, believers can trust God that all things will work together for good according to his eternal plan.

Appendix 2:

Isn't That Just Your Interpretation?

Atheist: Okay, I went back and read this entire book just like you asked, but I don't think you've made the case that Christianity is true.

Christian: Why not?

Atheist: Because it's just *your* interpretation.

Christian: Of course it's *my* interpretation, but that doesn't mean my interpretation is wrong.

Atheist: I say it *is* wrong!

Christian: Is that just *your* interpretation?

Atheist: So you're turning the tables on me.

Christian: Yes. All conclusions involve making an interpretation, including yours. And in order for you to know that my interpretation (Christianity) is objectively wrong, you would have to know what is objectively right. So what is that right interpretation?

Atheist: There are no objective interpretations.

Christian: Forgive me for doing this again, but is *that* an objective interpretation?

Atheist: Stop that!

Christian: Stop what, being logical? I'm just using the Road Runner tactic from chapter 1. When you say something that's self-defeating, I feel compelled to point it out. So how can you make the objective interpretation that there are no objective interpretations?

Atheist: Okay, so maybe there are objective interpretations.

Christian: Yes, there are. While you may interpret the evidence and conclude that Christianity is false, I may do the same and conclude it's true. But since opposites cannot both be true, one of us must be right, and the other one must be wrong. So who is right?

Atheist: I am.

Christian: Why?

Atheist: I just think I'm right.

Christian: But that's just an assertion. You must give evidence rather than just make assertions. In this book, we didn't make assertions that Christianity is true—we gave evidence every step of the way, from the question of truth all the way to the inspiration of the Bible. What evidence do you have that atheism is true?

Atheist: Evil and science.

Christian: That's not positive evidence for atheism but merely *perceived* obstacles to belief in Christianity. As we have seen, the existence of evil doesn't disprove God (appendix 1), and scientific discoveries actually support the Christian worldview (chapters 3–6).

Atheist: But if Christianity is true, it excludes too many people. After all, millions of people are not Christians.

Christian: That doesn't determine whether Christianity is true or not. After all, truth is not determined by how many people believe it. Truth is *discovered* by looking at the evidence. Is your interpretation (that Christianity is false) necessarily wrong because it excludes millions of Christians?

Atheist: No.

Christian: Neither is mine, then. Besides, as we saw when we talked about evil, Christianity doesn't exclude people—people exclude themselves from Christianity. Everyone knows that God exists. But because we all have free will, some people choose to suppress that knowledge so that they can follow their own desires. Paul talks about that in Romans chapter 1.

Atheist: Maybe so, but I find your conclusion extremely judgmental. And you know, you ought not judge!

Christian: Forgive me again, but if we ought not judge, then why are you judging me for judging?

Atheist: What's the matter, Mister Holy—you'd rather play logic games than believe what Jesus said?

Christian: It's not a mere game but an observation about the way things really are. It's self-defeating to tell me, "You ought not judge" when that's a judgment itself. Furthermore, you are making a judgment when you say Christianity is *not* true!

Atheist: Okay, but what about my second point. Don't you believe what Jesus said?

Christian: Why are you quoting the Bible? Do you believe it's true now?

Atheist: No, but you do. So why don't you believe what Jesus said?

Christian: I do. The problem is *you don't know what he said.* Jesus did *not* tell us not to judge. He simply told us not to judge hypocritically. He said, "Do not judge, or you too will be judged. For in the same way you judge others, you will be judged, and with the measure you use, it will be measured to you" (Matt. 7:1-2). He then went on to say, "Take the plank out of your own eye, and then your will see clearly to remove the speck from your brother's eye." In other words, when you judge, don't judge hypocritically. The Bible also *commands us to make judgments* when it tells us to "test everything" (1 Thess. 5:21), and not to "believe every spirit" (1 John 4:1) but to believe in Jesus Christ for eternal life (John 3:16).

Atheist: Are you done?

Christian: No. There's one more point: it would be impossible to live very long if you didn't judge good from evil. You make hundreds of vital decisions every day that can either hurt you or help you. When you make those decisions you are making judgments!

Atheist: Alright, I see that everyone makes judgments. And you are making judgments by interpreting the Bible the way you do. Who's to say that your interpretation is right?

Christian: You need to look at the context of the passage to discover the objective meaning.

Atheist: If objective interpretations are possible, then why are there so many different interpretations of the Bible?

Christian: Why do so many people get their math sums wrong? Is there no right answer to arithmetic problems?

Atheist: Language is different. I think that there are many interpretations of a sentence or a Bible verse that are true. That's why you get so many denominations.

Christian: So you are saying that sentences can be interpreted in only *one* way.

Atheist: No! . . . Didn't you hear what I just said? I said exactly the opposite is true. There are *many* valid interpretations.

Christian: If there are many valid interpretations, then why did you just correct me for misinterpreting what you said?

Atheist: I did?

Christian: Yes, you just told me that I misunderstood you. In effect, you said that my interpretation was wrong! Why did you do that if there are many valid interpretations?

Atheist: Because I knew what I meant, and it should have been obvious to you.

Christian: You're right. So let me ask you this: why is it that when you make a statement, you expect others to know what *you* mean, but when God makes a statement in the Bible, you give yourself the option of pouring any meaning you want into it?

Atheist: Okay, so maybe there are objective interpretations. But if there are, then why are there so many denominations?

Christian: For the same reason there are a lot of non-Christians. It's not because the truth is not *perceived*, it's because the truth is not *received*. In other words, we believe our own traditions and desires over the Word of God. Jesus spoke forcefully against doing this (Matthew 15; 23).

Atheist: Alright. I'm going to come clean with you.

Christian: It's about time!

Atheist: The real problem I have with Christianity is that it leads to intolerance. You Christians all think you have the truth!

Christian: Haven't you noticed that *everyone* thinks they have the truth? Those who say Christianity is false think they have *that* truth. Even those who say every religion is true think that's the truth!

Atheist: Okay, okay, you're right. I think atheism is true. But I'm not intolerant like most Christians!

Christian: Even if Christians are intolerant, that wouldn't mean Christianity is false.

Atheist: I realize that, but it's still a practical problem.

Christian: How so?

Atheist: Because people who think they have the truth want to impose that truth on others.

Christian: Do you mean politically?

Atheist: Yes.

Christian: I've got news for you: everyone involved in politics—including every non-Christian—is trying to impose what he or she thinks is the truth. So what's your point?

Atheist: My point is that Christians want to take away the rights of people!

Christian: Actually, Christianity is one of the few worldviews that can justify absolute human rights because it affirms that those rights are given to us by God. As our founders recognized, governments aren't meant to give or take away rights: governments are meant to secure rights that the people already possess. That's what we affirmed in our Declaration of Independence.

Atheist: But what about tolerance?

Christian: Christianity is one of the few worldviews that not only offers but champions religious tolerance. Since God doesn't force anyone to believe (in fact the purpose of this life is to make a *free choice*), most Christians recognize that government shouldn't try to force belief either.

Atheist: But during the Crusades, some Christians obviously thought differently!

Christian: They may have called themselves Christians, but they certainly were not following the teachings of Christ. Jesus never condoned such conduct.

Atheist: I think a completely secular government is the most tolerant of all. After all, there is religious freedom in secular countries in Europe.

Christian: Those countries do exist, but most of them are living off the remnants of the Christian worldview from previous generations. How much religious freedom is there in a self-declared atheistic country such as China, or how much was there in the former Soviet Union? Not much. And if you go to most Muslim countries today, you'll also find very little religious freedom. Last I checked, churches are not allowed in Saudi Arabia, and most other Muslim countries treat Christians as second-class citizens.

Atheist: That may be true for religious tolerance, but most Christians are not very tolerant about certain moral issues.

Christian: Do you think tolerance is an absolute moral obligation?

Atheist: You're trying to connect moral obligations with God again, aren't you?

Christian: There is no other connection. As we saw in chapter 7, there are no moral obligations or moral rights if there is no God. So why should anyone be tolerant if there is no moral obligation to be tolerant?

Atheist: Because it's the right thing to do.

Christian: That's just another assertion. As an atheist, you have no way to justify why anyone should be tolerant.

Atheist: Maybe not. But as a Christian, you do. So why don't you believe that we ought to be tolerant?

Christian: Actually, the supreme moral obligation is love—not tolerance. Tolerance says, "Hold your nose and put up with others." Love says, "Reach out and help others."

Atheist: Why can't you be tolerant *and* loving?

Christian: You can, but sometimes love requires you to be intolerant. For example, wouldn't it be unloving to tolerate murder, rape, theft, or racism?

Atheist: I suppose so.

Christian: Good, but we're getting a little off the subject. The focus of Christianity is spiritual, not social salvation. While Christians certainly have social obligations, Christ came to free us from our sins, not to free us from "the Romans."

Atheist: You wouldn't know that by the behavior of some Christians today.

Christian: You mean you don't like their biblical views on moral issues like abortion and homosexuality?

Atheist: Yes.

Christian: So?

Atheist: What do you mean, so? Those issues are important to me!

Christian: Are those issues so important to you that you're willing to give up truth itself in order to keep them?

Atheist: What are you talking about?

Christian: The issue is truth, not what you find politically or personally attractive. Do you think you ought to believe what's true?

Atheist: Of course. Every reasonable person would say yes to that!

Christian: So if Christianity is true, you ought to believe it regardless of the impact you think it might have on politics, moral issues, or any other facet of your life.

Atheist: That's hard to do.

Christian: Maybe. But it's a lot harder in the long run to believe error. Christ said, "If anyone would come after me, he must deny himself and take up his cross and follow me. For whoever wants to save his life will lose it, but whoever loses his life for me will find it. What good will it be for a man if he gains the whole world, yet forfeits his soul? Or what can a man give in exchange for his soul?" Do you really want to exchange your eternal soul for temporal political positions or personal preferences?

Atheist: If Christianity is true, that's the choice I have to make.

Christian: Yes. And God wants you to choose him. But he loves you so much that he'll respect either choice you make. Just remember that either choice you make will have consequences here and in eternity. And that's not just my interpretation.

Appendix 3:

Why the Jesus Seminar Doesn't Speak for Jesus

MANY CHRISTIANS HAVE been troubled recently by a group known as the "Jesus Seminar" that has made outlandish claims regarding the New Testament, casting doubt on 82 percent of what the Gospels ascribe to Jesus. One member, John Dominic Crossan, even went so far in his denial of the Resurrection as to claim that Jesus was buried in a shallow grave, dug up by dogs, and eaten! But the so-called Jesus Seminar does not speak for the real Jesus. There are at least seven reasons for this conclusion.

The Wrong Group—The Jesus Seminar, established in 1985, is comprised of seventy-plus "scholars" who are largely on the radical fringe. Some are atheists, and some are not even scholars (one is a filmmaker). Atheist founder Robert Funk acknowledged the radical nature of their work when he stated, "We are probing what is most sacred to millions, and hence we will constantly border on blasphemy." This is an honest and accurate disclosure.

The Wrong Motive—By their own admission their goal is to create a new "fictive" Jesus,[1] which involves deconstructing the old picture of Jesus in the Gospels and reconstructing one that fits modern man. In view of this, no one should look to their work for the real Jesus. They are making Jesus in their own image.

Moreover, their work is tainted by their confessed publicity seeking. They admitted, "We are going to try to carry out our work in full public view. We will not only honor the freedom of information, we will insist on the public disclosure of our work."[2] More bluntly, the Jesus Seminar sought publicity from the very beginning. A TV summit, numerous articles, interviews with the press, tapes, and even a possible movie are further indications of their aim to advertise.

The Wrong Procedure—Their procedure is prejudiced, attempting to determine truth by majority vote. This method is no better today than when most people believed the world was square. Having 70 largely radical "scholars" vote on what Jesus said is akin to giving 100 largely liberal members of Congress the chance to vote on higher taxes!

The Wrong Books—The Jesus Seminar vote is based in part on a hypothetical "Gospel of Q" (from German *Quelle,* meaning source) and a second-century *Gospel of Thomas,* which comes from Gnostic heretics. In addition to these, the Seminar appeals to a nonexistent *Secret Mark.* The result is that the apocryphal second-century *Gospel of Thomas* is considered more authentic than the earlier Mark or John.

The Wrong Assumptions—Their conclusions are based on radical presuppositions, one of which is their unjustified rejection of miracles. If God exists, then miracles are possible. Hence, any *a priori* rejection of miracles is a rejection of the existence of God. In light of their implicit atheism, there should be no surprise that they reject the Jesus of the Gospels.

Further, their conclusions are based on the unfounded assumption that Christianity was influenced by mystery religions. As we saw in chapter 12, this could not be the case. The monotheistic Jewish writers of Scripture would not be using polytheistic pagan sources and could not be dependent on sources that were later than their time.

The Wrong Dates—They posit unjustified late dates for the four Gospels (probably A.D. 70 to 100). By doing this they believe they are able to create enough time to conclude that the New Testament is comprised of myths about Jesus. But this is contrary to the facts, as we saw in chapters 9 and 10. The New Testament is early and contains even earlier source material.

The Wrong Conclusions—In the wake of destroying the basis for the real Jesus of the Gospels, the Jesus Seminar has no real agreement on who Jesus actually was: a cynic, a sage, a Jewish reformer, a feminist, a prophet-teacher, a radical social prophet, or an eschatological prophet. It's little wonder that something done by the wrong group, using the wrong procedure, based on the wrong books, grounded in the wrong presuppositions, and employing the wrong dates would come to the wrong conclusion!

Notes

INTRODUCTION
FINDING THE BOX TOP TO THE PUZZLE OF LIFE

1. Carl Sagan, *Cosmos* (New York: Random House, 1980), 4.
2. From the audiotape "Exposing Naturalistic Presuppositions of Evolution," at Southern Evangelical Seminary's 1998 Apologetics Conference. Tape AC9814. Posted online at www.impactapologetics.com.
3. Quoted in Plato, *Apology*, section 38.
4. All emphases in Scripture quotations have been added by the authors.
5. From Friedrich Nietzsche, *The AntiChrist*, section 47, quoted in Walter Kaufmann, *The Portable Nietzsche* (New York: Viking, 1968), 627.
6. Quoted in Os Guinness, *Time for Truth* (Grand Rapids, Mich.: Baker, 2000), 114.
7. C. S. Lewis, *The Screwtape Letters* (Westwood, N.J.: Barbour, 1961), 46.

CHAPTER 1
CAN WE HANDLE THE TRUTH?

1. C. S. Lewis, *The Abolition of Man* (New York: Macmillan, 1947), 35.
2. Frank Morison, *Who Moved the Stone?* (Grand Rapids, Mich.: Zondervan, 1977).
3. Frank Turek and Norman Geisler, *Legislating Morality* (Eugene, Ore.: Wipf & Stock, 2003). Previously published by Bethany, 1998.

CHAPTER 2
WHY SHOULD ANYONE BELIEVE ANYTHING AT ALL?

1. See James Sire, "Why Should Anyone Believe Anything At All?" in D. A. Carson, ed., *Telling the Truth* (Grand Rapids, Mich.: Zondervan, 2000), 93-101. See also James Sire, *Why Should Anyone Believe Anything At All* (Downers Grove, Ill.: InterVarsity Press, 1994).
2. There is, of course, inductive logic, deductive logic, and symbolic logic, but all of these are based in the same fundamental laws of thought.
3. David Hume, *An Inquiry Concerning Human Understanding*, xii, 3.
4. C. S. Lewis, "Learning in War-Time," in C. S. Lewis, *The Weight of Glory and Other Addresses* (Grand Rapids, Mich.: Eerdmans, 1965), 50.

5. Of course, according to Kant, we can know things about this phenomenal world of our senses such as scientific propositions. Also, Kant held that, while we cannot *know* anything about the real world (e.g., God), nevertheless, we can *posit* that there is a God and live *as if* he exists, even though we can't know anything about the way he really is. This Kant called "practical" reason.

6. In fact, we arrive at most decisions in life—from what we eat to whom we choose for friends—through observation and induction. For example, we don't have perfect information about the liquid in a Campbell's Soup can— we think it's edible and won't poison us—but we're not 100 percent certain. We are relying on our prior experience that Campbell's Soup is trustworthy, and we are concluding that there's actually Campbell's Soup and not poison in the can. Likewise, we don't have perfect information about the character of people we may meet. But after spending some time with them, we may conclude that they are trustworthy people. Are we 100 percent certain? No, because we are generalizing from our limited number of experiences. Our conclusion may be highly probable, but it is not certain. This is the case with many decisions we make in life.

7. Frank Turek and Norman Geisler, *Legislating Morality* (Eugene, Ore.: Wipf & Stock, 2003). Previously published by Bethany, 1998.

8. In addition to the Qur'an (read Suras 8 and 9 for yourself), see Norman Geisler and Abdul Saleeb, *Answering Islam,* 2nd ed. (Grand Rapids, Mich.: Baker, 2002). Appendix 5 lists twenty citations from the Qur'an that either command or condone violence against "infidels."

9. Those who disagree with the necessity of logic in finding truth are defeating themselves and proving our point. Why? Because they attempt to use logic to deny logic. This is like trying to use language to communicate that language cannot be used to communicate!

CHAPTER 3
IN THE BEGINNING THERE WAS A GREAT SURGE

1. Quoted in Hugh Ross, *The Creator and the Cosmos* (Colorado Springs: NavPress, 1995), 57.

2. All the galaxies are moving away from us, but that does not mean that we are at the center of the universe. To visualize how this can be, picture a balloon with black dots on it. When you blow up the balloon, all of the dots separate from one another whether they are near the center or not. The dots on opposite sides of the balloon (those farthest away from one another) separate more quickly than those next to one another. In fact, Hubble discovered a linear relationship between distance and speed, which showed that a galaxy twice as far from us moves away at twice the speed. This became known as Hubble's Law.

3. Quoted in Fred Heeren, *Show Me God* (Wheeling, Ill.: Daystar, 2000), 135.

4. Francis Bacon, *The New Organon* (1620; reprint, Indianapolis: Bobbs Merrill, 1960), 121.

5. David Hume, in J. Y. T. Greig, ed., *The Letters of David Hume*, 2 vols. (New York: Garland, 1983), 1:187.

6. You may have heard the First Law of Thermodynamics stated like this: "Energy can neither be created nor destroyed." That is a philosophical assertion, not an empirical observation. How could we know that energy was not created? There were no observers to verify it. A more accurate definition of the First Law, as far as observations go, is that "the total amount of energy in the universe (i.e., usable and unusable energy) remains constant." So as usable energy is consumed, it is converted into *un*usable energy, but the sum of the two remains the same. Only the proportion of usable to unusable changes.

7. Robert Jastrow, *God and the Astronomers* (New York: Norton, 1978), 48.

8. Quoted in Paul Davies, *The Cosmic Blueprint* (New York: Simon & Shuster, 1988), 20, emphasis added.

9. Words like "precede" and "before" usually imply time. We don't mean it that way, because there was no time "before" the Big Bang. For there can be no time before time began. What then could exist before time? The answer is, very simply, the Eternal! That is, the Eternal Cause that brought time, space, and matter into existence.

10. The entire debate is available on video at www.rzim.com.

11. Isaac Asimov, *Beginning and End* (New York: Doubleday, 1977), 148.

12. Anthony Kenny, *The Five Ways: St. Thomas Aquinas' Proofs of God's Existence* (New York: Schocken, 1969), 66.

13. Jastrow, *God and the Astronomers*, 15-16.

14. See Fred Heeren, *Show Me God*, 163-168; and Ross, *Creator and the Cosmos*, 19.

15. Heeren, *Show Me God*, 168.

16. See Michael D. Lemonick, "Echoes of the Big Bang," *Time*, May 4, 1992, 62.

17. Jastrow, *God and the Astronomers*, 11.

18. Ibid., 14.

19. "A Scientist Caught Between Two Faiths: Interview with Robert Jastrow," *Christianity Today*, August 6, 1982, emphasis added.

20. Arthur Eddington, *The Expanding Universe* (New York: Macmillan, 1933), 178.

21. Quoted in Heeren, *Show Me God*, 156.

22. Quoted in ibid., 157.

23. Quoted in ibid.

24. Quoted in ibid., 139.

25. For a detailed explanation and refutation of atheistic explanations for the

beginning of the universe, see William Lane Craig's article, "The Ultimate Question of Origins: God and the Beginning of the Universe," posted online at http://www.leaderu.com/offices/billcraig/docs/ultimatequestion.html; see also Norman Geisler, *Baker Encyclopedia of Christian Apologetics* (Grand Rapids, Mich.: Baker, 1999), 102-106.

26. See Jastrow, *God and the Astronomers*, 125.

27. See "'Baby Pic' Shows Cosmos 13 Billion Years Ago," CNN.com, February 11, 2003, at http://www.cnn.com/2003/TECH/space/02/11/cosmic.portrait/.

28. See Kathy Sawyer, "Cosmic Driving Force? Scientists' Work on 'Dark Energy' Mystery Could Yield a New View of the Universe," *Washington Post*, February 19, 2000, A1.

29. Stephen W. Hawking, *A Brief History of Time* (New York: Bantam, 1988), 136-139; see also Norman Geisler and Peter Bocchino, *Unshakable Foundations* (Minneapolis: Bethany, 2001), 107-110.

30. Quoted in Norman Geisler and Paul Hoffman, eds., *Why I Am a Christian: Leading Thinkers Explain Why They Believe* (Grand Rapids, Mich.: Baker, 2001), 66.

31. Jastrow, *God and the Astronomers*, 16 (emphasis ours).

32. Ibid., 28.

33. Ibid., 113-114.

34. V. J. Stenger, "The Face of Chaos," *Free Inquiry* 13 (Winter 1992–1993): 13.

35. See Cliff Walker, "An Interview with Particle Physicist Victor J. Stenger," at http://www.positiveatheism.com/crt/stenger1.htm. Interview date, November 6, 1999.

36. See "'Baby Pic' Shows Cosmos 13 Billion Years Ago."

37. George Will, "The Gospel from Science," *Newsweek*, November 8, 1998.

38. Albert Einstein, in *Science, Philosophy, and Religion: A Symposium* (New York: The Conference on Science, Philosophy and Religion in Their Relation to the Democratic Way of Life, 1941). Posted online at http://www.sacred-texts.com/aor/einstein/einsci.htm. Accessed October 15, 2003.

39. Jastrow, *God and the Astronomers*, 116.

CHAPTER 4
DIVINE DESIGN

1. Isaac Newton, "General Scholium," in *Mathematical Principles of Natural Philosophy* (1687) in *Great Books of the Western World*, Robert M. Hutchins, ed. (Chicago: Encyclopedia Britannica, n.d.), 369.

2. As is the case with most constants, this constant is dependent on others. For example, the gravitational interaction is also a function of the size of the moon, which is larger relative to its planet than most other moons.

3. Personal correspondence with Jeffrey A. Zweerink, research physicist, UCLA, October 23, 2003.

4. For the full text, and for more information on the accident, see the report of the Apollo 13 Review Board, posted on NASA's website. http://spacelink. msfc.nasa.gov/NASA.Projects/Human.Exploration.and.Development. of.Space/Human.Space.Flight/Apollo.Missions/Apollo.Lunar/Apollo. 13.Review.Board.Report/Apollo.13.Review.Board.Report.txt; see also http://solarviews.com/eng/apo13.htm#bang. For a transcript of the mission with explanatory commentary see: http://209.145.176.7/~090/awh/ as13.html.

5. For additional constants, see Hugh Ross, "Why I Believe in Divine Creation," in Norman Geisler and Paul Hoffman, eds., *Why I Am a Christian: Leading Thinkers Explain Why They Believe* (Grand Rapids, Mich.: Baker, 2001), chapter 8. More of these constants are being discovered all the time, so much so that Ross intends to update the list quarterly. Check his website at www.reasons.org. For more on why animal life is rare in the universe, see Peter Ward and Donald Brownlee, *Rare Earth: Why Complex Life Is Uncommon in the Universe* (New York: Copernicus, 2000).

6. Hugh Ross, "Why I Believe in Divine Creation," 138-141.

7. Quoted in Walter Bradley, "The 'Just-so' Universe: The Fine-Tuning of Constants and Conditions in the Cosmos," in William Dembski and James Kushiner, eds., *Signs of Intelligence* (Grand Rapids, Mich.: Baker, 2001), 168.

8. Quoted in Geisler and Hoffman, eds., *Why I Am a Christian,* 142.

9. Fred Hoyle, "The Universe: Past and Present Reflections," *Engineering and Science* (November 1981): 12.

10. For the president's complete remarks, see http://www.whitehouse.gov/news/ releases/2003/02/20030201-2.html.

11. The Second Commandment prohibits "graven images" for perhaps this very reason. Images limit the majesty of God. Idols are idols whether they are metal and mental.

12. See http://www.whitehouse.gov/news/releases/2003/02/20030201-2.html.

13. C. S. Lewis, *The Screwtape Letters* (Westwood, N.J.: Barbour, 1961), 14.

14. Quoted in Fred Heeren, *Show Me God,* vol. 1 (Wheeling, Ill.: Daystar, 2000), 239.

15. Dennis Overbye, "Zillions of Universes? Or Did Ours Get Lucky?" *The New York Times,* October 28, 2003, F1.

Chapter 5
The First Life: Natural Law or Divine Awe?

1. Information scientist Hubert Yockey, from the University of California at Berkeley, makes it clear that this comparison between the English alphabet

and the genetic alphabet is no analogy but one of mathematical identity. He writes, "It is important to understand that we are not reasoning by analogy. The sequence hypothesis applies directly to the protein and the genetic text as well as to written language and therefore the treatment is mathematically identical." See Hubert P. Yockey, "Self Organization, Origin-of-life Scenarios and Information Theory," *Journal of Theoretical Biology* 91 (1981): 16.

2. Richard Dawkins, *The Blind Watchmaker* (New York: Norton, 1987), 17-18, 116.

3. For a discussion from evolutionists of the numerous difficulties in suggesting that life is a product of natural law, see Peter Ward and Donald Brownlee, *Rare Earth* (New York: Copernicus, 2000), chapter 4.

4. For more on the problems with the Urey-Miller experiment and nine other discredited "evidences" for evolution, see Jonathan Wells, *Icons of Evolution: Science or Myth? Why Much of What We Teach About Evolution Is Wrong* (Washington, D.C.: Regnery, 2000).

5. Dawkins, *Blind Watchmaker*, 1.

6. Quoted in Phillip E. Johnson, *The Wedge of Truth* (Downers Grove, Ill.: InterVarsity Press, 2000), 153.

7. Ibid.

8. Klaus Dose, "The Origin of Life: More Questions than Answers," *Interdisciplinary Science Review* 13 (1998): 348; quoted in Lee Strobel, *The Case for Faith* (Grand Rapids, Mich.: Zondervan, 2000), 107.

9. Quoted in Strobel, *Case for Faith*, 107.

10. Chandra Wickramasinghe, interview by Robert Roy Britt, October 27, 2000. Posted online at http://www.space.com/searchforlife/chandra_sidebar_001027.html (emphasis added).

11. Michael Denton, *Evolution: A Theory in Crisis* (Bethesda, Md.: Adler & Adler, 1985), 264.

12. Hubert Yockey, *Information Theory and Molecular Biology* (Cambridge, New York: Cambridge University Press, 1992), 284, emphasis added.

13. Phillip E. Johnson, "The Unraveling of Scientific Materialism," *First Things* (November 1997): 22-25.

14. E-mail sent on July 10, 2001. The entire exchange that week can be read at http://www.arn.org/docs/pjweekly/pj_weekly_010813.htm.

15. Richard Lewontin, "Billions and Billions of Demons," *The New York Review of Books,* January 9, 1997, 31.

16. See Strobel, *Case for Faith*, 99-101.

17. The entire debate is on videotape, and can be viewed online at http://www.leaderu.com/offices/billcraig/docs/craig-atkins.html.

18. J. Budziszewski, *Written on the Heart: The Case for Natural Law* (Downers Grove, Ill.: InterVarsity Press, 1997), 54.

19. See Norman L. Geisler and Peter Bocchino, *Unshakable Foundations* (Minneapolis: Bethany, 2001). Anecdote from a personal conversation with Peter Bocchino, April 3, 2003.

20. Mortimer Adler, *Haves Without Have-Nots* (New York: Macmillan, 1991).

21. William Dembski, *The Design Revolution: Answering the Toughest Questions About Intelligent Design* (Downers Grove, Ill.: InterVarsity Press, forthcoming).

22. Albert Einstein, in a letter to Max Born, December 4, 1926, quoted in Elizabeth Knowles, ed., *The Oxford Dictionary of Quotations* (Oxford: Oxford University Press, 1999), 290.

23. Quoted in William Dembski and James Kushiner, eds., *Signs of Intelligence* (Grand Rapids, Mich.: Baker, 2001), 102.

CHAPTER 6
New Life Forms: From the Goo to You via the Zoo?

1. Carl Sagan, *Cosmos* (New York, Random House, 1980), 278.

2. Phillip E. Johnson, *Darwin on Trial* (Downers Grove, Ill.: InterVarsity Press, 1993), 27.

3. Jonathan Wells, *Icons of Evolution: Science or Myth? Why Much of What We Teach About Evolution Is Wrong* (Washington, D.C.: Regnery, 2000), 178.

4. See Norman L. Geisler and Peter Bocchino, *Unshakable Foundations* (Minneapolis: Bethany, 2001), 149-150; see also Jonathan Wells, *Icons of Evolution,* chapter 9, 211; and Lane P. Lester and Raymond G. Bohlin, *The Natural Limits of Biological Change* (Grand Rapids, Mich.: Zondervan, 1984), 88-89.

5. For more on Darwin's finches, see Wells, *Icons of Evolution,* 159-175.

6. Charles Darwin, *On the Origin of Species* (New York: Penguin, 1958), 171.

7. Michael Behe, *Darwin's Black Box: The Biochemical Challenge to Evolution* (New York: Touchstone, 1996), 39.

8. Ariel Roth, *Origins* (Hagerstown, Md.: Herald, 1998), 66.

9. Michael Behe, "Intelligent Design Theory as a Tool for Analyzing Biochemical Systems," in William Dembski, ed., *Mere Creation: Science, Faith, and Intelligent Design* (Downers Grove, Ill.: InterVarsity Press, 1998), 183, emphasis added.

10. Miller agrees with Behe that natural selection cannot favor the evolution of a nonfunctional system. But he deflects the argument by suggesting that a mousetrap in transition—while unable to catch mice—may function as a tie clip or keychain (see http://www.millerandlevine.com/km/evol/DI/ Mousetrap.html). This, of course, misses the point. Complex living things

can't randomly substitute one function for another and still survive. A living thing would die if one of its vital systems failed to perform its primary function, even if it was performing some other function during its Darwinian transition. In other words, it's the loss of the vital function that's important, not the fact that the intermediate system might be able to do something else in the meantime!

11. See several of Behe's responses to his critics at http://www.trueorigin.org/behe08.asp.

12. Michael Behe, "A Mousetrap Defended," 2000, http://www.trueorigin.org/behe05.asp.

13. Behe, *Darwin's Black Box*, 232-233.

14. E-mail sent to Phillip Johnson on July 10, 2001. The entire exchange that week can be read at http://www.arn.org/docs/pjweekly/pj_weekly_010813.htm.

15. See "Riken Finds Bigger Gap in Chimp, Human Genes," *Japan Times*, July 12, 2003. Posted online at http://www.japantimes.co.jp/cgi-bin/getarticle.pl5?nn20030712b6.htm. Accessed October 17, 2003.

16. Mouse Genome Sequencing Consortium, "Initial Sequencing and Comparative Analysis of the Mouse Genome," *Nature* 420 (December 5, 2002): 520-562.

17. Michael Denton, *Evolution: A Theory in Crisis* (Bethesda, Md.: Adler & Adler, 1985), 285.

18. Darwin, *On the Origin of Species*, 280.

19. Stephen J. Gould, "Evolution's Erratic Pace," *Natural History* 86 (1977): 13-14. More recently Robert B. Carroll, curator of vertebrate paleontology at the Redpath Museum at McGill University, affirmed Gould's assessment when he wrote, "What is missing are the many intermediate forms hypothesized by Darwin" ("Towards a New Evolutionary Synthesis," *Trends in Ecology and Evolution* 15 [2000]: 27-32).

20. Wells, *Icons of Evolution*, 37.

21. Ibid., 42.

22. Denton, *Evolution: A Theory in Crisis*, 286.

23. Wells, *Icons of Evolution*, 219.

24. See Norman Geisler, *Baker Encyclopedia of Christian Apologetics* (Grand Rapids, Mich.: Baker, 1999), 489; see also Wells, *Icons of Evolution*, 209-228.

25. Quoted in Wells, *Icons of Evolution*, 221.

26. Michael Behe, *Darwin's Black Box*, 22.

27. As we have seen, the same can be said for DNA similarity—it could just as well be the result of a common designer as of a common ancestor.

28. For a thorough defense of Intelligent Design, see William Dembski, *The Design Revolution: Answering the Toughest Questions About Intelligent Design* (Downers Grove, Ill.: InterVarsity Press, 2004).

29. William Dembski, *Intelligent Design: The Bridge Between Science and Theology* (Downers Grove, Ill.: InterVarsity Press, 1999), 244

30. Walter Bradley, interview by Lee Strobel, *The Case for Faith* (Grand Rapids, Mich.: Zondervan, 2000), 108.

31. Behe, *Darwin's Black Box,* 193.

32. Originally from a 1989 *New York Times* book review. Posted online at http://members.tripod.com/doggo/doggdawkins.html. Accessed May 15, 2003.

33. Richard Lewontin, "Billions and Billions of Demons," *The New York Review of Books,* January 9, 1997, 150.

34. Robert Jastrow, *God and the Astronomers* (New York: Norton, 1978), 114.

35. Fyodor Dostoevsky, *The Brothers Karamazov* (New York: Norton, 1976), 72.

36. Quoted in D. James Kennedy, *Skeptics Answered* (Sisters, Ore.: Multnomah, 1997), 154.

37. Strobel, *Case for Faith,* 91.

38. From the audiotape "Reaching Evolutionists," at Southern Evangelical Seminary's 2001 Apologetics Conference. Tape AC0108. Posted online at www.impactapologetics.com.

39. Wells, *Icons of Evolution,* 230.

40. Norman Geisler, *Baker Encyclopedia of Christian Apologetics* (Grand Rapids, Mich.: Baker, 1999); Norman Geisler, *Systematic Theology,* vol. 2 (Minneapolis: Bethany, 2003).

41. Some Christians fear that granting long time periods improves the plausibility of macroevolution. But as we saw in chapter 5, this is not so.

Chapter 7
Mother Teresa vs. Hitler

1. J. Budziszewski, *Written on the Heart: The Case for Natural Law* (Downers Grove, Ill.: InterVarsity Press, 1997), 208-209.

2. C. S. Lewis, *Mere Christianity* (New York: Macmillan, 1952), 19.

3. See J. Budziszewski, *What We Can't Not Know* (Dallas: Spence, 2003), 39.

4. See ibid.

5. Joseph Fletcher, *Situation Ethics: The New Morality* (Philadelphia: Westminster, 1966), 43-44.

6. Lewis, *Mere Christianity,* 45.

7. Ibid., 25.

8. For a transcript of the debate see http://www.renewamerica.us/archives/speeches/00_09_27debate.htm. Accessed May 20, 2003.

9. Contrary to popular opinion, atheists, like everyone else in politics, are trying to legislate morality. Our book *Legislating Morality* goes into detail on

this topic (Frank Turek and Norman Geisler, *Legislating Morality* [Eugene, Ore.: Wipf & Stock, 2003]). Previously published by Bethany, 1998.

10. See Lewis, *Mere Christianity,* 26.

11. Thanks to our friend Francis Beckwith for this example. See his book *Relativism: Feet Firmly Planted in Mid-Air,* coauthored with Greg Koukl (Grand Rapids, Mich.: Baker, 1998), for an outstanding critique of relativism.

12. Budziszewski, *What We Can't Not Know,* 114

13. For a complete discussion of how to resolve conflicting moral absolutes see Norman Geisler's, *Christian Ethics: Options and Issues* (Grand Rapids, Mich.: Baker, 1989), particularly chapter 7.

14. Feminist Naomi Wolf is a notable example. She admits that everyone knows an unborn child is a human being, and that abortion is a real sin that requires atonement. But instead of ending abortion, Wolf suggests that women who get abortions hold candlelight vigils at abortion facilities to show their sorrow! This sounds like an expiatory ritual similar to—forgive the comparison—that of the cannibals.

15. Frank Turek and Norman Geisler, *Legislating Morality* (Eugene, Ore.: Wipf & Stock, 2003). Previously published by Bethany, 1998.

16. Edward O. Wilson, "The Biological Basis of Morality," *The Atlantic Monthly,* April 1998. Posted online at http://www.theatlantic.com/issues/ 98apr/biomoral.htm. Accessed May 13, 2003.

17. Lewis, *Mere Christianity,* 22.

18. Jeffrey Schloss, Ph.D. (ecology and evolutionary biology), argues that even though certain altruistic and self-sacrificial behaviors can perhaps be explained in Darwinian terms, there are others that cannot be so explained; Schloss focuses especially on those who aided and hid potential Holocaust victims. See Jeffrey Schloss, "Evolutionary Account of Altruism and the Problem of Goodness by Design," in William Dembski, ed., *Mere Creation* (Downers Grove, Ill.: InterVarsity Press, 1998), 236-261.

19. Adolf Hitler, *Mein Kampf,* 4th printing (London: Hurst & Blackett, 1939), 239-240, 242.

20. Here is the entire quote: "The Races of Man.—At the present time there exist upon the earth five races or varieties of man, each very different from the other in instincts, social customs, and, to an extent, in structure. There are the Ethiopian or negro type, originating in Africa; the Malay or brown race, from the islands of the Pacific; the American Indian; the Mongolian or yellow race, including the natives of China, Japan, and the Eskimos; and, finally, *the highest type of all, the Caucasians,* represented by the civilized white inhabitants of Europe and America" (George William Hunter, *Essentials of Biology: Presented in Problems* [New York, Cincinnati, Chicago: American Book, 1911], 320, emphasis added).

21. Peter Singer, *Practical Ethics,* 1st ed. (Cambridge: Cambridge University

Press, 1979), 122-123; quoted in Scott Klusendorf, "Death with a Happy Face: Peter Singer's Bold Defense of Infanticide," *Christian Research Journal* 23, no. 1 (2001): 25. See also Helga Kuhse and Peter Singer, *Should the Baby Live?* (Brookfield, Vt.: Ashgate, 1994), 194-197.

22. James Rachels, *Created from Animals: The Moral Implications of Darwinism* (New York: Oxford University Press, 1990), 186.

23. Randy Thornhill and Craig Palmer, *A Natural History of Rape: Biological Bases of Sexual Coercion* (Cambridge, Mass.: MIT Press, 2001).

24. Quoted in Nancy Pearcey, "Darwin's Dirty Secret," *World* magazine, March 25, 2000.

25. Lewis, *Mere Christianity*, 21.

Chapter 8
Miracles: Signs of God or Gullibility?

1. This Being is a he, not an it; a person, not a thing. We know this Being has personality because he has done something only persons can do—he has made a choice, namely, the choice to create.

2. See Francis Beckwith, Norman Geisler, Ron Rhodes, Phil Roberts, Jerald Tanner, and Sandra Tanner, *The Counterfeit Gospel of Mormonism* (Eugene, Ore.: Harvest, 1998), chapter 2.

3. C. S. Lewis, *The Screwtape Letters* (Westwood, N.J.: Barbour, 1961), 46.

4. Antony Flew, "Miracles," in *The Encyclopedia of Philosophy,* Paul Edwards, ed., vol. 5 (New York: Macmillan and the Free Press, 1967), 346.

5. From the audiotape "Worldviews In Conflict," at Southern Evangelical Seminary's 2002 Apologetics Conference. Tape AC0213. Posted online at at www.impactapologetics.com.

6. We often hear Christians trying to explain the miraculous story of Jonah by appealing to supposed true accounts of fishermen surviving inside whales for some time. Even if those events are true, they are completely irrelevant. The story of Jonah is meant to be miraculous—namely, something only God could do. Certainly, a man would not survive in a great fish for three days and be vomited up on a particular land mass unless it was an act of God. If that appears unbelievable because the world doesn't regularly work that way, it's *meant* to appear that way! A miracle may not be a miracle if it can be explained by natural means. The bottom line is that the God who conducted the greatest miracle of all—the creation of the universe, including great fish and human beings—would have had no trouble orchestrating the Jonah miracle.

7. C. S. Lewis, *Miracles* (New York: Macmillan, 1947), 106.

8. Unlike moral laws, natural laws are not based on God's nature and thus are changeable. While God cannot violate moral laws—because he is the unchanging standard of morality—he can change or interrupt natural laws

at will. In fact, God could have created physical reality—including natural laws, the natural environment, and living things—with completely different characteristics than what we have now.

9. Posted online at http://hcs.harvard.edu/~gsascf/shield.html. Accessed June 1, 2003.

10. Most people falsely believe that the more they've played the lottery in the past, the greater chance they have to win this time. It doesn't matter how many times a person has played the lottery in the past; each lottery is a unique event unaffected by previous plays. It's 76 million to one (or whatever the improbable odds are) every time. Hume would suggest that the repeated past experience of losing should cause you to disbelieve it if you actually did win. But if one day you win, then you've really won, despite the fact that you may have lost it thousands of times before. Likewise, a miracle can occur regardless of how many times it hasn't occurred in the past.

11. Lewis, *Miracles*, 105.

12. Revised under the new title *Miracles and the Modern Mind* (Grand Rapids, Mich.: Baker, 1992).

13. For a detailed discussion, see Norman Geisler, *Signs and Wonders* (Wheaton, Ill.: Tyndale, 1988), chapter 8. See also Norman Geisler, *Baker Encyclopedia of Christian Apologetics* (Grand Rapids, Mich.: Baker, 1999).

14. The Bible: Ex. 4:1-5; Num. 16:5ff; 1 Kings 18:21-22; Matt. 12:38-39; Luke 7:20-22; John 3:1-2; Acts 2:22; Heb. 2:3-4; 2 Cor. 12:12. The Qur'an: Sura 3:184, 17:102; cf. Sura 23:45.

15. For a detailed discussion, see Geisler, *Signs and Wonders*, chapters 7 and 8. See the list on pages 107-108 (out of print).

16. For much more on this topic, see the article from which this chart is taken: "Miracles, False," in Geisler, *Baker Encyclopedia of Christian Apologetics*, 471-475.

17. On some of these occasions multiple miracles were performed. For example, Jesus is said to have healed "many" several times, usually as people from town gathered around (e.g., Mark 1:34; 3:10; 6:56; Luke 5:15; 6:18; 9:11). The apostles performed several miracles on single occasions as well (Acts 5:16; 8:7; 19:11-12).

18. Theologically, the three great periods of miracles have certain things in common: Moses needed miracles to deliver Israel and sustain the great number of people in the wilderness (Ex. 4:8). Elijah and Elisha performed miracles to deliver Israel from idolatry (see 1 Kings 18). Jesus and the apostles showed miracles to confirm establishment of the new covenant and its offer of deliverance from sin (Heb. 2:3-4).

CHAPTER 9
DO WE HAVE EARLY TESTIMONY ABOUT JESUS?

1. There is a version of this quotation where Josephus affirms that Jesus was the Messiah, but most scholars believe that Christians changed the quotation to read that way. According to Origen, a church father who was born in the late second century, Josephus was not a Christian. So it is unlikely he would claim that Jesus was the Messiah. The version we have quoted here is from an Arabic text that is believed to be uncorrupted.

2. Why didn't Josephus refer to Jesus more? We can surmise that as a historian for the emperor, Josephus had to choose his topics and words carefully. Domitian was particularly suspicious of anything that might be associated with sedition. This new sect called Christianity could have been considered seditious, because Christians had this strange new belief system and refused to worship Caesar and the Roman gods. As a result, Josephus certainly didn't want to alarm or upset his boss by writing too many favorable comments about Christianity. Nevertheless, these two references affirm the existence of Jesus and James and corroborate the New Testament accounts.

3. Josephus, *Antiquities*, 20:9.1.

4. See Acts 21:17-18; cf. 15:13.

5. The ten non-Christian sources are: Josephus; Tacitus, the Roman historian; Pliny the Younger, a Roman politician; Phlegon, a freed slave who wrote histories; Thallus, a first-century historian; Seutonius, a Roman historian; Lucian, a Greek satirist; Celsus, a Roman philosopher; Mara Bar-Serapion, a private citizen who wrote to his son; and the Jewish Talmud. For a complete listing of mentions of Christ from these sources, see Norman L. Geisler, *Baker Encyclopedia of Christian Apologetics* (Grand Rapids, Mich.: Baker, 1999), 381-385; see also Gary Habermas, *The Historical Jesus* (Joplin, Mo.: College Press, 1996), chapter 9.

6. Gary Habermas and Michael Licona, *The Case for the Resurrection of Jesus* (Grand Rapids, Mich.: Kregel, forthcoming).

7. Since Luke mentions Tiberius, the total number of authors for Tiberius is ten. See Habermas and Licona, *Case for the Resurrection of Jesus*. We've added the Jewish Talmud to the list assembled by Habermas and Licona because it was likely composed in the early second century, well within 150 years of Jesus' death. Hence, our count is 43 and 10 instead of the 42 and 9 suggested by Habermas and Licona.

8. Geisler, *Baker Encyclopedia of Christian Apologetics*, 531-537.

9. Ibid., 531-537, 547.

10. A few critics have offered possible non–New Testament alternatives. In order to be successful, they have had to change the number of letters on a line of ancient text from the 20s to the 60s in some cases. This many letters to a line

would be highly unusual. See Geisler, *Baker Encyclopedia of Christian Apologetics,* 547.

11. Quoted in David Estrada and William White, Jr., *The First New Testament* (Nashville: Nelson, 1978), 137.

12. Keep in mind that this is *not* the gap between the events and the original writings. That gap is even shorter, as we'll see later in this chapter.

13. See Williston Walker, Richard Norris, David Lotz, and Robert Handy, *A History of the Christian Church,* 4th ed. (New York: Scribner, 1985), 123-124.

14. For a breakdown of these quotations, see Norman Geisler and William Nix, *General Introduction to the Bible* (Chicago: Moody, 1986), 431.

15. For more details and for sources, see Geisler, *Baker Encyclopedia of Christian Apologetics,* 532.

16. Philip Schaff, *A Companion to the Greek Testament and the English Version,* 3rd ed. (New York: Harper, 1883), 177.

17. For more details and for sources, see Geisler, *Baker Encyclopedia of Christian Apologetics,* 532.

18. Fredric Kenyon, *Our Bible and the Ancient Manuscripts,* 4th ed., rev. A. W. Adams (New York: Harper, 1958), 23.

19. Paul Barnett, *Is the New Testament Reliable?* (Downers Grove, Ill.: InterVarsity Press, 1986), 38-40.

20. See Heb. 5:1-3; 7:23, 27; 8:3-5; 9:25; 10:1, 3-4, 11; 13:10-11.

21. See Barnett, *Is the New Testament Reliable?* 65.

22. See Paul Barnett, *Jesus and the Rise of Early Christianity* (Downers Grove, Ill.: InterVarsity Press, 1999), 343.

23. Colin J. Hemer, *The Book of Acts in the Setting of Hellenistic History* (Winona Lake, Ind.: Eisenbrauns, 1990), 376-382. For a summary of Hemer's reasons, see Geisler, *Baker Encyclopedia of Christian Apologetics,* 528.

24. Most, if not all, scholars date the origin of this material prior to A.D. 40. See Gary Habermas, *The Historical Jesus* (Joplin, Mo.: College Press, 1996), 152-157; see also Habermas and Licona, *Case for the Resurrection of Jesus,* forthcoming), chapter 7.

25. In addition, by writing "I delivered to you," Paul was reminding them that he had already given them that testimony earlier. So while he wrote them in, say, 56, he must have verbalized it to them during an earlier visit to Corinth, probably in A.D. 51. This also means Paul must have received it prior to 51, which means this information was in existence prior to then.

26. William Lillie, "The Empty Tomb and the Resurrection," in D. E. Nineham, et al., *Historicity and Chronology in the New Testament* (London: SPCK, 1965), 125.

27. William F. Albright, *Recent Discoveries in Bible Lands* (New York: Funk & Wagnalls, 1956), 136.

28. William F. Albright, "William Albright: Toward a More Conservative View," *Christianity Today,* January 18, 1963, 3.

29. If Luke really did interview eyewitnesses as he claims, then his Gospel contains early eyewitness testimony that should be considered just as reliable as if Luke had seen it himself. Eyewitness testimony is primary source material even if it was recorded later by someone else.

30. A. N. Sherwin-White, *Roman Society and Roman Law in the New Testament* (Oxford: Clarendon, 1963), 189.

31. William Lane Craig, *The Son Rises* (Eugene, Ore.: Wipf & Stock, 2001), 101.

32. William Lane Craig, "The Evidence for Jesus." Posted online at http://www.leaderu.com/offices/billcraig/docs/rediscover2.html. Accessed August 10, 2003.

33. Gary Habermas, *The Historical Jesus* (Joplin, Mo.: College Press, 1996), chapter 7.

34. Some scholars think there's other circumstantial evidence that Mark was written in the 30s. Mark mentions the high priest five times but doesn't name him. The three other Gospels identify him as Caiaphas. Why doesn't Mark identify him? Perhaps because Caiaphas was still the high priest when Mark was writing, so there was no need to name him. If this is true, then Mark was written by A.D. 37 because that's when Caiaphas's high priesthood ended (Josephus, *Antiquities,* 18:4.3).

35. Some scholars believe New Testament writers used written records that predate the Gospels. Luke 1:1 seems to confirm this. However, many liberal scholars suggest that the Gospels are not eyewitness accounts but were derived from one yet undiscovered source known as "Q." In the next chapter, we'll show why the New Testament writers *were* eyewitnesses. For an outstanding critique of biblical criticism and the idea that there was a "Q" source from which the New Testament writers drew, see former "Q" proponent Eta Linnemann, *Biblical Criticism on Trial* (Grand Rapids, Mich.: Kregel, 2001); see also Geisler, *Baker Encyclopedia of Christian Apologetics,* 618-621.

36. Craig Blomberg, *The Historical Reliability of the Gospels* (Downers Grove, Ill.: InterVarsity Press, 1987), 197.

37. For the debate on audiotape, see www.impactapologetics.com.

38. Incidentally, while we may not have documents from the 500, their inclusion with fourteen eyewitnesses identified by name makes their seeing the risen Christ an unlikely invention of Paul. We'll discuss this further in chapter 10.

CHAPTER 10
DO WE HAVE EYEWITNESS TESTIMONY ABOUT JESUS?

1. See Colin J. Hemer, *The Book of Acts in the Setting of Hellenistic History* (Winona Lake, Ind.: Eisenbrauns, 1990).

2. The threat of death even extended to Romans. See Paul Maier, *In the Fullness of Time* (Grand Rapids, Mich.: Kregel, 1991), 305.

3. A. N. Sherwin-White, *Roman Society and Roman Law in the New Testament* (Oxford: Clarendon, 1963), 189.

4. William Ramsay, *St. Paul the Traveller and the Roman Citizen* (New York: Putnam, 1896), 8.

5. See a complete listing of the miracles in Norman L. Geisler, *Baker Encyclopedia of Christian Apologetics* (Grand Rapids, Mich.: Baker, 1999), 485.

6. One reason Luke wrote Acts may have been to show Paul's innocence to officials in the Roman Empire. He certainly provided enough historical references to show that he was telling the truth. Of course, it would not have been wise of Luke to lie to Roman officials.

7. Craig L. Blomberg, *The Historical Reliability of John's Gospel* (Downers Grove, Ill.: InterVarsity Press, 2001), 63.

8. F. F. Bruce, *The New Testament Documents: Are They Reliable?* (Downers Grove, Ill.: InterVarsity Press, 1981), 82.

9. Quoted in ibid., 90-91.

10. See Blomberg, *Historical Reliability of John's Gospel,* 69-281. For other good discussions of John's historicity see Paul Barnett, *Is the New Testament Reliable?* (Downers Grove, Ill.: InterVarsity Press, 1986), 56-80; and Geisler, *Baker Encyclopedia of Christian Apologetics,* 388-395.

11. Barnett, *Is the New Testament Reliable?* 62.

12. See William D. Edwards, Wesley J. Gabel, Floyd E. Hosmer, "On the Physical Death of Jesus Christ," *Journal of the American Medical Association* 255, no. 11 (March 21, 1986): 1455-1463.

13. Skeptics might say, "Well, maybe he saw some other crucified person whose heart was punctured with a spear." That might explain it if this were the only eyewitness detail John gives us. But as we have seen, he's given us several other details, which strongly suggests he really was an eyewitness to the crucifixion of Jesus.

14. There may actually be more than those we have identified because we did not conduct an exhaustive search on every name that appears in the New Testament.

15. Pilate appears often in the New Testament: Roman governor of Judea, Matt. 27:2; Luke 3:1; causes slaughter of certain Galileans, Luke 13:1; tries Jesus and orders his crucifixion, Matt. 27; Mark 15; Luke 23; John 18:28-40; 19;

I DON'T HAVE ENOUGH FAITH TO BE AN ATHEIST

Acts 3:13; 4:27; 13:28; 1 Tim. 6:13; allows Joseph of Arimathea to take Jesus' body, Matt. 27:57-58; Mark 15:43-45; Luke 23:52; John 19:38.

16. Mark refers to the high priest but does not name him (14:53). Again, this leads some scholars to believe that Mark's account was written before A.D. 37 because that's when Caiaphas's reign ended. The theory here is that Mark was writing to a contemporary audience who already knew who the high priest was.

17. Josephus, *Antiquities,* 18:2.2.

18. See Matt. 26:3, 57; Luke 3:2; John 11:49; 18:13-14, 24, 28; Acts 4:6.

19. See "The Short List: The New Testament Figures Known to History," *Biblical Archaeological Review* 26, no. 6 (November/December 2002): 34-37.

20. See "The Short List: The New Testament Figures Known to History," *Biblical Archaeological Review* 26, no. 6 (November/December 2002): 34-37.

CHAPTER 11
THE TOP TEN REASONS WE KNOW THE
NEW TESTAMENT WRITERS TOLD THE TRUTH

1. For an explanation of these and more than 800 other verses critics have questioned, see Norman Geisler and Thomas Howe, *When Critics Ask* (Grand Rapids, Mich.: Baker, 1992).

2. It's interesting to note that the creed recorded in 1 Corinthians 15 does not include the women as eyewitnesses. Perhaps that's because the apostles recognized that a mention of women would add no further credibility to the fourteen male eyewitnesses specifically named there.

3. See Gary Habermas, *The Historical Jesus* (Joplin, Mo.: College Press, 1996), 205.

4. See Geisler and Howe, *When Critics Ask,* 21.

5. Simon Greenleaf, *The Testimony of the Evangelists* (1874; reprint, Grand Rapids, Mich.: Baker, 1984), 9-10.

6. *The Gospel of Peter.* See Ron Cameron, *The Other Gospels* (Philadelphia: Westminster, 1982), 80-81.

7. Even if one argues that Matthew's angel is an embellishment, that wouldn't disprove the historicity of the Resurrection. In fact, even the embellished Gospel of Peter is built on the historical fact of the Resurrection.

8. N. T. Wright, *The Resurrection of the Son of God* (Minneapolis: Fortress, 2003), 603.

9. J. P. Moreland, interview by Lee Strobel, *The Case for Christ* (Grand Rapids, Mich.: Zondervan, 1998), 250.

10. Paul's first letter to the Corinthians, which was written in the mid-50s A.D., deals with the issue of Communion as if it has been in practice there for quite some time. Paul says he passed on to the Corinthians previously what the Lord had passed on to him (1 Cor. 11:23). Paul's first visit to Corinth was

about A.D. 51, which is probably when he passed the practice of Communion on to them. This, of course, would mean Paul had to have received it even earlier.

11. Charles Colson, "An Unholy Hoax?" *Breakpoint* commentary, March 29, 2002 (No. 020329). Posted online at http://www.epm.org/Unholy Hoax.htm.

12. From a speech delivered at the Mississippi College School of Law, reported at http://tmatt.gospelcom.net/column/1996/04/24/.

13. For a discussion of the few Qur'anic passages that some Muslims believe speak of miracles, see Norman Geisler and Abdul Saleeb, *Answering Islam,* 2nd ed. (Grand Rapids, Mich.: Baker, 2002), 163-168.

14. See ibid., 163-174.

CHAPTER 12
DID JESUS REALLY RISE FROM THE DEAD?

1. Gary R. Habermas, *The Risen Jesus and Future Hope* (Lanham, Md.: Rowman & Littlefield, 2003).

2. While scholars are not unanimous on the empty tomb, a *majority* of them (about 75 percent) believe the tomb was empty. The other eleven facts stated here enjoy nearly unanimous scholarly support.

3. Habermas, *Risen Jesus and Future Hope,* 9-10.

4. William Lane Craig, in Paul Copan and Ronald Tacelli, eds., *Jesus' Resurrection: Fact or Figment? A Debate Between William Lane Craig and Gerd Lüdemann* (Downers Grove, Ill.: InterVarsity Press, 2000), 56.

5. In 1968, an ancient burial site was uncovered in Jerusalem containing about thirty-five bodies. It was determined that most of these had suffered violent deaths in the Jewish uprising against Rome in A.D. 70. One of these was a man named Yohanan Ben Ha'galgol. He was about twenty-four to twenty-eight years old, had a cleft palate, and a seven-inch nail was still driven through both of his feet. The feet had been turned outward so that the square nail could be hammered through at the heel, just inside the Achilles tendon. This would have bowed the legs outward as well, so that they could not have been used for support on the cross. The nail had gone through a wedge of acacia wood, then through the heels, then into an olive wood beam. There was also evidence that similar spikes had been put between the two bones of each lower arm. These had caused the upper bones to be worn smooth as the victim repeatedly raised and lowered himself to breathe (breathing is restricted with the arms raised). Crucifixion victims had to lift themselves to free the chest muscles and, when they grew too weak to do so, they died by suffocation. See Norman Geisler, *Baker Encyclopedia of Christian Apologetics* (Grand Rapids, Mich.: Baker, 1999), 48.

6. Quintilian, *Declarationes maiores* 6:9; referenced in Gary Habermas and Michael Licona, *The Case for the Resurrection of Jesus* (Grand Rapids, Mich.: Kregel, forthcoming).

7. William D. Edwards, Wesley J. Gabel, and Floyd E. Hosmer, "On the Physical Death of Jesus Christ," *Journal of the American Medical Association* 255, no. 11 (March 21, 1986): 1463.

8. Some skeptics claim that this was merely a subjective appearance in the mind of Paul because his companions did not see anyone (Acts 9) or understand what the voice said (Acts 9 and 22). But this conclusion is incorrect because Paul's companions did experience objective phenomena: 1) they did see a real light, they just didn't see a person; and 2) they did hear a real voice, they just didn't understand what it said.

9. See Gary Habermas, *The Historical Jesus* (Joplin, Mo.: College Press, 1996), 202-205.

10. Referenced by Origen (A.D. 185?–254?). See Habermas, *Historical Jesus*, 218. Phlegon's writings do not survive but are referenced by Origen and Julius Africanus. Skeptics might object to the use of quotations referenced by Christians like Origen, but this objection is unreasonable. While we can't check to see if Origen quoted Phlegon accurately, we can assume he did because Origen's audience at the time would have probably had access to Phlegon's original. It wouldn't make sense for Origen to make up or alter Phlegon's quote if it could be easily checked out at the time.

11. See Paul Maier, *In the Fullness of Time* (Grand Rapids, Mich.: Kregel, 1991), 202; see also Habermas, *Historical Jesus*, 176.

12. Maier, ibid.

13. Seutonius, *Claudius*, 25; quoted in Habermas, *Historical Jesus*, 191.

14. Muslims sometimes appeal to the *Gospel of Barnabas* as evidence, but this has proven to be a fraud. See Norman Geisler and Abdul Saleeb, *Answering Islam*, 2nd ed. (Grand Rapids, Mich.: Baker, 2002), appendix 3.

15. Paul Copan, ed., *Will the Real Jesus Please Stand Up? A Debate Between William Lane Craig and John Dominic Crossan* (Grand Rapids, Mich.: Baker, 1998), 65.

16. Ibid.

17. C. S. Lewis, *Christian Reflections*, Walter Hooper, ed. (Grand Rapids, Mich.: Eerdmans, 1967), 209.

18. Craig L. Blomberg, *The Historical Reliability of John's Gospel* (Downers Grove, Ill.: InterVarsity Press, 2001), 259.

19. See Edwin Yamauchi, "Easter—Myth, Hallucination or History?" *Christianity Today* (March 15, 1974; and March 29, 1974).

20. Gary Habermas and Michael Licona, *The Case for the Resurrection of Jesus* (Grand Rapids, Mich.: Kregel, forthcoming).

21. For a comprehensive treatment of these and other alternative theories for the Resurrection, see ibid.

22. Thanks to Gary Habermas for this point (personal conversation, July 29, 2003).

23. Quoted in Paul Copan and Ronald Tacelli, eds., *Jesus' Resurrection, Fact or Figment? A Debate Between William Lane Craig and Gerd Lüdemann* (Downers Grove, Ill.: InterVarsity Press, 2000), 181.

24. In ibid.

25. Copan, ed., *Will the Real Jesus Please Stand Up?* 61-62, emphasis added.

26. Recall our example from chapter 5 about evidence needing context: a man who cuts open a woman's stomach is a criminal or a hero depending on the context of the event. If it takes place in an alley and the man intends to harm her, he's a criminal; but if it takes place in a hospital delivery room, he's a hero.

27. See Paul Maier, *Eusebius: The Church History* (Grand Rapids, Mich.: Kregel, 1999), 57, 81.

28. A similar argument was made from the unusual exploits of Napoleon in the satire by Richard Whately titled *Historical Doubts Relative to Napoleon Bonaparte*. See H. Morely, ed., *Famous Pamphlets* (New York: Routledge, 1890).

29. Adapted from "Arise, Sir Knight," a sermon by James Allan Francis, in *The Real Jesus and Other Sermons* (Philadelphia: Judson, 1926), 123-124.

CHAPTER 13
WHO IS JESUS: GOD?
OR JUST A GREAT MORAL TEACHER?

1. Barry's testimony is taken from his chapter in Norman Geisler and Paul Hoffman, eds., *Why I Am a Christian: Leading Thinkers Explain Why They Believe* (Grand Rapids, Mich.: Baker, 2001), 205-221; and from our personal conversations with him.

2. When compared with the next oldest existing manuscript of Isaiah—the Masoretic text from A.D. 1000—the text is 95 percent identical, and the 5 percent variation consists mostly of slips of the pen and spelling differences (none of these variances affect any matter of doctrine). This is an example of the meticulous care Jewish scribes took in copying the Scriptures over the centuries. For more on Old Testament manuscripts, see Norman Geisler and William Nix, *General Introduction to the Bible* (Chicago: Moody, 1986), 357-382.

3. Larry R. Helyer, *Yesterday, Today and Forever: The Continuing Relevance of the Old Testament* (Salem, Wis.: Sheffield, 1996), 318.

4. Many Jewish rabbis down through the centuries, even before the time of Christ, took Isaiah 53 as a reference to the coming Messiah. See S. R. Driver

and A. D. Neubauer, *The Fifty-third Chapter of Isaiah According to Jewish Interpreters* (Oxford and London: Parker, 1877). For example, this work quotes rabbinic opinions saying that the following verses refer to the Messiah: "tender shoot" from verse 2 (page 22); "man of sorrows" from verse 3 (page 11); "He carried our infirmities" from verse 4 (page 23); "He was pierced for our transgressions" from verse 5 (page 24).

5. For a detailed explanation of this prophecy, see Harold Hoehner, *Chronological Aspects of the Life of Christ* (Grand Rapids, Mich.: Zondervan, 1978), 115-138.

6. So-called psychic predictions cannot compare to those of the Bible. For example, the *People's Almanac* (1976) did a study of the predictions of twenty-five top psychics. They found that 66 of the 72 (or 92 percent) were dead wrong. Those that were correct to some degree were vague or could be explained by chance or by a general knowledge of world circumstances. One prediction, for example, was that the United States and Russia would remain leading powers and there would be no world wars. Isn't that incredible? By contrast, some of the Bible's predictions are hundreds of years in advance where future circumstances could not be foreseen without divine help, and all of the Bible's predictions have proven to be 100 percent accurate. See Norman L. Geisler, *Baker Encyclopedia of Christian Apologetics* (Grand Rapids, Mich.: Baker, 1999), 475-478. See pages 544-546 for problems with the alleged Nostradamus predictions.

7. J. Barton Payne, *Encyclopedia of Biblical Prophecy* (Grand Rapids, Mich.: Baker, 1973), 665-670. Payne also identified 95 messianic prophecies for Christ's second coming (42 in the Old Testament, 53 in the New Testament).

8. Philip B. Payne, "Jesus' Implicit Claim to Deity in His Parables," *Trinity Journal*, 2 NS (1981), 17.

9. C. S. Lewis, *Mere Christianity* (New York: Macmillan, 1952), 54-55.

10. Ibid., 55-56.

11. Peter Kreeft, "Why I Believe Jesus Is the Son of God," in Geisler and Hoffman, eds., *Why I Am a Christian*, 228-229.

12. Quoted in Jeffrey L. Sheler, *Is the Bible True?* (San Francisco: HarperSanFrancisco, 1999), 208.

13. Lewis, *Mere Christianity*, 145.

14. See Geisler, *Baker Encyclopedia of Christian Apologetics*. The following comes from page 730: The Holy Spirit is called "God" (Acts 5:3-4). He possesses the attributes of deity, such as omnipresence (cf. Ps. 139:7-12) and omniscience (1 Cor. 2:10-11). He is associated with God the Father in creation (Gen. 1:2). He is involved with other members of the Godhead in the work of redemption (John 3:5-6; Rom. 8:9-17, 23-27; Titus 3:5-7). He is associated with other members of the Trinity under the "name" of God (Matt. 28:18-20). Finally, the Holy Spirit appears, along with the Father and

Son, in New Testament benedictions (e.g., 2 Cor. 13:14). Not only does the Holy Spirit possess deity but he also has a differentiated personality. That he is a distinct person is clear in that Scripture refers to "him" with personal pronouns (John 14:26; 16:13). Second, he does things only persons can do, such as teach (John 14:26; 1 John 2:27), convict of sin (John 16:7-8), and be grieved by sin (Eph. 4:30). Finally, the Holy Spirit has intellect (1 Cor. 2:10-11), will (1 Cor. 12:11), and feeling (Eph. 4:30).

Chapter 14
What Did Jesus Teach About the Bible?

1. The Jewish Old Testament contains the same material as the Protestant Old Testament, but the book divisions are different. The Protestant Old Testament splits Samuel, Kings, Chronicles, and Ezra–Nehemiah into two books each, and the twelve minor prophets into twelve separate books. So while they are numbered as 22 books in the Jewish Old Testament, these same books are split into 39 books in the Protestant Old Testament. The Roman Catholic Old Testament contains 11 additional books (seven listed separately and four inserted as pieces of other books) that are called the Apocrypha. These books were added by the Roman Catholic Church at the Council of Trent in 1546, largely in response to the reformation initiated by Martin Luther.

2. Except for its title, the chart is from Norman Geisler and William Nix, *General Introduction to the Bible* (Chicago: Moody, 1986), 85.

3. The Bible affirms what we know by general revelation—that there must be an unchanging standard of truth. The Bible claims that God is truth (Ps. 31:5; 33:4; John 14:6; 1 John 4:6); that God cannot lie (Heb. 6:18; Titus 1:2); and that God cannot change (Num. 23:19; 1 Sam 15:29; Ps. 102:26-27; Mal. 3:6; Heb. 13:8; James 1:17). For more on the attributes of God, see Norman Geisler, *Systematic Theology,* vol. 2 (Minneapolis: Bethany, 2003), part 1.

4. Quoted in Jeffrey L. Sheler, *Is the Bible True?* (San Francisco: Harper SanFrancisco, 1999), 78.

5. Ibid., 80.

6. Norman Geisler, *Baker Encyclopedia of Christian Apologetics* (Grand Rapids, Mich.: Baker, 1999).

7. For sermon tapes by Andy Stanley, see www.northpoint.org.

8. For a listing of biblical miracles, see "Miracles in the Bible," in Geisler, *Baker Encyclopedia of Christian Apologetics.*

9. This is not an argument from silence because the Bible is not silent on the nature, purpose, and function of these special apostolic miracles (see, for example, 2 Cor. 12:12; Heb. 2:3-4). This function of confirming apostolic revelation fits with their cessation, since they were not needed after the revelation was confirmed.

10. Bruce Metzger, interview by Lee Strobel, *The Case for Christ* (Grand Rapids, Mich.: Zondervan, 1998), 69.

11. Only Philemon, 2 Peter, James, and 3 John are not cited. Yet, Clement of Rome (writing A.D. 95–97) and/or Ignatius (A.D. 110) confirm Philemon, 2 Peter, and James even before Polycarp and Irenaeus. So the only book not cited as authentic by anyone in the first two centuries is the tiny letter called 3 John. See Geisler and Nix, *General Introduction to the Bible*, 294.

12. Irenaeus, *Adversus haereses*, 3.3.4.

13. From Geisler and Nix, *General Introduction to the Bible*, 294.

14. Luke, while technically not an apostle, possibly was one of the 500 who witnessed the resurrected Christ. But even if he was not, Luke had his writings confirmed by his traveling companion, the apostle Paul (1 Tim. 5:18; cf. Luke 10:7). Therefore, Luke's work is considered apostolic teaching.

15. See Norman Geisler and Thomas Howe, *When Critics Ask* (Grand Rapids, Mich.: Baker, 1992); and Norman Geisler, *Systematic Theology*, vol. 1 (Minneapolis: Bethany, 2002), chapter 27.

16. Augustine, *Reply to Faustus the Manichaean*, in P. Schaff, ed., *A Select Library of the Nicene and Ante-Nicene Fathers of the Christian Church*, 14 vols. (1st series, 1886–1894; reprint, Grand Rapids, Mich.: Eerdmans, 1952), 11.5.

17. Copyist errors have been found in manuscripts, but they are easily identified and known not to be in the original by comparing the many manuscripts in existence (see chapter 9). While no Bible originals have yet been found, earlier manuscripts of other works have survived. So it is possible that a Bible original may someday be discovered.

18. For example, at one time critics thought the Bible was wrong about a people known as the Hittites. There was no evidence of their existence outside of the Bible. That is, until their entire library was uncovered in Turkey. Likewise, critics thought that writing did not exist in Moses' time, so there was no way he could have written any of the Old Testament. That is, until they found the Ebla tablets in Syria, which predate Moses by 1,000 years. As research continues, the Bible continues to be affirmed.

Chapter 15
Conclusion: The Judge, the Servant King, and the Box Top

1. For a discussion of how God can be sovereign and humans remain free, see Norman Geisler, *Chosen but Free*, 2nd ed. (Minneapolis: Bethany, 2001).

2. Philip Yancey, *Disappointment with God* (New York: HarperCollins, 1988), 109-110.

3. Ibid.

4. C. Truman Davis, M.D., "A Physician Analyzes the Crucifixion: A Medical

Explanation of What Jesus Endured on the Day He Died." Posted online at http://www.thecross-photo.com/Dr_C._Truman_Davis_Analyzes_the_ Crucifixion.htm. Accessed October 9, 2003. Originally published in *Arizona Medicine,* March 1965, Arizona Medical Association. For additional information on the death of Christ see, William D. Edwards, Wesley J. Gabel, and Floyd E. Hosmer, "On the Physical Death of Jesus Christ," *Journal of the American Medical Association* 255, no. 11 (March 21, 1986): 1463.

5. C. S. Lewis, *The Great Divorce* (New York: Macmillan, 1946), 72.

6. C. S. Lewis, *Mere Christianity* (New York: Macmillan, 1943), 65.

7. For more on hell and objections to hell, see Norman Geisler, *Baker Encyclopedia of Christian Apologetics* (Grand Rapids, Mich.: Baker, 1999), 308-313.

8. For examples of Bible books where doubt and questions about God are expressed, see Job, many of the Psalms, Ecclesiastes, and Lamentations.

APPENDIX 1
IF GOD, WHY EVIL?

1. C. S. Lewis, *The Problem of Pain* (New York: Macmillan, 1959), 81.

2. Augustine, *The City of God,* 14.1.

3. James Madison, in *The Federalist,* Benjamin F. Wright, ed. (Cambridge, Mass.: Harvard University Press, 1961), 356.

4. For a more complete treatment of the problem of evil see Norman Geisler, *Baker Encyclopedia of Christian Apologetics* (Grand Rapids, Mich.: Baker, 1999). See also Peter Kreeft, *Making Sense Out of Suffering* (Ann Arbor, Mich.: Servant, 1986).

APPENDIX 3
WHY THE JESUS SEMINAR DOESN'T SPEAK FOR JESUS

1. See *Forum,* vol. 1 (March 1985).

2. Ibid., 7, 10.

General Index

Scripture Index

Norman Geisler is author or coauthor of some sixty books, including *The Baker Encyclopedia of Christian Apologetics* and his four-volume *Systematic Theology.* He has taught at the university and graduate level for nearly forty years and has spoken or debated in all fifty states and in twenty-five countries. He holds a Ph.D. in philosophy from Loyola University and now serves as president of Southern Evangelical Seminary, near Charlotte, North Carolina. For more information on Dr. Geisler and Southern Evangelical Seminary, visit www.SES.edu or call 1-800-77-TRUTH.

Frank Turek holds two masters degrees and is pursuing a doctorate in apologetics at Southern Evangelical Seminary, where he serves as vice president. He is a sought-after speaker who has appeared on numerous television and radio programs including *The O'Reilly Factor, Hannity and Colmes,* and *Politically Incorrect.* His first book, *Legislating Morality: Is It Wise? Is It Legal? Is It Possible?* (also coauthored with Dr. Geisler) won the Evangelical Christian Publishers Association's Gold Medallion award as the best book in its category. For more information on Frank Turek, or to schedule him for a speaking engagement, visit www.ambassadoragency.com or call 1-877-425-4700.